1-2-3® for DOS Release 2.3 QuickStart

Que® Development Group

Text and graphics developed by
Rick Winter

1-2-3® for DOS Release 2.3 QuickStart
Copyright © 1991 by Que® Corporation.

Library of Congress Catalog No.: 91-61979

ISBN: 0-88022-716-8

93 92 91   6 5 4 3 2 1

Interpretation of the printing code: the rightmost double-digit number is the year of the book's printing; the rightmost single-digit number, the number of the book's printing. For example, a printing code of 91-1 shows that the first printing of the book occurred in 1991.

Screen reproductions in this book were created by means of the program Collage Plus from Inner Media, Inc., Hollis, N.H.

1-2-3 for DOS Release 2.3 QuickStart is based on Releases 2.01, 2.2, and 2.3 of Lotus 1-2-3.

Publisher: Lloyd J. Short

Associate Publisher: Karen A. Bluestein

Acquisitions Manager: Terrie Lynn Solomon

Product Development Manager: Mary Bednarek

Managing Editor: Paul Boger

Book Designer: Scott Cook

Product Directors
Joyce J. Nielsen
Kathie-Jo Arnoff

Production Editor
Robin Drake

Technical Editor
Lynda A. Fox

Production Team
Claudia Bell
Brad Chinn
Jeanne Clark
Sandy Grieshop
Denny Hager
Bob LaRoche
Tad Ringo
Bruce Steed
Lisa Wilson

*Composed in Garamond and Macmillan
by Que Corporation*

Trademark Acknowledgments

Acknowledgments

Que Corporation thanks the following individuals for their contributions to this book:

Joyce Nielsen, for her thorough developmental work, and for ensuring high quality and technical accuracy in the final manuscript.

Kathie-Jo Arnoff, for her ongoing work on the development of the QuickStart series.

Rick Winter, for providing both original and revised material that adhered to the QuickStart format, and for doing so in a timely manner.

Lynda Fox, for her dedication to ensuring the book's technical accuracy.

Mary Bednarek and *Dorothy Aylward*, for supervising the flow of materials to and from the author and technical editor. Thanks also to Mary for her project management skills.

Paul Boger, for his proficient management of the editorial process.

The Que Production Department, for their skillful talents in producing a high-quality text that meets Que's standards of excellence.

Contents at a Glance

Table of Contents

Introduction

If you are new to Lotus 1-2-3—and have access to Release 2.01, 2.2, or 2.3—this book is for you. *1-2-3 for DOS Release 2.3 QuickStart* helps you grasp the basics of using 1-2-3—enabling you to begin creating your own worksheets (or modify existing worksheets created by others) with a minimum of effort. You don't even need to be familiar with computers—keyboard basics are covered, as well as how to install 1-2-3 Release 2.3 if it is not already installed on your computer.

1-2-3 for DOS Release 2.3 QuickStart is a step forward in the evolution of how a book is organized and structured. The book uses a tutorial approach, taking you through important concepts step-by-step, describing all the fundamentals you need to know about the program. The text supplies essential information and provides comments on what you see. Many illustrations help guide you through procedures or clarify difficult concepts.

Learning any new program can be an intimidating experience. *1-2-3 for DOS Release 2.3 QuickStart* is designed to help shorten your learning curve by allowing you to learn basic concepts quickly. Whether you are new to 1-2-3 or have tried unsuccessfully to learn the program, you will find *1-2-3 for DOS Release 2.3 QuickStart* a quick way to learn the fundamentals of 1-2-3.

What Does This Book Contain?

The chapters in *1-2-3 for DOS Release 2.3 QuickStart* are organized to take you from basic information to more sophisticated tasks, including printing reports and creating graphs.

Chapter 1, "An Overview of 1-2-3," shows you the wide range of 1-2-3's capabilities. You explore how 1-2-3 can be used for spreadsheet, graphics, and database applications.

Chapter 2, "Getting Started," explains how to start and leave 1-2-3 and teaches you the basics about using the keyboard and a mouse, understanding the 1-2-3 and Wysiwyg screens, and accessing 1-2-3's Help system. You also learn about the new 1-2-3 on-line tutorials.

Chapter 3, "Introducing Worksheet Basics," teaches you about the fundamental tasks of using a spreadsheet. You learn how 1-2-3 fits into the realm of integrated software and discover how to enter and edit data, move around in the worksheet, select commands from menus, and save and retrieve files.

Chapters 4, 5, and 6 cover all the basic concepts you need to begin creating 1-2-3 worksheets. Chapter 4, "Working with Ranges," teaches you how to use the range commands and specify ranges and shows you step-by-step how to perform formatting tasks. Chapter 5, "Building a Worksheet," shows you how to use the worksheet commands to improve the appearance of the worksheets you develop. And Chapter 6, "Modifying a Worksheet," explains how to modify your worksheet by moving and copying cell contents and finding and replacing the contents of cells.

Chapter 7, "Using Functions," introduces you to 1-2-3's selection of built-in functions for performing a variety of calculations. Among the functions illustrated are those for performing mathematical, statistical, and logical calculations.

Chapter 8, "Printing Reports," shows you how to set print specifications and organize your data for printing. You also learn to hide columns and rows, control paper movement, enhance a report by adding headers and footers, and change the page layout.

In Chapter 9, "Printing with Wysiwyg," you learn about the add-in feature Wysiwyg, which provides a "what-you-see-is-what-you-get" display. Wysiwyg offers presentation-quality printing techniques such as the use of different font styles and sizes, including graphs along with data in your printed output, and shading, outlining, or underlining selected ranges.

Chapter 10, "Managing Files," describes how to use passwords to protect your worksheets, how to save and retrieve parts of files, and how to link cells between different files. This chapter also explains how to delete and list your files as well as how to import files from other software programs (such as dBASE) into 1-2-3.

Chapter 11, "Creating and Printing Graphs," teaches you how to produce graphs with 1-2-3 and the PrintGraph program. This chapter takes you from selecting graph types to adding titles and legends. In addition, the chapter shows you how to print and preview graphs.

Chapter 12, "Enhancing and Printing Graphs in Wysiwyg," shows you how to use Wysiwyg to enhance your graphs. This chapter includes adding text and drawings to your graph.

Chapter 13, "Managing Data," explains how to use 1-2-3 for data management. You learn to create and modify a database, and sort and search for specific records.

Chapter 14, "Understanding Macros," gives you an introduction to the concept of simple keystroke macros. This chapter teaches you to plan, position, create, name, and edit simple macros. The chapter includes macros you can use to start your own macro library.

The book concludes with two appendixes. Appendix A shows you how to install 1-2-3 Release 2.3. Appendix B is a summary of Allways commands for 1-2-3 Release 2.2 users (and for 1-2-3 Release 2.01 users who purchased Allways separately).

Who Should Use This Book?

1-2-3 for DOS Release 2.3 QuickStart is designed to be a quick guide for new 1-2-3 users. Whether you are sitting down with 1-2-3 for the first time or have tried many times to learn enough about 1-2-3 to use it efficiently, *1-2-3 for DOS Release 2.3 QuickStart* gives you enough information to get you started quickly. The book highlights important concepts and takes you through important information by providing steps and explanations interwoven with examples and illustrations.

What Do You Need To Run 1-2-3 Release 2.3?

There are no prerequisites for using this book or for using 1-2-3. The assumption is, of course, that you have the software, the hardware, and a desire to learn to use the program.

The following hardware is required to run 1-2-3 Release 2.3:

- An IBM PC or compatible computer.
- A hard disk with at least 7M available disk space.
- DOS version 2.1 or later.
- At least 384K of RAM. To run the Wysiwyg add-in, 512K is required. To run additional add-ins, 640K is required.
- A monitor that supports VGA, EGA, CGA, or the Hercules Graphics Adapter.
- A printer (optional).

What Is New in 1-2-3 Release 2.3?

This book discusses new features available with Release 2.3 of 1-2-3. This version of 1-2-3 has been enhanced with such additional features as the following:

- Wysiwyg, a what-you-see-is-what-you-get spreadsheet publishing add-in, lets you use different fonts, underlining, outlining, and shading on selected ranges. You can combine text and graphics on printed output. Once you are in Wysiwyg, you can make changes to a worksheet or graph and see how the final printed output will look.
- Mouse support, with and without Wysiwyg. You can quickly select commands and highlight ranges with a mouse.
- Dialog boxes, which allow you to keep track of available choices. They show current settings for options and allow you to change the options through the keyboard or the mouse directly in the dialog box. You can also change options through the regular command menu displayed above the box. 1-2-3 automatically displays dialog boxes when you use print, graph, database, and some worksheet commands.

- Three new add-ins in addition to Wysiwyg. The Auditor add-in allows you to find errors in your worksheet formulas. The Tutor add-in teaches you how to use 1-2-3. The Viewer add-in allows you to look at files before you retrieve them to help locate the right file to retrieve.

- Two tutorials, 1-2-3-Go! and Wysiwyg-Go!, which teach you how to use 1-2-3 and Wysiwyg.

- Background printing, which lets you continue working on a worksheet while it is printing.

- Encoded printing, which allows you to print your output to a disk. The file on disk will have specific instructions for the printer, including all enhancements. You do not need to be in 1-2-3 to print the encoded file.

- Two new graph types—mixed (a combination of bar and line) and HLCO (high-low-close-open, for stock analysis).

- Additional graph features that allow you to change the orientation of the graph, show stacked lines, change the border around the graph, and create 3-D effects.

Release 2.3 also incorporates the following features that were added to the previous version, Release 2.2:

- An Undo feature, which allows you to reverse the last command or action taken. Not only can you undo a mistake, but you can also try unfamiliar commands freely, knowing that you can undo many unsatisfactory results.

- File linking, which lets you use formulas to link the cell(s) of one worksheet to the cells in other worksheets. When one of the linked worksheets is retrieved, it is automatically updated.

- Minimal recalculation, which requires no special action on your part; only relevant formulas are recalculated when you make changes to the worksheet. This feature results in faster, more responsive worksheets.

- Search and replace, which lets you search for the occurrence of a string in a selected range and gives you the option of replacing some or all instances with a different string.

- Group options in /**Worksheet** and /**Graph** commands that simplify multiple column-width changes and graph-range definitions.

- Enhanced graph images that make line, bar, and stacked-bar graphs easier to read. Grid lines appear behind bars.

- Macro names can be descriptive names up to 15 characters long, increasing readability and tracking.

Where To Find More Help

After you learn the fundamentals presented in this book, you may want to learn more advanced applications of 1-2-3. Que Corporation has a full line of 1-2-3 books you can use. Among these are *Using 1-2-3 for DOS Release 2.3, Special Edition*; *1-2-3 for DOS Release 2.3 Quick Reference*; and *1-2-3 Beyond the Basics*. For more information on how to use DOS commands, new computer users can also benefit from reading Que's *MS-DOS 5 QuickStart*.

You can use 1-2-3's context-sensitive Help feature and the new on-line tutorials (1-2-3-Go! and Wysiwyg-Go!) to answer some of your questions while working with 1-2-3. These features are explained and illustrated in Chapter 2, "Getting Started."

Should all else fail, contact your computer dealer or Lotus Product Support (1-617-253-9150). In Canada, contact Lotus Product Support at 1-416-979-9412.

To subscribe to Lotus PROMPT for technical assistance, call 1-800-223-1662 and supply the PROMPT identification number provided with your software. In Canada, contact Lotus PROMPT at 1-800-668-8236.

Conventions Used in This Book

A number of conventions are used in *1-2-3 for DOS Release 2.3 QuickStart* to help you learn the program. This section provides examples of these conventions to help you distinguish among the different elements in 1-2-3.

References to keys are as they appear on the keyboard of the IBM Personal Computer and most compatibles. The function keys, F1 through F10, are used for special situations in 1-2-3. In the text, the function key name and the corresponding function key number are usually listed together, such as Graph (F10).

Direct quotations of words that appear on the screen are spelled as they appear on the screen and are printed in a `special typeface`. Information you are asked to type is printed in **boldface.** The slash and the first letter in each command from the 1-2-3 menu system also appears in boldface: **/R**ange **F**ormat **C**urrency. Also, the colon and the first command letter of Wysiwyg commands are in boldface: **:T**ext **E**dit.

Elements printed in uppercase include range names (SALES), functions (@PMT), modes (READY), and cell references (A1..G5).

If you use a mouse, this book assumes that it is a standard two or three button mouse and that it is configured normally for right-handed people. The left mouse button acts as the Enter key. The right mouse button, in most cases, is the equivalent of pressing Esc.

Conventions that pertain to macros deserve special mention here:

1. Single-character macro names (Alt-character combinations) appear with the backslash (\) and single-character name in lowercase: \a. In this example, the \ indicates that you press the Alt key and hold it down while you also press the A key.

2. 1-2-3 menu keystrokes in a macro line appear in lowercase: /rnc.

3. Range names within macros appear in uppercase: /rncTEST.

4. In macros, representations of direction keys, such as {DOWN}; function keys, such as {CALC}; and editing keys, such as {DEL}, appear in uppercase letters and are surrounded by braces.

5. Enter is represented by the tilde (~).

When two keys appear together, for example Ctrl-Break, you press and hold down the first key as you also press the second key. Other key combinations, such as Alt-F4, are pressed in the same manner. When two keys appear together and are not hyphenated, such as End Home, the first key is pressed and released before the second key is pressed.

Within the tables and step-by-step instructions, some keys appear similar to actual keys on the keyboard. Blue lines point out the most important areas of the illustrations.

Examples that use a mouse are provided as an alternative to using the keyboard to perform a similar function. A mouse is not required to use Release 2.3 and Wysiwyg efficiently. However, with practice, you may find that using a mouse will allow you to complete routine tasks more quickly and accurately.

Note: Most screens included in this book were captured with the Wysiwyg add-in active. Most screens also display a worksheet grid (added with the Wysiwyg command **:D**isplay **O**ptions **G**rid **Y**es). Chapter 2 explains how to load Wysiwyg into memory temporarily, as well as how to configure your system to load and invoke Wysiwyg automatically each time you start 1-2-3.

An Overview of 1-2-3

1

Before you put your fingers on the keyboard to start using 1-2-3, you need to know the range of capabilities of this software package. If you are inheriting a spreadsheet created by someone else, coming up to speed with 1-2-3 may require little more of you than simply entering data. If, on the other hand, someone has handed you the 1-2-3 package and said, "Prepare a sales forecast for product A," your task may seem a bit intimidating. Whether you are an experienced or a new spreadsheet user, this chapter shows you some of the many features of 1-2-3 and describes how they can fit into your day-to-day tasks.

As you read through this chapter, ask yourself which of the 1-2-3 features you'll be using most often. Will you be maintaining an accounts receivable spreadsheet? Perhaps your department is in charge of setting up a database to track inventory. Will you be responsible for printing reports and graphs? Whatever the application, read the appropriate overview sections closely, and look for references at the ends of these sections for the chapters in the book that deal more specifically with that topic.

The 1-2-3 electronic spreadsheet

1-2-3 graphics

1-2-3 database management

1-2-3 printed reports and graphs

Macros and the advanced macro commands

Key Terms in This Chapter

Electronic spreadsheet	The electronic replacement for the accountant's pad.
Worksheet	The 1-2-3 spreadsheet.
Wysiwyg	An acronym for "what-you-see-is-what-you-get"—the name of the spreadsheet publishing add-in provided with Release 2.3.
Direction keys	The keys that allow movement within the 1-2-3 worksheet—including PgUp, PgDn, Home, End, Tab, and the arrow keys.
Cell	The intersection of a row and a column in the 1-2-3 worksheet.
Cell pointer	The highlighted bar that allows you to enter data within the worksheet area and identifies the current cell.
Formula	An action performed on a specified cell or group of cells. For example, the formula +A1+B1 sums the contents of cells A1 and B1.
Function	A shorthand method of using formulas. For example, instead of typing the formula +A1+B1+C1+D1+E1, you can use the @SUM function @SUM(A1..E1).
Command	A menu selection used to carry out an operation within the worksheet.
Mouse	A device which attaches to your computer that allows you to quickly choose cells and commands with a click of one of its buttons.

Whether you are an experienced computer user who is new to the 1-2-3 program, or you are using a computer for the first time, you will find that the fundamentals of 1-2-3 can be quickly grasped. If you start by learning the most basic concepts of 1-2-3 and then gradually build on your knowledge and experience, you'll be amazed by how easily you'll learn the program. If, however, you jump right in and start using string functions or macros right away, you may find yourself running into snags. This book uses an easy, step-by-step approach to demonstrate the fundamental tasks you can perform with 1-2-3.

What Is a Spreadsheet?

Sometimes known as a ledger sheet or accountant's pad, a *spreadsheet* is a specialized piece of paper on which information is recorded in columns and rows. Spreadsheets usually contain a mix of descriptive text and accompanying numbers and calculations. Typical business applications include balance sheets, income statements, inventory sheets, and sales reports.

Although you may be unfamiliar with business applications for spreadsheets, you already use a rudimentary spreadsheet if you keep a checkbook. Similar to an accountant's pad, a checkbook register is a paper grid divided by lines into rows and columns. Within this grid, you record the check number, the date, a transaction description, the check amount, any deposits, and a running balance.

NUMBER	DATE	DESCRIPTION OF TRANSACTION	PAYMENT/DEBT (−)	✔	FEE (IF ANY) (−)	DEPOSIT/CREDIT (+)	BALANCE $1000 00
1001	9/3/89	Department Store Credit	51 03				948 97
1002	9/13/89	Electric	95 12				853 85
1003	9/14/89	Grocery	74 25				779 60
1004	9/15/89	Class Supplies	354 57				425 03
	9/16/89	Deposit				250 00	675 03
1005	9/21/89	Telephone	49 43				625 60

A manual checkbook register.

What happens when you make an invalid entry in your checkbook register, or you have to void an entry? Such procedures are messy because you have to erase or cross out entries, rewrite them, and recalculate everything. The limitations of manual spreadsheets are apparent even with this simple example of a checkbook register.

For complex business applications, the dynamic quality of an electronic spreadsheet such as 1-2-3 is indispensable. You can change one number and recalculate the entire spreadsheet in an instant. Entering new values is nearly effortless. Performing calculations on a column or row of numbers is accomplished with formulas—usually the same type of formulas that calculators use.

1

Compare the manual checkbook register to the following electronic one. Notice that the electronic checkbook register is set up with columns and rows. Columns are marked by letters across the top of the spreadsheet; rows are numbered along the side. Each transaction is recorded in a row, the same way you record data in a manual checkbook.

An "electronic" checkbook register.

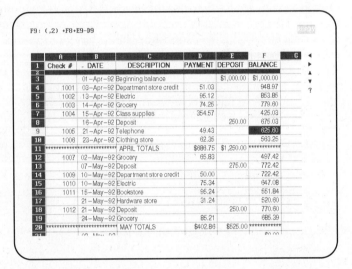

Assigning column letters and row numbers lends itself well to creating *formulas.* Note the following formula in the upper left corner of the electronic checkbook:

+F8+E9–D9

These instructions to 1-2-3 translate to

Previous BALANCE plus DEPOSIT minus PAYMENT

As you can see from this simple example, formulas let you establish mathematical relationships between values stored in certain places on your spreadsheet. Formulas let you easily make changes to a spreadsheet, and you can quickly see the results. In the electronic checkbook, if you delete an entire transaction (row), the spreadsheet automatically recalculates itself. You can also change an amount and not worry about recalculating your figures, because the electronic spreadsheet updates all balances.

If you forget to record a check or deposit, 1-2-3 lets you insert a new row at the location of the omitted transaction and enter the information. Subsequent entries are moved down one row, and the new balance is automatically

1

calculated. Inserting new columns is just as easy. Indicate where you want the new column to go, and 1-2-3 inserts a blank column at that point, moving existing information to the right of that column.

What if you want to know how much you have spent at the local department store since the beginning of the year? With a manual checkbook, you have to look for each check written to the store and total the amounts. Not only does this task take considerable time, but you may overlook some of the checks. An electronic checkbook can sort your checks by description so that all similar transactions are together. You then create a formula that totals all the checks written to the department store, for example.

This simple checkbook example demonstrates how valuable an electronic spreadsheet is for maintaining financial data. Although you may choose not to use 1-2-3 to balance your personal checkbook, an electronic spreadsheet is an indispensable tool in today's modern office.

The 1-2-3 Electronic Spreadsheet

1-2-3 has a number of capabilities, but the foundation of the program is the electronic spreadsheet. The framework of this spreadsheet contains the graphics and data management elements of the program. Graphics are produced through the use of spreadsheet commands. Data management occurs in the standard row-and-column spreadsheet layout.

Release 2.3 provides two additional dynamic features: Wysiwyg (an acronym for "what-you-see-is-what-you-get") and mouse control. Wysiwyg is an add-in program providing state of the art desktop publishing features for enhancing on-screen and printed 1-2-3 worksheets and graphics. With Wysiwyg you can create presentation-style reports and graphics in minutes. Whether or not Release 2.3 is active, you can use a mouse to quickly move around the worksheet, select commands and files, and specify ranges.

The importance of the spreadsheet as the basis for 1-2-3 cannot be overemphasized. All the commands for the related features of 1-2-3 are initiated from the same main menu as the spreadsheet commands, and all the commands have the same format. For example, all the commands for graphics display refer to data in the spreadsheet, and they use this data to draw graphs on the screen. For easy data management, the database is composed of records that are actually rows of cell entries in a spreadsheet. When Wysiwyg is active in Release 2.3, you have access to an additional menu—the Wysiwyg menu—which enables you to enhance the on-screen image and the printed output.

1

1-2-3's integrated electronic spreadsheet replaces traditional financial modeling tools, reducing the time and effort needed to perform even sophisticated accounting tasks.

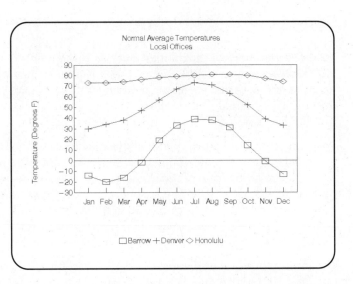

With 1-2-3's graphics capabilities, you can create seven different graph types, and see worksheets and graphics together on-screen.

1

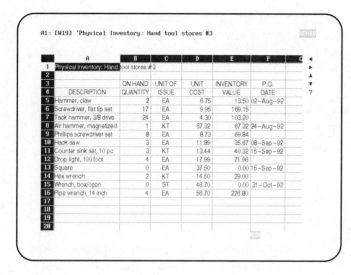

1-2-3's database commands and statistical functions help to manage and manipulate data.

The Size of 1-2-3's Worksheet

With 256 columns and 8,192 rows, the 1-2-3 worksheet contains more than 2,000,000 cells. The columns are lettered from A to Z, AA to AZ, BA to BZ, and so on, to IV for the last column. The rows are sequentially numbered from 1 to 8192.

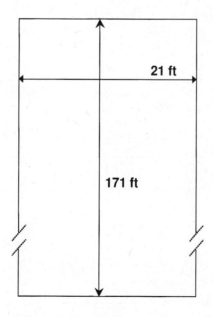

21 ft

171 ft

A good way to visualize the spreadsheet (or *worksheet*) is as a giant sheet of grid paper that is about 21 feet wide and 171 feet long.

1

Although the 1-2-3 worksheet contains so many columns and rows, there are some limitations to using the entire sheet. If you imagine storing just one character in each of the 2,097,152 available cells, you end up with a worksheet that is far larger than the standard 640K random-access memory (RAM) of an IBM PC.

1-2-3 Releases 2.2 and 2.3 require at least 320K of RAM. If you want to use the Wysiwyg add-in feature (provided with 1-2-3 Release 2.3), you must have a hard disk on your computer and at least 512K of RAM.

The Worksheet Window

Because the 1-2-3 grid is so large, you cannot view the entire worksheet on the screen at one time. The screen thus serves as a *window* onto a small section of the worksheet. To view other parts of the worksheet, you can use the *direction keys* (Tab, PgUp, PgDn, Home, End, and arrow keys) to move the cell pointer around the worksheet. When the cell pointer reaches the edge of the current window, the window shifts to follow the cell pointer across and up (or down) the worksheet.

To illustrate the window concept, imagine cutting a one-inch square hole in a piece of cardboard. If you place the cardboard over this page, you will be able to see only a one-inch square piece of text. The rest of the text is still on the page; the data is simply hidden from view. When you move the cardboard around the page (the same way that the window moves when the direction keys are used), different parts of the page become visible.

The default 1-2-3 worksheet displays 8 columns (each 9 characters wide) and 20 rows.

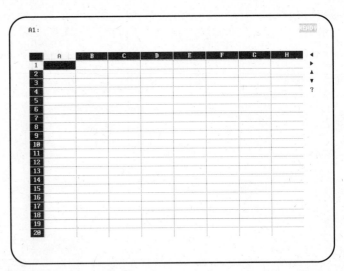

You can change the default number of columns that are displayed by narrowing or widening one or more of the columns. In Release 2.3, Wysiwyg allows you to change the height of individual rows, as well as change the width of columns.

Cells

Each column in a 1-2-3 worksheet is assigned a letter; each row is assigned a number. The intersections of the columns and rows are called *cells*. Cells are identified by their column and row coordinates. The cell located at the intersection of column A and row 15, for example, is called A15. The cell located at the intersection of column X and row 55 is named X55. Cells can be filled with two types of information: labels, which are text entries; or values, which consist of numbers and/or formulas.

A *cell pointer* allows you to enter information into the current cell. In 1-2-3, as in most spreadsheets, the cell pointer looks like a highlighted rectangle on the computer's screen. The cell pointer typically is one row high and one column wide.

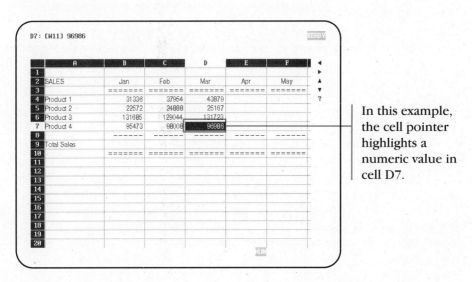

In this example, the cell pointer highlights a numeric value in cell D7.

The direction keys on your keyboard move the cell pointer around the worksheet. Release 2.3, however, offers you another way to move the cell pointer: by moving a mouse and clicking a mouse button. These methods of navigating the 1-2-3 worksheet are discussed in detail in Chapter 2.

Formulas

1-2-3 allows mathematical relationships to be created between cells. Suppose, for example, that the cell named C1 contains the formula

$$+A1+B1$$

Cell C1 then displays the sum of the contents of cells A1 and B1. (The + sign before A1 tells 1-2-3 that what you have entered into this cell is a formula, not text.) The cell references serve as variables in the equation. Each time you modify the contents of cell A1 and/or B1, the sum in cell C1 automatically reflects these changes.

You now know that only a portion of the entire 1-2-3 worksheet is visible at one time. Although you see only values in the cells, 1-2-3 stores all the data, formulas, and formats in memory. A simple 1-2-3 worksheet displays values, not the formulas "behind" them.

In this example, the cell pointer is positioned on C1, and its formula is displayed at the top left of the screen.

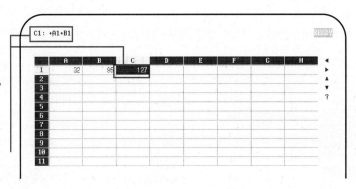

"What If" Analysis

1-2-3 allows you to play "what if" with your model. After you have built a set of formulas into 1-2-3's worksheet, you can modify and recalculate the worksheet with amazing speed, using several sets of assumptions. If you use only paper, a pencil, and a calculator to build your model, every change requires recalculation of each correlation. If the model has 100 formulas and you change the first one, you must make 100 manual calculations so that the change flows through the entire model. If you use a 1-2-3 worksheet, however, the same change requires pressing only a few keys—the program does the rest. This capability permits you to perform extensive "what if" analyses.

Suppose, for example, that you want to forecast sales for two products over the next six months and to recalculate the revenue totals for different discounts.

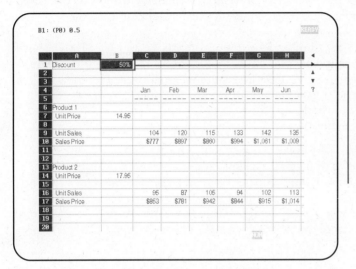

If you enter 50% into B1 as the discount rate, 1-2-3 calculates the sales price figures.

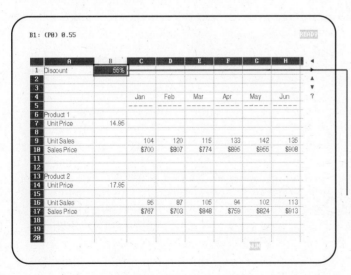

If you change the discount rate from 50% to 55%, 1-2-3 automatically recalculates the new sales price figures.

1

With 1-2-3's Undo feature, you have even greater flexibility in playing the "what if" game with your worksheet. By inserting a new value, you can see the implications throughout the worksheet. If the results are unsatisfactory, simply use the Undo feature (press Alt-F4), and the worksheet returns to its previous condition. The Undo feature is explained in greater detail in Chapter 3.

Functions

You can create simple formulas, involving only a few cells, when you refer to the cell addresses and use the appropriate operators (+, –, /, and *). Each formula is stored in memory, and only its value appears in the cell.

You can create complex formulas when you use 1-2-3's functions. These *functions* are shortcuts to help you make common mathematical computations with a minimum of typing. Functions are like abbreviations for long and cumbersome formulas. The @ sign signals 1-2-3 that an expression is a function. For instance, you can use the shorter @SUM function @SUM(A1..E1) instead of typing the formula +A1+B1+C1+D1+E1.

Building applications would be difficult without 1-2-3's capacity for calculating mathematical, statistical, logical, financial, and other types of formulas. 1-2-3 comes with many functions that let you create complex formulas for a wide range of applications, including business, scientific, and engineering applications. You learn more about 1-2-3's functions in Chapter 7.

Commands

1-2-3 has many commands that help you perform a number of tasks in the worksheet. You use these commands at every phase of building and using a worksheet application. Commands are activated by pressing the slash (/) key, and commands from the Wysiwyg menu are executed by pressing the colon (:) key. Each of these actions displays a separate menu of commands from which you choose the command you want. Although some of the options appearing on the main 1-2-3 and Wysiwyg menus are identical, they are used for different purposes. Chapter 3 tells you how commands are selected, and Chapter 4 begins a discussion of specific commands.

The 1-2-3 main menu enables you to format the worksheet; name ranges; erase, copy, and move data; perform calculations; store files; protect worksheet cells; protect files with passwords; print the worksheets; and do much more, such as create graphs and retrieve files. The Wysiwyg menu lets you enhance the appearance of text and numbers you enter, as well as enhance the look of reports and graphs you print.

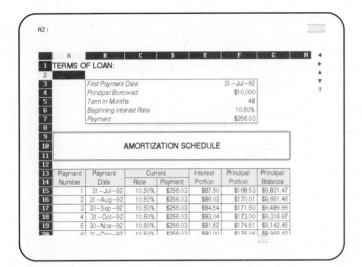

A 1-2-3 worksheet enhanced with lines, shadows, and fonts selected with Wysiwyg commands.

1-2-3 Graphics

The spreadsheet alone makes 1-2-3 a powerful program, with all the functions many users need. The addition of graphics features, which accompany the spreadsheet, makes 1-2-3 a tool you can use to present data visually and to conduct graphic "what if" analyses. You can quickly design and alter graphs as worksheet data changes—without using commands to redefine a modified graph. This means that you can change graphs almost as fast as 1-2-3 recalculates data.

1-2-3 Release 2.3 has seven basic graph types: bar, stacked bar, line, pie, XY (scatter), HLCO (high-low-close-open), and mixed (bar and line). You have an exceptional amount of flexibility in your choices of graph formats, colors, shading, labels, titles, and subtitles.

In Release 2.3, Wysiwyg allows you to choose colors from a palette of more than 200 colors, and also enables you to add symbols and other graphic elements to your graphs. The process of creating and printing graphs is covered in Chapter 11; using Wysiwyg to enhance the appearance of graphs is the subject of Chapter 12.

You can represent up to six ranges of data on a single graph (except for pie graphs and scatter diagrams). You can create, for example, a line graph with six different lines.

1

The line graph is the default graph type for 1-2-3. That is, if you do not specify a particular type, 1-2-3 displays the data as a line graph.

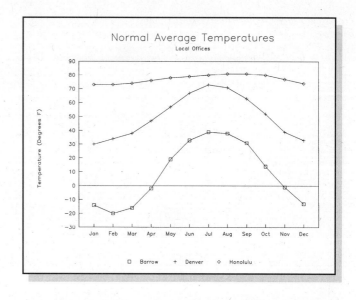

The bar graph, typically used to show the trend of numeric data across time, often compares two or more data items.

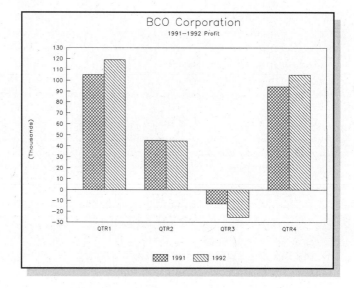

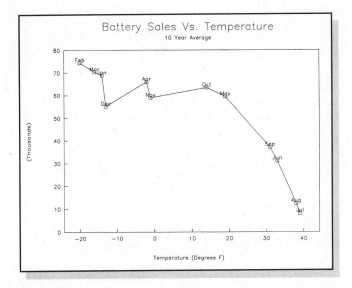

The XY (scatter) graph compares one numeric data series to another, determining whether one set of values appears to depend on the other.

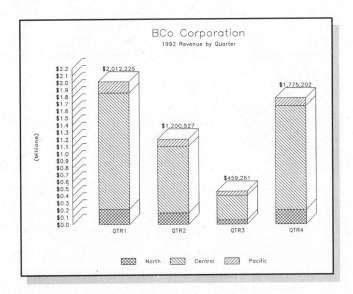

The stacked-bar graph includes two or more data series that total 100 percent of a specific category.

The pie graph shows only one data series, in which the parts total 100 percent of a specific numeric category.

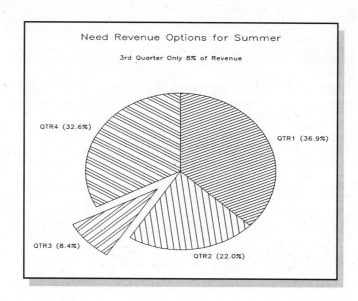

The HLCO (high-low-close-open) graph is used to track stock performance over time.

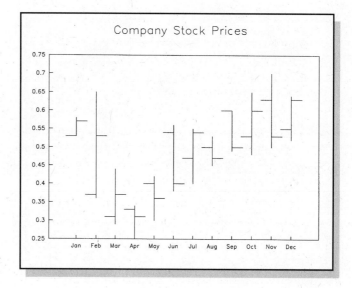

1

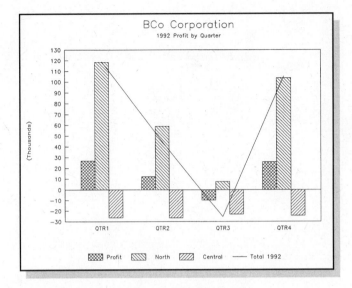

The mixed graph shows a combination bar-and-line graph to track two different types of data, such as sales performance against advertising expenses.

1-2-3 Database Management

The row-and-column structure that is used to store data in a spreadsheet program is similar to the structure of a relational database. When you use 1-2-3's true database management commands and functions, you can sort, query, extract, and perform statistical analyses on data in up to 8,191 records (with up to 256 fields of information).

One important advantage of a 1-2-3 database over independent database programs is that its database commands are similar to others used in the 1-2-3 program. This similarity allows you to learn the use of the 1-2-3 database manager along with the rest of the 1-2-3 program.

A row in 1-2-3 is equal to a record in a conventional database. In that record, you might store a client's name, address, and phone number.

1

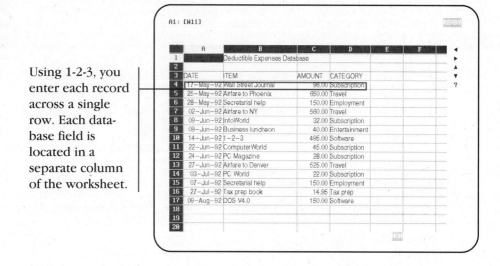

Using 1-2-3, you enter each record across a single row. Each database field is located in a separate column of the worksheet.

1-2-3 has sophisticated facilities for performing sort and search operations. You can sort the database on any number of items and by numerous criteria, and you can find a particular record with a few simple keystrokes. These and other database operations are explained further in Chapter 13.

Printed Reports and Graphs

By using 1-2-3's commands for printing, you can print worksheet data and graphs for either draft review or formal presentations. You can send data and graphs directly from 1-2-3 to the printer or save worksheet data in a text file so that the data can be incorporated in another program, such as a word processing program. You also can save data and graphs to a file format that retains your selected report enhancements (such as boldface type, underlining, and italic) so that you can print later with an operating system command.

With the printing commands from the Wysiwyg menu, you can combine text and graphics anywhere on a page for sophisticated, publishing-quality output; you can preview all pages, including text and graphics, before printing; you can print in portrait or landscape mode on laser printers; and you can automatically compress a worksheet print range to fit a single page.

One of the major benefits of printing with Release 2.3 is that as soon as you start printing, you can return to work within the worksheet on-screen while the printing job runs in the background. Chapters 8 and 9 discuss printing in greater detail.

Macros and the Advanced Macro Commands

Two other features help to make 1-2-3 the most powerful and popular integrated spreadsheet, graphics, and database program. When you use 1-2-3's macros and advanced macro commands, you can automate and customize 1-2-3 for your particular applications.

By using 1-2-3 macros, you can reduce multiple keystrokes to a two-keystroke operation. Simply press two keys, and 1-2-3 does the rest—whether you're formatting a range, creating a graph, or printing a worksheet.

You can create a macro, for example, to format a cell to display currency. Suppose that you place numbers requiring currency and other different formats in several adjacent cells. Because 1-2-3 formats cells in range groups (contiguous cells), you have to use quite a few keystrokes to format several adjacent cells with different formats. You can create a macro that will, in effect, "record" your actions as you specify the keystrokes to format a cell to display currency. Then, after you assign a name and save the macro, you can format a cell with currency by simply typing a single keystroke combination instead of seven keystrokes.

A number of enhancements in Releases 2.2 and 2.3 make the macro capability even more powerful and easier to use than in earlier releases of 1-2-3. These enhancements include the following:

- You can use descriptive words (up to 15 characters)—instead of single letters—to name macros.
- The Learn feature allows you to record keystrokes to build macros automatically.
- STEP mode provides an echo of each command at the bottom of the screen while you run the macro—to help you find macro errors.
- The Macro Library Manager add-in lets you create an external file of macros available for all worksheets.

Macros and the advanced macro commands are covered in Chapter 14.

Think of simple keystroke macros as the building blocks for advanced macro command programs. When you begin to add advanced macro commands to simple keystroke macros, you control and automate many of the actions required to build, modify, and update 1-2-3 models. At the most sophisticated level, 1-2-3's advanced macro commands are used as a full-fledged programming language for developing custom business applications.

1

When you use 1-2-3's advanced macro commands, you see what kind of power is available for your 1-2-3 applications. For the applications developer, the set of advanced macro commands is much like a programming language (such as BASIC), but the programming process is significantly simplified by all the powerful features of 1-2-3's spreadsheet, database, and graphics commands. 1-2-3 offers 50 "invisible" commands—the advanced macro commands—that give you a greater range of control over your 1-2-3 applications.

Summary

In this overview chapter, you saw how one of the simplest examples of a spreadsheet—a checkbook register—becomes easier to use in electronic form. You were introduced to the features of 1-2-3's spreadsheet, such as its size, window, and cells. You learned how 1-2-3 worksheets are designated and can be recalculated for "what if" analyses. And you learned about 1-2-3's powerful commands and functions, with which you can build formulas for a wide variety of applications.

The chapter gave you a glimpse of 1-2-3's flexible graphics capabilities. You had a quick view of 1-2-3's database and its power for managing and reporting on stored data. The chapter touched on macros and the advanced macro commands, which allow you to automate and customize your use of 1-2-3 and its graphics and database capabilities.

Specifically, you learned the following key information about 1-2-3:

- The 1-2-3 worksheet contains 8,192 rows and 256 columns. All rows on the 1-2-3 worksheet are assigned numbers. All columns on the 1-2-3 worksheet are assigned letters.

- Wysiwyg, an add-in program provided with Release 2.3, enables you to enhance 1-2-3 worksheets and graphics through commands available in a separate Wysiwyg menu.

- A cell is the intersection of a column and a row. Cells are identified by their column and row coordinates (A2, B4, and G10, for example).

- The cell pointer is the highlighted rectangle that allows you to enter data into the worksheet.

- Formulas can be used in 1-2-3 to create mathematical relationships between cells.

- 1-2-3's functions are built-in formulas that automatically perform complex operations.

- Commands are initiated by pressing the slash (/) key to display a command menu. In Release 2.3, Wysiwyg commands can be initiated by pressing the colon (:). You can also use a mouse to access the 1-2-3 and Wysiwyg menus in Release 2.3.

- 1-2-3's graphics capability lets you create seven types of graphs from worksheet data. Many options are available for enhancing the appearance of these graphs.

- Each row of a 1-2-3 database corresponds to a database record. With the database features available in 1-2-3, you can perform complex operations, such as sorting and searching records.

- Macros and the advanced macro commands deliver exceptional power to 1-2-3 by automating both simple and complex tasks into two-keystroke operations.

The power of 1-2-3 is best realized by actually using the program. The next chapter shows you how to get started.

Getting Started

2

This chapter helps you get started using 1-2-3 and Wysiwyg. Before you begin, be sure that 1-2-3 is installed on your computer system. Follow the instructions in your Lotus documentation or the Appendix of this book to complete the installation. Even if you have already installed 1-2-3, you may want to check the Appendix to make sure that you haven't overlooked any important details.

The information in this chapter will be useful if you are new to computers or 1-2-3. If you find this introductory material too basic and want to begin using the 1-2-3 worksheet immediately, you can skip to Chapter 3. However, if you want to begin using the mouse and/or Wysiwyg, you should first read the sections of this chapter that relate to these topics.

Starting 1-2-3 and Wysiwyg

Exiting 1-2-3

Learning the keyboard

Understanding mouse terminology

The 1-2-3 and Wysiwyg screens

The 1-2-3 help system and tutorial

2

Key Terms in This Chapter

Lotus 1-2-3 Access Menu	The Lotus menu system that links all of 1-2-3's different programs. It includes options for accessing the main 1-2-3 program, printing graphs, modifying installation settings, and translating files between 1-2-3 and other software programs.
Alphanumeric keys	The keys in the center section of the computer keyboard. Most of these keys resemble those on a typewriter keyboard.
Numeric keypad	The keys on the right side of the Personal Computer AT and enhanced keyboards. This keypad is used for entering and calculating numbers, for moving the cell pointer in the worksheet area, or for moving the cursor and menu pointer in the control panel.
Function keys	The 10 keys on the left side of the Personal Computer AT keyboard or the 12 keys at the top of the enhanced keyboard. These keys are used for special 1-2-3 functions, such as accessing help, editing cells, and recalculating the worksheet.
Control panel	The area above the reverse-video border of the 1-2-3 worksheet. The control panel contains three lines that display important information about the contents of a cell, command options and explanations, special prompts or messages, and mode indicators.
Worksheet area	The largest part of the 1-2-3 screen, where data that has been entered into the worksheet is displayed.
Status line	A single line located at the bottom of the 1-2-3 screen that displays information such as the file-and-clock indicator, error messages, and status indicators.
Icon panel	The area on the right side of the screen containing five icons for use with a mouse.

Starting 1-2-3

Getting into 1-2-3 is quite easy. Starting from DOS, you can go directly to a fresh worksheet or you can enter 1-2-3 by way of the Lotus 1-2-3 Access Menu, which provides several menu options. The following discussion shows you both ways to begin.

Starting 1-2-3 from DOS

Starting 1-2-3 directly from DOS is a shortcut and requires less memory than using the Lotus 1-2-3 Access Menu. In the following instructions, the assumption is that the 1-2-3 program is on drive C of your hard disk, in a subdirectory named \123R23. To start 1-2-3, follow these steps:

1. With the C> system prompt displayed on your screen, change to the \123R23 directory by typing **cd\123R23** and pressing ⏎Enter.
2. Start 1-2-3 by typing **123** and pressing ⏎Enter.

After a few seconds, the 1-2-3 logo appears. The logo remains on-screen for a few seconds. Then the worksheet is displayed, and you're ready to use 1-2-3.

Starting 1-2-3 from the Lotus 1-2-3 Access Menu

Lotus devised the Lotus 1-2-3 Access Menu as a way to move quickly between the programs in the 1-2-3 package. For example, the Lotus 1-2-3 Access Menu has a series of menus that enable you to translate between 1-2-3 and other programs, such as dBASE, Symphony, and Multiplan.

To start the Lotus 1-2-3 Access Menu, follow these steps:

1. With the C> system prompt displayed on your screen, change to the \123R23 directory by typing **cd\123R23** and pressing ⏎Enter.
2. Start the Lotus 1-2-3 Access Menu by typing **lotus** and pressing ⏎Enter.

33

2

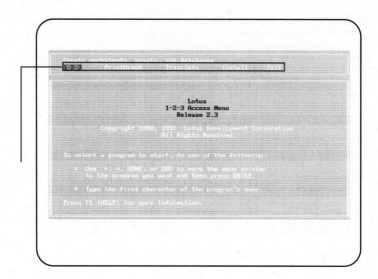

The Lotus 1-2-3
Access Menu
screen appears.

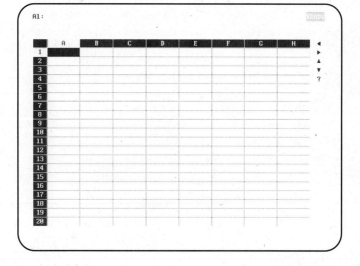

The 1-2-3 option,
logically enough,
starts the main
1-2-3 program.

34

2

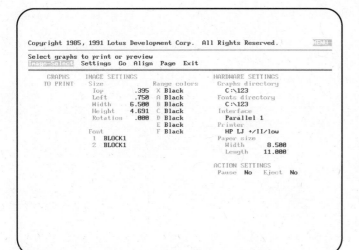

The **P**rintGraph
option begins the
1-2-3 PrintGraph
program for
graph printing.
You can also use
Wysiwyg to print
graphs from
within the 1-2-3
worksheet.

```
                Lotus  1-2-3  Release 2.3 Translate Utility
      Copr. 1985, 1991  Lotus Development Corporation  All Rights Reserved

   What do you want to translate FROM?

              1-2-3 1A
              1-2-3 2.2 through 2.3
              dBase II
              dBase III
              DIF
              Enable 2.0
              Multiplan (SYLK)
              SuperCalc4
              Symphony 1.0
              Symphony 1.1 through 2.2
              VisiCalc


           Move the menu pointer to your selection and press ENTER
                 Press ESC to end the Translate utility
                 Press F1 (HELP) for more information
```

The Translate
option accesses
the 1-2-3 Trans-
late utility, which
allows you to
translate files
between 1-2-3
and other soft-
ware programs.

35

2

The Translate utility provides links among different versions of 1-2-3, and also between 1-2-3 and other software programs, such as dBASE, Symphony, and Multiplan. An example of using the Translate utility is included in Chapter 10 of this book. For further information, refer to the Lotus documentation or Que's *Using 1-2-3 for DOS Release 2.3,* Special Edition.

The **Install** option accesses the 1-2-3 Install program, which changes the options set during installation.

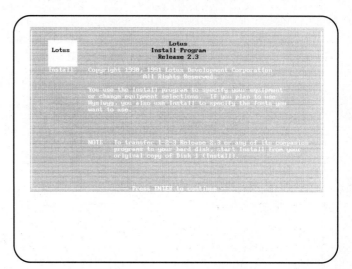

See the Lotus documentation or the Appendix of this book for specific installation instructions.

Exit quits the 1-2-3 program and returns you to DOS.

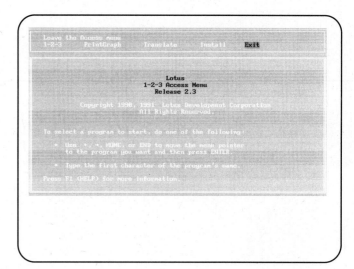

Starting Wysiwyg

2

To take advantage of the new Wysiwyg features of 1-2-3 Release 2.3, you have to load the Wysiwyg add-in into memory. This multistep procedure must be performed each time you start 1-2-3 unless you set 1-2-3 to load and invoke Wysiwyg automatically. You can save time by configuring your system to load and invoke Wysiwyg automatically. The automatic and manual methods of loading Wysiwyg are presented in the following sections.

Starting Wysiwyg Automatically

If you choose the automatic method of loading and invoking Wysiwyg, you need to complete the following procedure only once. Wysiwyg will then load and invoke each time you access 1-2-3. This automatic method is the recommended procedure for accessing Wysiwyg.

To configure your system to load and invoke Wysiwyg automatically, follow these steps:

1. Call up the 1-2-3 menu by pressing ⃞/.
2. Select Worksheet **G**lobal **D**efault **O**ther **A**dd-In **S**et.

   Note: To select commands from menus, press the first letter of the command (⃞W ⃞G ⃞D ⃞O ⃞A ⃞S in this example) or highlight each command and press ⏎Enter. If you use a mouse, point to a command and click the left mouse button. Chapter 3 discusses command selection in detail.

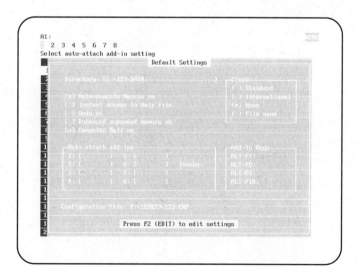

1-2-3 displays up to eight choices for add-ins.

3. Select a number from 1 to 8. If this is the first add-in you are setting up to load automatically, select **1**.

4. From the list of files that appears, type or highlight **WYSIWYG.ADN** and press ⏎Enter.

5. Select **No**-key.

   Note: Although you can choose to attach Wysiwyg with a function key, it is recommended that you select the **No**-key option.

6. Select **Yes** to automatically activate Wysiwyg each time you load 1-2-3.

7. To save this setting and return to the 1-2-3 worksheet, select **Quit Update Quit**.

The next time you start 1-2-3, and each time thereafter, the 1-2-3 worksheet loads, and then Wysiwyg loads automatically.

Starting Wysiwyg Manually

If you choose the manual method of loading Wysiwyg, you must complete the entire procedure that follows each time you access 1-2-3. This option is preferable if you will seldom need the spreadsheet publishing features offered with Wysiwyg (requiring additional memory and processing time).

To load Wysiwyg manually, follow these steps:

1. Call up the 1-2-3 menu by pressing /.

2. Select **Add-In**. (You can also access the /Add-in menu by pressing and holding the Alt key and pressing F10.)

   Note: To select commands from menus, press the first letter of the command (A in this example) or highlight the command and press ⏎Enter. If you use a mouse, point to a command and click the left mouse button. Chapter 3 discusses command selection in detail.

3. Select **Attach**.

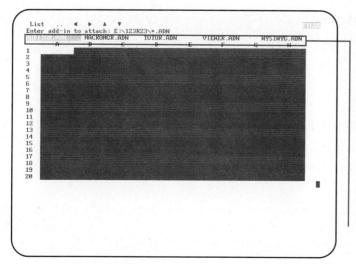

A list of add-in files appears. In addition to Wysiwyg, the spreadsheet auditor, macro library manager, 1-2-3 tutor, and file viewer are other options that come with 1-2-3 Release 2.3.

4. Type or highlight **WYSIWYG.ADN** and press ⏎Enter.

5. Select **No-key**.

    Note: Although you can choose to attach Wysiwyg to a function key, it is recommended that you select the **No-key** option.

    Once you make your selection, the Wysiwyg copyright screen appears, and then the Wysiwyg worksheet appears.

6. To return to the 1-2-3 worksheet, select **Quit**.

Exiting 1-2-3

There are two ways to leave the 1-2-3 program to return to DOS: by using the /System command or the /Quit command. Both commands are accessible from the 1-2-3 main menu. To access the main menu, press the slash (/) key. The **S**ystem and **Q**uit commands are listed among the options on this menu.

2

Using /System To Leave 1-2-3 Temporarily

The /System command returns you to the DOS system prompt, but you do not exit the 1-2-3 program—your departure is only temporary.

To leave 1-2-3 temporarily, follow these steps:

1. Call up the 1-2-3 menu by pressing ⌷.

   Note: Mouse users can access a menu by moving the mouse pointer to the area above the worksheet frame. This action automatically generates the 1-2-3 or Wysiwyg menu (depending on which menu was used most recently). Click the right mouse button to toggle between the two menus.

The 1-2-3 main menu is displayed.

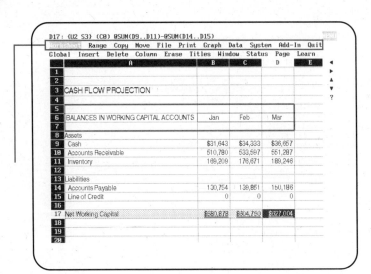

2. Select **System**.

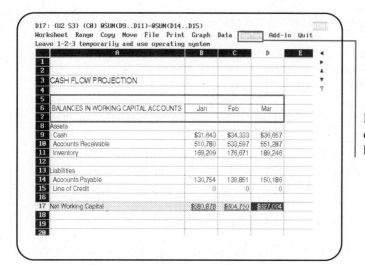

Here, the **System** command is highlighted.

After you select the **System** command, the DOS prompt is displayed.

3. While at the DOS level, perform the desired system operation (such as changing drives or directories, copying files, or accessing other programs).

4. To return to the 1-2-3 worksheet, type exit and press ↵Enter. You return to the current worksheet, in the exact place where you issued the /System command.

The Advantages of Using /System

/System is a useful command when you need to check the amount of space remaining on disk before you copy a file to it, or when you want to see how large a particular worksheet is before you load the worksheet. /System saves you the trouble of quitting the 1-2-3 program, issuing the appropriate DOS commands, and then getting back into the worksheet.

The /System command is particularly useful for giving you access to your system's file-handling commands. For example, if you want to save your worksheet but your data diskette is full, you can use the /System command to suspend 1-2-3 processing while you prepare a new diskette using the DOS FORMAT command. After you return to 1-2-3 by typing **exit** and pressing Enter, you can save your worksheet to the new diskette with the /File Save command.

The Limitations of Using /System

You should be aware of two potential problems in using the /System command. First, if you have a large worksheet that takes up most memory, the /System command may fail because there is not enough memory to run another program. If the /System command fails, 1-2-3 displays the error message `Insufficient memory to invoke DOS`, and the ERROR indicator appears in the upper right corner of the screen. If this happens, you can press Esc to return to your worksheet.

The second problem is that certain programs you run from 1-2-3 by using the /System command may cause 1-2-3 to abort when you try to return by typing **exit** and pressing Enter. You can safely invoke from 1-2-3 DOS file-management commands such as FORMAT, COPY, ERASE, DIR, and DISKCOPY, and most business-application programs. Starting one of the many memory-resident utility programs, however, causes 1-2-3 to abort when you type **exit** and press Enter. Before trying to use the /System command during an important 1-2-3 session, take a few minutes to experiment with the programs you want to use.

2

Using /Quit To Exit 1-2-3

The /Quit command from the 1-2-3 main menu allows you to exit both the worksheet and the 1-2-3 program. You are asked to verify this choice before you exit 1-2-3, because your data will be lost if you quit 1-2-3 without saving your file.

To exit 1-2-3, follow these steps:

1. Call up the 1-2-3 menu by pressing ⌷ or moving the mouse pointer to the top of the screen (and clicking the right mouse button to switch to the 1-2-3 menu, if necessary).

   Note: If you haven't saved your file, do so now by selecting **F**ile **S**ave. Next, enter the file name. If the file name already exists, select **R**eplace to update the current file. Then press ⌷ again before proceeding with the next step. The process of saving files is explained in the next chapter.

2. Select **Q**uit.

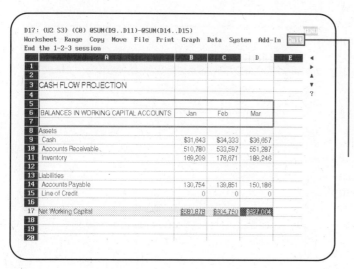

Here, the **Quit** command is highlighted.

2

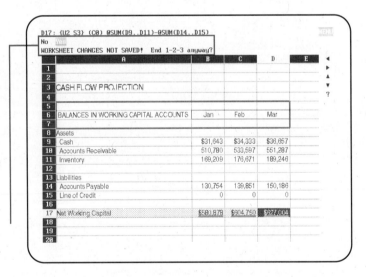

```
D17: (U2 S3) (C0) @SUM(D9..D11)-@SUM(D14..D15)                    TEXT
┌────┐
│ No │ Yes
└────┘
End 1-2-3 session (Remember to save your worksheet first)
                             A              B        C        D      E    ◄
 1                                                                        ►
 2                                                                        ▲
 3   CASH FLOW PROJECTION                                                 ▼
 4                                                                        ?
 5
 6   BALANCES IN WORKING CAPITAL ACCOUNTS    Jan      Feb      Mar
 7
 8   Assets
 9     Cash                                $31,643  $34,333  $36,657
10     Accounts Receivable                 510,780  533,597  551,287
11     Inventory                           169,209  176,671  189,246
12
13   Liabilities
14     Accounts Payable                    130,754  139,851  150,186
15     Line of Credit                            0        0        0
16
17   Net Working Capital                  $580,878 $604,750 $627,004
18
19
20
```

You are asked to verify that you want to exit.

3. Select **Yes**.

If you have made changes in your current worksheet but have not saved them with **/File Save**, 1-2-3 beeps and displays a reminder when you try to exit.

```
D17: (U2 S3) (C0) @SUM(D9..D11)-@SUM(D14..D15)                    TEXT
┌────┐
│ No │ Yes
└────┘
WORKSHEET CHANGES NOT SAVED!  End 1-2-3 anyway?
                             A              B        C        D      E    ◄
 1                                                                        ►
 2                                                                        ▲
 3   CASH FLOW PROJECTION                                                 ▼
 4                                                                        ?
 5
 6   BALANCES IN WORKING CAPITAL ACCOUNTS    Jan      Feb      Mar
 7
 8   Assets
 9     Cash                                $31,643  $34,333  $36,657
10     Accounts Receivable                 510,780  533,597  551,287
11     Inventory                           169,209  176,671  189,246
12
13   Liabilities
14     Accounts Payable                    130,754  139,851  150,186
15     Line of Credit                            0        0        0
16
17   Net Working Capital                  $580,878 $604,750 $627,004
18
19
20
```

4. If you have already made changes to the file since it was last saved and you want to abandon these changes, select **Yes**.

    Otherwise, if you need to save the file before exiting 1-2-3, select **No**. Then use **/File Save** to save your file before you exit 1-2-3.

2

Note: If you started 1-2-3 from the Lotus 1-2-3 Access Menu, you return to the Lotus 1-2-3 Access Menu when you select /Quit. To exit the Lotus 1-2-3 Access Menu and return to the operating system, select **Exit**.

Learning the Keyboard

Before you begin learning 1-2-3, you need to get to know your keyboard. Each of the two most popular keyboards consists of these sections: the alphanumeric keys in the center, the numeric keypad with direction keys on the right, and the function-key section on the left or across the top. The enhanced keyboard, the standard keyboard for all new IBM personal computers and most compatibles, also has a separate grouping of direction keys.

The original IBM Personal Computer AT keyboard

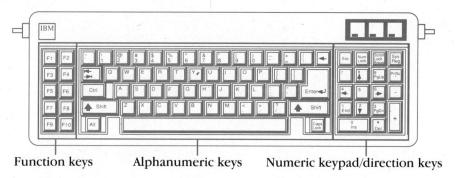

Function keys   Alphanumeric keys   Numeric keypad/direction keys

The Enhanced Keyboard   Function keys

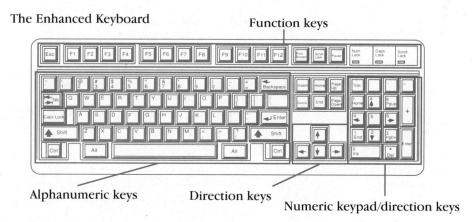

Alphanumeric keys   Direction keys   Numeric keypad/direction keys

2

The Alphanumeric Keys

Most of the alphanumeric keys on the computer keyboard perform the same actions as those on a typewriter. In 1-2-3 several of the keys have special functions. For example, the slash (/) key accesses the 1-2-3 menu, the colon (:) key accesses the Wysiwyg menu, and the period (.) key defines a range of cells. Table 2.1 highlights each of these important keys.

Table 2.1
The Special Keys

Key	Action
Esc	Returns to the previous menu; erases the current entry during editing, or the range or command specification; returns from a help screen; clears error messages from the screen.
Tab	Moves the cell pointer one screen to the right.
Shift Tab	Moves the cell pointer one screen to the left.
Caps Lock	Activates capitalization of all alphabetic characters when keys for those characters are pressed. Displays the CAPS indicator in the status line when active. Remains in effect until you press this key again (acts as a toggle).
Shift	Changes lowercase letters and characters to uppercase. When not in Num Lock mode, enables typing of numbers on the numeric keypad.
Ctrl	When used with the left- or right-arrow key, moves the cell pointer one screen to the left or right in READY mode or moves the cursor five characters to the left or right in EDIT mode; when used with Break, returns 1-2-3 to READY mode or halts execution of a macro.
Alt	When used with other keys, invokes macros, activates Step mode, performs an Undo, or executes other commands.
Space bar	Inserts a space within a cell entry; moves the menu pointer one item to the right when selecting commands from a menu.

2

Key	Action
⬅Backspace	Erases the previous character in a cell during cell definition; erases the character to the left of the cursor during editing. Cancels a range during some prompts that display the old range.
↵Enter	Accepts an entry into a cell or selects a highlighted menu command.
.	Defines a range of cells or anchors one corner when defining a range. Also used as a decimal point.
:	Calls up the Wysiwyg menu.
/	Calls up the 1-2-3 main menu; also functions as a division sign in formulas.
<	Used as an alternative to the slash (/) for calling up the 1-2-3 main menu; also used in logical formulas.
Scroll Lock	Scrolls the entire window one row or column when the cell pointer is moved. Displays the SCROLL indicator in the status line when active. Acts as a toggle.
Pause	Pauses a macro, a recalculation, and some commands until you press any key. On AT keyboards, Pause is Ctrl Num Lock .
Num Lock	Activates the numeric representation of keys in the numeric keypad. Displays the NUM indicator in the status line when active. Acts as a toggle.
Ins	Changes 1-2-3 from insert mode to overtype mode during editing. When pressed, causes the OVR indicator to be displayed in the status line and enables new characters to overwrite existing text. Acts as a toggle.
Del	When a cell containing an entry is highlighted, erases the cell entry (similar to the /Range Erase command). Also deletes the character above the cursor during the editing process.

2

The Numeric Keypad and Direction Keys

The keys in the numeric keypad are used mainly for data entry and for moving the cell pointer or cursor. The enhanced keyboard has separate direction keys for this movement function.

To use the numeric keypad to enter numbers rather than to position the cell pointer or cursor, you can either press Num Lock before and after you enter the numbers and then move to the next cell, or hold down Shift only when you press the number keys.

Neither way is ideal, because you have to switch between functions. If you have an enhanced keyboard, you don't have this problem because your keyboard has a special set of direction keys that have no other purpose. If you don't have an enhanced keyboard, you can create a simple macro that lets you enter numbers and move to the next cell without having to press Shift or Num Lock.

The Function Keys

You use the function keys F1 through F10 for special tasks, such as accessing Help, editing cells, and recalculating the worksheet. Although the enhanced keyboard has 12 function keys (F1 through F12), 1-2-3 uses only the first 10 of these.

In addition to pressing the function key alone, 1-2-3 also uses the Alt key in conjunction with function keys. To use the Alt-function key combination, first hold down the Alt key, and then press the function key. In Release 2.3, if you use the Ctrl key with the F1 key, you can display the last Help screen that was viewed.

A plastic function-key template that describes the actions of each function key or Alt-function key combination on the enhanced keyboard is provided with the Lotus software. Another version of the template is provided for users with AT or compatible keyboards. Table 2.2 explains the operations of the function keys.

2

Table 2.2
The Function Keys

Key	Action
F1	**(Help)** Accesses 1-2-3's context-sensitive help system, and displays a cross-referenced Help index. Also explains error messages that appear in a dialog box on-screen.
F2	**(Edit)** Shifts 1-2-3 to EDIT mode. Also allows you to activate a dialog box displayed on-screen.
F3	**(Name)** Displays a list of names in the control panel any time a command or formula can accept a range name or file name. Pressing F3 a second time switches to a full-screen display.
F4	**(Abs)** In READY mode, predefines ranges in 1-2-3 or Wysiwyg, allowing multiple commands to then be executed on that range. In EDIT mode, changes a cell address or range from relative to absolute to mixed.
F5	**(GoTo)** Moves the cell pointer to the specified cell coordinates (or range name).
F6	**(Window)** Moves the cell pointer to the other side of a split screen. Also toggles the display of dialog boxes on-screen.
F7	**(Query)** Repeats the most recent /Data **Q**uery operation.
F8	**(Table)** Repeats the most recent /Data **T**able operation.
F9	**(Calc)** Recalculates all formulas in the worksheet. If entering or editing a formula, converts the formula to its current value.
F10	**(Graph)** Displays the current graph on-screen, if one exists.
Alt F1	**(Compose)** Allows you to create characters not found on the normal keyboard, such as bullets and foreign currency symbols.

continued

2

Table 2.2 (continued)

Key	Action
Alt F2	**(Step)** Steps through macros one step at a time, allowing you to find errors.
Alt F3	**(Run)** Generates a list of range names in the worksheet, allowing you to select the name of a macro to run.
Alt F4	**(Undo)** When Undo is activated, reverses all actions made since 1-2-3 was last in READY mode.
Alt F5	**(Learn)** Records keystrokes to a defined learn range to create a macro. Press again to stop recording keystrokes.
Alt F7	**(App1)** Activates an add-in program assigned to this key combination, if one has been assigned.
Alt F8	**(App2)** Activates an add-in program assigned to this key combination, if one has been assigned.
Alt F9	**(App3)** Activates an add-in program assigned to this key combination, if one has been assigned.
Alt F10	**(App4)** Activates an add-in program assigned to this key combination, if one has been assigned. Otherwise, displays the /Add-In menu.
Ctrl F1	**(Bookmark)** Displays the last Help screen that was viewed.

Understanding Mouse Terminology

To use a mouse, you have to load a mouse driver before starting 1-2-3. 1-2-3 does not provide the mouse driver; the company that manufactures the mouse does. Directions for adding a mouse driver are in the documentation you received with your mouse.

Your mouse can replace some of the activities normally done from the keyboard. The mouse pointer, a small arrow appearing on-screen, points to the center of the screen when 1-2-3 is loaded. Pressing either the right or left mouse button enables you to use the mouse and mouse pointer to select commands, switch between the 1-2-3 and Wysiwyg menus, move the cell and

2

menu pointers, select ranges, and choose options on dialog boxes. Before using the mouse, you should become familiar with additional terms such as point, click, click-and-drag, icon, and icon panel.

To *point* means to move the mouse until the tip of the arrow is pointing on something. For example, if you are instructed to point to (or highlight) cell B5, then you must move the mouse until the tip of the arrow is over cell B5.

When you *click* the mouse, you press and immediately release one of the two buttons on the mouse. (If your mouse has three buttons, only the two outside buttons are active. The center button is not used in 1-2-3.) Normally, you only click a mouse button after you point with the mouse. The left button on the mouse acts as the Enter key. The right button has two functions. The right button usually acts as the Esc key; if you are typing text into a cell, for example, pressing the right button erases the text from the edit line and returns 1-2-3 to READY mode. The second function of the right mouse button is to switch between the 1-2-3 menu and the Wysiwyg menu.

With the Install program, you can reverse the operations of the mouse buttons. That is, you can make the right button the Enter button and the left button the Esc/Switch menu button. This is helpful if you are left-handed because reversing the buttons enables you to use your index finger on the primary button and your middle finger on the secondary button.

Click-and-drag is a combination of pointing, clicking, and moving the mouse. You normally use this method to highlight a worksheet range.

To click-and-drag, follow these steps:

1. Move the mouse pointer to the desired beginning location, such as the upper left corner of a range.
2. Press and hold the left mouse button; do not release the button at this time (this anchors the cell pointer).
3. Move the mouse to the desired ending location, such as the lower right corner of a range, and release the mouse button. The desired range is highlighted.
4. Click the left mouse button again to finish specifying the range.

For example, to select a range from B5 through D10, point to cell B5, press and hold the left mouse button and point to cell D10; then release the left mouse button and press the left button again.

2

An *icon* is a character that represents an action. These characters are displayed on the right side on the screen—within the *icon panel*. There are four triangles and one question mark. When you point and click on one of the icons, you invoke an action.

Clicking any of the triangles has the same action as pressing one of the arrow keys; the cell pointer moves one cell in the direction indicated by the triangle. Clicking the question mark selects Help, just as if you pressed the Help (F1) function key.

When a mouse is installed, the five mouse icons appear within the icon panel—on the right side of the Release 2.3 screen.

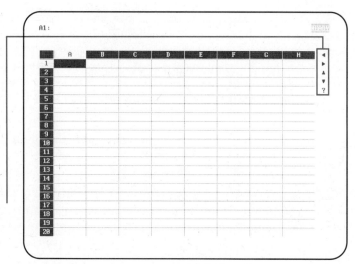

Understanding the 1-2-3 Screen

The 1-2-3 display is divided into three main parts: the control panel at the top of the screen, the worksheet area, and the status line at the bottom of the screen. (If you have a mouse, the screen also includes an icon panel with five icons, located on the right side of the screen or on the first line of the screen when you use some commands, such as /**File R**etrieve). The worksheet frame separates the control panel from the worksheet area. This frame contains the letters and numbers that mark the columns and rows of the worksheet area. The sections that follow describe each of these areas in more detail.

2

Control panel

Worksheet area

Worksheet frame

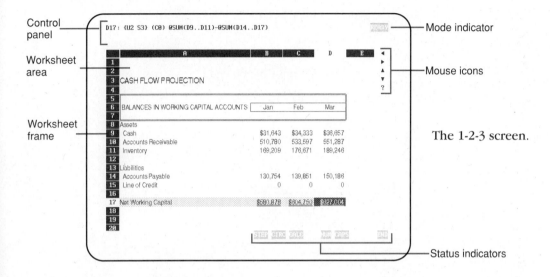

The 1-2-3 screen.

Mode indicator

Mouse icons

Status indicators

The Control Panel

The *control panel*, the area above the reverse-video border, can show three lines of information. The control panel contains data about the current cell as well as the menu commands.

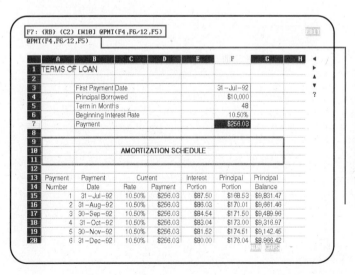

The first line of the control panel shows information about the current cell (the cell highlighted by the cell pointer).

2

In this example, the control panel includes the following cell information:

F7: {RB} (C2) [W10] @PMT(F4,F6/12,F5)

This line displays the address of the cell (F7), followed by the Wysiwyg format (right bottom line), display format (C2 for *Currency*, *2* decimal places), the column width (10 characters), and the content of the cell (in this case, a formula). When applicable, this line also shows the protection status of the cell (U if unprotected or PR if protected). The upper right corner of the first line always displays the mode indicator (EDIT in this example). Mode indicators are explained in detail later in this chapter. When Wysiwyg is active, information applicable to Wysiwyg, such as row height, graph, and text format, also appears on this line.

The second line of the control panel contains any characters that are being entered or edited or displays the options in a menu. The preceding example shows a formula to be edited.

This example shows the 1-2-3 main menu with the Worksheet menu option highlighted.

	F7: {RB} (C2) [W10] @PMT(F4,F6/12,F5)						MENU

Worksheet Range Copy Move File Print Graph Data System Add-In Quit
Global Insert Delete Column Erase Titles Window Status Page Learn

	A	B	C	D	E	F	G	H
1	TERMS OF LOAN							
2								
3		First Payment Date				31−Jul−92		
4		Principal Borrowed				$10,000		
5		Term in Months				48		
6		Beginning Interest Rate				10.50%		
7		Payment				$256.03		
8								
9								
10			AMORTIZATION SCHEDULE					
11								
12								
13	Payment	Payment	Current	∗	Interest	Principal	Principal	
14	Number	Date	Rate	Payment	Portion	Portion	Balance	
15	1	31−Jul−92	10.50%	$256.03	$87.50	$168.53	$9,831.47	
16	2	31−Aug−92	10.50%	$256.03	$86.03	$170.01	$9,661.46	
17	3	30−Sep−92	10.50%	$256.03	$84.54	$171.50	$9,489.96	
18	4	31−Oct−92	10.50%	$256.03	$83.04	$173.00	$9,316.97	
19	5	30−Nov−92	10.50%	$256.03	$81.52	$174.51	$9,142.45	
20	6	31−Dec−92	10.50%	$256.03	$80.00	$176.04	$8,966.42	

NUM CAPS

The third line of the control panel provides explanations of the current menu item or the next hierarchical menu. As you move the menu pointer from one item to the next in a command menu, the explanation on the third line of the control panel changes to correspond with the highlighted option.

The Worksheet Area

The largest part of the 1-2-3 screen is composed of the *worksheet area*. As described in Chapter 1, the 1-2-3 worksheet consists of 256 lettered columns

2

and 8,192 numbered rows, yet only a portion of the worksheet is displayed on the screen at any time. All information entered into the worksheet is stored in cells. A cell is the intersection of a column and a row.

The Worksheet Frame

To the left and above the worksheet area is the *worksheet frame*. When you first start 1-2-3, the letters A–H appear at the top of each column and the numbers 1–20 appear at the left of each row. As you move around the worksheet, the column letters and row numbers change and 1-2-3 highlights the current column and row to indicate your position.

The Status Line

The status line is the bottom line of the 1-2-3 screen. This line normally displays the current date and time, but you can change it to reflect the current file name or to display neither date and time nor file name. The current date and time can be displayed in the status line in two different formats. This line also contains any status indicators, described in the following sections.

The 1-2-3 Indicators

The 1-2-3 screen can display two different types of indicators. The mode indicators appear in the upper right corner of the control panel. The status indicators appear within the status line along the bottom of the screen. The 1-2-3 indicators are summarized in table 2.3. The next few sections explain each of these types of indicators.

Table 2.3
The 1-2-3 Indicators

Indicator	Description
The Mode Indicators	
COLOR	Wysiwyg is prompting you to select a color from its palette of colors.
CYCLE	You selected the Wysiwyg command **:**Graph Edit Select Cycle.

continued

Table 2.3 (*continued*)

Indicator	Description
DRAG	You selected the Wysiwyg command **:G**raph **E**dit **A**dd **R**ectangle or **E**llipse.
EDIT	F2 has been pressed. A cell entry is being edited, or you are editing settings in a dialog box.
ERROR	1-2-3 encountered an error, and a dialog box is displaying the error on-screen. Press F1 to display an explanation of the error.
FILES	1-2-3 is waiting for you to select a file name from a list of file names.
FIND	1-2-3 is in the middle of a /**D**ata **Q**uery **F**ind operation.
FRMT	You pressed /**D**ata **P**arse **F**ormat-Line **E**dit and 1-2-3 is waiting for you to edit the format line.
HELP	You pressed F1 (Help) causing 1-2-3 to display a pop-up help screen. Press Esc to return to the worksheet.
LABEL	A label is being entered.
MENU	A list of command choices is displayed because you pressed / or < from READY mode.
NAMES	1-2-3 is waiting for you to select from a list of range names, graph names, or attached add-in names.
PAN	You selected the Wysiwyg command **:G**raph **E**dit **V**iew **P**an.
POINT	1-2-3 is waiting for you to point to a cell, or Wysiwyg is waiting for you to select a point on a diagram.
READY	1-2-3 is waiting for a command or cell entry. This is the default mode when you start 1-2-3.
SELECT	Wysiwyg is waiting for you to select an item.
SETTINGS	You pressed a command that allows you to change a number of settings. 1-2-3 displays a dialog box. Change the settings through the command line, with the mouse, or by pressing F2 and choosing the highlighted letters.

2

Indicator	Description
SIZE	Wysiwyg is asking you to resize an object.
STAT	1-2-3 is displaying the status of the current worksheet.
TEXT	You selected the Wysiwyg command **:T**ext **E**dit.
VALUE	A number or formula is being entered.
WAIT	1-2-3 is in the middle of a command or process and cannot respond to other commands until the indicator disappears.
WYSIWYG	With Wysiwyg loaded in memory, a menu of Wysiwyg commands is displayed because you pressed the colon (**:**) key from READY mode.

The Status Indicators

CALC	The file is set to manual recalculation and there has been a change since the last calculation. Press F9 (Calc) to recalculate the worksheet and clear the indicator.
CAPS	Caps Lock has been pressed and is active. All letters are entered as uppercase. Acts as a toggle.
CIRC	A circular reference (a formula that refers to itself) has been found. The **/W**orksheet **S**tatus command or the Auditor add-in can be used to display the location of the circular reference.
CMD	A 1-2-3 macro is executing.
END	The End key has been pressed and is active, waiting for you to press a direction key. Acts as a toggle.
LEARN	You have pressed Alt-F5, and 1-2-3 is now recording all your keystrokes in a Learn range that you defined with **/W**orksheet **L**earn.
MEM	Random-access memory is almost exhausted. If you continue to enter data, you can receive a `Memory full` error message.
NUM	Num Lock has been pressed and is active. You can use the numeric keypad to enter numbers without using Shift. Acts as a toggle.

continued

2

Table 2.3 (*continued*)

Indicator	Description
OVR	The Ins key has been pressed while in EDIT mode—1-2-3 replaces any keystrokes above the cursor with the typed characters. Acts as a toggle.
PRT	Indicates a background print (started with either the /**P**rint Background or the **:P**rint Background command) is in progress.
RO	The current file is read-only. The file can only be saved with a different name. Applies to files used on a network or multiuser system. Sometimes occurs if you run out of memory while reading a file.
SCROLL	Scroll Lock has been pressed and is active. Whenever you use an arrow key, the entire window moves in the direction of the arrow. Acts as a toggle.
SST	A macro is in single-step execution (STEP mode).
STEP	You turned on single-step mode for macros, but you are not currently running a macro. When you start a macro, this indicator changes to SST.
UNDO	The Undo feature has been activated with the /**W**orksheet **G**lobal **D**efault **O**ther **U**ndo **E**nable command. You can press Alt-F4 to reverse changes made since 1-2-3 was last in READY mode.

The Mode Indicators

One of 1-2-3's modes is always in effect, depending on what you are doing. The mode indicator is shown in reverse video in the upper right corner of the screen, within the control panel. For example, READY appears whenever data can be entered into the worksheet or whenever the menu can be invoked.

2

VALUE is displayed as the mode indicator when you enter numbers or formulas; and LABEL appears when you enter letters, as in a title or label. You see the EDIT indicator after you press Edit (F2) in order to edit a formula or label in the control panel.

The Status Indicators

Other indicators report the status of the worksheet. They include general message indicators, such as CALC and LEARN, and warnings, such as CIRC and MEM. These indicators appear in reverse video along the bottom line of the screen. Note that when an error occurs, 1-2-3 beeps and displays a dialog box in the worksheet. For more information on the error, press F1. To clear the error and return to READY mode, press Esc.

The status indicators NUM, CAPS, and SCROLL represent the keyboard's Num Lock, Caps Lock, and Scroll Lock keys, respectively. These keys are "lock" keys because they can temporarily lock the keyboard into a certain function. When a lock key is active, 1-2-3 displays the key's indicator in reverse video in the lower right corner of the screen. Many keyboards also use different lights that show when a particular lock key is active. Each lock key is a toggle, which means that pressing the key repeatedly turns its function alternately on and off. Therefore, to turn off a lock key that is on, you simply press it again.

Two other status indicators used within 1-2-3 are OVR for the Ins key and END for the End key. When OVR appears in reverse video at the bottom of the screen, you know that 1-2-3 is in overtype mode. That is, whatever you type while in EDIT mode replaces existing characters, numerals, or symbols.

The Interactive Dialog Boxes

When you can change a number of options at one time, Lotus provides dialog boxes. These special status screens show what the current settings are and allow you to change the options directly on the screen or through command menus. When you choose certain options on dialog boxes, an additional pop-up dialog box may appear to offer you further options. Chapter 3 describes how to make choices in the dialog boxes.

2

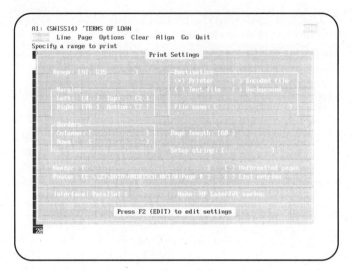

This is an example of the Print Settings dialog box.

The Mouse Icons

When you use certain commands that require listing files or range names, 1-2-3 removes the mouse icons from the right side of the screen and displays them on the first line of the screen. When prompted for a file name, in addition to the five original icons, 1-2-3 will display icons that help you choose the drive and directory.

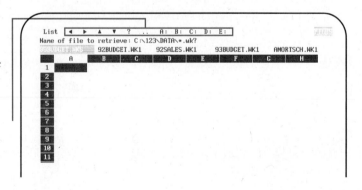

When you choose /**File Retrieve**, 1-2-3 displays additional icons.

As explained earlier, when you have a mouse loaded, the right side of the screen displays an icon panel for use with the mouse. Table 2.4 describes the function of each of these symbols. To select an icon, place the mouse pointer on the icon and click the left mouse button. Click and hold down the button to scroll continuously.

Table 2.4
The Icon Panel

Symbol	Function
◄	Moves the cell pointer one cell to the left
►	Moves the cell pointer one cell to the right
▲	Moves the cell pointer up one cell
▼	Moves the cell pointer down one cell
?	Activates a help screen
..	Go to parent directory (for example, if C:\123\DATA is the current directory, choosing .. will display the C:\123 directory)
A:, B:, C:	Change to the A:, B:, C:, or additional drives

Accessing the 1-2-3 Help System and On-Line Tutorial

One of the biggest selling points of 1-2-3 is its user-friendliness. Lotus tries to ensure that the spreadsheet program is easy to learn and use. The program offers you two basic kinds of assistance: a context-sensitive help system available with the touch of a key, and the 1-2-3 on-line tutorial that can be accessed from within the worksheet or from DOS.

The 1-2-3 Help System

1-2-3 has a context-sensitive help system. In other words, when you need clarification on a particular topic, you can press Help (F1) at any time and read the displayed information or select the topic you need from the list that appears. If you press Help (F1) while in READY mode, the Help Index appears. Choose any of the topics in the Help Index to get to the other help screens. You can use the keyboard or the mouse to navigate through help.

Using the 1-2-3 Help System with the Keyboard

When you want general help, or specific help on a command or function, use the following procedure.

61

2

To access the help screen for a specific financial function, you can type the @ sign and function name—for example, @**PMT**. Then press Help (F1).

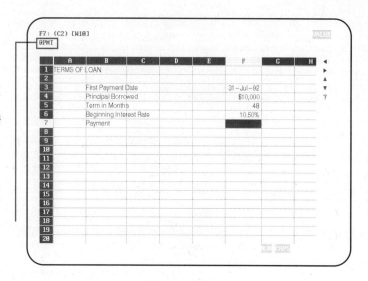

A context-sensitive pop-up screen about how to use the @PMT function appears.

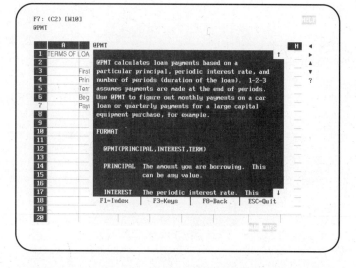

Read the screen. If necessary, to scroll the screen down, press the down-arrow key. For other keys to move around Help, see table 2.5.

If you want to go to the Help Index, press F1.

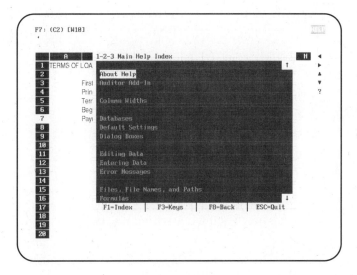

From the Help Index, you can choose many different topics.

To choose a help topic, use your arrow keys to point to the topic and press Enter.

To return to READY mode, press Esc.

Table 2.5
Navigation Keys for Help Screens

Key	Function
→, ↓, or Tab⇄	Moves the pointer to the next help topic. If there are no more help topics, scrolls the screen down one line at a time.
↑, ←, or ⇧Shift Tab⇄	Moves the pointer to the previous help topic. Otherwise, scrolls the screen up one line at a time.
End	Moves to the last help topic on-screen.
↵Enter	Displays the highlighted help topic.
Esc	Leaves help and returns to the worksheet.
F1	Shows the Help Index.
F3	Displays this list of help keys.
F8	Goes to the previous help screen.

continued

2

Table 2.5 (*continued*)

Key	Function
Home	Moves to the first help topic on-screen.
PgDn	Moves down one screen.
PgUp	Moves up one screen.

Using the 1-2-3 Help System with the Mouse

You can also use the mouse to navigate around the Help system. When you want general help, or specific help on a command or function, use the following procedure.

Move the mouse pointer to the ? icon and click the left mouse button.

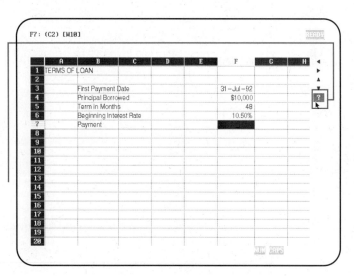

Read the screen. If necessary, to scroll the screen down, click on the down arrow in the pop-up screen. To scroll up, click on the up arrow. To return to the previous help screen, click on the F8=Back cell on the bottom of the pop-up screen.

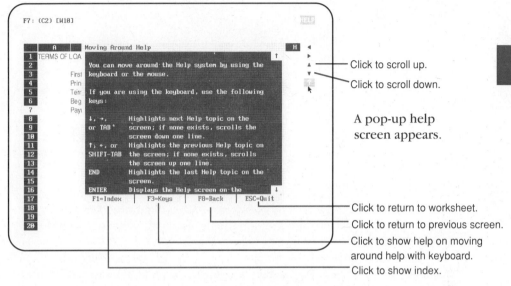

Click to scroll up.

Click to scroll down.

A pop-up help
screen appears.

Click to return to worksheet.

Click to return to previous screen.

Click to show help on moving
around help with keyboard.

Click to show index.

If you want to go to the Help Index, click on the `F1=Index` cell.

To choose a help topic, click on the topic.

To return to READY mode, click the left mouse button on the `ESC=Quit` cell or press the right mouse button.

If you are working from the Wysiwyg command menu, pressing Help (F1) or clicking on the **?** icon brings up a Wysiwyg help screen. To get to the Wysiwyg help index, press F1 from READY mode, press End, and press Enter.

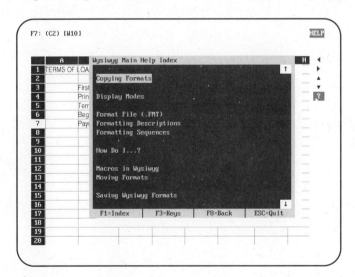

The Wysiwyg
Help Index
screen displays
many topics to
help you use
Wysiwyg.

The On-Line Tutorial

Lotus offers a series of self-paced lessons in an on-screen tutorial called *1-2-3-Go!* The lessons are arranged in order of increasing difficulty and build on each other. The Tutorial does not cover all of 1-2-3's functions and commands, but it includes enough information to give you a basic understanding of the program. Before you use the Tutorial, you must successfully install 1-2-3 on your hard disk and then attach the tutorial through the add-in key. You can also access the tutorial from your operating system by typing **LEARN123**. If you want to learn more about Wysiwyg, type **LEARNWYS** at the operating system prompt.

The best approach to using the Tutorial is to complete one section at a time. Then work with 1-2-3 for a while before you tackle the more advanced topics in subsequent lessons. To see some of the things that 1-2-3 can do and learn about how to operate the tutorial, choose the section titled Read Me First. For an introduction on how to start creating a worksheet, choose Section 1—Building a Worksheet. After you feel comfortable with all the material in the first two sections, you can try the other sections.

To use the on-screen tutorial from 1-2-3, follow these steps:

1. From within 1-2-3, select /Add-in (or press and hold the ⟨Alt⟩ key and press ⟨F10⟩).
2. Select Attach.
3. Type or highlight **TUTOR.ADN** and press ⟨↵Enter⟩.

    1-2-3 prompts you to choose a function key to activate the tutor.

4. If you think that you will want to use the tutor again in the current session, select **7**, **8**, **9**, or **10**.

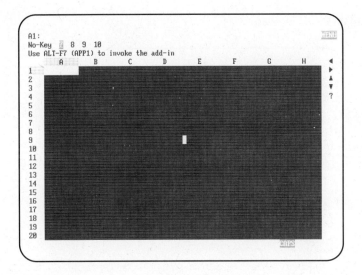

In this example, choose **7**.

5. When 1-2-3 returns to the Add-in menu, select **Invoke**.

6. To go to the tutor, type or highlight **TUTOR** and press ⏎Enter.

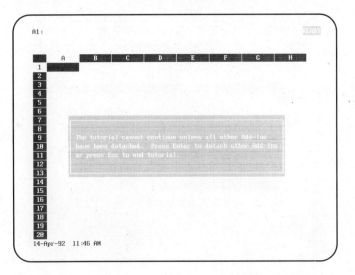

If other add-ins are present, 1-2-3 prompts you with this message.

67

7. If you have any other add-ins attached, press ↵Enter

2

The 1-2-3-Go!
screen appears.

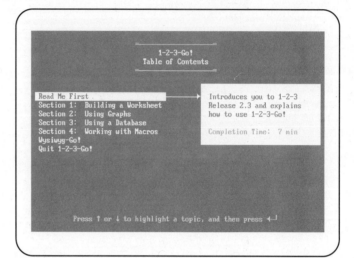

8. Select one of the sections by moving the highlighted bar and pressing
↵Enter

For example,
press ↵Enter to
begin the section
titled "Read Me
First."

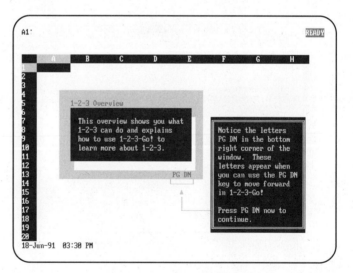

9. Follow the instructions on the screen.

10. If for some reason you want to quit in the middle of the tutorial, press the key combination you selected in step 4 (Alt F7 in this example) and choose Quit 1-2-3-Go!

Note: In this example, you chose an add-in function key for the tutor. Therefore, after you return to 1-2-3, you can press the key combination you selected (Alt-F7) to run the tutor again.

To run the on-screen tutorials from your operating system, follow these steps:

1. At the operating system prompt, change to your 1-2-3 directory.

   For example, at the ⌐ \> prompt, type **CD \123R23** and press ↵Enter

2. To start 1-2-3-Go!, type **LEARN123** and press ↵Enter

   Or

   To start Wysiwyg-Go!, type **LEARNWYS** and press ↵Enter

3. Select one of the sections by moving the highlighted bar and pressing ↵Enter.

4. Follow the instructions on the screen.

Summary

This chapter presented the information you need to use 1-2-3 for the first time. You learned how to start and exit 1-2-3 from either DOS or the Lotus 1-2-3 Access Menu, and how to start Wysiwyg. You also learned how to access the PrintGraph, Translate, and Install programs. The parts of the 1-2-3 screen and how 1-2-3 uses the keyboard and mouse also were presented. In addition, you learned how to use the on-line help facility and the 1-2-3 on-line tutorial.

Specifically, you learned the following key information about 1-2-3:

■ You can start 1-2-3 directly from DOS by typing 123 and pressing Enter from the \123R23 directory.

■ To start 1-2-3 from the Lotus 1-2-3 Access Menu (allowing entry into other 1-2-3 programs such as PrintGraph and Translate), type **lotus** (instead of **123**) and press Enter from the appropriate drive and directory.

■ To take advantage of the new Wysiwyg features of 1-2-3 Release 2.3, you have to load the Wysiwyg add-in into memory. This procedure must be performed each time you start 1-2-3—unless you set 1-2-3 to load and invoke Wysiwyg automatically.

■ The /System command enables you to leave 1-2-3 temporarily so that you can perform DOS commands. To return to the current 1-2-3 worksheet, type **exit** and press Enter from DOS.

■ Use the /Quit command to exit the worksheet and the 1-2-3 program. 1-2-3 allows you the option of canceling this choice when changes are made to the worksheet since it was last saved.

■ Most keyboards contain alphanumeric keys in the center of the keyboard, a numeric keypad and direction keys on the right side, and function keys on the left side or across the top.

■ You can use a mouse (if one is installed) to perform some of the activities normally handled from the keyboard. Pressing a mouse button enables you to select commands, switch between the 1-2-3 and Wysiwyg menus, move the cell and menu pointers, select ranges, and activate a pop-up dialog box.

■ The 1-2-3 screen consists of three main areas: the control panel (three lines at the top of the screen), the worksheet area (the major portion of the screen), and the status line (one line at the bottom of the screen). When a mouse is installed, the screen also contains an icon panel with five icons for use with the mouse (located on the right side of the screen).

■ The mode indicator is always displayed in the top right corner of the screen. The status indicators are displayed at different times in the status line at the bottom of the screen.

- 1-2-3 provides a context-sensitive help system that you can access by pressing Help (F1). You can also access an index for both 1-2-3 and Wysiwyg with several options from which you can choose a particular topic.

- 1-2-3's on-screen tutorial teaches basic concepts and skills for using 1-2-3. This tutorial is accessed through the /Add-in menu (or the Alt-F10 key combination).

Now that you are familiar with the 1-2-3 and Wysiwyg environment, you are ready to begin using 1-2-3 to enter data and formulas. The next chapter presents information on entering and editing data and formulas, and moving around the worksheet. Chapter 3 also presents additional information about using Wysiwyg.

2

Introducing
Worksheet
Basics

In Chapter 1, you learned that 1-2-3 is an integrated program that can do much more than make spreadsheet calculations. Depending on your business needs or assigned tasks, you can use 1-2-3 to create worksheets, generate presentation-quality reports, develop simple or complex databases, and produce graphics that illustrate worksheet data.

This chapter explores some of the simpler operations in 1-2-3: moving around the worksheet; selecting commands from menus; entering and editing data; using formulas and functions; and naming, saving, and retrieving files. This chapter also shows you how to use the mouse in Release 2.3 to navigate the worksheet and select commands and files from menus.

If you have used other spreadsheet programs, you are probably familiar with some of the concepts discussed in this chapter. If this is your first experience with spreadsheets, however, the basics discussed in this chapter are informative and helpful.

Moving around
the worksheet

Selecting
commands from
menus

Entering and
editing data

Entering
formulas and
functions

Using Undo

Naming, saving,
and retrieving
files

3

Key Terms in This Chapter

Cursor	The underscore that appears inside the cell pointer or within the control panel in EDIT mode.
Range name	An alphanumeric name given to a cell or a rectangular group of cells.
Menu pointer	The rectangular bar that highlights menu commands.
Data	Labels or values entered into a worksheet cell.
Label	A text entry entered in the worksheet.
Value	A number or formula entered in the worksheet.
Label prefix	A single aligning character typed before a label.
Operator	A mathematical or logical symbol that specifies an action to be performed on data.
Order of precedence	The order in which an equation or formula is executed; determines which operators act first.
Wild card	A character such as a question mark (?) or asterisk (*) that represents any other single or multiple character(s).
Dialog box	A status screen that shows you current options for a command and allows you to change those options on-screen.

Moving around the Worksheet

After you start entering data in your worksheet, you need some easy ways to move the cell pointer quickly and accurately. Remember that the 1-2-3 worksheet is immense—it contains 8,192 rows, 256 columns, and more than 2,000,000 cells. You may have many blocks of data of various sizes in widely separated parts of the worksheet. 1-2-3 provides several ways to quickly move the cell pointer to any location in the worksheet.

Remember that the cell pointer and the cursor are not the same. The *cell pointer* is the bright rectangle that highlights an entire cell in the worksheet area. The *cursor* is the underscore that is sometimes inside the cell pointer and sometimes in the control panel. The cursor indicates on-screen where keyboard activity takes effect; the cell pointer indicates the cell that is affected. Whenever you move the cell pointer, the cursor—inside the cell pointer— moves with it.

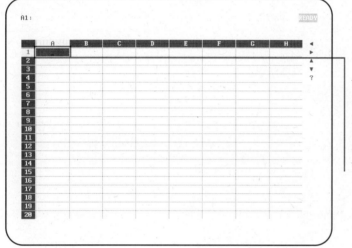

When you start 1-2-3, the cell pointer appears automatically in cell A1 of the worksheet.

You control the cell pointer either with keyboard keys or with a mouse. (To use a mouse, you must have a mouse driver loaded and a mouse attached to the computer.) The following section shows you how to use your keyboard to move the cell pointer around the worksheet. In a subsequent section, you learn how to use a mouse to navigate the worksheet.

Keyboard Control of the Cell Pointer

When 1-2-3 is in READY mode, the program is ready for you to enter data into the highlighted cell. To enter data in another cell, use the direction keys to move the cell pointer to the new location. See the tables in this chapter for explanations of the direction keys.

When you begin to enter data, the READY mode indicator changes to LABEL or VALUE, depending on whether you are entering text or numbers. The cursor disappears from the cell pointer and appears in the control panel, where the action is taking place.

When you enter
text, the READY
mode indicator
automatically
changes to
LABEL.

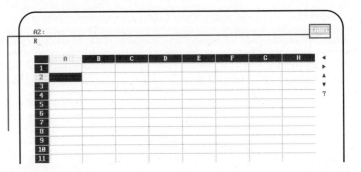

The POINT mode indicator signifies that you can position the cell pointer or
highlight a range in your worksheet.

When 1-2-3 is in
POINT mode, you
can point out a
range with the
direction keys.

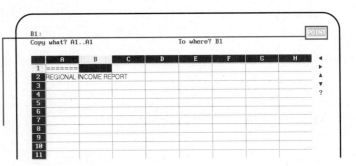

The direction
keys have differ-
ent actions when
you are editing in
EDIT mode,
making a cell
entry, or entering
a command.

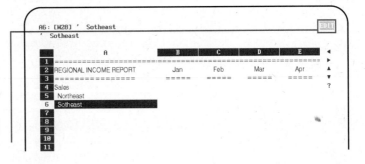

To edit a label or value in EDIT mode, move the cursor in the control panel
with the Home, End, and left- and right-arrow keys. The actions of direction
keys are described in table 3.1.

Table 3.1
Direction Keys

Key	Action
←	Moves the cell pointer one column to the left in the worksheet; in the control panel, moves the cursor one character to the left in EDIT mode or the menu pointer one item to the left in MENU mode
→	Moves the cell pointer one column to the right in the worksheet; in the control panel, moves the cursor one character to the right in EDIT mode or the menu pointer one item to the right in MENU mode
↑	Moves the cell pointer up one row
↓	Moves the cell pointer down one row
Tab⇄ or Ctrl→	Moves the cell pointer one screen to the right in the worksheet; in the control panel, moves the cursor five characters to the right in EDIT mode
⇧Shift Tab⇄ or Ctrl←	Moves the cell pointer one screen to the left in the worksheet; in the control panel, moves the cursor five characters to the left in EDIT mode
PgUp	Moves the cell pointer up one screen
PgDn	Moves the cell pointer down one screen
Home	Returns the cell pointer to cell A1 from any location in the current worksheet; when used after the End key, positions the pointer at the lower right corner of the current worksheet
End	When used before any arrow key, moves the cell pointer (in the direction of the arrow key) to the next boundary between a blank cell and a cell containing data
F5 (GoTo)	Moves the cell pointer to the cell coordinates (or range name) you specify

3

3

Using the Basic Direction Keys

The arrow keys on the numeric keypad (or on the separate pad of the enhanced keyboard) are the basic keys for moving the cell pointer with the keyboard. The cell pointer moves in the direction of the arrow on the key as long as you hold down the key. When you reach the edge of the screen, the worksheet continues scrolling in the direction of the arrow.

Scrolling the Worksheet

You can scroll the worksheet—one screen at a time—to the right by pressing the Tab key and to the left with Shift-Tab (hold down the Shift key while pressing Tab). You can also scroll the worksheet by holding down the Ctrl key and pressing the right- or left-arrow key. To get the same effect up or down, use the PgUp and PgDn keys to move up or down one screen at a time. Scrolling provides quick ways of paging through the worksheet.

In this income worksheet, the cell pointer is positioned at cell A1.

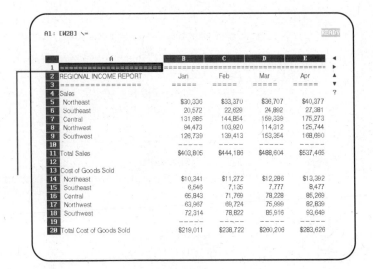

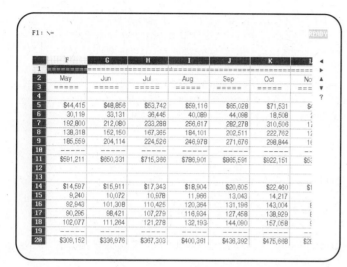

When you press Tab, the worksheet scrolls one screen to the right. The cell pointer now appears in cell F1 and columns F through K (and a portion of column L) appear on-screen.

3

If you then press Shift-Tab, the worksheet scrolls one screen to the left. In this example, the cell pointer returns to its original location at cell A1.

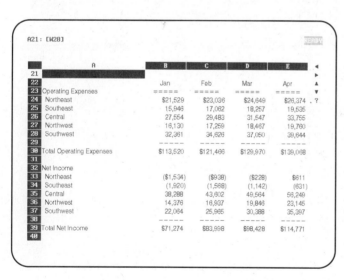

When you press PgDn, the worksheet scrolls down one screen. The cell pointer now appears in cell A21 and rows 21 through 40 display on-screen.

If you then press PgUp, the worksheet scrolls up one screen, and the cell pointer returns to its original location at cell A1.

Pressing the Scroll Lock key to activate the scroll function makes the worksheet appear to move in the opposite direction of the arrow key you press—no matter where the cell pointer is positioned on the screen. For example, if the cell pointer is positioned in cell A1 and you press the Scroll Lock key followed by the right-arrow key, the entire worksheet (not just the cell pointer) moves one column to the right. Learning 1-2-3 is usually easier without activating the scroll function with the Scroll Lock key.

Using the Home and End Keys

The Home key provides a quick way to return to the beginning of the current worksheet when 1-2-3 is in READY or POINT mode. Pressing Home makes the cell pointer return to cell A1 from anywhere in the worksheet.

When you press Home in READY mode, the cell pointer moves to cell A1.

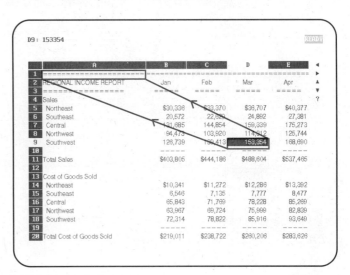

Pressing the Home key in POINT mode is a handy way to quickly highlight a range of data you plan to move or copy.

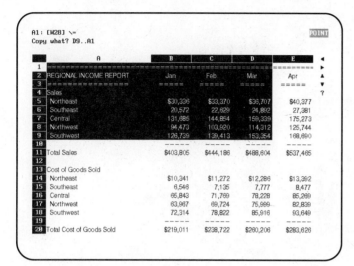

When you press Home in POINT mode, the cell pointer highlights a rectangle. One corner appears at A1, with the opposite corner at the original position of the cell pointer.

The Home and End keys have different actions in EDIT mode. For example, in EDIT mode, the Home key moves the cursor in the control panel.

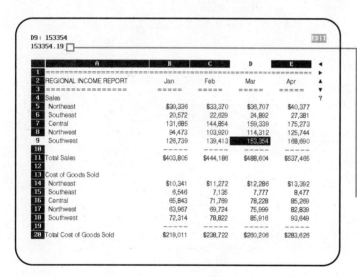

When you press F2 (Edit), the cursor appears in the control panel after the last character of your cell entry.

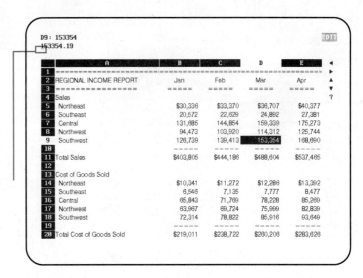

When you press Home in EDIT mode, the cursor moves to the first character in the cell entry.

1-2-3 uses the End key in a unique way. When you press an arrow key after you have pressed and released the End key, the cell pointer moves in the direction of the arrow key to the next boundary between a blank cell and a cell containing data. Because the cell pointer moves only to the next boundary, any gaps (blank lines) in your blocks of data will slow this procedure.

As the following example illustrates, you can use the End key with the arrow keys to quickly reach the borders of the worksheet area in a worksheet.

To learn how the End key works with the arrow keys, follow these steps:

1. Move the cell pointer to the edge of a contiguous range of cells.

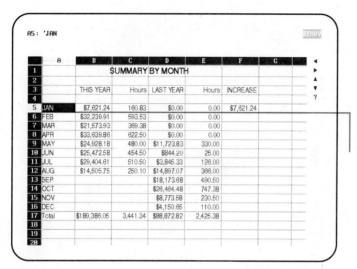

In this example, start at cell A5.

3

2. Press `End`.

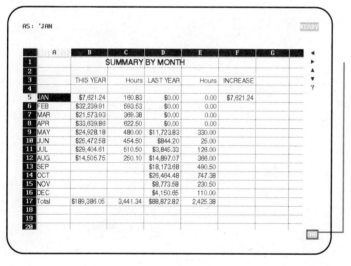

Notice that 1-2-3 displays the End status indicator. This means that the cell pointer will travel to the end of the direction you indicate.

3. Press `→`.

3

The cell pointer
jumps to the right
boundary of the
range, to cell F5.

F5: (C2) [W10] +B5-D5

	A	B	C	D	E	F	G
1			SUMMARY BY MONTH				
2							
3		THIS YEAR	Hours	LAST YEAR	Hours	INCREASE	
4							
5	JAN	$7,621.24	160.83	$0.00	0.00	$7,621.24	
6	FEB	$32,239.91	593.53	$0.00	0.00		
7	MAR	$21,573.93	369.38	$0.00	0.00		
8	APR	$33,639.86	622.50	$0.00	0.00		
9	MAY	$24,928.18	480.00	$11,723.83	330.00		
10	JUN	$25,472.58	454.50	$844.20	25.00		
11	JUL	$29,404.61	510.50	$3,845.33	126.00		
12	AUG	$14,505.75	250.10	$14,897.07	366.00		
13	SEP			$18,173.68	490.50		
14	OCT			$26,464.48	747.38		
15	NOV			$8,773.58	230.50		
16	DEC			$4,150.65	110.00		
17	Total	$189,386.05	3,441.34	$88,872.82	2,425.38		
18							
19							
20							

4. Press End, and then press ↓.

Because there are
no cells below F5,
the cell pointer
moves all the way
to the bottom of
the worksheet, to
cell F8192.

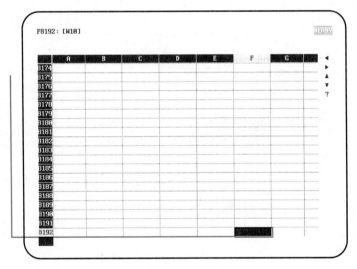

F8192: [W10]

84

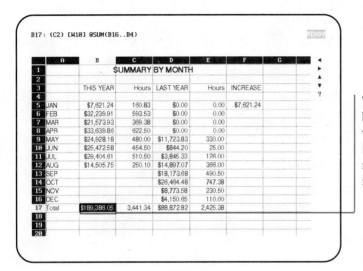

To return to the
beginning of the
worksheet, press
[Home]. Then
move to cell B17
in this example.

3

5. Press [End], and then press [↑].

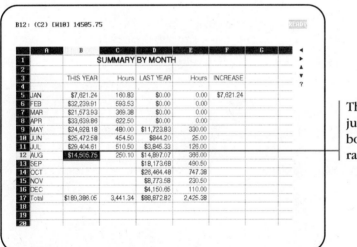

The cell pointer
jumps to the next
boundary of the
range, to cell B12.

When you use the End key followed by the Home key, the cell pointer moves
to the cell of the last occupied column and last occupied row of your
worksheet.

If the cell pointer is originally positioned at cell A1, you can press End and
then Home when prompted for a range to print.

3

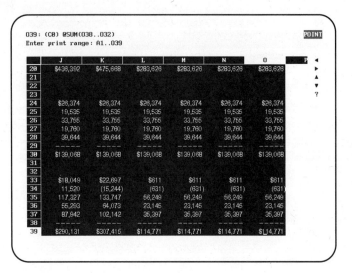

1-2-3 highlights
the entire range
to print.

If you practice with the End key, you can speed up many commands that
require you to specify a range.

Using the GoTo (F5) Key

The GoTo (F5) key gives you a way to jump directly to any cell location.

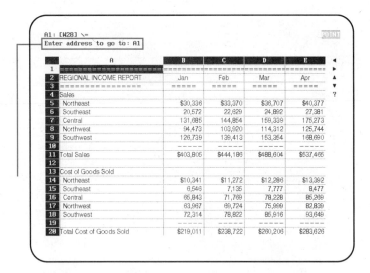

When you press
GoTo (F5), 1-2-3
prompts you for
the new cell
address.

In response to the prompt, type the desired cell address. When you work on a large worksheet, you might forget the cell addresses for specific parts of the worksheet and then have difficulty using the GoTo (F5) key. You can, however, use range names with the GoTo (F5) key so that you don't have to remember cell addresses.

You can assign a range name to a cell or a rectangular group of cells. Then you can press the GoTo (F5) key and type the range name instead of the cell address. When the range name refers to more than one cell, the cell pointer moves to the upper left corner of the range. (Ranges and range names are discussed in detail in Chapter 4.)

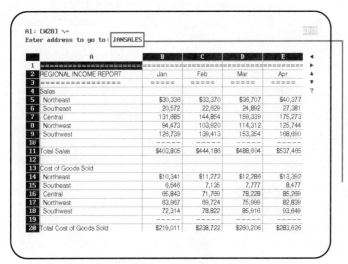

In this example, JANSALES (a range that begins in cell B5) is specified as the location to go to.

Mouse Control of the Cell Pointer

You can use the left mouse button to move the cell pointer when 1-2-3 is in READY or POINT mode. There are several ways to move the cell pointer with the mouse. The simplest way is to point to a cell on-screen and click the left mouse button. Another way is to use the icons on the right side of the worksheet. The five icons in the icon panel include four solid triangles, each pointing in a different direction. Pointing to one of the triangles and clicking the left mouse button moves the cell pointer one cell in the direction of the triangle.

3

If you click the triangle that points to the right, the cell pointer moves one cell to the right—from cell A1 to B1 in this example.

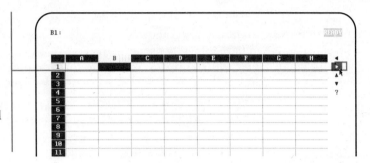

If you hold down the left mouse button while pointing to a triangle icon, the cell pointer keeps moving in the direction of the triangle. If you want to move the cell pointer to a cell not shown on the display, point to the appropriate triangle and hold down the left mouse button until the worksheet starts to scroll. When you reach the row or column you want, release the mouse button.

You can drag the cell pointer around the worksheet by positioning the mouse pointer on the cell pointer, pressing and holding the left mouse button and moving the cell pointer to the desired location. This method also allows you to move the cell pointer to a cell not shown on the display—when the mouse pointer moves past the edge of the worksheet, the screen begins scrolling. When you release the mouse button, the scrolling stops.

For example, suppose that the cell pointer is in cell A5. To move the cell pointer to a cell not currently shown on the screen, such as Z5, position the mouse pointer on cell A5, and then hold the left mouse button and move—or drag—the mouse pointer to the right beyond the far right column displayed on-screen. When you move the mouse beyond the last displayed column, the entire worksheet scrolls to the left, and the column letter shown in the first line of the control panel changes. When you get to column Z, release the mouse button. This method works similarly if you want to move to a cell above, below, to the left, or to the right of the cells displayed on-screen.

You can use the End key with the triangles in the icon panel to move the cell pointer to the next boundary between a blank cell and a cell containing data. Simply press and release the End key on the keyboard, and then click the triangle representing the direction you want the cell pointer to move. This procedure provides the same results as using the End key with the arrow keys on the keyboard (described in a previous section).

Selecting Commands from Menus

The 1-2-3 main menu is always available whenever you start 1-2-3. To speed up procedures, you can select a number of options from certain commands through dialog boxes. Release 2.3 offers an additional menu system with the Wysiwyg spreadsheet publishing add-in program. If you want to use the Wysiwyg menu, however, you must first load the Wysiwyg feature into memory. As you learned in Chapter 2, you can install the Wysiwyg program so that it loads automatically whenever you start 1-2-3.

The 1-2-3 and Wysiwyg menus offer several hundred command options, but you will probably use only a small portion of these on a frequent basis. Although some of the command options appearing in both the 1-2-3 and Wysiwyg main menus are the same (such as the Worksheet, Print, and Graph options), they are used to perform different types of tasks.

A helpful aspect of menus is the ease of selecting commands. From the keyboard, you can either point to the menu option you want and press Enter, or you can just type the first letter of the command. (A later section of this chapter discusses how to select menu commands if you are using a mouse.) To point to a command on the menu, use the left- and right-arrow keys on the keyboard. You can use the space bar interchangeably with the right-arrow key to move the menu pointer to the right. The left-arrow key can be used to move the menu pointer to the left. After you highlight the desired command, press Enter.

If you move the menu pointer to the last command of a menu and press the right-arrow key again, the menu pointer reappears on the first command of the menu. Similarly, if the menu pointer is on the first command of a menu, press the left-arrow key to move to the last command. Note that you can also move the menu pointer to the end of the command line by pressing the End key or to the beginning of the line by pressing the Home key.

The other way to select a command from the keyboard is to enter its first letter. When you become familiar with the commands in 1-2-3's various menus, you will learn that typing is much faster than pointing. To select a menu command from the keyboard, you can either point or type.

Pointing to Commands

1. Call up the 1-2-3 menu by pressing ⌷/⌷ or call up the Wysiwyg menu by pressing ⌷:⌷ .
2. Use ⌷←⌷ or ⌷→⌷ to move the menu pointer until the desired command is highlighted.

3

The menu pointer, the rectangular bar that highlights menu selections, is positioned on the Copy option of the 1-2-3 menu.

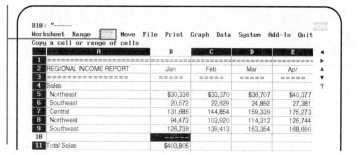

3. Press ⏎Enter.

4. Continue this process, selecting the desired commands from the 1-2-3 or Wysiwyg menu and responding to any resulting prompts until the task is complete.

Typing Commands

1. Call up the 1-2-3 menu by pressing ⌙ or call up the Wysiwyg menu by pressing :.

2. Select the desired command by typing the first letter of the command.

In this example, pressing C selects the Copy command from 1-2-3's main menu and takes you directly to a prompt.

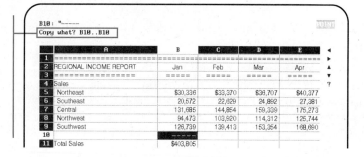

3. Continue selecting commands from the 1-2-3 or Wysiwyg menu and responding to any resulting prompts until the task is complete.

If you make the wrong command selection, you can press Esc at any time to return to the previous menu. For instance, if you realize that you should have selected Insert, not Delete, from the 1-2-3 /Worksheet menu, press Esc once to return to the /Worksheet menu. You can press Esc as many times as necessary to return to any location in the series of menus or to leave MENU mode completely. To return to READY mode in one step, press Ctrl-Break. Table 3.3 describes the keys you can use to move around the 1-2-3 and Wysiwyg menus.

Table 3.3
Moving around the 1-2-3 and Wysiwyg Menus

Key	Action
⁄	Displays the 1-2-3 main menu from READY mode
:	Displays the Wysiwyg main menu from READY mode
→ or space bar	Moves the menu pointer one option to the right
←	Moves the menu pointer one option to the left
End	Moves to the last menu option
Home	Moves to the first menu option
↵Enter	Chooses the highlighted menu option
First letter of menu option	Chooses the menu option that begins with that letter (each option of a menu begins with a different letter)
Esc	Goes back to the last menu one step at a time until reaching READY mode
Ctrl Break	Goes back to READY mode in one step

Using the 1-2-3 Menu

As discussed in the previous section, the procedure for selecting commands from the 1-2-3 menu is simple. To select a command from the 1-2-3 main menu, make certain that 1-2-3 is in READY mode, and press the slash (/) key.

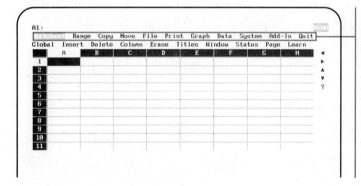

As soon as you press /, the mode indicator in the upper right corner of the screen changes to MENU and the 1-2-3 main menu appears on the second line of the control panel.

91

The third line of the control panel contains either a brief explanation of the highlighted command or the menu that results from choosing the highlighted command. As you point to different commands by moving the menu pointer across the menu, a new explanation (or menu) appears as each command is highlighted. This assistance is displayed at all levels of menus.

Here, the third line of the control panel displays an explanation of the command that is highlighted.

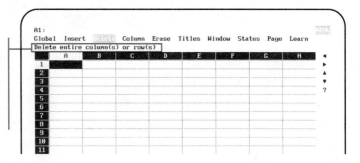

The 1-2-3 main menu provides the command options for building and modifying your worksheet and graphics applications. Table 3.4 summarizes the selections on the 1-2-3 main menu.

Table 3.4
Selections on the 1-2-3 Main Menu

Selection	Description
Worksheet	Changes global worksheet settings; inserts and deletes columns or rows; sets column widths, windows, and titles; erases the worksheet from memory; displays worksheet status; inserts page breaks; and records keystrokes in the worksheet
Range	Formats, erases, names, justifies, protects and searches ranges of data, aligns labels, restricts data entry, converts formulas to values, and transposes columns and rows
Copy	Copies ranges of data and formats
Move	Moves ranges of data and formats
File	Accesses, saves, combines, erases, lists, and imports files; extracts parts of files; changes current directory; and controls file administration

Selection	Description
Print	Enables you to print worksheets and graphs to a printer or file
Graph	Creates, resets, views, saves, names, and adds enhancements to graphs
Data	Performs sorts, queries, and regressions on 1-2-3 databases; fills a range; creates tables of values; calculates frequency distribution; multiplies and inverts matrixes; and converts labels
System	Returns you to DOS temporarily while the current worksheet remains in memory
Add-In	Loads, activates, or removes 1-2-3 add-in programs
Quit	Returns to READY mode

Using Dialog Boxes

When you choose some commands, such as /Worksheet Global, /Graph, /Print Printer, /Data Sort and /Data Query, 1-2-3 displays a special status screen called a *dialog box*. A dialog box shows the current settings associated with the command.

In addition to showing the settings, dialog boxes allow you to select settings from the screen rather than through menus. The different parts of dialog boxes include option buttons, check boxes, text boxes, pop-up dialog boxes, command buttons, and list boxes.

Option buttons appear as parentheses. If an option is selected, an asterisk (*) appears within the parentheses. *Check boxes* appear as square brackets ([ ]). An item is selected if an X appears within the square brackets. *Text boxes* allow you to fill in the entry, whether it is text, numbers, or range names, depending on what the command requires.

The /**W**orksheet
Global dialog
box.

Option button

Check box

Text box

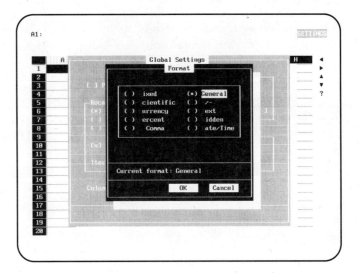

When a command requires further options, 1-2-3 may show a *pop-up dialog box* with more choices or a *list box* allowing you to choose an item from a list.

The /**W**orksheet
Global **F**ormat
pop-up dialog
box allows you to
select additional
formatting
options.

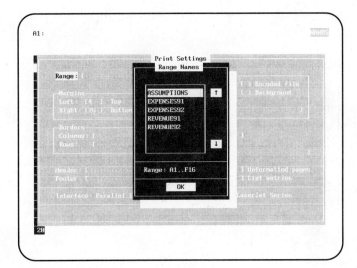

3

Pressing Names (F3) from the Print Setting Range text box produces a list of range names.

To use a dialog box with the keyboard, press Edit (F2). 1-2-3 will highlight a character from each of the options (usually the first letter). Move the pointer to the option or press the letter of the option you want to change.

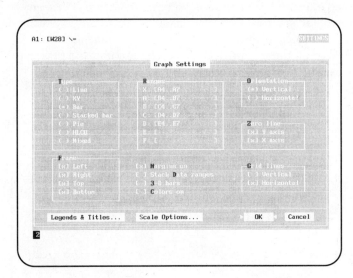

When you press Edit (F2), 1-2-3 allows you to choose a character from the keyboard for each item.

To use a dialog box with the mouse, move the mouse pointer to an option and click the left mouse button.

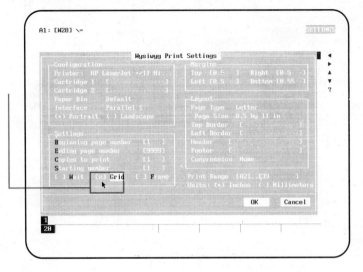

You can click on the Grid check box in the Wysiwyg Print Settings dialog box.

After you press Edit (F2) or choose an item with the mouse, the dialog box shows at least one *command button,* located at the bottom of the box. Command buttons allow you to accept or cancel dialog box settings or move to another dialog box. OK is the most common command button. OK means that you are satisfied with all selections on the dialog box and want to get out of the dialog box. Choose OK by pressing Enter when the command button is highlighted, or by clicking on the command button. Other command buttons include Cancel and choices that produce another dialog box. Command buttons that produce another dialog box end in an ellipses (...).

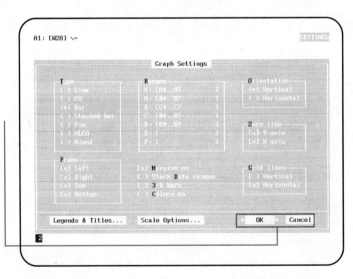

When you press Edit (F2), the dialog box shows command buttons on the bottom.

Using the Wysiwyg Menu

In addition to the 1-2-3 menu and dialog boxes, Release 2.3 includes a Wysiwyg menu to enhance your 1-2-3 worksheets. The Wysiwyg menu is not available for use until you load and invoke the program, just like other add-in programs available for 1-2-3. To select a command from the Wysiwyg menu, make certain that 1-2-3 is in READY mode, and press the colon (:) key.

```
A1: [W28] \=                                          WYSIWYG
Worksheet Format Graph Print Display Special Text Named-Style Quit
Column  Row  Page
              A                 B          C          D          E        ◄
 1   ===============================================================    ►
 2  'Sales by Quarter         Qtr 1      Qtr 2      Qtr 3      Qtr 4     ▲
 3   ===============================================================    ▼
 4   Product 1              $123,876   $149,850   $200,799   $177,822    ?
 5   Product 2               $65,012   $102,932    $98,723    $89,074
 6   Product 3               398,212    401,234    442,029    442,983
 7   Product 4               298,383    302,938    343,983    347,293
 8                          --------   --------   --------   --------
 9   Total Sales            $885,483   $956,954 $1,085,534 $1,057,172
10
11
```

As soon as you press : , the mode indicator in the upper right corner of the screen changes to WYSIWYG and the Wysiwyg main menu appears in the second line of the control panel.

The format of the Wysiwyg menu is similar to that of the 1-2-3 menu, because the third line of the control panel also contains either a brief explanation of the highlighted command or the menu that results from choosing the highlighted command (as shown in the preceding figure). As you point to different commands by moving the menu pointer across the Wysiwyg menu, a new explanation (or menu) appears as each command is highlighted. Table 3.5 summarizes the selections on the Wysiwyg main menu.

Table 3.5
Selections on the Wysiwyg Main Menu

Selection	Description
Worksheet	Sets column widths, row heights, and page breaks
Format	Adds boldface, italics, lines, shading, colors, fonts, and drop shadows
Graph	Inserts a graph into a worksheet range, and enhances and sizes the graph
Print	Prints the formatted worksheet or graph, and specifies page layout and enhancement options

continued

3

Table 3.5 (*continued*)

Selection	Description
Display	Alters screen characteristics such as colors, size of cells, grid lines, and intensity
Special	Copies, moves, imports, and exports formats
Text	Edits, aligns, and reformats a range of text
Named-Style	Assigns names to commonly used format combinations
Quit	Returns to READY mode

The next section discusses how to use a mouse to select commands from both the 1-2-3 and Wysiwyg menus.

Using the Mouse To Select Menu Commands

When you move the mouse pointer into the control panel area at the top of the screen, a menu automatically appears as if you had pressed the slash (/) or colon (:) key from the keyboard.

If you move the mouse pointer to the control panel, a menu automatically appears.

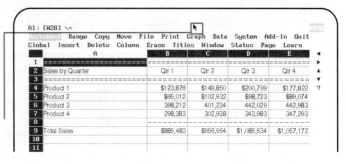

The menu that results (1-2-3 or Wysiwyg) is the last menu used in the current 1-2-3 session. If a menu has not yet been used in the current session, the 1-2-3 menu will appear first. Pressing the right mouse button while the mouse pointer is in the control panel area switches between the 1-2-3 and Wysiwyg menus.

98

Using a mouse to select an option from a menu is easy. To select a 1-2-3 or Wysiwyg command with the mouse, follow these steps:

1. Move the mouse pointer to the control panel to automatically display a 1-2-3 or Wysiwyg menu. If necessary, press the right mouse button to switch between menus.

2. Click the left mouse button on the desired menu option. You select all options from resulting menus in the same way.

Continue clicking the left mouse button on the desired commands from the 1-2-3 or Wysiwyg menu. Respond to any resulting prompts by typing from the keyboard and pressing Enter to accept the entry. You can scan the different menu items and view their descriptions on the third line of the control panel by pressing and holding the left mouse button while you move the mouse pointer across the menu. When you release the mouse button, you select the command that was last highlighted.

While the mouse pointer is in the control panel and a menu is displayed, you can press the right button one or more times to return to previous menus. Moving the mouse pointer back to the worksheet area removes the menu from the screen and returns 1-2-3 to READY mode.

Using the mouse can greatly increase your speed and productivity. Experiment with using the mouse, the keyboard, or a combination of both to find which method works best for you.

Entering Data into the Worksheet

You can enter data into a cell by highlighting the cell with the cell pointer and typing the entry. To complete the entry, press Enter or any of the direction keys discussed in this chapter. If you press a direction key to complete the entry, the cell pointer also moves one cell in the selected direction. Using this method eliminates one step in data entry operations because you do not need to press the Enter key *and* a direction key after every entry.

If you are using a mouse, you can complete an entry by clicking one of the triangle keys in the icon panel. Note that this action has the same effect as pressing an arrow key on the keyboard to complete the entry—the cell pointer moves one cell in the specified direction.

If you enter data into a cell that already contains information, the new data replaces the earlier information. This is one way to change data in a cell; other methods involve using the Edit (F2) key or using the Wysiwyg :Text Edit command to edit data directly in a cell. Explanations of each of these procedures appear later in this chapter.

3

There are two types of cell entries: labels and values. Labels are text entries, and values can be either numbers or formulas (including functions, which 1-2-3 treats as built-in formulas). The type of entry can be determined from the first character you enter. Your entry is treated as a value (a number or a formula) when you start with one of the following characters:

0 1 2 3 4 5 6 7 8 9 + − . (@ # $

When you begin your entry with a character other than one of the preceding ones, 1-2-3 treats your entry as a label.

A value—whether a number, formula, or function—can be used for computing purposes. A label is a collection of characters and cannot logically be used in a calculation.

Entering Labels

Labels are commonly used in 1-2-3 for row and column headings, titles, explanation, and notes, and they play an important role in worksheet development. Without labels in a worksheet, you might know that column H is January data and row 11 is Inventory Assets, but how would someone else who is not familiar with the worksheet know?

Labels make values more evident in a worksheet and help you find information quickly.

A1: 'TERMS OF LOAN

	A	B	C	D	E	F	G	H
1	TERMS OF LOAN							
2								
3		First Payment Date				31−Jul−92		
4		Principal Borrowed				$10,000		
5		Term in Months				48		
6		Beginning Interest Rate				10.50%		
7		Payment				$256.03		
8								
9								
10	AMORTIZATION SCHEDULE							
11								
12								
13	Payment	Payment		Current	Interest	Principal	Principal	
14	Number	Date	Rate	Payment	Portion	Portion	Balance	
15	1	31−Jul−92	10.50%	$256.03	$87.50	$168.53	$9,831.47	
16	2	31−Aug−92	10.50%	$256.03	$86.03	$170.01	$9,661.46	
17	3	30−Sep−92	10.50%	$256.03	$84.54	$171.50	$9,489.96	
18	4	31−Oct−92	10.50%	$256.03	$83.04	$173.00	$9,316.97	
19	5	30−Nov−92	10.50%	$256.03	$81.52	$174.51	$9,142.45	
20	6	31−Dec−92	10.50%	$256.03	$80.00	$176.04	$8,966.42	

A label can be up to 240 characters long and can contain any string of characters and numbers. A label that is too long for the width of a cell continues (for display purposes) across the cells to the right, as long as the neighboring cells contain no other entries.

When you make an entry into a cell and the first character does not indicate a value entry, the assumption is that you are entering a label. After you type the first character, 1-2-3 shifts to LABEL mode.

You can control how labels are displayed in the cell. By preceding a text entry with a label prefix, you can tell 1-2-3 to left-justify ('), center (^), right-justify ("), or repeat (\) a label when it is displayed. The following sections cover each of these options.

Aligning Labels

Because the default position for displaying labels is left-justified, you don't have to type the label prefix when entering most labels—1-2-3 automatically supplies it for you. When your labels consist of numbers followed by text (as in addresses), you must use a label prefix before 1-2-3 will accept the entry into a cell.

When you enter only a number as a label—for example, the year 1991—the assumption is that you are entering a value. You need some way to signal that you intend this numeric entry to be treated as text. You can indicate this by using one of the label prefixes. In this case, you can enter 1991 as a centered label by typing **^1991**.

To align labels as you enter them into the worksheet, you must first type a label prefix. Use the following label prefixes for label alignment:

'	Left-justifies
"	Right-justifies
^	Centers

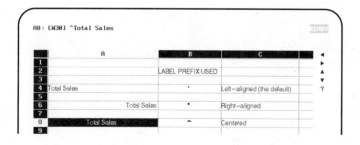

You can use label prefixes to align labels three different ways.

3

3

1-2-3 alone does not correctly center or right-align text that overflows a cell. However, if you have Wysiwyg in memory, you can correct this problem by preceding a label entry with a double caret (^ ^) to center, or a double quotation mark (" ") to right-justify the entry.

Repeating Label Characters

An additional label prefix is available for repeating one or more characters in a single cell. For example, you can use the repeat character—a backslash (\)—to create a separator line that fills an entire cell.

To repeat characters within a single cell, follow these steps:

1. Move the cell pointer to the cell that will contain the repeating label.

   For example, move the cell pointer to cell A11 to use the repeat character that creates a separator line.

2. Press ⌐\⌐ and then type the character(s) to be repeated within the highlighted cell.

   In this example, type ⌐\⌐⌐=⌐ to fill cell A11 with equal signs.

3. Press ⌐⏎Enter⌐ to enter the label into the highlighted cell.

Cell A11 is now filled with equal signs. Repeat these steps in adjoining cells to form the remainder of the separator line.

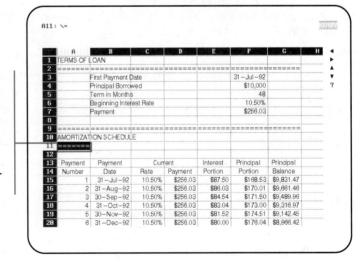

Controlling Label Prefixes

You can control label prefixes in several different ways. If you want to change the alignment of a range of labels after the labels are entered, use the 1-2-3 /**R**ange Label command. You can also use the Wysiwyg **:T**ext **E**dit command or the Edit key (F2) (explained later in this chapter) to edit individual cells.

For example, suppose that you enter two rows of labels and then decide that you want the labels to be centered. You can change the alignment of a range of existing labels by using the /**R**ange Label command. (You learn more about ranges in Chapter 4.)

To align a range of labels, follow these steps:

1. Select /**R**ange Label.

2. Select one of the following alignment choices: **Left**, **Right**, or **Center**.

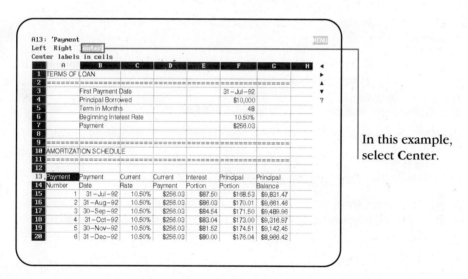

In this example, select Center.

3. Specify the range of cells to be aligned.

    In this example, highlight the range A13..G14; then press ↵Enter.

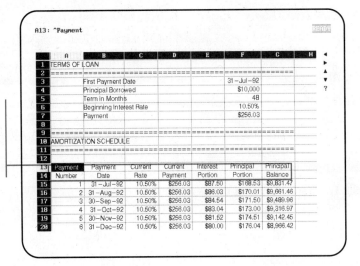

The cells are now centered, with each label in the range preceded by a caret (^).

If you want to set the alignment of an entire worksheet to the left, right, or center *before* you enter labels, you can use the /Worksheet Global Label-Prefix command. This command will not change the alignment of existing labels, however. The alignment of existing labels can be changed by using the /Range Label command, the :Text Edit command, or Edit (F2).

To set the alignment of labels for the entire worksheet, follow these steps:

1. Select /Worksheet Global Label-Prefix.

2. Select one of the following alignment choices: **Left**, **Right**, or **Center**.

You can use the /Worksheet Global command to check the current alignment settings for the worksheet. This information appears near the bottom of the resulting screen.

Entering Numbers

As you know, values in 1-2-3 consist of numbers and formulas. 1-2-3 worksheets use numbers for many different types of applications—especially those that involve data entry.

The rules for entering numbers are the following:

- A number must begin with the numerals 0 through 9, a decimal point, a minus sign (–), or a dollar sign ($). If you type a plus sign (+) before a number you enter or if you enter a number in parentheses, the + and the ( ) will not appear in the cell.

104

- You can end a number with a percent sign (%), which causes 1-2-3 to automatically divide the number preceding the sign by 100.
- A number cannot have more than one decimal point.
- You can enter a number in scientific notation, which is called **Sci** format in 1-2-3 (for example, 1.234E+06).
- You cannot enter spaces after numbers.
- Do not start a number entry with one or more spaces. If you do, 1-2-3 treats the entry as a label. This does not cause an immediate error, but 1-2-3 treats the cell contents as zero the next time the number is used in a formula.

If you do not follow these rules, 1-2-3 beeps when you press Enter and automatically shifts to EDIT mode as if Edit (F2) were pressed.

Entering Formulas

In addition to simple values, you can enter formulas into cells. Enter formulas either by typing the formula into the cell or by pointing with the keyboard or the mouse, which entails moving the cell pointer so that 1-2-3 enters the cell addresses for you.

Suppose that you want to create a formula that adds a row of numbers. For example, you want to add the amounts in cells B4, B5, B6, and B7, and place the result in cell B9. To do this by typing, enter **+B4+B5+B6+B7** into cell B9. The + sign at the beginning of the formula indicates that a formula, not a label, is to be entered. 1-2-3 then switches to VALUE mode, the appropriate mode for entering numbers and formulas.

To enter a formula with cell addresses by pointing, follow these steps:

1. Begin with the cell pointer highlighting the cell that will hold the formula, and then press +

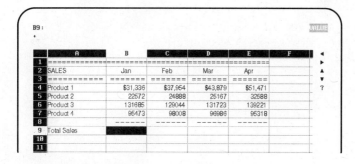

In this example, move the cell pointer to cell B9 and press +

2. Move the cell pointer to the first cell address of the formula and press +.

3

In this example, highlight cell B4 and press +.

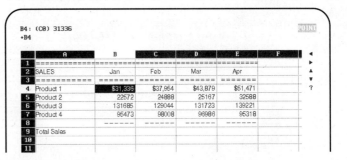

The mode indicator in the upper right corner of the screen shifts from VALUE to POINT as you move the cell pointer to cell B4. Notice that the address for the cell appears after the plus sign in the second line of the control panel—in this case, +B4.

When you press + again, the cell pointer moves immediately from cell B4 back to the beginning cell—in this example, to cell B9. The mode indicator also shifts back to VALUE.

3. Move the cell pointer to the next cell address of the formula and press +.

In this example, highlight cell B5 and press +.

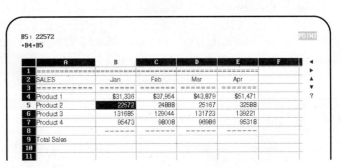

4. Continue pointing and entering plus signs until the formula is complete.

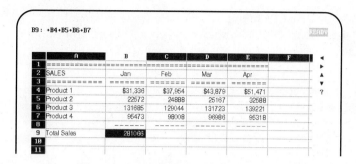

In this example, move the cell pointer to cell B6 and press +; then highlight cell B7 and press ↵Enter.

3

5. Press ↵Enter to complete the operation.

Remember that you can use a combination of typing and pointing (with or without a mouse) to enter a formula that contains one or more cell addresses. Use the method that works best for you. The easiest method is to point when cells are close to the one you are defining and to type references to distant cells. You get the same results with either method, and you can mix and match the two techniques within the same formula.

Using Mathematical Operators in Formulas

Operators are symbols that indicate arithmetic operations in formulas, and they are either logical or mathematical. Logical operators are discussed in Chapter 13, "Managing Data." The mathematical operators are the following:

Operator	Meaning
^	Exponentiation
+, –	Positive, negative
*, /	Multiplication, division
+, –	Addition, subtraction

This list indicates, from the top down, the order of precedence—that is, the order in which these operators are evaluated. For example, exponentiation takes place before multiplication, and division occurs before subtraction. Operations inside a set of parentheses are always evaluated first, and operators at the same level of precedence are evaluated in order from left to right.

Consider the following formula:

$+F4*C6-G2 \char`\^ C7$

107

The plus sign (+) indicates the beginning of a formula (rather than a label). The asterisk (*) tells 1-2-3 to multiply the values stored in cells F4 and C6. The minus sign (–) subtracts the result of the second element (G2 $\wedge$ C7) from the first (+F4*C6). The caret ($\wedge$) indicates exponentiation.

The first operator to be evaluated in a formula is exponentiation—the power of a number. In the formula $8+2 \wedge 3$, for example, $2 \wedge 3$ (2 to the power of 3) is evaluated before the addition. The answer is 16 (8+8), not 1000 (10 to the power of 3).

The next set of operators to be evaluated indicates the sign of a value (whether it is positive or negative). Notice the difference between a + or – sign that indicates a positive or negative value and a + or – sign that indicates addition or subtraction. When used as signs, these operators are evaluated before multiplication and division; when used as indicators of addition and subtraction, they are evaluated after multiplication and division. For example, 5+4/–2 is evaluated as 5+(–2), with 3 as the answer. The – sign indicates that 2 is negative, then 4 is divided by –2, and finally 5 is added to –2, resulting in the answer of 3.

You can use parentheses to override the order of precedence. Consider the order of precedence in the following formulas, in which cell B3 contains the value 2, cell C3 contains the value 3, and cell D3 contains the value 4. Notice how parentheses affect the order of precedence and the results in the first two formulas.

Formula	Evaluation	Result
+C3–D3/B3	3–(4/2)	1
(C3–D3)/B3	(3–4)/2	–0.5
+D3*C3–B3 $\wedge$ C3	(4*3)–(2 $\wedge$ 3)	4
+D3*C3*B3/B3 $\wedge$ C3–25/5	((4*3*2)/(2 $\wedge$ 3)–(25/5))	–2

Correcting Errors in Formulas

It is easy to make errors when you enter formulas—especially when you enter formulas that are complex. 1-2-3 provides ways to help you discover and correct these sometimes inevitable errors.

If you try to enter a formula that contains a logical or mathematical error, the program will beep, change to EDIT mode, and move the cursor to the section of the formula where the problem most likely exists. You can then correct the error and continue.

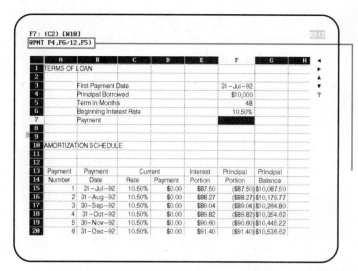

The formula shown in the control panel contains an error.

3

If you don't know what the problem is, give yourself time to think by converting the formula to a label. To do this, follow these steps (while in EDIT mode):

1. To convert a formula to a label from EDIT mode, press $\boxed{\text{Home}}$, (apostrophe), and then press $\boxed{\text{↵Enter}}$.

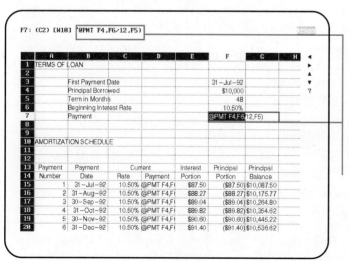

The formula shown in the control panel has been converted to a label.

2. After you correct the formula, delete the apostrophe by pressing F2 to switch to EDIT mode. Next press Home, followed by Del; then press ↵Enter.

The corrected formula is shown in the control panel.

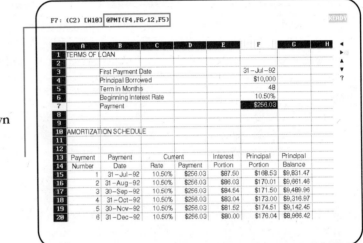

If your formula is long and complex, break it down into logical segments and test each segment separately. Using smaller segments helps to debug the formula. Also, because 1-2-3 limits individual cell entries to 240 characters, the reduced size may be necessary for the program to accept the formula.

Common errors include open parentheses and commas that are missing from built-in formulas (functions). What appears to be a logical error may be only a missing punctuation mark. When 1-2-3 beeps to indicate a formula error, check the formula for a missing parenthesis or comma near the cursor.

Formulas that contain embedded or trailing spaces result in errors. To find a trailing space, press the End key while in EDIT mode. If the cursor is more than one character beyond the end of a formula, you can delete the trailing spaces with the Backspace key.

1-2-3 provides two commands to help you examine and analyze your formulas. The /**P**rint **P**rinter **O**ptions **O**ther **C**ell-Formulas command (discussed in Chapter 8) prints a list of all the formulas (one per line) in your worksheet. The /**R**ange **F**ormat **T**ext command (discussed in Chapter 4) displays existing formulas (instead of values) in their worksheet locations.

Using Functions in Formulas

Like most electronic spreadsheets, 1-2-3 includes built-in functions. These functions fall into eight basic categories: (1) mathematical and trigonometric, (2) date and time, (3) financial, (4) statistical, (5) database, (6) logical, (7) string, and (8) special. Some of 1-2-3's functions are described in the text that follows. You can learn more about 1-2-3's functions in Chapter 7.

The *mathematical* and *trigonometric* functions perform standard arithmetic operations such as computing absolute value (@ABS) or square root (@SQRT), rounding numbers (@ROUND), and computing the sine (@SIN), cosine (@COS), and tangent (@TAN).

The *date* and *time* functions, such as @DATE and @TIME, convert dates and times to serial numbers. The serial numbers allow you to perform date and time arithmetic or to document your worksheets and reports.

The *financial* functions calculate returns on investments (@IRR and @RATE), loan payments (@PMT), present values (@NPV and @PV), future values (@FV), and compound growth periods (@TERM and @CTERM).

The *statistical* functions perform standard calculations on lists, such as summing values (@SUM), calculating averages (@AVG), finding minimum and maximum values (@MIN and @MAX), and computing standard deviations and variances (@STD and @VAR).

The *database* functions perform statistical calculations on a field of a database, based on certain criteria. These functions, such as @DSUM and @DAVG, have names and uses similar to the statistical functions.

The *logical* functions, such as @IF, @TRUE, and @FALSE, let you perform conditional tests. You can use these functions to test whether a condition is true or false.

The *string* functions help you manipulate text. You can use string functions to repeat text characters (@REPEAT), to convert letters to uppercase or lowercase (@UPPER or @LOWER), and to change strings to numbers and numbers to strings (@VALUE and @STRING).

The *special* functions perform a variety of tasks. For example, @CELL and @CELLPOINTER can return up to 10 different characteristics of a cell, including its width, format, type of address, and prefix.

3

3

Entering a 1-2-3 Function

As noted earlier, 1-2-3 has a variety of functions that perform many different tasks—from simple arithmetic to complex statistical analysis and depreciation calculations. Functions consist of three parts: the @ sign, a function name, and an argument or range. Note that range refers to the range of the cells that the function will use.

Consider the following function:

@SUM(B1..E1)

This formula uses the @SUM function to compute the total of the range of four cells from B1 through E1. The @ sign signals that the entry is a function. SUM is the name of the function being used.

You can enter function names with upper- or lowercase letters; this book uses uppercase letters to denote 1-2-3 functions. The statement (B1..E1) is the *argument* (in this case, a range). A function's arguments, always enclosed in parentheses, specify the cell or range of cells on which the function will act. This function tells 1-2-3 to compute the sum of the numbers in cells B1, C1, D1, and E1, and to display the result in the cell containing the formula.

Some functions can be quite complex. For example, you can combine several functions in a single cell by having one function use other functions as its arguments. The length of an argument, however, is limited. Functions, like formulas, can contain only 240 characters per cell.

When you enter a function that requires a cell address, you can enter the address by typing or pointing.

To enter the formula @SUM(B7..B4) by pointing, follow these steps:

1. Move the cell pointer to the cell that will contain the formula, and type @SUM(For this example, move the cell pointer to cell B9.

The @ sign, function name, and opening parenthesis are typed.

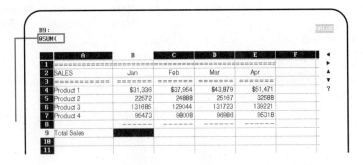

2. Move the cell pointer to a corner of the range and press ⎡.⎤.

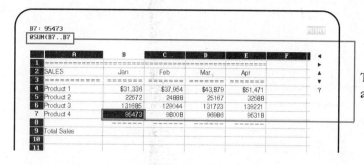

The cell pointer is anchored at B7.

3. Press ⎡↑⎤ three times.

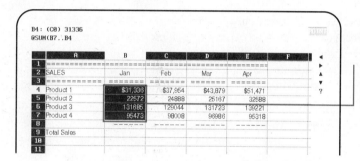

The range of cells between B7 and B4 is highlighted.

4. Type the closing parenthesis ()) and press ⎡↵Enter⎤.

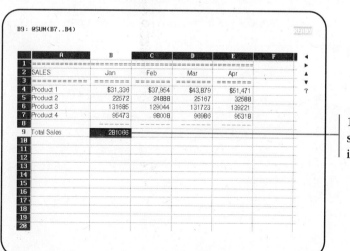

1-2-3 enters the sum of B7..B4 into cell B9.

Note: You can also use a mouse to specify ranges used in functions. Specifying ranges with a mouse is covered in detail in Chapter 4.

Editing Data in the Worksheet

One of the first things you need to be able to do when entering data into a 1-2-3 worksheet is to modify the contents of cells without retyping the complete entry. You can easily change an existing cell entry by using the Edit (F2) key from the keyboard or by using the Wysiwyg **:Text E**dit command that allows you to edit text directly in the worksheet.

Using the Edit (F2) Key

To edit data with the Edit (F2) key, begin by moving the cell pointer to the appropriate cell and pressing Edit (F2). After you press Edit (F2), the mode indicator in the upper right corner of the screen changes to EDIT. The contents of the cell are duplicated in the second line of the control panel (the edit line), the cursor appears at the end of the entry, and you are ready for editing.

When you first press Edit (F2), 1-2-3 is in *insert mode*. Any new characters you type are inserted at the cursor, and any characters on the right side of the cursor are pushed one position to the right. If you activate *overtype mode* by pressing the Ins key, any new character you type replaces the character directly above the cursor, and the cursor moves one position to the right. When 1-2-3 is in overtype mode, the indicator OVR appears at the bottom of the screen. Pressing the Ins key again switches 1-2-3 back to insert mode.

To edit the contents of a cell with the keyboard, follow these steps:

1. Highlight the appropriate cell and press [F2] (Edit).

   Notice that the mode indicator changes to EDIT.

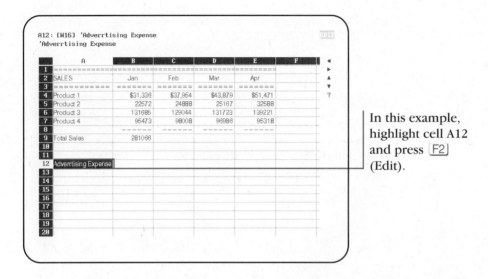

In this example, highlight cell A12 and press ⌞F2⌟ (Edit).

2. With the contents of the cell displayed in the second line of the control panel, move the cursor to the part of the entry you want to edit (by pressing ⌞←⌟ or ⌞→⌟).

    In this example, use ⌞←⌟ to move the cursor to the second *r*.

3. Use one or more of the editing keys described in table 3.6 to modify the cell's contents.

    In this example, press ⌞Del⌟ to delete the character above the cursor.

4. Press ⌞⏎Enter⌟ (or type any new characters and then press ⌞⏎Enter⌟) to complete the edit and return 1-2-3 to READY mode.

You can also use Edit (F2) when you enter data into a cell for the first time. If you make a mistake while you enter the data, you can correct the error without retyping the entire entry. Table 3.6 provides a listing of the key actions available with the Edit (F2) key.

Table 3.6
Key Actions Available with Edit (F2)

Key	Action
⌞←⌟	Moves the cursor one position to the left
⌞→⌟	Moves the cursor one position to the right
⌞Tab⌟ or ⌞Ctrl⌟⌞→⌟	Moves the cursor five characters to the right

continued

115

3

Table 3.6 (*continued*)

Key	Action
⬆Shift Tab⁚ or Ctrl ←	Moves the cursor five characters to the left
Home	Moves the cursor to the first character in the entry
End	Moves the cursor one position to the right of the last character in the entry
←Backspace	Deletes the character to the left of the cursor
Del	Deletes the character above the cursor
Ins	Toggles between insert and overtype modes
Esc	Clears the edit line; when pressed again, abandons changes and leaves EDIT mode
F2 (Edit)	In EDIT mode, returns you to VALUE or LABEL mode; in these modes, you can use the direction keys to enter the data and move the cursor

Wysiwyg Editing

The :Text Edit command on the Wysiwyg menu provides you with additional editing features. With this command, you can enter and edit a range of labels in the worksheet (instead of in the control panel). The process is similar to that of editing a paragraph within a word processing program, because Wysiwyg treats the range that you specify for editing as a "paragraph." Also, when you select a range to edit, the text will wrap around to the next line as you type—without having to press Enter at the end of each line.

When you choose :Text Edit and specify a cell or range of cells, a vertical-line cursor appears in front of the first character in the label in the worksheet. The entry does not appear in the control panel. Move the cursor by using the arrow keys on the keyboard, or clicking the triangle icons with the mouse. Delete characters using Del and Backspace; insert characters by typing them from the keyboard. Complete the edit by pressing Esc or clicking the right mouse button. When you finish, the format reference {Text} appears in the cell contents line of the control panel.

116

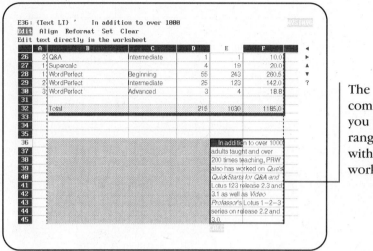

The **:Text Edit** command allows you to edit a range of data within the worksheet area.

Table 3.7 lists the editing keys available when you use the **:Text Edit** command in Wysiwyg. Notice that more editing keys are available this way than by using the Edit (F2) key; some of the same keys used with both methods have different meanings. While you are using **:Text Edit**, you can use F3 to display a menu to change text format, such as fonts, bold, italics, and others.

Table 3.7
Key Actions Available with :Text Edit

Key	Action
←	Moves the cursor one position to the left in the range
→	Moves the cursor one position to the right in the range
↑	Moves the cursor up one row in the range
↓	Moves the cursor down one row in the range
Tab↹ or Ctrl→	Moves the cursor to the end of the word
⇧Shift Tab↹ or Ctrl←	Moves the cursor to the beginning of the word
PgUp	Moves the cursor up one screen
PgDn	Moves the cursor down one screen

continued

117

3

Table 3.7 (*continued*)

Key	Action
Home	Moves the cursor to the first character in the line; when pressed a second time, moves the cursor to the first character of the paragraph (range)
End	Moves the cursor to the last character in the line; when pressed a second time, moves the cursor to the last character of the paragraph (range)
↵Enter	Starts a new line
←Backspace	Deletes the character to the left of the cursor
Del	Deletes the character to the right of the cursor
Ins	Toggles between insert and overtype modes
Esc	Completes the edit and returns 1-2-3 to READY mode
Ctrl ↵Enter	Creates an end-of-paragraph symbol and begins a new line
F3	Displays a menu of different formats that can be applied to the text in the range

Using the Undo Feature

When you use electronic spreadsheet packages, you can destroy hours of work by using the wrong commands or typing over existing entries. For example, if you type over a complicated formula, you can replace the old version with a new (incorrect) version. It is easy to confuse the command to delete rows or columns (/Worksheet Delete) with the command to erase a range (/Range Erase) and delete a row or column while intending merely to erase data. The results can be difficult to recover from—particularly when formulas depend on those deleted rows or columns.

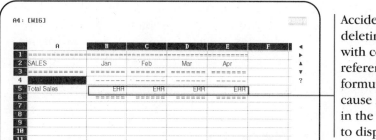

Accidentally deleting rows with cells that are referenced by formulas can cause many cells in the worksheet to display ERR.

3

The Undo feature, which is activated by pressing the key combination Alt-F4 (hold down the Alt key and press F4), in most cases returns the worksheet to its previous appearance and condition before the most recent command or entry. You can undo only the last command, and if you change your mind about what was just undone, you can again use Undo (Alt-F4) to "reverse" the undo.

Press Alt-F4 (Undo) to undo the last command.

Using the command that resets (clears) all range names (/**R**ange **N**ame **R**eset), instead of the command that deletes individual range names (/**R**ange **N**ame **D**elete), is another common mistake that can create frustration—especially when many range names are used in a worksheet. Undo is a quick solution for recovering the lost range names. You must, however, catch errors immediately because the only command you can reverse is the last one you entered.

119

3

The Undo feature also has other uses. Every user is sometimes apprehensive about using certain commands because of the possibility of unexpected results or potential disasters. With Undo you can proceed with a command, having confidence that if you don't like the results you can reverse them. However, note that some commands cannot be reversed—especially those that involve changes to a file on disk, such as /File Erase.

Activating and Deactivating Undo

Initially, the Undo feature is disabled; therefore you must use commands to enable Undo. To turn on the Undo feature, select the command /Worksheet Global Default Other Undo Enable.

To make this change permanent—so that the Undo feature is active each time you access 1-2-3—you must also select the command /Worksheet Global Default Update before exiting 1-2-3. You can use the /Worksheet Global Default Status command to check whether or not the Undo feature is enabled. When the Undo feature is available, the UNDO status indicator appears when 1-2-3 is in READY mode.

In order for the Undo feature to work, 1-2-3 creates a temporary backup copy of the entire worksheet whenever you start a command or cell entry. This information is stored in your computer's temporary memory (RAM). Storing this data takes up space and limits the worksheet size you can build with 1-2-3.

As a worksheet grows in size, the amount of memory reserved for holding a backup copy of the last worksheet image becomes exhausted, and you may not be able to use the Undo feature. Under these circumstances, you can deactivate the Undo feature temporarily with the /Worksheet Global Default Other Undo Disable command.

This command makes the Undo feature unavailable, but it creates more room for your worksheet to grow. If you later start to work on another worksheet (before exiting 1-2-3), you can reactivate the Undo feature with the command /Worksheet Global Default Other Undo Enable.

If you become accustomed to the Undo feature and rely on it heavily for security, avoid building worksheets so large that they prevent your use of Undo.

What Can't Be Undone?

There is no way to undo some commands. You cannot "unerase," "unsave," or "unextract" a disk file; neither can you "unprint" your last printed output.

120

You can undo most other commands, however, including the entire sequence of commands associated with creating graphs, setting up ranges for data query commands, and all "undo-able" steps embedded within a macro.

Naming, Saving, and Retrieving Files

The sections that follow explain file operations that beginning 1-2-3 users need most often—naming, saving, and retrieving files. For more information about other file operations, including deleting and listing files; specialized operations such as protecting files with passwords; combining, linking, and transferring files; and using the Translate Utility, see Chapter 10.

Naming Files

1-2-3 file names are up to eight characters long with a three-character extension.

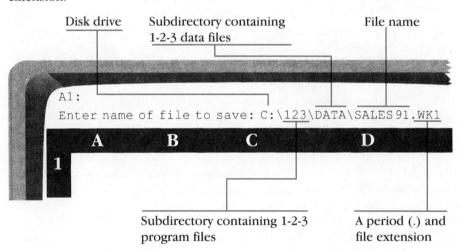

The basic rules for naming files are the following:

- File names may include the characters A through Z, the numbers 0 through 9, the hyphen (–), and the underscore (_). Depending on your system, you may be able to use other special characters, but 1-2-3 will not accept the characters <, >, or *. Although 1-2-3 separates the file name from the three-letter extension with a period (.), the

121

3

program does not accept the period within the file name. Therefore, the following file names are illegal:

CH<15>.WK1

TOM*BBS.PRN

SALES.91.WK1

- File names should not contain blank spaces. For example, SALES RPT.WK1 is not a valid file name.
- 1-2-3 converts lowercase letters to uppercase letters in file names.

You determine the eight-character file name, but 1-2-3 creates the extension based on the file format. The basic file extensions follow:

- WK1 is the extension automatically added to names of worksheet files saved with the /File Save command. If you choose to back up an existing file while saving, the BAK extension is assigned to the previous version of the file.

- PRN is the extension automatically added to names of 1-2-3 files that you save in text (ASCII) format with the /Print File command. PRN files can be printed or imported into 1-2-3 and other programs.

- PIC is the extension automatically added to names of graph files saved with the /Graph Save command. You must issue this command *after* creating the file within 1-2-3 and *before* printing the graph from 1-2-3's PrintGraph program.

- ENC is the extension automatically added to names of files that you save in encoded format with the /Print Encoded command. Encoded files can be printed from DOS.

Note: Release 2.3 can read older 1-2-3 worksheets with WKS extensions, but 1-2-3 writes the new files with WK1 extensions when you save the worksheet. If you want to run WK1 files with earlier versions of 1-2-3, you need to use the Translate Utility (discussed in Chapter 10.) If you want to use a Release 3.x file (extension WK3) in Release 2.3, the file must first be saved with the WK1 extension from within 1-2-3 Release 3.x. If this procedure is used, however, certain formatting created in Release 3.x may be lost in the translation.

In addition to creating files with the WK1, BAK, PRN, PIC, and ENC extensions, 1-2-3 enables you to supply your own extension. Simply enter the file name according to the previously listed rules, enter a period, and add an extension of one to three characters. Note that 1-2-3 does not display any file name with your special extension when the program lists worksheet, print, or graph files. The /File Retrieve command, for example, displays all worksheet (WK1 and WKS) files except for those with your special extensions. To retrieve your special file, type the file name, including the period and extension, after the `Name of file to retrieve:` prompt.

Remember to be descriptive when you think of a name for the new file. Choose a file name that relates something about the file's contents. This will prevent confusion once you have created several different files and need to access a particular file quickly. The following figure provides some good examples of file names:

File name	Description
INV_JUN	Inventory worksheet for June
PRO_REST	*Pro forma* worksheet for a planned restaurant
EMPLSTDP	Employee list for the Data Processing Department

If you work with many different worksheets containing basically the same information, you should use similar names without, of course, using the same names. For example, if you use the name SALES91 for a sales worksheet for the year 1991, you can name the sales worksheets for 1992 and 1993 SALES92 and SALES93, respectively. This naming technique will help you recall file names later.

Saving Files

Computerized spreadsheets have one danger that is not as common in the paper-and-pencil world. If you keep track of your business accounts manually, you can simply get up from your desk and walk away when you decide to quit working. There's nothing to "exit," nothing to turn off (except, perhaps, a calculator), and usually nothing that might cause your work to vanish from your desk. Unless they are misplaced or accidentally thrown away, the materials you use in a manual accounting system remain safely on your desk until morning.

With electronic spreadsheets—and with computer files in general—the risks of power outages or human errors can be costly in terms of data and time loss. If you exit 1-2-3 without saving your file, any work that you have done since the last time you saved the file is lost. You can recover the data only by retyping it into the worksheet. You should make an effort, therefore, to save your files frequently—at least once every half hour to one hour (depending on how many changes are made).

To save a new or existing file with the keyboard, follow these steps:

1. Select /**F**ile **S**ave.

When you save a new worksheet file, 1-2-3 automatically supplies a list of the worksheet files on the current drive and directory.

You can press ⌷F3⌷ (Name) to view a full-screen list of all worksheet files on the current drive and directory.

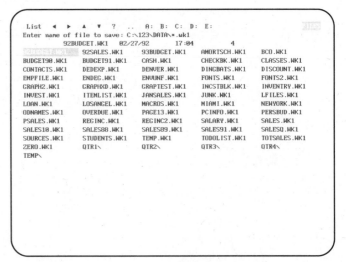

2. Highlight one of the displayed worksheet file names or type a new file name.

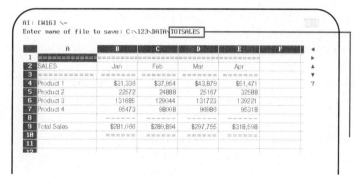

Remember to choose descriptive file names that identify the files for ease in locating them later.

3. Press ⏎Enter. 1-2-3 automatically supplies a WK1 extension for a new file and saves the file on disk.

If you are saving an existing file, another menu appears with the options **C**ancel, **R**eplace, and **B**ackup. To update the current file on disk, select **R**eplace.

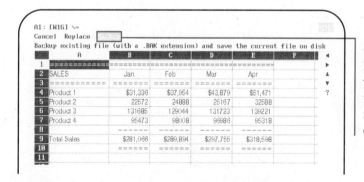

Choose the **B**ackup option if you want to save the latest changes made to an existing file.

Backup is an alternative to the **C**ancel and **R**eplace options of /**F**ile **S**ave. Backup renames the older version of your file—using the same file name— and adds BAK as the file extension. The current version of your file is then saved with the WK1 extension. This process allows you always to have available your two most recent worksheet versions.

3

Saving on the Hard Disk and on a Floppy Disk

If you use a hard disk system, you may want to save your worksheets on the hard disk as well as on a floppy disk. To do this, follow these steps:

1. To save your worksheet on the hard disk, select /**F**ile **S**ave, type the file name after the hard disk drive and directory prompt and press ⏎Enter.

    Note: If you are saving a file that has been previously saved, highlight (or type) the existing file name, press ⏎Enter, and select **R**eplace.

2. To save your worksheet on a floppy disk, select /**F**ile **S**ave, and press the Esc key one or more times—until the prompt Enter name of file to save: is all that remains.

3. Type the disk drive designation (for example **A:**), followed by the file name and press ⏎Enter.

For example, type
A:TOTSALES and
press ⏎Enter.

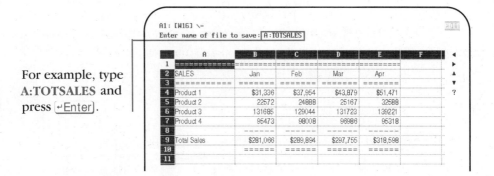

Checking Disk Space before Saving

As you use 1-2-3, you soon have several worksheet files that take up significant disk space. Although hard disk users generally don't have to worry about running out of disk space when saving, floppy disk users need to check the amount of disk space periodically. You need to monitor the amount of disk space your files use, however, no matter what type of system you use. Nothing is worse than getting the message Disk full after you have worked on an important worksheet and are attempting to save it.

You can avoid this problem by using 1-2-3's /**S**ystem command. Whenever you select /**S**ystem, 1-2-3 steps aside and displays the DOS prompt. Even though the DOS prompt is displayed, 1-2-3 and your current worksheet are still in memory.

At the DOS prompt, type **CHKDSK** and press Enter to see how much space is
available on your disk.

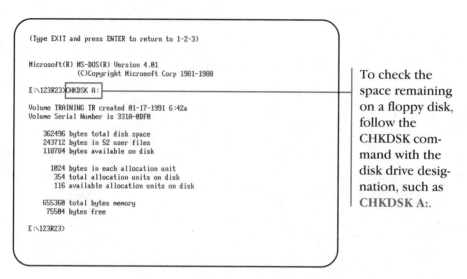

To check the
space remaining
on a floppy disk,
follow the
CHKDSK com-
mand with the
disk drive desig-
nation, such as
CHKDSK A:.

You also can use the FORMAT command of DOS to format a new diskette if
you need one (see your DOS manual).

If you are using a hard disk system, and your hard disk is almost full, you can
erase some of the old files before saving the new files. (First make sure that
you have a proper backup of the old files.)

When you finish the DOS operations, type **exit** and press Enter to return to
the 1-2-3 worksheet. Now you can save the current worksheet.

One point to remember: when you use /System to exit to DOS, do not start
any program from DOS that will alter memory, such as a memory-resident
program. If you do, you won't be able to return to the 1-2-3 worksheet, and
you will lose any work you have not saved.

Retrieving Files

To call a file back into memory from disk, use the /**F**ile **R**etrieve command. If
you are just starting 1-2-3, this command brings a new file into memory.
Otherwise, this command replaces the current file with the new file. Therefore, be sure you have saved the current file with /**F**ile **S**ave before retrieving a
new file. Release 2.3 provides a prompt to warn you to save the file.

127

To retrieve a file with the keyboard, follow these steps:

1. Select /**File R**etrieve.

2. If you have not saved your current file, 1-2-3 beeps and indicates that worksheet changes are not saved. Select **Yes** to erase the file in memory or **No** to cancel the command and allow you to save the current file.

1-2-3 displays a partial list of worksheet files in the current drive and directory.

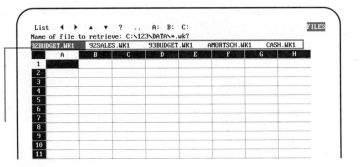

The files displayed have the WK1 extension. Any WKS files from older versions of 1-2-3 are also listed.

3. If you don't see the file name you want, press F3 (Name).

1-2-3 displays a full-screen list of file names in the current drive and directory.

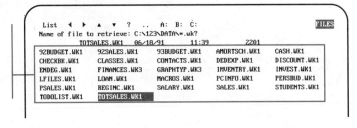

When you highlight a file name on the full screen, you also see the date and time the file was created, as well as its size.

4. Select the desired file name by highlighting or typing it; then press ↵Enter.

Using Wild Card Characters for File Retrieval

When you retrieve files, you can use wild cards with 1-2-3. Wild cards—the asterisk (*) and the question mark (?)—are helpful when you need to limit the number of files that are displayed on-screen, or when you are unsure of the exact spelling of a file you want to retrieve.

If you want to display only those file names that begin or end with a certain character or characters, use the asterisk (*). For example, you can type **S*** and then press ⏎Enter at the `Name of file to retrieve:` prompt.

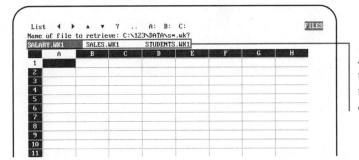

All the file names that begin with the letter S are displayed.

You can use the asterisk (*) wild card in place of any combination of characters; the question mark (?) wild card stands for any one character. The asterisk can be used by itself or following other characters. According to these rules, SALES*.WK1 is acceptable, but *91.WK1 is not. The question mark wild card, on the other hand, can be used in any character position. Therefore, instead of the incorrect retrieval name *91.WK1, you can enter **?????91.WK1**.

Retrieving Files from Subdirectories

1-2-3 keeps track of subdirectory names as well as file names. When you issue the **/File Retrieve** command, for example, subdirectories of the current directory are displayed with the file names.

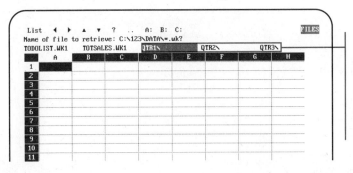

The backslash (\) symbol following a name (within a list of file names) indicates a subdirectory name.

3

When you select a subdirectory name, 1-2-3 displays the list of files in that subdirectory.

This screen shows the files in the QTR1 subdirectory.

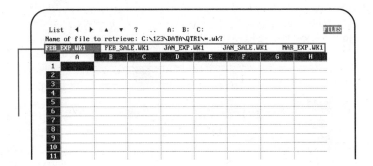

When you need to access a file that is on a different drive—or one that is in a directory that is not a subdirectory of the current directory—use the Esc key or the Backspace key after selecting /File Retrieve. When you press Esc while the default path name shows in the control panel, 1-2-3 changes to EDIT mode. You can then edit the file specification just as you would any label entry. When you press Esc a second time, 1-2-3 erases the current drive and directory specification. You can then enter the specification for the drive and directory you want.

You can use the Backspace key to erase the path name, one entire subdirectory at a time. To reverse the process, select a subdirectory name from the list of files and press Enter.

Some valid file names, with their drive and directory specifications, are the following:

File name	Description
B:\SAMPLE1.WK1	Worksheet file on drive B
C:\123R23\SAMPLE1.WK1	Worksheet file in subdirectory \123R23 on drive C
C:\123R23\DATA*.PIC	List of all PIC files in subdirectory DATA of subdirectory \123R23 on drive C (1-2-3 displays the list and waits for you to select a specific file name)
A:*.*	List of all files on drive A (1-2-3 displays all file names and waits for you to select a specific file name)

130

Summary

This chapter on 1-2-3 basics covered many important concepts that are essential for beginning 1-2-3 users. You learned about moving the cell pointer around the worksheet using the keyboard and the mouse; selecting commands from the 1-2-3 and Wysiwyg menus; entering and editing data, formulas, and labels; using the Undo feature; and naming, saving, and retrieving 1-2-3 files.

Specifically, you learned the following key information about 1-2-3:

■ The arrow keys move the cell pointer horizontally and vertically, one cell at a time. When used with the End key, however, they can move the cell pointer quickly—even to the remote borders of 1-2-3's large worksheet.

■ The PgUp, PgDn, Tab, and Shift-Tab keys help you move around the worksheet one screen at a time (up, down, right, and left, respectively).

■ The Home key moves the cell pointer to the upper left corner of a worksheet—usually to cell A1. When you specify a cell address for the GoTo (F5) function key, you make the cell pointer jump almost instantly to any cell in the worksheet.

■ Commands are selected with the keyboard from 1-2-3's menu system by pressing slash (/) and from Wysiwyg's menu system by pressing colon (:). Next either point to the desired command and press Enter or directly select the command by typing the first letter of the menu command.

■ To select 1-2-3 or Wysiwyg commands with a mouse, move the mouse pointer to the control panel to display a menu. Press the right mouse button to toggle between menus. Commands are selected by clicking the left mouse button on the desired command.

■ Two types of data can be entered into a 1-2-3 worksheet: labels and values. Labels are text entries, and values include numbers, formulas, and functions.

■ Label prefixes are used to affect how text data is displayed in individual cells. The label prefixes include ' (left-justify), " (right-justify), ^ (center), and \ (repeat label). The /Range Label command aligns labels in a range of cells, and the /Worksheet Global Label-Prefix command changes the alignment of labels for the entire worksheet.

3

3

- A strength of 1-2-3 is its capacity to accept and compute complex numerical data, formulas, and functions. 1-2-3's functions, always identified by the @ sign preceding the function's name, are used within formulas to provide exceptional power in worksheets.

- The Edit (F2) key is used to modify any data that has been entered (or is currently being entered) into the worksheet. The direction keys are used to move the cursor in the control panel while editing a cell entry. In Wysiwyg, you can use :Text Edit to edit a range of data within the worksheet itself.

- The Undo feature, activated by pressing Alt-F4, enables you to "undo" the previous command before the next command is executed. To use Undo, you must first select the command /Worksheet Global Default Other Undo Enable. To release the extra memory required by Undo, you can temporarily deactivate the Undo feature with the /Worksheet Global Default Other Undo Disable command.

- File names used in 1-2-3 Release 2.3 can be no more than eight characters in length, followed by a period (.) and a three-character extension. File extensions include WK1 for worksheet files, BAK for backup worksheet files, PRN for ASCII print files, PIC for graph files, and ENC for encoded print files.

- The /File Save command is used to save the current worksheet file. If the file name already exists, 1-2-3 prompts you to Replace the existing file or Cancel the command. The Backup option ensures that the previous two versions of the worksheet will always be available.

- The /File Retrieve command is used to call an existing file into memory. 1-2-3 provides a list of worksheet files (and subdirectories) located in the current directory. The wild-card characters * and ? are used to limit the files displayed with the /File Retrieve command.

The 1-2-3 basics provided in this chapter will enable you to begin working with ranges, which are discussed in the next chapter.

Working with Ranges

This chapter (with the next two chapters) teaches you the principles of using commands and shows you how to use some of the fundamental 1-2-3 commands needed to build worksheets. Although most of the commands discussed in this chapter are from the /Range menu, some options from the /Worksheet menu are also included. Chapters 4, 5, and 6 discuss the commands you use to create a worksheet.

To make sense of the command structure, you first need to understand the concept of ranges. While some commands affect the entire worksheet, others affect only certain cells or groups of cells. 1-2-3 uses the term *range* for a rectangular block of cells, and many useful 1-2-3 actions are built around the range concept. This chapter explains the concept of ranges and shows you how to use them with specific commands.

Ranges offer many advantages that make your work less tedious and more efficient. When you use ranges, you can execute commands that affect all the cells in a group rather than one individual cell. For example, you can format a block of cells to display as currency by executing a single command on the specified range of cells.

When you use range names instead of cell addresses, you can quickly process blocks of cells in commands and formulas. A descriptive range name will help you and others recognize the nature of the data that the range contains. You can use the range name with the GoTo (F5) key to move the cell pointer quickly to that range in the worksheet.

Designating a range

Using range names

Erasing ranges

Formatting cell contents

Key Terms in This Chapter

Range	A rectangular group of cells used in a worksheet operation. For example, the rectangular area A5..D10 is a range.
Range commands	Commands used to manipulate cells in ranges. You can access the /**R**ange commands through the **Range** option on the 1-2-3 main menu.
Range name	An alphanumeric name of up to 15 characters given to a rectangular group of cells.
Preselecting a range	Selecting the range to be affected by one or more commands with the F4 key before a command is issued.
Range name table	A list of all range names and their corresponding cell addresses. This list is produced with the /**R**ange **N**ame **T**able command.
Formatting	The process of changing the way data is displayed in the worksheet. Formatting is accomplished with the /**R**ange **F**ormat or /**W**orksheet **G**lobal **F**ormat commands.

Using the Mouse

To use a mouse with 1-2-3 Release 2.3, you need a mouse, mouse software, and a graphics monitor and graphics card that support a mouse. You can use a mouse to select commands and files, specify ranges, move the cell pointer within the worksheet, and make selections in a dialog box. Refer to the following sections of the specified chapters for further information on using the mouse.

- Chapter 2— "Understanding Mouse Terminology"
- Chapter 3— "Mouse Control of the Cell Pointer"
  "Using Dialog Boxes"
  "Using the Mouse To Select Menu Commands"
- Chapter 4— "Using the Mouse To Specify Ranges"

What Is a Range?

1-2-3's definition of a range is a rectangular block of adjacent cells. The smallest possible range is one cell, and the largest is the entire worksheet. Remember that ranges are specified by the cells in the upper left and lower right corners of the range.

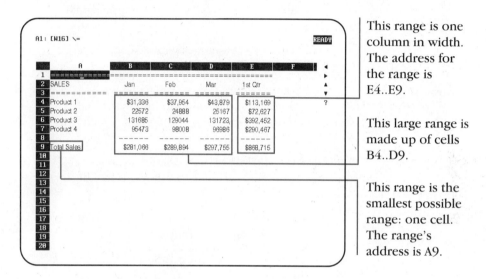

This range is one column in width. The address for the range is E4..E9.

This large range is made up of cells B4..D9.

This range is the smallest possible range: one cell. The range's address is A9.

Access the range commands by selecting /Range from the 1-2-3 main menu. You then see the following menu of commands:

Format Label Erase Name Justify Prot Unprot Input Value Trans Search

Table 4.1 provides a brief description of the actions of each of these commands.

Table 4.1
Selections on the /Range Menu

Selection	Description
Format	Changes the display of values or formula results in a cell or range of cells
Label	Aligns text labels in a cell or range of cells
Erase	Deletes the contents of a cell or range of cells

continued

Table 4.1 (*continued*)

Selection	Description
Name	Assigns, modifies, or deletes a name associated with a cell or range of cells
Justify	Fits text within a desired range by wrapping words to form complete paragraphs with lines of approximately the same length
Prot (Protect)	Prevents changes to cell ranges when /Worksheet Global Protection is enabled
Unprot (Unprotect)	With /Worksheet Global Protection active, enables changes to a range of cells and identifies (through increases in intensity or changes of color) which cells' contents can be changed
Input	With /Worksheet Global Protection active, restricts movement of the cell pointer to unprotected cells in a range
Value	Copies formulas in a range to their values in another specified range (or the same range)
Trans (Transpose)	Reorders columns of data into rows or rows of data into columns
Search	Finds or replaces a string of data within a specified range

Designating a Range

Many commands act on ranges. For example, the /Range Erase command prompts you for the range to erase. You can respond to a prompt for a range in the following ways:

- Type the addresses of the upper left and lower right cells in the range.
- Use the direction keys or the mouse to highlight the cells in the range.
- Type the range name or press Name (F3) to display a list of range names and select the range name you want.
- Preselect a range with the F4 key to allow multiple commands to be performed on a single range.

Each method is covered in the following sections.

Typing Range Addresses

Using the typing method, you specify a range by typing the address of the
upper left and lower right corners. Be sure to separate the two addresses with
one or two periods. 1-2-3 always stores a range with two periods, but you only
need to type one period.

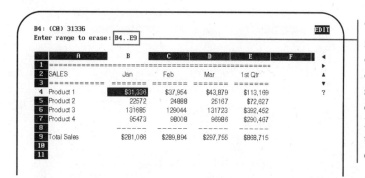

To specify the
range B4..E9, you
can type B4..E9
or B4.E9. 1-2-3
stores the range
containing B4,
E4, B9, and E9 as
the four range
corners.

You can type cell addresses to specify a range in several situations: when the
range does not have a range name, when the range you want to specify is far
from the current cell, or when you know the addresses of the range. Experienced 1-2-3 users rarely type cell addresses; they highlight a range in POINT
mode or use range names instead.

Highlighting a Range

The second method, that of highlighting the cells in the range in POINT
mode, is used most often. You can point to and highlight a range in commands and functions just as you can point to a single cell in a formula.

Following the prompt to enter a range, 1-2-3 displays the address of the cell
pointer in the control panel. This single cell, shown as a one-cell range, is
anchored. The default range with most /Range commands is an anchored one-
cell range. When the cell is anchored, you highlight a range as you move the
cell pointer.

When a range is highlighted, the cells of the range appear in reverse video (or
in a different color if you have a color monitor). Reverse video, or the use of a
different color, allows ranges to be specified easily, with little chance for error.

137

As you move the cell pointer, the reverse-video or colored rectangle expands until you finish specifying the range.

Suppose, for example, that you select the /**R**ange Erase command. 1-2-3 displays the prompt `Enter range to erase:`.

4

The location of the cell pointer marks the beginning of the anchored range.

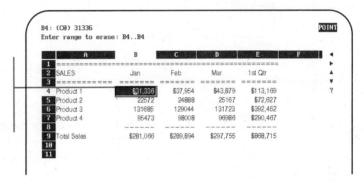

To clear an incorrectly highlighted range, press Esc or Backspace. The highlight collapses to the anchored cell only, and the anchor is removed—allowing you to move the cell pointer to the correct location at the beginning of the range.

You can use the End key with the direction keys to quickly highlight large ranges. Use the End key to move the cell pointer to the boundaries of contiguous data ranges.

After you press End ↓ followed by End →, the range B4..E9 is highlighted and the address appears in the control panel.

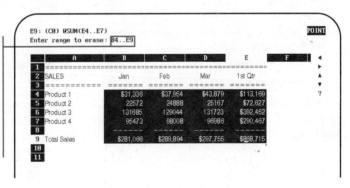

138

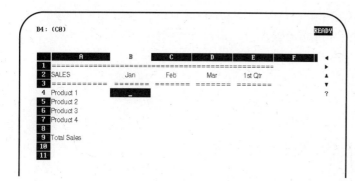

When you press Enter, 1-2-3 executes the command using the highlighted range, and the cell pointer returns to the originating cell.

Pointing (or highlighting) is faster and easier than typing the range addresses. You also make fewer errors by pointing than by typing, because you can see the range as you specify it. A later section of this chapter shows you how to highlight a range with a mouse.

Typing a Range Name

Another way to specify a range is to type an existing range name at the prompt. Range names, which should be descriptive, can contain as many as 15 characters and can be used in formulas and commands.

The use of range names is advantageous for several reasons. Range names are easier to remember than cell addresses, and it may be faster to use a name than to point to a range in another part of the worksheet. Range names also make formulas easier to understand. For example, when you see the range name NOV_SALES_R1 (rather than the cell address) in a formula, you have a better chance of remembering that the entry represents "November Sales for Region 1." The process of assigning names to ranges is described in a later section of this chapter.

Using the Mouse To Specify Ranges

You can use a mouse to quickly specify ranges in a worksheet. Click-and-drag the mouse to designate ranges.

To specify a range with a mouse, follow these steps:

1. Click the left mouse button on the upper left corner of the range, and hold the button down.

2. Drag the mouse to the lower right corner of the range.

139

3. Release the mouse button. The desired range is highlighted.

4. Click the left mouse button again or press ⏎Enter to continue to the next step in the procedure.

Note: You can cancel the highlighted range by clicking the right mouse button or by pressing Esc.

Preselecting a Range

Before issuing one or more commands, you can select the range to be affected by the command(s). This technique is called *preselecting* a range. When you preselect a range, you can issue several formatting commands that affect the same range. The range that you preselect remains selected. For example, if you want to change the font of some numbers and then outline the cells that contain the numbers, preselect the range and perform both commands. Ranges can be preselected either from the keyboard or with a mouse. To preselect a range from the keyboard, follow these steps:

1. Move the cell pointer to the upper left corner of the range.

2. Press F4.

The mode indicator changes from READY to POINT and an anchored range address appears in the control panel.

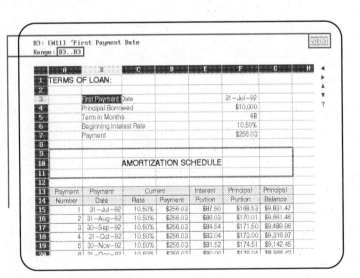

3. Highlight the range using the direction keys and press ⏎Enter.

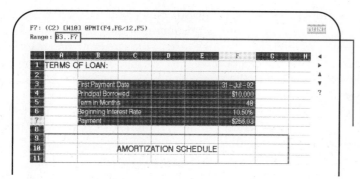

In this example, the range B3..F7 has been preselected.

4. Select one or more commands to be performed on the range (such as **:Format Italics Set**).

5. When you finish working with the preselected range, simply move the cell pointer (using a direction key) or press (Esc).

To preselect a range with the mouse, follow these steps:

1. Move the cell pointer to the upper left corner of the range.

2. Press and hold the (Ctrl) key and click the left mouse button.

   The mode indicator changes from READY to POINT and an anchored range address appears in the control panel. You can now release the (Ctrl) key (but not the mouse button).

3. Highlight the range by dragging the mouse pointer to the lower right corner of the range, and then release the mouse button.

4. Select one or more commands to be performed on the range (such as **:Format Italics Set**).

5. When you finish working with the preselected range, click either mouse button.

Dealing with Remembered Ranges

1-2-3 remembers ranges previously specified with certain commands by highlighting the range when the command is reissued. These commands include **/Data**, **/Graph**, **/Print**, and **/Range Search** from the 1-2-3 menu, and **:Graph** and **:Print** from the Wysiwyg menu. If the previous range is what you need, press Enter to select the highlighted range. If you want to specify a new range, first press Backspace to cancel the old range (the cell pointer moves to the current worksheet cell). Then specify the range with the keyboard or mouse.

141

In addition to using Backspace to cancel a previous range, you can also use Esc or the right mouse button. When you use this method, the cell pointer moves to the upper left corner of the old range, not to the current worksheet cell. For example, suppose that the cell pointer is in cell M1, and you want to print this part of the worksheet. The range previously printed was A2..G18. When you choose the /**Print** **P**rinter **R**ange command, 1-2-3 remembers the old range. If you press Backspace now, 1-2-3 cancels the old range and returns the cell pointer to cell M1. If you press Esc or the right mouse button, 1-2-3 cancels the old range but moves the cell pointer to cell A2, the upper left corner of the old range.

Using Range Names

Range names can contain as many as 15 characters and should describe the range's contents. The advantage of naming ranges is that they are easier to understand than cell addresses. For example, the phrase SALES_MODEL25 is a more understandable way of describing the sales for Model #25 than its cell coordinates. (Note that the underscore is part of the range name.)

Range names can be useful tools for processing commands and generating formulas. Whenever you must designate a range that has been named, you can respond with the range name instead of entering cell addresses or pointing to cell locations. 1-2-3's /**R**ange **N**ame command lets you tag a specific range of the worksheet with any name you choose. After naming the range, you can type the name and press Enter instead of typing the cell addresses that indicate the range's boundaries. You can also use a range name to jump from one part of the worksheet to another.

The /**R**ange **N**ame command, for example, lets you give the name SALES1 to the cells in the range B4..D4.

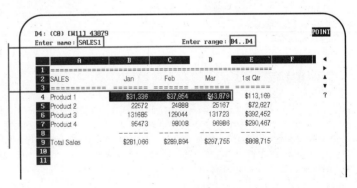

The simplest way to compute the sum of this range is to use the function @SUM(SALES1). In a similar way, you can use the function @MAX(SALES1) to determine the maximum value in the range. In functions and formulas, you can always use range names in place of cell addresses.

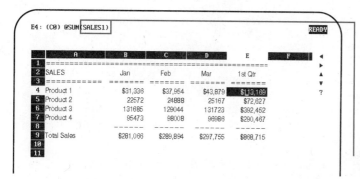

When you name the range, you can use it in a formula or in response to a command prompt that asks for a range.

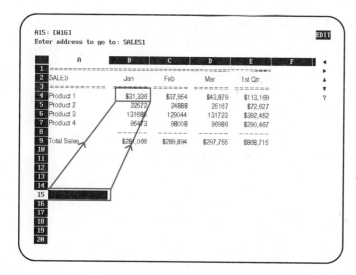

Type **SALES1** after pressing F5 (GoTo) and the cell pointer moves to cell B4—the first cell (upper left corner) of the range named SALES1.

After you establish a range name, 1-2-3 automatically uses that name, instead of cell addresses, throughout the worksheet. For example, any formulas in the worksheet that refer to a named range include that name within the formula (rather than the cell addresses of the range).

You can also designate the ranges of cells to be printed or to be extracted and saved to another worksheet. If you set up special names corresponding to different areas and you want to print or extract and save these areas to

143

another worksheet, you can enter a predefined range name rather than actual cell addresses. For example, if you want to print a portion of a worksheet, you can use the command **/Print Printer Range**. Then you can type an existing range name, such as PART_1 or PART_5, in response to the prompt for entering a print range.

You can name ranges in one of two ways. You can either issue the **/Range Name Create** command to create a new range name or you can select **/Range Name Labels** to use a label already in the worksheet as a name for a range.

When you create a name, you assign a name to one or more cells. When you use the **Labels** option, you pick up a label from the worksheet and make it the range name of a one-cell range above, below, to the left, or to the right of the label. You can assign more than one label at a time, but each label applies only to one adjacent cell.

Naming a Group of Cells

The **/Range Name Create** command is ideal when you need to give a name to a multicell range. To use **/Range Name Create** to specify a name for any range, even one cell, follow these steps:

1. Select **/Range**.

Range is the second option on the 1-2-3 main menu.

```
B4: (C0) [W15] 113169                                          MENU
Worksheet  Range  Copy  Move  File  Print  Graph  Data  System  Add-In  Quit
Format  Label  Erase  Name  Justify  Prot  Unprot  Input  Value  Trans  Search
        A              B             C          D          E          F
 1  ===================================
 2  SALES          1st Qtr
 3  =========  ===========
 4  Bill                $113,169
 5  Mary                 $72,627
 6  John                $392,452
 7  Cindy               $290,467
 8                  ------------
 9  Total Sales         $868,715
10
11
```

2. Select **Name Create**.
3. At the prompt `Enter name:` type the range name you want, and then press `⏎Enter`. Do not use a name that can be confused with a cell address, such as Q1.

   For this example, type **QTR1** and press `⏎Enter`.

144

4. At the prompt `Enter range:` select the range you want to name by typing the cell addresses, highlighting the range, or typing an existing range name; then press ⏎Enter.

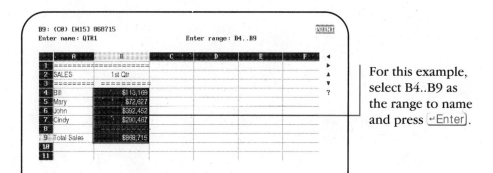

For this example, select B4..B9 as the range to name and press ⏎Enter.

4

Naming a Single Cell

If you need to assign names to a series of one-cell entries with adjacent labels or to a series of columns or rows with headings, use the /**R**ange Name **L**abels command. This command is similar to /**R**ange Name **C**reate except that the names for ranges are taken directly from adjacent cells. These names must be text entries (labels); you cannot use numeric entries and blank cells to name adjacent cells with the /**R**ange Name **L**abels command.

To use /**R**ange Name **L**abels to assign names to single-cell entries, follow these steps:

1. Position the cell pointer on the first label you want to use as a range name. Remember that you can use this command only on adjacent cells.

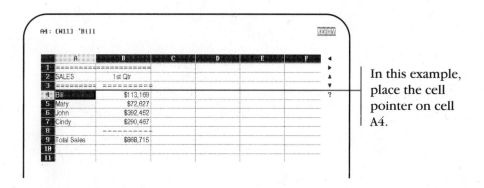

In this example, place the cell pointer on cell A4.

2. Select /**R**ange **N**ame **L**abels.

3. Select the appropriate option: **Right, Down, Left,** or **Up,** depending on the location of the cells to be named.

In this example, select **Right** because the range you want to name is to the right of the current cell.

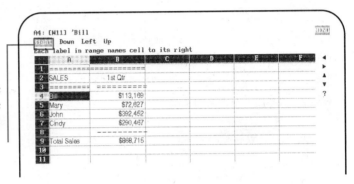

4. At the prompt `Enter label range:` select the cells containing the labels you want to use as range names; then press ⏎Enter.

   In this example, select the range A4..A7; then press ⏎Enter.

Deleting Range Names

You can delete range names individually or all at once. The /**R**ange **N**ame **D**elete command allows you to delete a single range name, and the /**R**ange **N**ame **R**eset command causes all range names to be deleted. The second command is powerful; use it with caution. Note that these commands only delete range names, not the actual ranges themselves.

To delete a single range name, follow these steps:

1. Select /**R**ange **N**ame **D**elete.

2. When 1-2-3 displays a list of range names, select the range name you want to delete, and then press ⏎Enter.

146

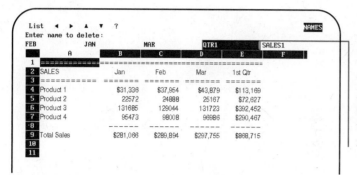

In this example, the range name QTR1 is highlighted. Press (↵Enter) to delete the highlighted range name.

To delete all the range names in a worksheet, select /**R**ange **N**ame **R**eset.

Note: Use this command with caution. 1-2-3 deletes all range names as soon as you enter the command, without giving you a chance to verify your selection. Of course, if the Undo feature is active, you can use Alt-F4 to reverse this command.

If you delete a range name, 1-2-3 no longer uses that name and reverts to using the range's cell address. For example, @SUM(SALES1) returns to @SUM(B4..D4). The contents of the cells within the range, however, remain intact. To erase the contents of ranges, use the /**R**ange **E**rase command, which is explained later in this chapter.

Listing Range Names

Suppose that you select the /**R**ange **E**rase command and then you can't remember the name of the range you want to erase. You can use the Name (F3) function key to produce a list of the range names in the current worksheet.

To display a list of the range names in the current worksheet, follow these steps:

1. Make sure that the worksheet is in POINT or VALUE mode, and then press (F3) (Name).

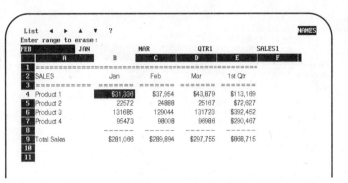

In this example, F3 (Name) was pressed in POINT mode.

2. If the range names extend beyond the right edge of the control panel, use the arrow keys to display the additional names.

3. To display a full-screen list of range names, press F3 a second time.

1-2-3 displays the entire list of range names (or as much of it as the screen can hold).

4. Move the cell pointer to the desired name and press ↵Enter. 1-2-3 then returns you to the worksheet.

You can use the space bar, the arrow keys, and the Home and End keys to select the name of the range you want to use. You can also press Tab or Shift-Tab to move right or left one screen (or line) at a time.

Note: If you want to print the displayed list of range names, hold down Shift and press PrtSc. (If you have an enhanced keyboard, press Print Screen.) Using Shift-PrtSc or Print Screen while your printer is turned on prints whatever appears on the screen.

To move the cell pointer to a certain range, use the Name (F3) key with the GoTo (F5) key to select the range name. When you press GoTo (F5) and then Name (F3), 1-2-3 displays an alphabetical list of your worksheet's range names

148

in the control panel. To designate the range you want to go to, select a name from the list by using the space bar, arrow keys, Home and End keys, and Tab or Shift-Tab. When you press Enter, the list disappears, and the cell pointer is positioned at the beginning of the selected range.

Creating a Table of Range Names

If you have created several range names in your worksheet, you can document them in a table in the worksheet. 1-2-3 provides the /**R**ange **N**ame **T**able command to perform this task.

To create a table of range names, follow these steps:

1. Move the cell pointer to the location where you want the upper left corner of the table to appear.

    For example, move the cell pointer to a cell located a few rows below the data in the worksheet.

2. Select /**R**ange **N**ame **T**able.

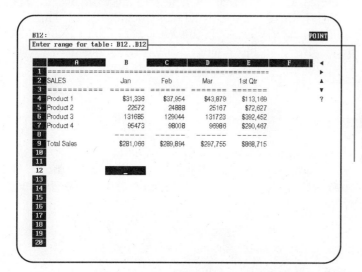

1-2-3 asks for the location of the table.

3. Press Enter to select the current location of the cell pointer.

4

149

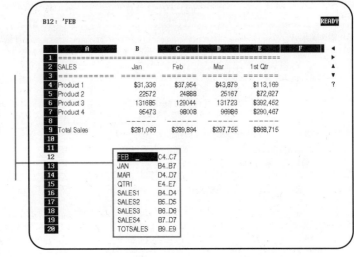

1-2-3 produces a table with all the range names in a column and with the referenced ranges to the immediate right.

4

Note: Creating a table of range names is simple, but you must be careful where you place the table. Make certain that the table will not write over an important part of the worksheet. The range-name table includes range names and addresses at the time the table is created. This list is *not* automatically updated when you create, delete, or move ranges. For an up-to-date table, you must re-create the table with the /**R**ange Name **T**able command.

Erasing Ranges

With the /**R**ange Erase command, you can erase sections of the worksheet. You can use this command on ranges as small as a single cell or as large as the entire worksheet. (However, a simpler way to erase a single cell is to highlight the cell and press Del.)

To erase a range, follow these steps:

1. Select /**R**ange Erase.
2. When 1-2-3 prompts you to supply a range, select the range you want to erase and press ⏎Enter.

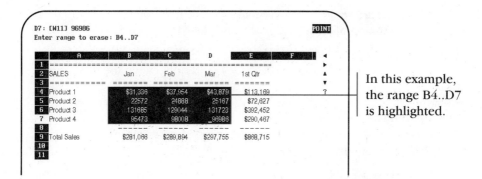

In this example, the range B4..D7 is highlighted.

Note: Although you can indicate a range to be erased by typing the cell addresses of the range or by entering a range name, highlighting the range lets you see the boundaries of the range you want to erase before 1-2-3 erases the range. Highlighting helps to prevent accidental erasure of important data.

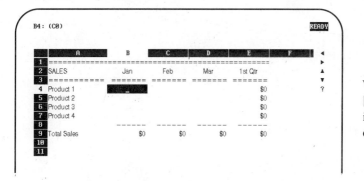

When you press (↵Enter), 1-2-3 immediately erases the range.

After you erase a range, you can recover it with the Undo feature if it is enabled (immediately press Alt-F4 to "undo" the /**R**ange **E**rase command). Otherwise, if the Undo feature is not active, you have to reenter all the data in order to restore the range (if the file was saved before the range was erased, you can retrieve the file again with /**F**ile **R**etrieve).

Formatting Cell Contents

You now know that 1-2-3 expects you to enter data in a certain way. If, for example, you try to enter **1,234**, the program beeps, switches to EDIT mode, and waits for you to remove the comma. You get the same result if you try to enter **10:08 AM**—in this case, the colon and the AM are the offenders. If you try to enter **$9.23**, the program accepts the entry, but removes the **$**.

1-2-3 would have limited usefulness if you could not change the way data is displayed on-screen. You can, however, control not only the display of data with commas, time, and currency, but also with a variety of other formats. You determine formats with one of the options of the /**R**ange Format or /**W**orksheet Global Format commands. The next chapter discusses the /**W**orksheet commands.

Table 4.2 provides examples of the formats that are available in 1-2-3. These formats primarily affect the way numeric values are displayed in a worksheet. Notice that **Text** format causes a formula to appear in a cell as a formula rather than a value and **Hidden** format affects the display of every kind of entry.

Cell formats specified with /**R**ange Format are automatically displayed within parentheses in the first line of the control panel. The worksheet's default cell format, however, does not appear in the control panel. You can use the /**W**orksheet **S**tatus command to view the current default worksheet format.

Table 4.2
1-2-3 Format Options

		Examples	
Format	*Description*	*Data entered*	*Result*
Fixed	Controls the number of decimal places displayed	**15.56**	16
Sci	Displays large or small numbers, using scientific (exponential) notation	**–21034567**	-2E+07
Currency	Displays currency symbols and commas	**234567.75**	$234,568
, (Comma)	Inserts commas to mark thousands and multiples of thousands	**1234567**	1,234,567

Format	Description	Examples	
		Data entered	**Result*
General	Displays values with up to 10 decimal points or uses scientific notation; the default format in a new worksheet	**26.003**	26.003
+/–	Creates horizontal bar graphs or time-duration graphs; useful for computers that cannot display graphs	**4.1** **–3**	++++ - - -
Percent	Displays a decimal number as a whole number with a % sign	**0.25**	25%
Date	Displays serial-date numbers. **/Range Format Date Time** sets time formats	**@DATE(91,8,1)** **@NOW**	01-Aug-91 07:48 AM
Text	Displays formulas as text, not the computed values that 1-2-3 normally displays	**+B5+B6** **@SUM(C4..C8)**	+B5+B6 @SUM(C4..C8)
Hidden	Hides contents from the display and does not print them; hidden contents are still evaluated	**289**	
Reset	Returns the format to the current **/Worksheet Global** format		

*The data displayed when formatted with no decimal places

4

Setting Range and Worksheet Global Formats

Although you frequently use the /Range Format command to format individual ranges in your worksheet, you can also change the default format for the entire worksheet. The /Worksheet Global Format command controls the format of all cells in the worksheet and the /Range Format command controls specific ranges.

Generally, you use the /Worksheet Global Format command when you are just starting to enter data in a worksheet. Be sure to choose a format that the majority of cells will use. After you set all the cells to that format, you can use the /Range Format command to override the Global format setting for specific cell ranges.

The /Range Format command takes precedence over the /Worksheet Global Format command. This means that whenever you change the global format, all the affected numbers and formulas will change automatically unless they were previously formatted with the /Range Format command. In turn, when you format a range, the format for that range will override any already set by /Worksheet Global Format.

Although the /Range Format command is generally used on cells that contain data, you can choose to select a format for cells that are now blank but will eventually contain data. Any information put in these cells later will be displayed according to the format you chose with /Range Format.

After you use /Range Format, the cells may display asterisks (*****). This indicates that the column is too narrow to display the formatted values. Use /Worksheet Column Set-Width to change the width of a column.

To change the format of a cell or range of cells, follow these steps:

1. Select /Range Format.

2. From the resulting menu, select the desired type of format.

In this example, select Currency.

3. If you are prompted to enter the number of decimal places, type a new number and press ↵Enter or just press ↵Enter to accept the default number.

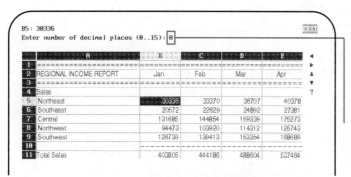

In this example, type 0 for zero decimal places and press ↵Enter.

4. Highlight the range you want to format.

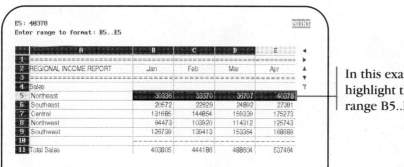

In this example, highlight the range B5..E5.

5. Press ↵Enter to complete the command.

The cell pointer appears in the first cell of the formatted range; the control panel indicates the format—in this case, (C0) for Currency with no decimal places.

	A	B	C	D	E
1					
2	REGIONAL INCOME REPORT	Jan	Feb	Mar	Apr
3					
4	Sales				
5	Northeast	$30,336	$33,370	$36,707	$40,378
6	Southeast	20572	22629	24892	27381
7	Central	131685	144854	159339	175273
8	Northwest	94473	103920	114312	125743
9	Southwest	126739	139413	153354	168689
10					
11	Total Sales	403805	444186	488604	537464

B5: (C0) 30336   READY

General Format

General format is the default format for all new worksheets. When numbers appear in General format, commas that separate thousands and multiples of thousands are not displayed. Trailing zeros to the right of the decimal point are also suppressed. General format uses scientific notation for numbers too large or too small to be displayed normally.

Fixed Format

1-2-3's Fixed format is similar to General format because it does not display commas or dollar signs. Fixed format, however, lets you choose the number of decimal places to be displayed (up to 15).

Scientific (Sci) Format

Sci (Scientific) format causes 1-2-3 to display numbers in exponential form (scientific notation). Unlike General format, Sci format lets you control the number of decimal places and therefore the amount of precision to be displayed.

Currency Format

Currency format displays numbers in cells with a dollar sign ($) before each entry, and with commas to separate thousands and multiples of thousands. Negative values appear in parentheses ( ). Although the dollar sign is the default, other symbols can be used as currency indicators. Currency format also allows you to control the number of decimal places (up to 15).

Comma (,) Format

The **,** (Comma) format is similar to **C**urrency format, except that no dollar signs appear in the number display. Commas separate hundreds from thousands, hundreds of thousands from millions, and so on. Parentheses ( ) identify negative numbers. After you choose the **,** (Comma) format, you can specify the number of decimal places you want. Only in **C**urrency and **,** (Comma) formats are negative values displayed within parentheses. In other formats, negative values are preceded by a minus sign.

The +/– Format

The **+/–** format creates a horizontal bar "graph" of plus or minus signs within the cell, depending on the value of the number you enter in the cell. Asterisks appear if the size of the bar graph exceeds the column width. If you enter zero in a cell, a period (.) appears on the graph and displays left-justified in the cell.

You can use this format to mark a value in a long column of numbers. As you scan the column, the +'s and –'s stand out and are easy to locate.

Percent Format

The **P**ercent format is used to display percentages. When you select this format, you also select the number of decimal places. The values displayed in the worksheet are the values you enter, multiplied by 100 and followed by a percent sign. When you use the **P**ercent format, remember to enter numbers with the correct decimal point. To display 12%, for example, you must enter **.12**, not **12**. You can also enter the value as **12%** and 1-2-3 will display the number as 0.12 until you format it.

Date and Time Formats

1-2-3 represents any given date internally as an integer equal to the number of days from December 31, 1899, to the given date. For example, January 1, 1900, is represented by the number 1; December 31, 2099 (the last date in 1-2-3's calendar), is represented by 73050. To enter a date into the worksheet, you can use one of the three date functions: @DATE, @DATEVALUE, or @NOW.

1-2-3 calculates a period of hours as a fraction expressed in decimals. The calculations are based on a 24-hour clock (military time). You can use one of the time functions (@TIME, @TIMEVALUE, or @NOW) to enter a time into

157

the worksheet. You can specify many date and time formats with the /Range Format Date and /Worksheet Global Format Date commands.

Text Format

Text format displays formulas as they are entered in the command line, not the computed values that 1-2-3 normally displays. Numbers that are entered with this format are displayed as in General format.

The two most important applications of this format are setting up table ranges for /Data Table commands and debugging. Because you can display all the formulas on-screen with the Text format, finding and correcting problems is a relatively easy task. You usually have to widen the cell width to see your complete formulas when you use this technique.

Hidden Format

The /Range Format Hidden command suppresses the cell contents for any given range. If you want to hide all the cells in a column or range of columns, instead use the /Worksheet Column Hide command, discussed in the next chapter.

Although a cell with Hidden format appears as a blank cell on-screen, its contents appear in the control panel when you highlight the cell, and the contents are still available for calculations or formulas. All the formulas and values can be calculated and readjusted when values are changed. The contents of hidden cells within a range to be printed do not appear on your printed copy.

Reset Format

The /Range Format Reset command resets the format of the indicated range to the global default setting. When the format of a range is reset, the format indicator for any cell within the range disappears from the control panel. The Reset option does not appear on the /Worksheet Global Format menu.

Controlling the International Formats

1-2-3 enables you to control the punctuation and currency sign displayed by , (Comma) and Currency formats, and to control the way the date and time are displayed when you use the special International Date and Time formats. To control these settings globally for the worksheet, use the /Worksheet

Global Default Other International command. This command allows you to choose the format 1-2-3 uses for displaying the date and time, currency symbols, negative values (with a minus sign or parentheses), and punctuation.

Summary

This chapter showed you how to create worksheets with many of the /Range commands. You learned how to use the /Range commands to create and name ranges, delete range names and erase ranges, move quickly to a named range, and display existing range names in the control panel or on the full screen. You also learned how to format a cell or a range of cells to determine how values and formula results appear on-screen.

Specifically, you learned the following key information about 1-2-3:

- A range in 1-2-3 is defined as a rectangular block of adjacent cells. Ranges are identified by the cell addresses of their upper left and lower right corners, separated by one or two periods. An example of a range is C4..G17.

- A range can be designated by typing the cell addresses; highlighting the range with the direction keys or the click-and-drag technique of the mouse; or typing an existing range name.

- You can use the F4 key to preselect a range. This enables you to perform many commands on a single range without having to respecify the range after each command.

- You use the /Range Name Create and /Range Name Labels commands to name ranges of cells within the worksheet. The Create option is commonly used to name new multicell ranges. The Labels option is useful for naming a series of one-cell entries with adjacent labels, or a series of columns or rows with headings.

- The /Range Name Delete and /Range Name Reset commands can delete one or all range names, respectively. Use the Reset option with caution; all range names are deleted immediately with its selection, and 1-2-3 does not require verification of this command.

- To list all ranges named in the current worksheet, press Name (F3) in POINT or VALUE mode (when 1-2-3 prompts for a range or when you create a formula).

- You can use the Name (F3) key with the GoTo (F5) key to select the name of a range where you want to move the cell pointer. If you press GoTo (F5) and then press Name (F3), 1-2-3 displays an alphabetical list of your worksheet's range names in the control panel.

4

159

■ The /**R**ange **N**ame **T**able command lists all range names and their corresponding locations within the worksheet. You should execute this command in a remote portion of the worksheet to avoid over-writing your worksheet data.

■ The /**R**ange **E**rase command erases single-cell or multicell ranges. You can denote a range to be erased by typing the cell addresses of the range, entering a range name, or highlighting the range. Highlighting is the preferred method because it allows you to see the boundaries of the range you want to erase before 1-2-3 erases the range. Single-cell ranges can be erased by highlighting the cell and pressing Del.

■ The /**R**ange **F**ormat command changes the way data is displayed in the worksheet. Some available formatting options within 1-2-3 include **C**urrency, **F**ixed, **P**ercent, **T**ext, **H**idden, and **,** (Comma).

The next chapter discusses the various tasks that can be performed with both the /**W**orksheet and **:W**orksheet commands, such as setting column widths and row heights, creating windows, freezing titles, inserting and deleting rows and columns, and protecting the worksheet.

Building a Worksheet

After you enter and format some data, you can use commands from 1-2-3's /Worksheet menu and Wysiwyg's **:**Worksheet menu to control the way your data is displayed and organized. In the last chapter, you learned how to manipulate data in specified ranges. This chapter shows you how to use commands that affect the entire worksheet at once.

In this chapter, you learn how to establish global settings for your worksheet; change column widths and row heights; insert and delete columns and rows; recalculate formulas; protect certain areas of your worksheet; and perform other tasks. The next chapter shows you how to modify your worksheet by making more substantial changes.

Erasing worksheets

Setting column widths

Splitting screens

Inserting rows and columns

Hiding columns

Protecting worksheets

5

Key Terms in This Chapter

/Worksheet commands	1-2-3 commands that affect the entire worksheet or certain defined areas of the worksheet. The /Worksheet command is found on the 1-2-3 main menu.
:Worksheet commands	Wysiwyg commands that adjust column widths and row heights, and add or remove horizontal and vertical page breaks. The :Worksheet command is found on the Wysiwyg main menu.
Global Settings dialog box	The dialog box that appears on-screen when you select /Worksheet Global.
Windows	Two separate screens that appear, either horizontally or vertically, after you execute the /Worksheet Window command. Windows allow you to view different parts of the worksheet at the same time.
Automatic recalculation	A default 1-2-3 setting indicating that the worksheet is calculated each time a cell's content changes.

Using the Mouse

To use a mouse with 1-2-3 Release 2.3, you need a mouse, mouse software, and a graphics monitor and graphics card that support a mouse. You can use a mouse to select commands and files, specify ranges, move the cell pointer within the worksheet, and make selections in a dialog box. Refer to the following sections of the specified chapters for further information on using the mouse.

- Chapter 2—"Understanding Mouse Terminology"
- Chapter 3—"Mouse Control of the Cell Pointer"
  "Using Dialog Boxes"
  "Using the Mouse To Select Menu Commands"
- Chapter 4—"Using the Mouse To Specify Ranges"

Using Worksheet Commands

1-2-3 offers a group of commands that perform some tasks similar to the /Range commands, but affect the entire worksheet or preset segments of the worksheet. With /Range commands, you define the range of cells affected by the commands. You do not have the same freedom with the /Worksheet and :Worksheet commands; they affect the whole worksheet, including entire columns or rows.

/Worksheet is the first command option on the 1-2-3 main menu. When you select /Worksheet, 1-2-3 offers the following group of commands:

> Global Insert Delete Column Erase Titles Window Status Page Learn

Table 5.1 provides a brief description of the actions of each of these commands.

Table 5.1
Selections on the /Worksheet Menu

Selection	Description
Global	Sets formats that affect the entire worksheet
Insert	Inserts blank columns and rows in the worksheet
Delete	Deletes entire columns and rows from the worksheet
Column	Sets column widths; hides and redisplays columns
Erase	Removes the entire worksheet from memory
Titles	Freezes or unfreezes the display of titles
Window	Splits the screen into two windows or restores the original screen
Status	Displays the current status of global worksheet settings and hardware configuration
Page	Inserts a character that controls page breaks in a printed worksheet
Learn	Records keystrokes used in macros (see Chapter 14)

Understanding the Global Settings Dialog Box

When you use the /**W**orksheet **G**lobal commands, 1-2-3 displays a dialog box showing all the current global settings.

The Global Settings dialog box shows the global column width, format, label prefix, protection settings, recalculation mode, and zero display that are in effect.

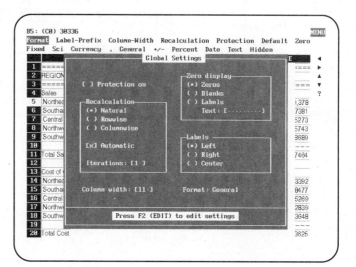

If you would rather see the body of your worksheet instead of the Global Settings dialog box, you can suppress this dialog box (and other dialog boxes) by pressing the Window (F6) key. This key acts as a toggle; when you press it again, you see the dialog box again.

Erasing the Worksheet

The /**W**orksheet **E**rase command clears the worksheet from the screen and memory. The effect is the same as if you quit 1-2-3 and restarted it from the operating system. You can use this command to create a new worksheet—with no data and the default worksheet settings. This command does not erase the worksheet file stored on disk.

Be sure that you understand the difference between the /**W**orksheet **E**rase command and the /**R**ange **E**rase command. The /**R**ange **E**rase command can remove the contents of every cell in the worksheet, except those that are protected. The /**R**ange **E**rase command does not, however, alter any of the global settings, such as column widths, cell formats, and print settings. After you issue the /**W**orksheet **E**rase command, the worksheet is exactly as it was when you loaded 1-2-3.

To erase the worksheet from the screen and the computer's memory, follow these steps:

1. Select /**W**orksheet.

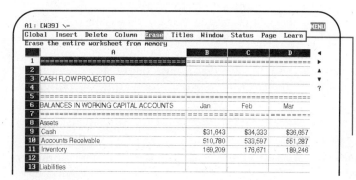

1-2-3 displays the menu of **Worksheet** commands.

2. Select **E**rase.

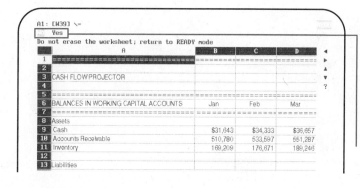

Because this command is potentially destructive, 1-2-3 prompts you for verification.

3. To erase the worksheet, select **Y**es.

   Or

   If you change your mind or need to save your file before erasing the worksheet, select **N**o.

Note: After a worksheet has been erased with /Worksheet Erase, you cannot recover it—unless the Undo feature is active and Alt-F4 is pressed before you issue the next command. You should always save worksheets you want to keep before you clear the worksheet with this command.

Setting Column Widths

You can control the worksheet's column widths to accommodate data entries that are too wide for the default column width. You can also reduce column widths to give the worksheet a better appearance when a column contains narrow entries. With 1-2-3, you have several options for setting column widths: one column at a time with the keyboard, one column at a time with the mouse, all the columns in the worksheet at once, or a range of contiguous columns.

Suppose that you are setting up a worksheet of cash flow projections and want to display long labels in the first column. You can set the width of the first column of your worksheet individually, and then set the other columns to any smaller width you choose. The sections that follow provide the necessary steps to carry out the commands for changing column widths.

Setting the Width of a Single Column

To change the width of a single column, you can use the /Worksheet Column Set-Width command. (**Note:** The Wysiwyg :Worksheet Column Set-Width command performs the same operation.) You can also use the mouse to quickly change the width of a single column. The following examples describe each of these methods.

To change the width of a single column from the keyboard, follow these steps:

1. Position the cell pointer within the column whose width you want to change.

2. Select /Worksheet Column.

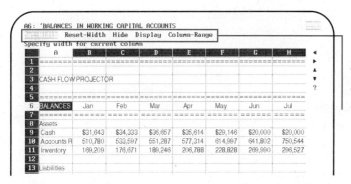

The options for changing widths appear.

3. Select **Set-Width**.

4. At the prompt `Enter column width`: either type a width between 1 and 240 or press ⬅ or ➡ until the desired column width is displayed.

   The advantage of using the left- and right-arrow keys is that the column width expands and contracts each time you press a key. To get a good idea of what the width requirements are, experiment when you enter the command.

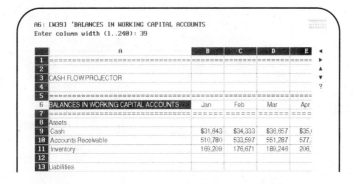

In this example, press ➡ until the long label shows completely.

5. Press ⏎Enter to complete the command.

To return the width of a single column to the default width of nine characters, use the /**Worksheet Column Reset-Width** command. (You can also use the Wysiwyg **:Worksheet Column Reset-Width** command to perform the same task.)

To change the width of a single column with the mouse, follow these steps:

1. Position the mouse pointer within the top border of the worksheet and point to the vertical line that marks the right side of the column to be sized.

2. Press and hold the left mouse button. A double-headed arrow pointing left and right appears in the top border.

3. To increase the width of the column, move the mouse to the right. To decrease the width of the column, move the mouse to the left.

A thin vertical line appears under the double-headed arrow, marking the boundary of the column.

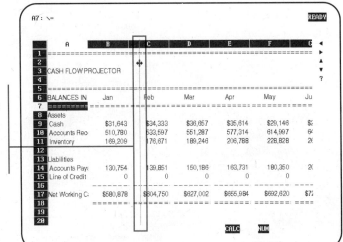

4. Release the left mouse button when the desired column width is marked.

To use a mouse to return a column to the default width of nine characters, move the mouse pointer to the vertical line that marks the right side of the column. Press and hold Shift and click the left mouse button.

Setting the Widths of All Columns at Once

You can set all the column widths in the worksheet at one time with the command /Worksheet Global Column-Width. This command is normally used in the early stages of worksheet creation. Many of the /Worksheet Global commands have corresponding /**R**ange commands that affect only certain areas of the worksheet; in this case, the corresponding commands are the /**W**orksheet Column Set-Width and /**W**orksheet Column Column-Range Set-Width commands.

To change the widths of all columns in the worksheet at one time, follow these steps:

1. Select /**W**orksheet **G**lobal. The Global Settings dialog box appears.

2. Press ⌈F2⌋ or click the left mouse button in the dialog box to edit the settings.

3. Select **C**olumn width.

4. Type the column width between 1 and 240 and press ⌈↵Enter⌋.

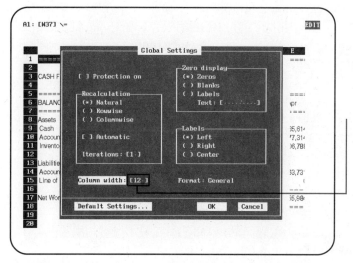

In this example, type **12**.

Note: The /**W**orksheet **G**lobal **C**olumn-Width command does not alter the width of columns already set with either the /**W**orksheet Column Set-Width or /**W**orksheet Column Column-Range commands.

In this example, all columns (except column A) have a width of 12 characters.

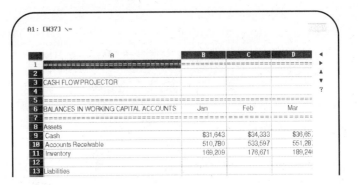

5. Select the OK command button at the bottom of the dialog box; then press Esc or the right mouse button until you return to READY mode.

You also can change global column widths exclusively with menu commands. Select /Worksheet Global Column-Width. Type the column width or press ← or → until the desired column width is displayed. Press Enter to complete the command.

Setting the Width of Contiguous Columns

If you want to set a group of adjacent columns to the same width, use the /Worksheet Column Column-Range Set-Width command. This command keeps you from having to set each adjacent column individually.

To change the widths of contiguous columns, follow these steps:

1. Position the cell pointer on the first or last column in the range of columns whose widths you want to change.

2. Select /Worksheet Column Column-Range Set-Width.

3. At the prompt Enter range for column width change: highlight cells in the range of columns you want to change; then press ⏎Enter.

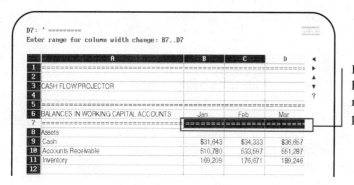

In this example, highlight the range B7..D7 and press ↵Enter.

4. At the prompt Select a width for range of columns:, either type a width between 1 and 240, or press ← or → until the desired column width is displayed; then press ↵Enter.

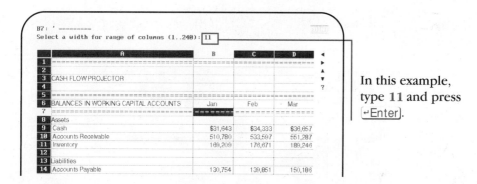

In this example, type 11 and press ↵Enter.

Note: The **R**eset-Width option, on the same menu as **S**et-Width, does not prompt you for a specific width, but returns the widths of all selected columns to the default column-width setting.

To verify the global column-width setting, use the /Worksheet **S**tatus command. Refer to the section "Checking the Status of Global Settings" later in this chapter.

Setting Row Heights

The Wysiwyg features of 1-2-3 Release 2.3 make it possible to view a variety of type fonts on-screen. However, many fonts are too large to fit in a normal size cell (with a default height of 14 points). When you format a cell to display a large font, 1-2-3 automatically adjusts the height of the row to compensate for the size of the font. Wysiwyg also lets you adjust the row height manually. You can use the mouse to quickly set the height of a single row. To adjust the height of a range of rows (as well as a single row), use the Wysiwyg command **:W**orksheet **R**ow **S**et-Height. The following procedures describe each of these methods.

To adjust the height of a single row with the mouse, follow these steps:

1. Position the mouse pointer within the left border of the worksheet and point to the horizontal line that marks the bottom of the row to be sized.

2. Press and hold the left mouse button. A double-headed arrow pointing up and down appears in the left border.

3. To increase the height of the row, move the mouse down. To decrease the height of the row, move the mouse up.

A thin horizontal line appears to the right of the double-headed arrow, marking the boundary of the row.

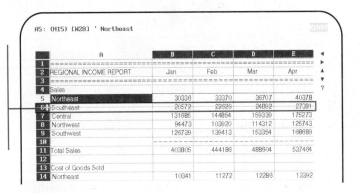

4. Release the left mouse button when the desired row height is marked.

To adjust the height of a range of rows (or a single row) with the keyboard, follow these steps:

1. Select **:W**orksheet **R**ow **S**et-Height.

2. At the prompt Select the rows to set height to: highlight the range of rows to set; then press ⏎Enter.

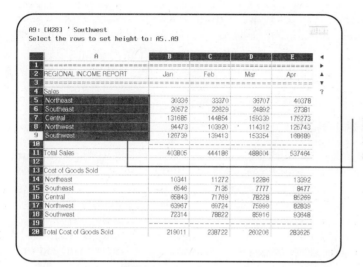

In this example, rows 5 through 9 are highlighted.

3. At the prompt `New row height in points`: either type a point size between 1 and 255, or press ⬆ or ⬇ until the desired row height is displayed; then press ⏎Enter.

In this example, specify 18 as the point size and press ⏎Enter.

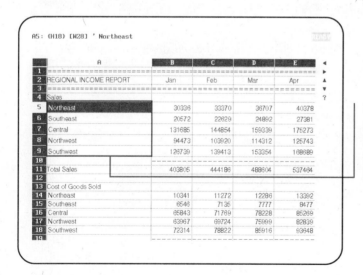

Rows 5 through 9 display an increased row height of 18 points.

5

173

Note: Once you set the height of a row or rows by using **:**Worksheet **R**ow Set-Height, the height does not automatically adjust when you change the font size for that row. To make the row sizes automatically adjust again, select the command **:**Worksheet **R**ow **A**uto, and select the rows you want to reset.

Splitting the Screen

Sometimes the size of a 1-2-3 worksheet can be unwieldy. For example, if you want to compare data in column A with data in column N, you need to be able to "fold" the worksheet so that you can see both parts at the same time. To do this, you can split the 1-2-3 screen display into two windows, either horizontally or vertically. This feature helps you to overcome some of the inconvenience of not being able to see the entire worksheet at one time. By splitting the screen with the /Worksheet **W**indow command or with the mouse, you can make the changes in one area and immediately see their effects in the other.

The Horizontal and Vertical options of the /Worksheet **W**indow menu split the screen in the manner indicated by their names. The screen splits at the point at which the cell pointer is positioned when you select the command Horizontal or Vertical. In other words, you don't have to split the screen exactly in half. Remember that the dividing line requires specifying either one row or one column, depending on whether you split the screen horizontally or vertically.

To split the screen into two horizontal or two vertical windows with the keyboard, follow these steps:

1. Position the cell pointer at the location where you want to split the screen.

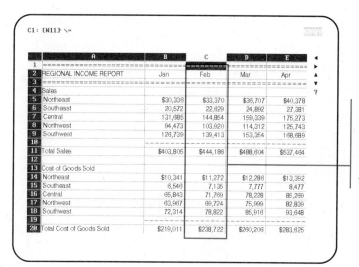

In this example, position the cell pointer in any row of column C to split the screen vertically.

2. Select /Worksheet Window.

3. Select either Horizontal or Vertical to split the screen.

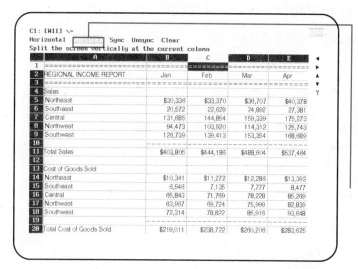

To compare two columns that cannot be seen together on the 1-2-3 screen, select Vertical.

M1: \=

	A	B		M	N	O
1	=============================		1	=========	=========	
2	REGIONAL INCOME REPORT	Jan	2	Dec	TOTAL	
3	=============================		3	=========	=========	
4	Sales		4			
5	Northeast	$30,336	5	$86,555	$648,731	
6	Southeast	20,572	6	58,694	$439,912	
7	Central	131,685	7	375,714	$2,815,994	
8	Northwest	94,473	8	269,541	$2,020,227	
9	Southwest	126,739	9	361,601	$2,710,219	
10			10			
11	Total Sales	$403,805	11	$1,152,105	$8,635,083	
12			12			
13	Cost of Goods Sold		13			
14	Northeast	$10,341	14	$26,683	$208,273	
15	Southeast	6,546	15,	16,892	$131,840	
16	Central	65,843	16	169,904	$1,326,131	
17	Northwest	63,967	17	165,063	$1,288,347	
18	Southwest	72,314	18	186,599	$1,456,445	
19			19			
20	Total Cost of Goods Sold	$219,011	20	$565,141	$4,411,036	

In this example, the screen is split vertically into two windows.

To split the screen into two horizontal or two vertical windows with the mouse, follow these steps:

1. Position the mouse pointer in the upper left corner of the worksheet frame. For a horizontal window, move to the line above row number 1. For a vertical window, move to the line to the left of column letter A.

2. Press and hold the left mouse button. A double-headed arrow appears. The arrow points up and down for horizontal windows, left and right for vertical windows.

3. To create two horizontal windows, move the mouse down. To create two vertical windows, move the mouse to the right.

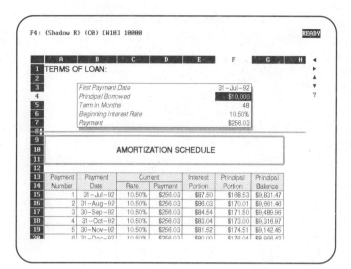

In this example, moving the mouse down displays a horizontal line—indicating the position of the horizontal window.

4. Release the left mouse button when you reach the desired position of the window.

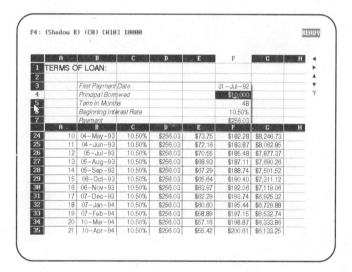

In this example, the screen is now split horizontally into two windows.

177

After you use the Horizontal option to split the screen, the cell pointer appears in the top window. When you specify a Vertical division, the cell pointer appears in the left window. To jump the division between the windows, use the Window (F6) function key, or click the left mouse button on a cell in the opposite window.

After the screen is split, you can change the screen display so that the windows scroll independently rather than together (the default mode). To scroll the windows independently, select /Worksheet Window Unsync. This command can be reversed by selecting the command /Worksheet Window Sync.

In Sync (synchronized) screen mode, when you scroll one window, the other window automatically scrolls too.

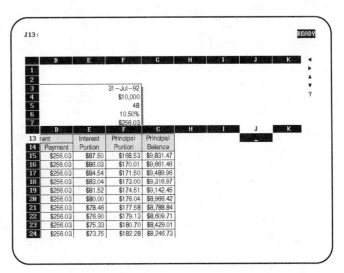

Horizontally split screens keep the same columns in view, and vertically split screens keep the same rows in view.

178

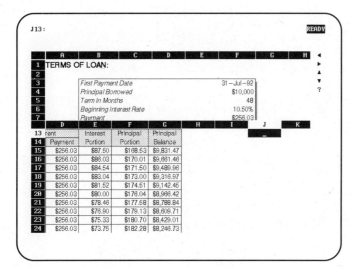

In Unsync (unsynchronized) screen mode, windows are controlled independently of each other in all directions. You can even display the same cells in two different windows.

5

To return to the single-window screen after selecting the **H**orizontal or **V**ertical options, select /**W**orksheet **W**indow **C**lear. When you use the **C**lear option, the single window takes on the settings of the top or left window, depending on how the screen was split.

Freezing Titles on the Screen

If you need to freeze rows and/or columns along the top and left edges of the worksheet so that they remain in view as you scroll to different parts of the worksheet, use the /**W**orksheet **T**itles command. The /**W**orksheet **T**itles command is similar to the /**W**orksheet **W**indow command. With both commands, you can see one area of a worksheet while you work on another area. The unique function of the /**W**orksheet **T**itles command, however, is that it freezes all the cells to the left or above (or both) the cell pointer's position so that those cells cannot move off the screen.

Because the default screen shows 20 rows by 8 columns (with the original column widths and row heights), you have to shift the screen if your data is outside of this screen area. In fact, you may have to scroll the screen several times in order to enter or view all the information.

179

Suppose that you want to keep on-screen the headings in rows 1–14 of this example, and the payment numbers and dates in columns A and B.

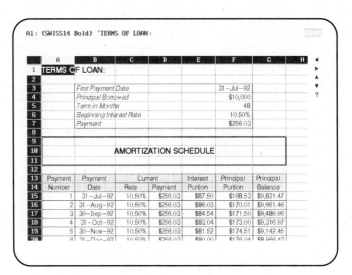

5

To freeze worksheet titles on the screen, follow these steps:

1. Position the cell pointer one cell below and to the right of the rows and/or columns you want to freeze.

   In this example, position the cell pointer in cell C15 to freeze columns A and B, and rows 1–14.

2. Select /**W**orksheet **T**itles.

3. Select **B**oth, **H**orizontal, or **V**ertical. The **B**oth option allows you to freeze rows and columns above and to the left of the cell pointer.

In this example, select **B**oth.

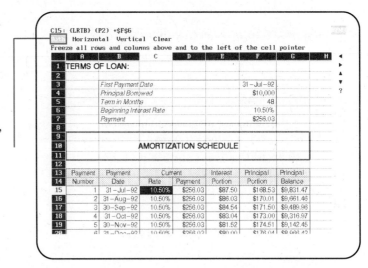

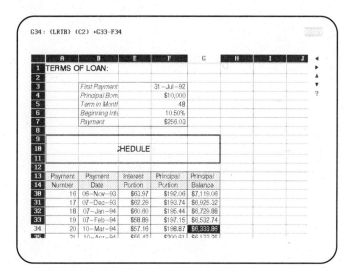

Now, no matter where you move the cell pointer, rows 1–14 and columns A and B are always displayed.

5

When you freeze columns and/or rows, you cannot move the cell pointer into the frozen area while 1-2-3 is in READY mode. If you try to move the cell pointer into the frozen area, 1-2-3 beeps. Similarly, the Home key moves the cell pointer only to the upper left cell in the unfrozen area. (Normally, the Home key moves the cell pointer to cell A1.) You can avoid this restriction, however, by using the GoTo (F5) key to move the cell pointer to the frozen titles area.

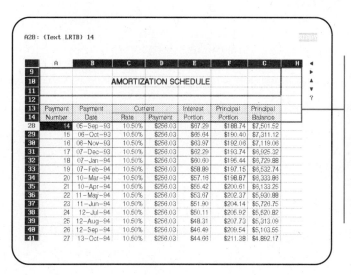

Here, /Worksheet Titles Horizontal was used to keep the row(s) above the cell pointer frozen on-screen. Rows 9–14 remain at the top of the screen when you scroll up and down.

Here, /Worksheet Titles Vertical was used to keep the column(s) to the left of the cell pointer frozen on-screen. Columns A and B remain on the left side of the screen when you scroll left and right.

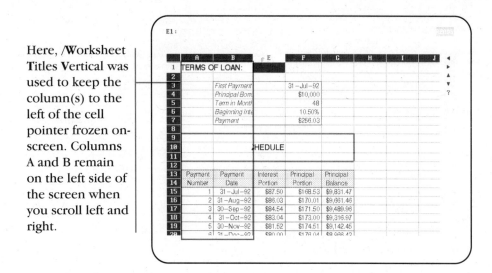

To unlock the frozen worksheet titles, use the /Worksheet Titles Clear command. Now you can move the cell pointer freely throughout the worksheet.

Inserting Columns and Rows

Suppose that you are finished creating a worksheet, but you want to enhance its general appearance. You can improve it by inserting blank columns and rows in strategic places to highlight headings and other important items. Whether you want to insert additional data or add blank rows or columns to separate sections of your worksheet, you can use the /Worksheet Insert command to insert columns or rows. You can insert multiple adjacent columns and rows each time you invoke this command.

To insert a new column or row into the worksheet, follow these steps:

1. Position the cell pointer at the location of the new column or row to be inserted.

   For example, position the cell pointer in column D to add a new column of data.

2. Select /Worksheet Insert.

3. Select Column or Row.

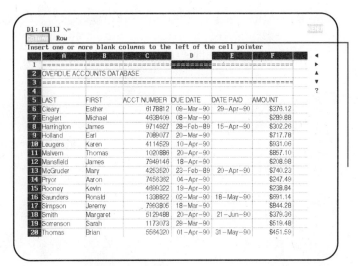

In this example,
select **Column** to
insert a new
column in the
worksheet.

4. In response to the prompt, designate the range where you want to
   insert the new column(s) or row(s). If you want to insert more than
   one column or row, use the arrow keys or the mouse to highlight
   multiple columns or rows.

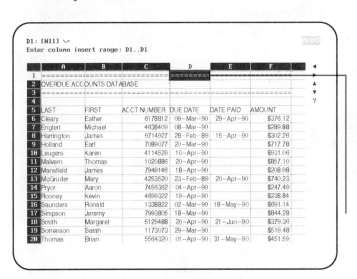

In this example,
be sure to
position the
cell pointer in
column D
to insert a
single column.

5. Press ⏎Enter to complete the command. Existing worksheet data is moved to the right of the cell pointer if you are inserting a column, or below the cell pointer if you are inserting a row.

In this example, when you press ⏎Enter, a blank column is displayed, ready for you to enter new data in the database.

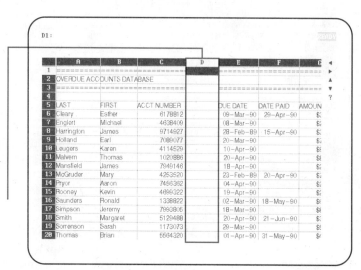

When you insert columns, 1-2-3 automatically shifts all data to the right of the new column—one column to the right, and modifies all the cell formulas for the change. If you insert rows, 1-2-3 inserts a blank row—all data located below the new row is automatically shifted down one row, and any formulas are modified. 1-2-3 does not have the capability of inserting or deleting partial columns and rows.

Deleting Columns and Rows

You can delete single (or multiple) columns or rows with the /Worksheet Delete command. After you select this command, you then choose **Column** or **Row** from the menu that appears on-screen. If you choose **Row**, 1-2-3 asks you to specify a range of rows to be deleted; the range you specify needs to include only one cell from each row to be deleted.

To delete existing columns or rows from the worksheet, follow these steps:

1. Position the cell pointer at the location of the first row or column to be deleted.

   For example, position the cell pointer in row 6.

184

2. Select /**Worksheet D**elete.

3. Select **C**olumn or **R**ow.

   For example, select **R**ow to delete rows from the worksheet.

4. In response to the prompt, designate the range where you want the column(s) or row(s) deleted.

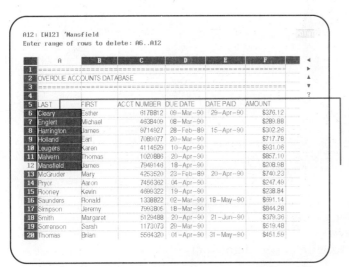

In this example, highlight rows 6 through 12 (in any column).

5. Press ⏎Enter to complete the command.

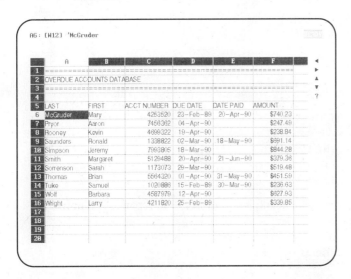

The original data in rows 6 through 12 is removed from the worksheet, and the data that originally appeared below these rows moves up.

185

Remember that /Worksheet Delete is different from /Range Erase. /Range Erase simply erases data from a cell or range of cells—not entire columns or rows of data.

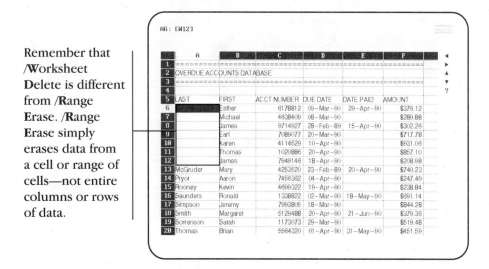

If you plan to use the command /Worksheet Delete to delete a column or row containing values, keep in mind that all formulas in the worksheet that still refer to these cells will then result in ERR. Also remember that when you use the /Worksheet Delete command, the columns or rows you delete may be gone forever. This command deletes entire columns or rows, not just the range of cells you specify in those columns or rows.

If the Undo feature is enabled, you can undo the deletion by pressing Undo (Alt-F4) before executing another command. Otherwise, the only remedies are to re-create the missing data or retrieve the worksheet file again. The latter approach works only if you have saved a copy of your worksheet that contains the missing data.

Hiding Columns

With the /Worksheet Column Hide command, you can suppress the display of one or more columns. One important use of this command is to suppress the display of unwanted columns when you are printing reports. When you hide intervening columns, a report can display data from two or more separated columns on a single page.

Other uses of this command include suppressing the display of sensitive information (such as financial statements), hiding the display of cells that have a numeric value of zero, and fitting noncontiguous columns on-screen. The procedures that follow describe how to hide and redisplay columns.

To hide one or more columns, follow these steps:

1. Select /**Worksheet Column Hide**.

2. Specify the columns to hide by either typing or highlighting the range.

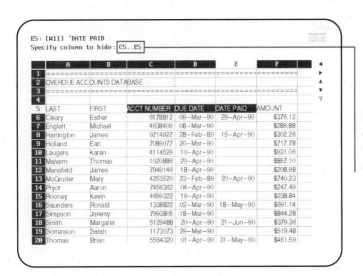

In this example, columns C through E are specified.

3. Press ↵Enter, and the specified columns are hidden from view.

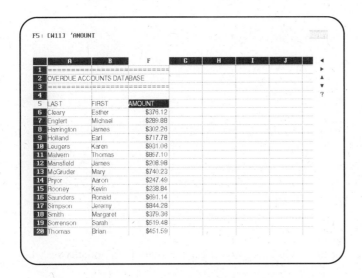

In this example, columns C through E are now hidden.

5

Although the hidden columns do not appear on the display, numbers and formulas in hidden columns are still present, and cell references to cells in hidden columns continue to work properly. You can tell which columns are missing only by noting the break in column letters at the top of the display. The hidden columns are temporarily redisplayed, however, when you use certain commands, such as /Copy or /Move; the hidden columns are marked with an asterisk (such as C*) during this temporary display.

This screen shows how hidden columns are temporarily displayed when using /Copy.

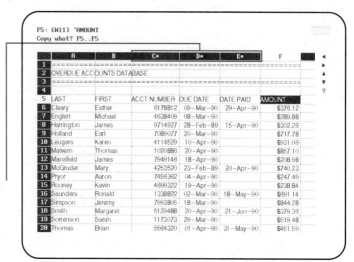

To redisplay hidden columns, follow these steps:

1. Select /**W**orksheet **C**olumn **D**isplay.

2. At the prompt `Specify hidden columns to redisplay:` enter the range of columns to redisplay.

188

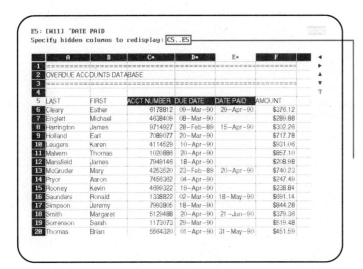

In this example, specify columns C through E.

3. Press ⏎Enter, and the hidden columns are redisplayed.

Suppressing the Display of Zeros

The /Worksheet Global Zero command enables you to suppress the display in the worksheet of all cells that have a numeric value of zero. For example, this technique is useful for preparing reports for a presentation where cells showing $0.00 would look odd. As an alternative, you may choose to have a label (such as No Charge), instead of a blank, displayed in zero-value cells.

You can enter formulas and values for all the items in the report, including the zero items, and then display the results with all the zeros removed or replaced by a label. The actual formula or value is displayed in the control panel when the cell pointer highlights a cell that contains a zero, or a formula that evaluates to zero.

Suppose that you have a worksheet that lists product codes and their associated costs. In some cases, the costs are $0.00, perhaps entered in error.

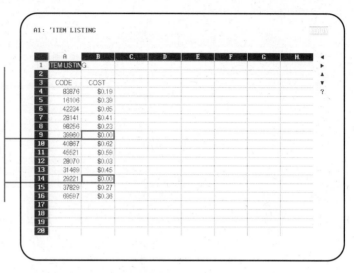

To suppress the display of zeros or to substitute a label for zero entries, follow these steps:

1. Select /**W**orksheet **G**lobal. The Global Settings dialog box appears.

2. Press ⎡F2⎦ or click the left mouse button in the dialog box to edit the settings.

3. Select **Z**ero display.

4. With the keyboard or mouse, select one of the following:

Selection	Description
Zeros	Displays zeros (the default)
Blanks	Suppresses zeros
Labels	Displays a specified label

5. If you chose **L**abels in step 4, select **T**ext; then type the label to appear in place of zeros in the worksheet and press ⎡↵Enter⎦.

190

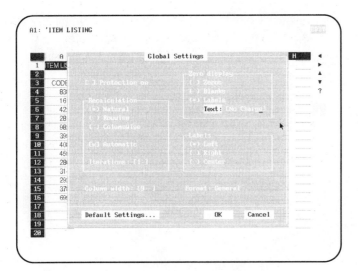

In this example, select **Labels** and **Text**; then type **No Charge** and press ↵Enter.

6. Select the OK command button at the bottom of the dialog box; then press Esc or the right mouse button until you return to READY mode.

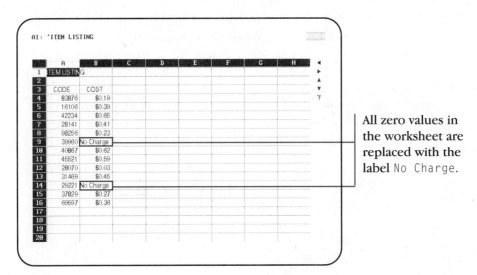

All zero values in the worksheet are replaced with the label No Charge.

You can also change zero display exclusively with menu commands. Select /Worksheet Global Zero. Then choose No, Yes, or Label. If you choose Label, type the label and press Enter.

If you want the zeros visible again, use the command /Worksheet Global Zero No. When you use the /File Save command to save your worksheet, the zero suppression or label substitution features of this command are not saved with the worksheet. Therefore, these features are not present when you retrieve a file.

Note: This command is not selective; all cells in the worksheet with a zero value are affected by the substitution. A cell with the value .004 would be displayed as 0.00 if a 2-decimal place format were used. Because the value is not truly zero, it would therefore not be changed by the /Worksheet Global Zero command.

Recalculating the Worksheet

One of the primary functions of a spreadsheet program is to recalculate cells with formulas when a value or formula in one of the cells changes. 1-2-3 provides two basic recalculation methods: automatic and manual. Using automatic recalculation, the default, 1-2-3 recalculates the formulas that are affected whenever a cell in the worksheet changes. In manual recalculation, the worksheet is recalculated only when the user requests it, either from the keyboard with the Calc (F9) key or from a macro.

1-2-3 also provides three orders of recalculation: the natural order and two linear orders, either columnwise or rowwise. Natural order is the default, but you can choose any of the three orders. You also can choose the number of times worksheets are recalculated. You select the recalculation options by using the /Worksheet Global Recalculation command. The recalculation options are described in Table 5.2.

Table 5.2
Selections on the /Worksheet Global Recalculation Menu

Selection	Description
Order of Recalculation	
Natural	1-2-3 does not recalculate any cell until the cells that it depends on have been recalculated. This is the default setting.
Columnwise	Recalculation begins at cell A1 and continues down column A, then goes to cell B1 and down column B, and so forth.

Selection	Description
Rowwise	Recalculation begins at cell A1 and proceeds across row 1, then goes across row 2, and so forth.
Method of Recalculation	
Automatic	The worksheet is recalculated whenever a cell changes. This is the default setting.
Manual	The worksheet is recalculated only when you press F9 (Calc).
Number of Recalculations	
Iteration	The worksheet is recalculated a specified number of times when you change cell contents in automatic recalculation, or press F9 (Calc) in manual recalculation. The default is one iteration per recalculation.

As a beginning 1-2-3 user, you may not need to change the recalculation settings at all. 1-2-3's default settings are **A**utomatic recalculation (meaning that each time a cell's content changes, the program automatically recalculates any formulas that are affected), and **N**atural order (meaning that 1-2-3 does not recalculate any given cell until after the cells that it depends on have been recalculated). To save processing time, you can switch to **M**anual recalculation so that 1-2-3 recalculates the worksheet only when you press Calc (F9).

For more specialized applications, the **C**olumnwise or **R**owwise recalculation method can be used. Be extremely careful when you use these orders of recalculation, however; if they are used improperly, they can produce erroneous values on the worksheet.

For more information on automatic, manual, and iterative recalculation, and natural, columnwise, and rowwise orders of recalculation, refer to Que's *Using 1-2-3 for DOS Release 2.3*, Special Edition. You'll find an in-depth discussion and examples on using the recalculation options.

Protecting the Worksheet

1-2-3 has special features that protect areas of a worksheet from possible destruction. Using a series of commands, you can set up ranges of cells that cannot be changed without special effort. In fact, columns and rows that contain protected cells cannot be deleted from the worksheet. These commands are particularly beneficial when you are setting up worksheets in which data will be entered by people who are not familiar with 1-2-3.

Protecting the Entire Worksheet

When you first create a worksheet, the global protection feature is not active, enabling you to make changes and add data anywhere in the worksheet. The /Worksheet Global Protection Enable command turns on the worksheet's protection system.

This protection system may be thought of as a series of barriers set up around all the cells in the worksheet. The barriers go down when the worksheet is first loaded, and all the cells in the worksheet can be modified. This arrangement is appropriate because you want to have access to everything in the worksheet when you first begin entering data.

After you finish making all your entries in the worksheet, you may want to make sure that certain areas are not modified, or you may want to set up areas with forms for data input and not allow the cell pointer to move anywhere else. To accomplish either of these tasks, you must first enable the protection feature with the /Worksheet Global Protection Enable command. After this command is issued, all the cells in the worksheet are protected. In other words, this command restores all the barriers in the worksheet.

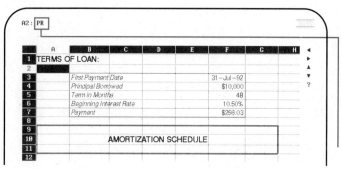

All cells in the worksheet are protected as indicated by the PR in the first line of the control panel.

Turning Off Protection in a Range

You can selectively unprotect certain cells or ranges with the /**R**ange Unprot command. In effect, you "tear down the barriers" that surround these individual cells or ranges of cells. You can reprotect these cells at any time by issuing the /**R**ange **P**rot command.

To turn off protection for a cell or range of cells in your worksheet, follow these steps:

1. Select /**R**ange Unprot.

2. Highlight the range of cells where you want to add or change data.

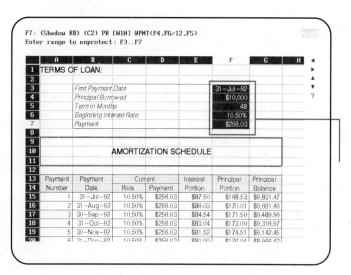

In this example, highlight the range F3..F7.

3. Press ⏎Enter to complete the command.

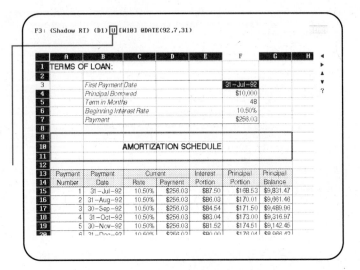

Unprotected cells are identified by a U in the control panel.

Suppose that you create a worksheet that includes a number of long and important formulas. You may want to protect these formulas against accidental deletion by using 1-2-3's protection capability. But what if you need to make a change in several of these formulas? You can move around the worksheet, unprotecting cells, changing the formulas, and then protecting the cells again. Or you can use the /Worksheet Global Protection Disable command to lower the barriers around all the cells. After making the necessary changes, you can restore protection to all the cells by using the /Worksheet Global Protection Enable command again.

Restricting Movement to a Particular Range

For even more protection, you can limit the movement of the cell pointer by using the /Range Input command. You must use this command, which allows movement only to cells unprotected with the /Range Unprot command, to set up special data input areas.

For example, suppose that you create a simple worksheet in which every cell is protected except those in the range F3..F7, whose cells were unprotected with the /Range Unprot command.

To restrict input to unprotected cells in the worksheet, follow these steps:

1. Select /**R**ange Input.

2. Highlight the range of cells that includes the unprotected cells in the data input area; then press ⏎Enter.

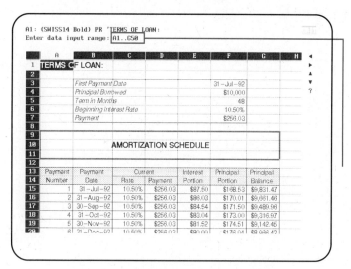

In this example, specify the range A1..G50 and press ⏎Enter.

Note: You should include the entire data input area (including protected areas) when specifying a range for the /**R**ange Input command. This range should include all cells that are unprotected with /**R**ange Unprot.

3. After the range is entered, the first cell of the data input area moves to the upper left corner of the screen, and the cell pointer jumps immediately to the first unprotected cell in the range.

5

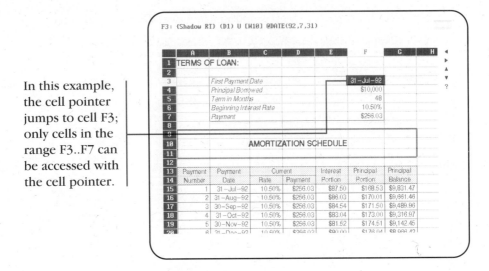

F3: {Shadow RT} (D1) U [W10] @DATE(92,7,31)

In this example, the cell pointer jumps to cell F3; only cells in the range F3..F7 can be accessed with the cell pointer.

You can now begin to enter or edit data in the unprotected cells. To move the cell pointer to the next unprotected cell after completing an entry, use the arrow keys.

The /**R**ange **I**nput command remains in effect until you press either the Enter key or the Esc key. The cell pointer then returns to the upper left corner of the data input range, and the worksheet returns to the same position on the screen as before the /**R**ange **I**nput command was issued.

Checking the Status of Global Settings

Use the /**W**orksheet Global, /**W**orksheet Global **D**efault, and /**W**orksheet **S**tatus commands to check the status of all global settings for the worksheet. These commands display dialog boxes on-screen, giving you an easy way to view the worksheet settings without having to experiment to find the settings.

When you select /**W**orksheet **G**lobal, the Global Settings dialog box appears.

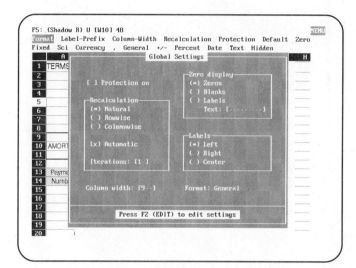

The Global Settings dialog box shows the current settings.

This example of the Global Settings dialog box indicates the following:

- Global protection is disabled.
- The recalculation method is automatic, with natural order and one iteration per recalculation.
- The default column width is nine characters.
- Zeros will be displayed as zeros rather than blanks or labels (covered in a previous section of this chapter).
- Labels will be left aligned (covered in Chapter 3).
- The cell display format is **G**eneral (covered in Chapter 4).

When you select /**W**orksheet **G**lobal **D**efault, the Default Settings dialog box appears.

The Default
settings dialog
box shows the
status of the
current directory,
Undo feature,
warning bell,
clock indicator,
add-ins, and other
features.

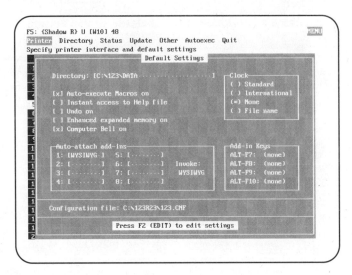

When you select /Worksheet Status, the Worksheet Status dialog box appears.

The Worksheet
Status dialog box
indicates the
available memory,
where a circular
reference may
exist, and other
features.

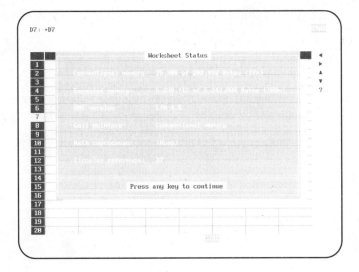

200

Entering a Page-Break Character

You can use a 1-2-3 command to enter a manual page break in the worksheet. The /Worksheet **P**age command inserts a blank row at the cell-pointer location.

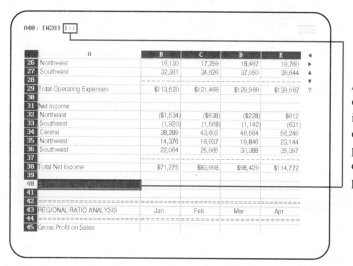

A page-break character (::) is inserted in the cell where the cell pointer was originally positioned.

The vertical bar (|) that precedes the page-break character (visible only in the control panel) tells 1-2-3 not to print the row. (This symbol is discussed in detail in Chapter 8.)

To enter a page-break character into a worksheet, follow these steps:

1. Position the cell pointer in the first column of the range to be printed, at the row location where you want a new page to begin.
2. Select /Worksheet **P**age.

Use a page-break character when printing a range from the worksheet. Although printing is not covered in detail until Chapter 8, the best time to insert page-break characters is while you are building the worksheet. As you become more experienced in building worksheets and printing reports, you will learn to think of printed pages as you build. Thinking ahead saves time and minimizes confusion when you're ready to print.

A page break is effective only when positioned at the left edge of the range being printed. If you add data to cells in the page-break row, the contents of those cells do not print when the page break is in effect.

You can remove a page break character by typing over it, deleting the row with /Worksheet Delete Row, or erasing the cell with /Range Erase.

The /Worksheet Page command works in conjunction with the /Print commands. When you print with Wysiwyg, the :Worksheet Page Row command allows you to set page breaks within rows, just like /Worksheet Page. You can also use the :Worksheet Page Column command to tell Wysiwyg where to break a page on the right margin. Chapter 8 discusses these commands in more detail.

Summary

5

This chapter showed you how the versatile /Worksheet commands can erase an entire worksheet, set column widths (individually or globally), split the screen into horizontal or vertical windows, and freeze titles for scrolling. The Wysiwyg :Worksheet commands can set column widths and row heights, and insert page breaks. You also learned how to insert and delete columns and rows, hide columns, suppress the display of zeros, recalculate and protect the worksheet, check the status of the global settings, and insert page breaks in a printed report.

Specifically, you learned the following key information about 1-2-3:

- The /Worksheet Erase command erases the worksheet from memory, but does not erase the file on disk.

- The /Worksheet Column Set-Width command changes the width of a single column. To reset the column to its original default, use /Worksheet Column Reset-Width. You can use the :Worksheet Column Set-Width and :Worksheet Column Reset-Width commands in Wysiwyg to perform the same functions.

- The /Worksheet Global Column-Width command changes the column width of all columns in the worksheet, except for those already changed.

- The /Worksheet Column Column-Range Set-Width command sets the width of contiguous columns. To reset these columns to the default, select /Worksheet Column Column-Range Reset-Width.

- The :Worksheet Row Set-Height command allows you to change the height of selected rows in Wysiwyg. The :Worksheet Row Auto command returns the height of selected rows to the current default.

■ You can use the mouse to quickly set individual column widths and row heights. Position the mouse pointer on the right column boundary or the bottom row boundary in the worksheet border, press and hold the left mouse button and move the mouse pointer in the direction of the desired column width or row height. Then release the mouse button.

■ The /Worksheet Window command splits the screen so that two different parts of the worksheet can be viewed at the same time. Worksheets can be split with the Horizontal or Vertical options. Use /Worksheet Window Clear to return to a single worksheet. You can also use a mouse to split the screen horizontally or vertically.

■ The /Worksheet Titles command freezes titles along the top and left borders of the worksheet so that the titles remain in view when scrolling the worksheet. The /Worksheet Titles Clear command unfreezes the titles.

■ The /Worksheet Insert command can insert one or more columns or rows into the worksheet. To delete one or more columns or rows, use /Worksheet Delete.

■ The /Worksheet Column Hide command temporarily removes columns of data from the screen. Hidden columns also do not print when included in a print range. These columns can be restored with the /Worksheet Column Display command.

■ The /Worksheet Global Zero command suppresses the display of zeros in the worksheet. Blank cells or labels, instead of zeros, are displayed on-screen. The actual value (or formula) is displayed in the control panel when a zero-valued cell is highlighted.

■ The /Worksheet Global Recalculation command changes the method, order, and number of iterations used in worksheet recalculation.

■ The /Worksheet Global Protection command allows you to turn protection on or off in a worksheet. /Range Unprot can then unprotect individual cells or ranges in the worksheet, to allow entry only in those cells.

5

■ The /**R**ange **I**nput command restricts input to only unprotected cells in a protected data-input range. The cell pointer moves only among the unprotected cells.

■ The /**W**orksheet **G**lobal, /**W**orksheet **G**lobal **D**efault, and /**W**orksheet **S**tatus commands display dialog boxes that indicate the worksheet's current global settings. These settings can be modified in the dialog boxes with the keyboard or a mouse.

■ The /**W**orksheet **P**age command inserts a blank row that contains a page-break character (::). This character indicates where a new page should begin when a worksheet is printed. The **:W**orksheet **P**age command allows you to specify both row and column page breaks when you print in Wysiwyg.

5

The next chapter shows you how to use the /**C**opy and /**M**ove commands to modify your worksheet data. You also learn how to use 1-2-3's search-and-replace feature.

Modifying a Worksheet

6

As you begin to create your own worksheets using the basic concepts and commands described in earlier chapters, you need to modify your worksheets by moving and copying data from one location to another. 1-2-3 provides the capacity to move and copy data—saving you hours of work when building and modifying your worksheets.

This chapter shows you how to improve your worksheets by moving and copying data effectively. You also learn how to search for and replace a specific string of data in a range of cells in the worksheet.

Moving the
contents of cells

Copying the
contents of cells

Searching for and
replacing cell
contents

Key Terms in This Chapter

Relative cell address	A cell reference that adjusts for a new location when used in a formula copied to that location. This cell address is the default.
Absolute cell address	A cell reference that does not adjust for a new location when used in a formula copied to that location.
Mixed cell address	A cell reference that combines both relative and absolute cell addressing; used when copying a formula to a new location.
Search string	A set of characters used with the /Range Search command to find specified text in a range of cells.

Using the Mouse

To use a mouse with 1-2-3 Release 2.3, you need a mouse, mouse software, and a graphics monitor and graphics card that support a mouse. You can use a mouse to select commands and files, specify ranges, move the cell pointer within the worksheet, and make selections in a dialog box. Refer to the following sections of the specified chapters for further information on using the mouse.

- Chapter 2—"Understanding Mouse Terminology"
- Chapter 3—"Mouse Control of the Cell Pointer"
    "Using Dialog Boxes"
    "Using the Mouse To Select Menu Commands"
- Chapter 4—"Using the Mouse To Specify Ranges"

Moving the Contents of Cells

In the days of manual spreadsheets, the process of moving data around on the page was called cutting and pasting because scissors and glue were used to move sections of the spreadsheet. 1-2-3 lets you cut and paste sections of the worksheet automatically.

With the /Move and /Copy commands, you can move and copy the contents of cells and ranges of cells from one part of the worksheet to another. The difference between moving and copying is that data that is moved from one location to another disappears from the first location; data that is copied appears in both locations.

Moving Data

Suppose that you want to move the contents of the range C2..D3 to the range E2..F3 on your worksheet. To move a range within a single worksheet, follow these steps:

1. Select /**M**ove.

2. At the prompt `Move what?` specify the range you want to move; then press ⏎Enter.

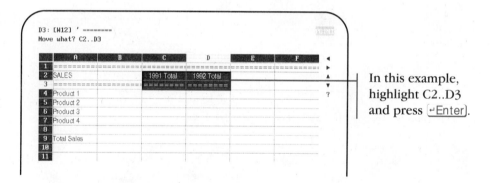

In this example, highlight C2..D3 and press ⏎Enter.

3. At the prompt `To where?` highlight the upper left cell of the new location; then press ⏎Enter.

Note: Highlighting the entire range at the `To where?` prompt is not necessary.

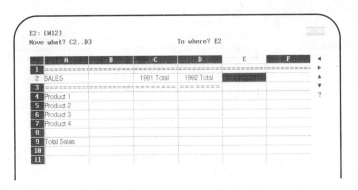

In this example, highlight cell E2 and press ⏎Enter.

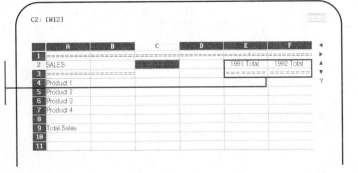

1-2-3 moves the specified range to the new location.

The cell pointer returns immediately to where it was when you initiated the /Move command. Remember that the cell pointer does not have to be positioned at the beginning of the starting range when you start the /Move command. You can always press Esc (or the right mouse button) to free the cell pointer and move it to the correct location.

Tips for Moving

Remember the following tips whenever you intend to move data:

- When you move a range of cells, the range where cells are copied to is completely overwritten by the range that is moved. Any cell contents are lost. If there are cells with formulas that depend on the cell addresses in the receiving range, the cells containing these formulas evaluate to ERR.

- If the Undo feature is enabled (with the /Worksheet Global Default Other Undo Enable command), you can reverse the effects of a /Move operation by pressing Alt-F4 before executing another command.

- Highlight ranges (rather than type ranges) to be moved to help avoid errors. Remember that you can also use the click-and-drag mouse technique to highlight the ranges when moving data.

- Use the End key for pointing to large ranges quickly. This method almost always reduces the number of required keystrokes for a move operation. If there are gaps (blank cells) within the blocks of data, however, the End key procedure is less useful because the cell pointer goes to the boundaries of each gap.

Copying the Contents of Cells

You will often want to copy the contents of cells to other locations in a worksheet. When you copy data, you also copy with it cell formats and protection status of the copied cell(s). In 1-2-3, you can copy data in the following ways:

- Copy the contents of one cell to another cell.
- Copy the contents of one cell to every cell in a range.
- Copy from one range to another range of equal size.
- Copy from one range to a larger range.

The procedure used for each copy operation is basically the same. To copy a range, follow these steps:

1. Select /Copy.
2. At the prompt `Copy what?` specify the cell or range you want to copy.
3. At the prompt `To where?` specify the cell or range where the data is to be copied.

The only elements that change are the dimensions and locations of the `Copy what?` and `To where?` ranges. Remember that you can type the coordinates of each range from the keyboard, type a range name, or highlight (point to) the ranges in POINT mode (with the keyboard or a mouse).

Copying Data

The basic methods of copying data within a worksheet are described in the text that follows.

209

Method 1: Copying from one cell to another cell

1. Select /Copy.

2. At the prompt `Copy what?` highlight the cell whose contents you want to copy; then press ⏎Enter. If the cell pointer is located in the cell to be copied, just press ⏎Enter.

In this example, press ⏎Enter to select cell A1 as the range to copy.

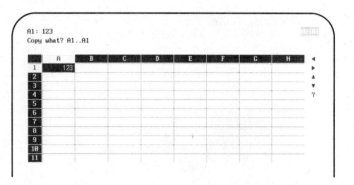

6

3. At the prompt `To where?` highlight the cell where you want the data copied. Then press ⏎Enter.

In this example, specify the range where the copy will go by high-lighting cell A2 and pressing ⏎Enter.

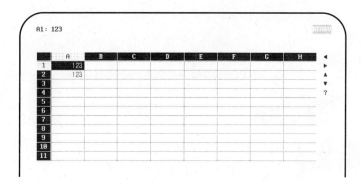

In this copy operation, the contents of cell A1 have been copied to cell A2.

Method 2: Copying from one cell to a range of cells

1. Select /Copy.

2. At the prompt `Copy what?` highlight the cell whose contents you want to copy; then press ⏎Enter. If the cell pointer is located in the cell to be copied, just press ⏎Enter.

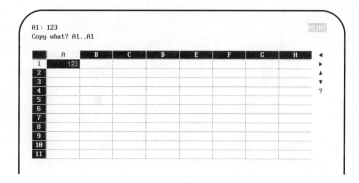

In this example, press ⏎Enter to select cell A1 as the range to copy.

3. At the prompt `To where?` highlight the range of cells where you want the data copied; then press ⏎Enter.

211

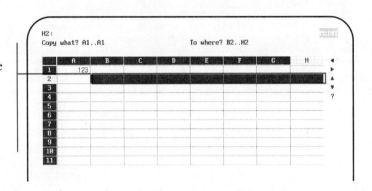

In this example, specify the range where the copy will go by high-lighting B2..H2 and pressing ⏎Enter.

6

The contents of cell A1 have been copied to each cell in the range B2..H2.

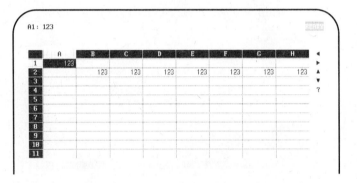

Method 3: Copying from one range to another range of equal size

1. Select /Copy.

2. At the prompt `Copy what?` highlight the range of cells whose contents you want to copy; then press ⏎Enter.

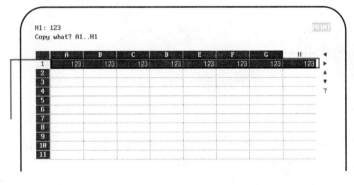

In this example, highlight the range A1..H1 and press ⏎Enter.

3. At the prompt `To where?` highlight the first cell of the range where you want the data copied; then press ⏎Enter.

Note: With this method of copying, highlighting the entire range to receive the copy is not necessary.

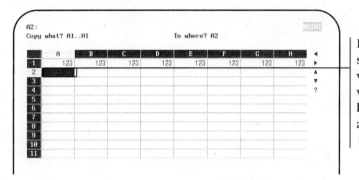

In this example, specify the range where the copy will go by highlighting cell A2 and pressing ⏎Enter.

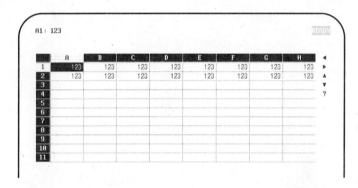

The range A1..H1 has been copied to the range A2..H2.

Method 4: Copying from one range to a larger range

1. Select /Copy.
2. At the prompt `Copy what?` highlight the range of cells whose contents you want to copy; then press ⏎Enter.

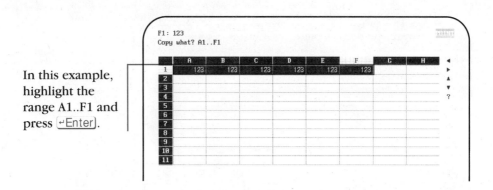

In this example, highlight the range A1..F1 and press ⏎Enter.

3. At the prompt To where? highlight only the first cells in the rows or columns to which you want the data copied; then press ⏎Enter.

6

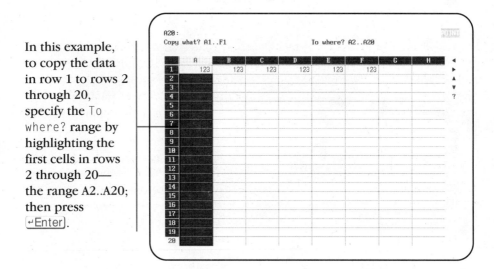

In this example, to copy the data in row 1 to rows 2 through 20, specify the To where? range by highlighting the first cells in rows 2 through 20— the range A2..A20; then press ⏎Enter.

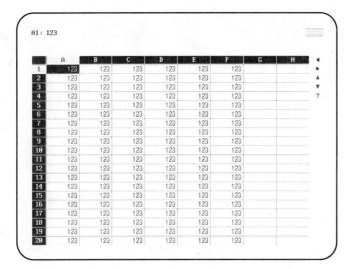

The range A1..F1 has been copied to the larger range A2..F20.

Think of this type of copying as an extension of the previous type. The results of this copy operation could have been reached by repeating the copy command 19 times and specifying 19 different single-row `To where?` ranges. The first range would be A2, the second would be A3, the third A4, and so on. The results are the same for either method, but you can save a great deal of time by copying to the A2..A20 range, as shown.

The best way to learn how the copy command works with different ranges is to experiment on your own. After a while, the rules of copying become second nature to you.

Addressing Cells

Although the connection may not be obvious, the way you address cells is tied closely to copy operations. Two different methods of addressing cells can be used when copying: *relative* and *absolute*. These two methods of referencing cells are important for building formulas. The type of addressing you use when you reference cells in formulas can affect the results produced by these formulas when you copy them to different locations in the worksheet. The following sections cover relative and absolute addressing as well as the combination of both methods—known as *mixed addressing*.

215

Referencing Cells with Relative Addressing

Relative addressing, 1-2-3's default for referencing cells, means that when you copy a formula, unless you specify otherwise, the addresses of the cells in the formula are adjusted automatically to fit the new location. Suppose that you have summed the contents of one column, and you need to sum the contents of several adjacent columns, but you don't want to enter the @SUM function over and over again.

To copy a formula with a relative address, follow these steps:

1. Select /Copy.

2. At the prompt Copy what? highlight the cell containing the formula to be copied; then press ⏎Enter.

In this example, highlight cell B11 and press ⏎Enter.

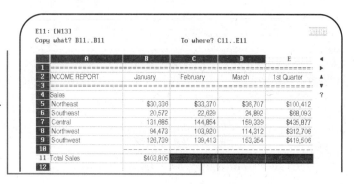

3. At the prompt To where? highlight the range of cells where you want the formula copied; then press ⏎Enter.

In this example, specify the range to receive the copy by highlighting C11..E11 and pressing ⏎Enter.

6

216

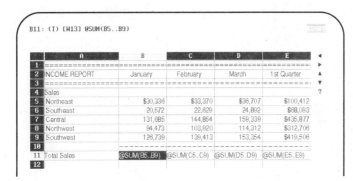

B11: (T) [W13] @SUM(B5..B9)

	A	B	C	D	E
1	====	====	====	====	====
2	INCOME REPORT	January	February	March	1st Quarter
3	====	====	====	====	====
4	Sales				
5	Northeast	$30,336	$33,370	$36,707	$100,412
6	Southeast	20,572	22,629	24,892	$68,093
7	Central	131,685	144,854	159,339	$435,877
8	Northwest	94,473	103,920	114,312	$312,706
9	Southwest	126,739	139,413	153,354	$419,506
10					
11	Total Sales	@SUM(B5..B9)	@SUM(C5..C9)	@SUM(D5..D9)	@SUM(E5..E9)
12					

1-2-3 copies the @SUM function to all the cells in the specified To where? range, C11..E11.

Note: In the preceding example, the range of formulas appears in **Text** format (rather than the resulting values) to show how each copied formula adjusts to its new location.

Notice that the cell references in the original function @SUM(B5..B9) refer to column B. When you copy the formula one column to the right, the cell references also change one column to the right. The cell references in the copy change from column B in the original formula to column C (C5..C9) in the copied formula. Cell references in formulas copied to cells D11 and E11 also change relative to where the original copy was.

Referencing Cells with Absolute Addressing

In some cases, a formula has an important address that should not be changed when the formula is copied. To keep an address absolute, enter a dollar sign ($) before the cell's column letter and before the cell's row number. For example, $E$11 is an absolute address.

Now that you have summed the contents of several columns of sales, you want to calculate the percentage of sales represented by each month of the quarter. In this example, the best way to do this is to copy a formula that contains an absolute address. When you create the formula in cell B13, place a $ before the E and before the 11 in the second part of the formula.

To copy a formula with an absolute address, follow these steps:

1. Select /Copy.

2. At the prompt Copy what? highlight the cell containing the formula with an absolute address to be copied. Then press ↵Enter.

217

```
B13: (P2) [W13] +B11/$E$11
Copy what? B13..B13
```

	A	B	C	D	E
1	============	========	========	========	=========
2	INCOME REPORT	January	February	March	1st Quarter
3	============	========	========	========	=========
4	Sales				
5	Northeast	$30,336	$33,370	$36,707	$100,412
6	Southeast	20,572	22,629	24,892	$68,093
7	Central	131,685	144,854	159,339	$435,877
8	Northwest	94,473	103,920	114,312	$312,706
9	Southwest	126,739	139,413	153,354	$419,506
10					
11	Total Sales	$403,805	$444,186	$488,604	$1,336,595
12					
13	Percent of Sales	30.21%			
14					
15					
16					
17					
18					
19					
20					

In this example, highlight cell B13 and press ⏎Enter. Note that cell B13 contains an absolute address ($E$11) in the formula +B11/$E$11.

3. At the prompt To where? highlight the range of cells where you want the formula with the absolute address to be copied. Then press ⏎Enter.

```
E13: [W13]
Copy what? B13..B13                    To where? C13..E13
```

	A	B	C	D	E
1	============	========	========	========	=========
2	INCOME REPORT	January	February	March	1st Quarter
3	============	========	========	========	=========
4	Sales				
5	Northeast	$30,336	$33,370	$36,707	$100,412
6	Southeast	20,572	22,629	24,892	$68,093
7	Central	131,685	144,854	159,339	$435,877
8	Northwest	94,473	103,920	114,312	$312,706
9	Southwest	126,739	139,413	153,354	$419,506
10					
11	Total Sales	$403,805	$444,186	$488,604	$1,336,595
12					
13	Percent of Sales	30.21%			
14					
15					
16					
17					
18					
19					
20					

In this example, specify the range to receive the copy by highlighting C13..E13 and pressing ⏎Enter.

218

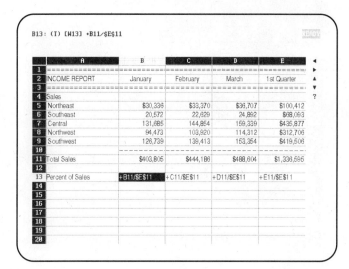

The range of formulas in row 13 is displayed in text format to show how each copied formula is adjusted to its new location.

Note that the first address of each formula varies, but the second address remains absolute as $E$11 in all four formulas.

Mixing Relative and Absolute Addressing

In some cases, a formula has an important address that cannot be changed as the formula is copied. The last section discussed absolute addresses, which do not change at all when the address is copied. You also can create a mixed address, which can sometimes change, depending on the direction of the copy operation. Mixed addressing refers to a combination of relative and absolute addressing. Because a cell address has a column and a row, you can make either portion absolute, while leaving the other part relative.

If you plan to copy cells with absolute addresses, you must prepare the cells to be copied by preceding them with dollar signs ($) in both their column and row designations. The dollar signs tell 1-2-3 that the cells have been changed to absolute addresses.

If you want to copy the formula from cell C10 to cell C17, the formula in C10 must contain one mixed address, one absolute address, and one relative address.

C10: (C0) [W7] +$B7*(1-$B$1)*C9

	A	B	C	D	E	F	G	H
1	Discount	50%						
2								
3								
4			Jan	Feb	Mar	Apr	May	Jun
5								
6	Product 1							
7	Unit Price	14.95						
8								
9	Unit Sales		104	120	115	133	142	135
10	Sales price		$777					
11								
12								
13	Product 2							
14	Unit Price	17.95						
15								
16	Unit Sales		95	87	105	94	102	113
17	Sales Price							
18								
19								
20								

When the formula in C10 is copied to C17, a mixed address ($B14) is used at the beginning of the formula.

C17: (C0) [W7] +$B14*(1-$B$1)*C16

	A	B	C	D	E	F	G	H
1	Discount	50%						
2								
3								
4			Jan	Feb	Mar	Apr	May	Jun
5								
6	Product 1							
7	Unit Price	14.95						
8								
9	Unit Sales		104	120	115	133	142	135
10	Sales price		$777					
11								
12								
13	Product 2							
14	Unit Price	17.95						
15								
16	Unit Sales		95	87	105	94	102	113
17	Sales Price		$853					
18								
19								
20								

Each mixed address refers to the respective unit price of each product. In this example, column B is absolute and row 14 is relative. Also contained in the formula is an absolute address ($B$1) which refers to the discount percentage, and a relative address (C16), which refers to the monthly unit sales for each product.

220

Using the Abs (F4) Key To Change a Cell Address

There are two ways to enter dollar signs for absolute or mixed addresses in a formula. You can type the dollar signs as you create the formula, or you can use the Abs (F4) key to have 1-2-3 enter the dollar signs for you. Use the Abs (F4) key in POINT or EDIT mode to make a cell address absolute, mixed, or relative. (Remember that in READY mode, if you are not entering or editing a formula, you can use the F4 key to prespecify a range.) The Abs (F4) key is a four-way toggle. Simply press the F4 key repeatedly (while in POINT or EDIT mode) until you get the kind of cell reference you want.

To change a cell address with the Abs (F4) key, follow these steps:

1. Highlight the cell containing the formula you want to change; then press F2 (Edit).

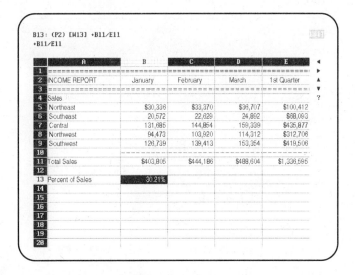

In this example, highlight cell B13 and press F2 (Edit).

2. Move the cursor in the edit line until you are beneath a cell address in the control panel; then press F4 (Abs) once to change the address to absolute.

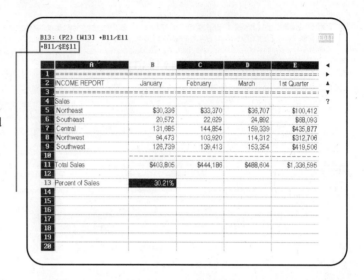

In this example, move the cursor under the second cell address, and then press ⌊F4⌋ (Abs) to change E11 to $E$11.

Press ⌊F4⌋ additional times to cycle through the references as shown in table 6.1.

3. At any point during the process, press ⌊↵Enter⌋ to accept the formula with relative, absolute, or mixed cell references.

Table 6.1
Using Abs (F4) in EDIT Mode To Change Address Type

Absolute Key	Col, Row Reference	Example
Before ⌊F4⌋ (Abs) pressed	Both Relative	+B11/**E11**
Press ⌊F4⌋ (Abs) once	Both Absolute	+B11/**$E$11**
Press ⌊F4⌋ (Abs) twice	Row Absolute	+B11/**E$11**
Press ⌊F4⌋ (Abs) three times	Column Absolute	+B11/**$E11**
Press ⌊F4⌋ (Abs) four times	Both Relative	+B11/**E11**

Transposing Rows and Columns

For copy operations that are difficult to perform with 1-2-3's normal /Copy commands, 1-2-3 has two specialized copy commands: /**R**ange **T**rans (Transpose) and /**R**ange **V**alue. The /**R**ange **T**rans command copies columns into rows and rows into columns.

222

The /**Range** **Value** command, explained in the next section, copies the values (but not the formulas) from one range to another. The /**Range** **Trans** command copies only values, but also copies each row of the original range into the corresponding column of the range receiving the copy, or each column of the original range into the corresponding row of the range receiving the copy. The result is a transposed copy of the original range. Suppose that you want to transpose the data in three rows to columnar format. To transpose the data, follow these steps:

1. Select /**Range** **Trans**.

2. At the prompt `Transpose what?` highlight the range of cells you want to transpose; then press `⏎Enter`.

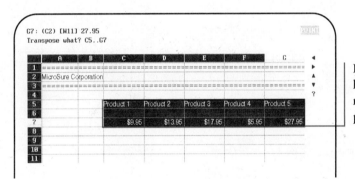

In this example, highlight the range C5..G7 and press `⏎Enter`.

3. At the prompt `To where?` highlight the columns to which you want the data copied.

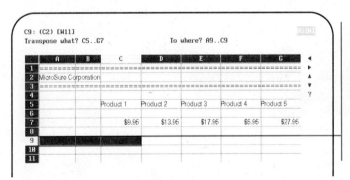

In this example, highlight the single worksheet range of A9..C9. Three columns must be highlighted because the original data covers three rows.

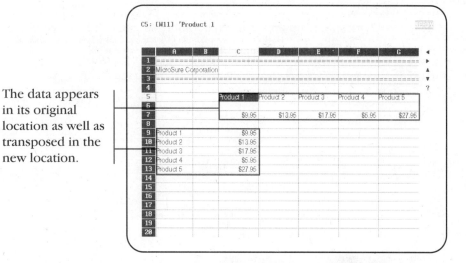

The data appears in its original location as well as transposed in the new location.

Note: Even if the original range contains formulas, /**R**ange **T**rans will convert the formulas to values in the destination range.

Converting Formulas to Values

The /**R**ange **V**alue command lets you copy only the values of the cells in one range to another range. This command is useful whenever you want to preserve the current formula values of a range of cells instead of having only the changed values after the worksheet has been updated. An important function of the /**R**ange **V**alue command is its capacity to convert formulas to values. You don't have to worry, therefore, about formulas that depend on cell references.

To convert formulas to values when copying, follow these steps:

1. Select /**R**ange **V**alue.

2. At the prompt `Convert what?` highlight the range of formulas to be copied; then press (⏎Enter).

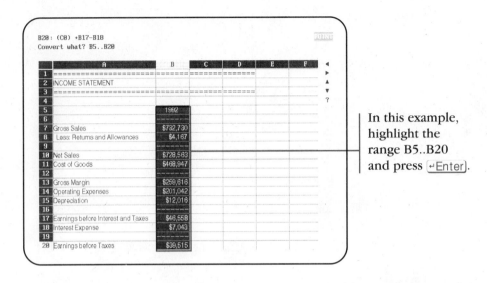

In this example, highlight the range B5..B20 and press ↵Enter.

6

3. At the prompt To where? highlight the first cell in the range where you want the values copied; then press ↵Enter.

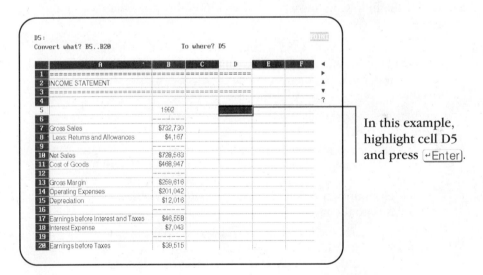

In this example, highlight cell D5 and press ↵Enter.

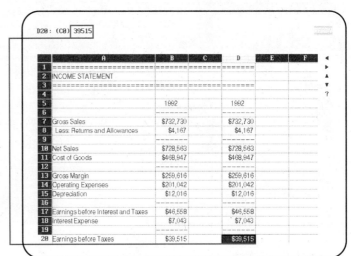

Notice that the formula in cell B20 has become a value in cell D20.

Tips for Copying

Remember the following tips whenever you intend to copy data within the worksheet:

- When you copy a cell, 1-2-3 automatically copies the format of the cell with it. This automatic format-copying feature saves you from having to set the format for an entire range of cells before (or after) copying to them.

- Sometimes the original and destination ranges overlap when you copy. The general rule is to avoid overlapping the end points of both ranges to prevent problems with the copy operation. If you do overlap them, you may get mixed results. You can, however, overlap ranges without error when the original and destination ranges have the same upper left boundary (such as when using /Range Value to copy formulas onto themselves).

- Note particularly the finality of the /Copy command when you disable the Undo feature. If you copy over the contents of a cell, you have no way to retrieve the contents. Make sure that you have properly designated your ranges before you complete the command. You can retrieve the worksheet again if it has already been saved, but all changes made since the last save are lost.

Searching for and Replacing Cell Contents

Looking for a word or string of characters in a large worksheet can be time-consuming and tedious. 1-2-3 offers a feature that allows you to search for text easily. If necessary, you can replace a specified string of characters with other text everywhere the string occurs. Frequent users of word processing software are familiar with this capability. It can be particularly useful for changing all occurrences of a particular misspelling to the correct spelling.

Whether you want to find the first occurrence of a string or you want to replace it with another string, you start with the same command, /**R**ange **S**earch. 1-2-3 performs the search column-by-column in the defined search range. The following section shows you how to search for a given string, and the subsequent section shows you how to search for a string and replace it with another string.

6

Searching for the Occurrence of a String

To search a specified range for a particular string in labels and/or formulas, follow these steps:

1. Select /**R**ange **S**earch.
2. Highlight the range you want to search; then press ⏎Enter.

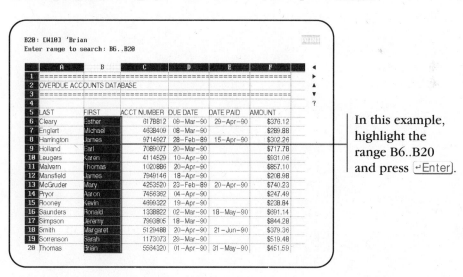

In this example, highlight the range B6..B20 and press ⏎Enter.

3. Define the string you want to search for and then press ⏎Enter . Note that the search string is not case-sensitive; you can enter the string in upper- or lowercase characters.

In this example, to search for all occurrences of James in the highlighted range, type james ; then press ⏎Enter .

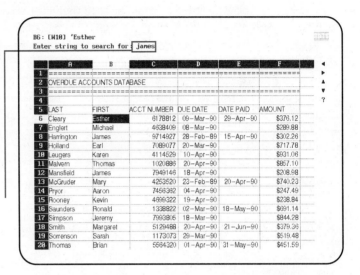

4. Indicate whether to search for formulas, labels, or both formulas and labels by selecting **F**ormulas, **L**abels, or **B**oth.

To check only cells that contain labels, select **L**abels.

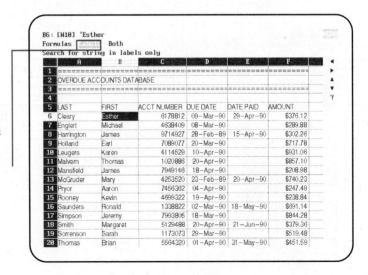

5. Select **F**ind to find a particular string in the range of labels that are selected.

   1-2-3 highlights the first appearance of the string.

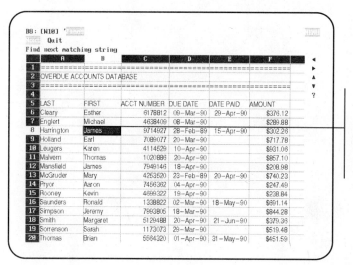

In this example, the first occurrence of James in the search range is highlighted by the cell pointer.

6. To see the next appearance of the string, select **N**ext.

   The second occurrence of the string, if present, is highlighted by the cell pointer.

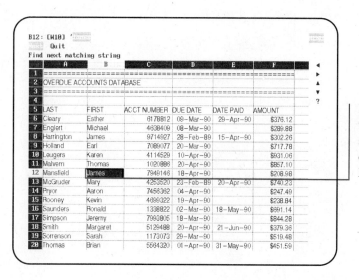

In this example, the next appearance of James in column B is highlighted.

6

7. At each of the successive prompts, select **Next** until 1-2-3 finds the last occurrence of your string in the range.

   Note: If you want to end the search before all occurrences of the string have been found, select **Quit**.

When 1-2-3 cannot locate another string, an error message is displayed.

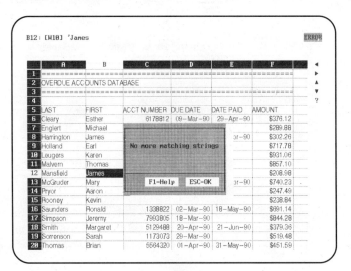

8. Press ⏎Enter or Esc to return to READY mode.

Replacing One String with Another String

To replace a string in the worksheet with another specified string, you follow a procedure similar to that which finds a string within a range. You must, however, supply the string of characters that will replace the existing string.

To search a range for a particular string and replace that string with another string, follow these steps:

1. Select **/R**ange **S**earch.

2. Highlight the range you want to search; then press ⏎Enter.

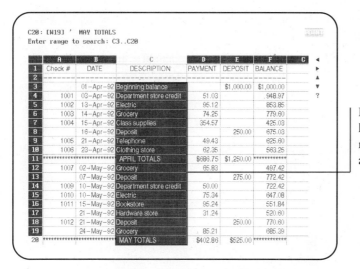

In this example, highlight the range C3..C20 and press ↵Enter.

3. Define the string you want to search for; then press ↵Enter. Note that the search string is not case-sensitive.

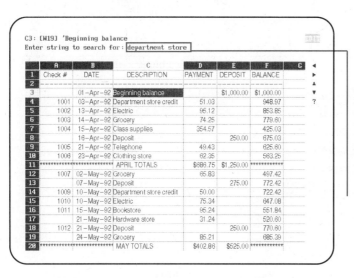

To search for Department store in the highlighted range, type **department store**; then press ↵Enter.

4. Indicate whether to search for formulas, labels, or both formulas and labels by selecting Formulas, **L**abels, or **B**oth.

If you need to correct a large range of formulas by changing a recurring cell reference, select Formulas.

For this example, select **L**abels.

5. Select **R**eplace to replace occurrences of the specified string with another string.

6. Define the string that will be used to replace occurrences of the specified search string; then press ⏎Enter. Note that this string *is* case-sensitive; your use of uppercase and lowercase characters in your definition will be copied to the replacement string.

In this example, to replace the occurrences of Department store with JCPenney, type **JCPenney** and press ⏎Enter.

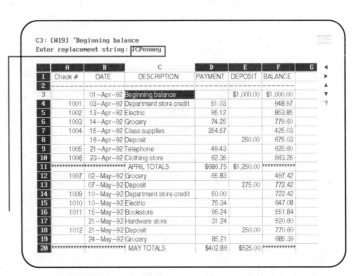

1-2-3 highlights the first occurrence of the search string and provides a menu with four options: **R**eplace, **A**ll, **N**ext, and **Q**uit.

7. Select one of the four options.

Replace completes the first instance of search and replace, and positions the cell pointer on the second occurrence—again offering you the same four menu options.

All replaces every matching string with the new string.

Next lets you highlight the next occurrence of the search string without making the replacement—allowing you to use **R**eplace selectively.

Quit ends the search and returns 1-2-3 to READY mode.

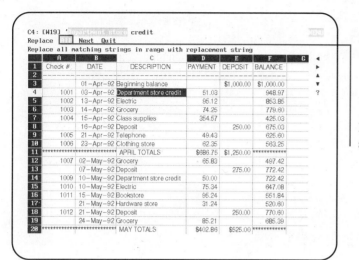

For this example, select **All**.

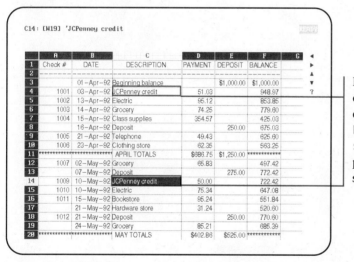

Note how all occurrences of the string `Department store` are replaced with the string `JCPenney`.

When 1-2-3 cannot locate another appearance of the string after you select **R**eplace or **N**ext, an error message is displayed. Press Enter or Esc to return to READY mode.

Tips for Using the Search-and-Replace Feature

Remember the following tips when using 1-2-3's search-and-replace feature:

- To protect your worksheet data from unexpected results, save your worksheet before executing a search-and-replace.

- If you confine your search to a given range, you can accelerate the search, and you're less likely to accidentally replace strings you want left undisturbed.

- The search string can consist of more than a single word. In fact, the string can be as long as 240 characters and can contain many words.

- The string you are searching for is not case-sensitive. 1-2-3 will find any string that matches the characters you type, regardless of whether you type the string in uppercase, lowercase, or a combination of these.

- Unlike the search string, the replacement string is case-sensitive. The substitution will consist of precisely what you type, in keeping with your use of uppercase and lowercase.

- The /Range Search command will not search hidden columns. The command can be used, however, to search individual cells that have been formatted with the /Range Format Hidden command.

Summary

In this chapter, you learned that when building a worksheet, you can use the /Move command to relocate cells and cell ranges, and the /Copy command to duplicate the contents of cells and cell ranges throughout a worksheet. By specifying relative, absolute, or mixed addressing, you can control cell references for formulas you use in your worksheets. You also learned that 1-2-3 provides a search-and-replace feature that allows you to find and/or replace specified strings of data in your worksheets.

Specifically, you learned the following key information about 1-2-3:

- The /Move command enables you to move the contents of one or more cells to any location in a worksheet. The data that is moved appears only in the new location.

- The /Copy command enables you to copy information to other parts of a worksheet. Once copied, the data appears in both locations.

- The End key, in combination with the arrow keys, can be used with the /Move and /Copy commands to quickly move or copy large ranges of data.

- Two types of cell addresses that are helpful when copying formulas are relative and absolute cell addresses. Combinations of relative and absolute cell addresses are called mixed cell addresses. Dollar signs are used to indicate which cell addresses are absolute or mixed.

- When creating or modifying relative, absolute, and mixed cell addresses, the Abs (F4) key can be used to toggle between the different types of cell references.

- The /Range Trans command copies data from columns into rows and rows into columns.

- The /Range Value command copies a range of formulas to their equivalent values in another (or the same) range.

- The /Range Search command finds a specified string of data in a range. This string can also be replaced with a new string.

6

The next chapter covers some of 1-2-3's built-in functions. Functions are used in formulas to perform complex calculations. A few of the categories of functions discussed include mathematical, financial and accounting, and string functions.

Using Functions

7

In addition to creating formulas, you can use a variety of ready-made formulas provided by 1-2-3. These built-in formulas—called functions—enable you to take advantage of 1-2-3's analytical capability. Functions are helpful when used with business, engineering, scientific, and statistical applications. You can use many of these powerful functions even in the simplest of worksheets. You can use functions by themselves, in your own formulas, or in macros and advanced macro-command programs to calculate results and solve problems.

1-2-3 Release 2.3 comes with an Auditor add-in that helps analyze formulas in your worksheet. The Auditor lists all cells (precedents) that provide data for a specified formula. The Auditor also identifies all formulas (dependents) that use a specified cell. In addition, the Auditor finds all formulas in a specified range and cells involved in circular references. For more information, refer to your Lotus 1-2-3 documentation.

1-2-3 provides the following types of functions:

- Mathematical and trigonometric
- Date and time
- Financial
- Statistical
- Database
- Logical
- String
- Special

Entering a 1-2-3 function

Using mathematical and trigonometric functions

Using date and time functions

Using financial functions

Using statistical functions

Using database functions

Using logical functions

Using string functions

Using special functions

Key Terms in This Chapter

Functions	1-2-3's built-in formulas that perform many different types of calculations.
Arguments	Inputs needed by most functions to perform their calculations.
Syntax	The format of a specific function.

This chapter first describes the basic steps for using 1-2-3 functions and then covers each of these groups in more detail. Several tables briefly describe all 1-2-3 functions. However, separate sections expand on the most commonly used 1-2-3 functions. Refer to Que's *Using 1-2-3 for DOS Release 2.3*, Special Edition, for additional coverage of each of 1-2-3's functions.

7

Using the Mouse

To use a mouse with 1-2-3 Release 2.3, you need a mouse, mouse software, and a graphics monitor and graphics card that support a mouse. You can use a mouse to select commands and files, specify ranges, move the cell pointer within the worksheet, and make selections in a dialog box. Refer to the following sections of the specified chapters for further information on using the mouse.

- Chapter 2—"Understanding Mouse Terminology"
- Chapter 3—"Mouse Control of the Cell Pointer"

    "Using Dialog Boxes"

    "Using the Mouse To Select Menu Commands"
- Chapter 4—"Using the Mouse To Specify Ranges"

Entering a 1-2-3 Function

If you have not yet reviewed Chapter 3, you should study the section of that chapter that introduces functions before you continue with this chapter. In Chapter 3 you learn about the eight groups of functions that this chapter covers and the steps used to enter a specific function.

This chapter does not include numbered steps for entering each function because you enter all functions with the same procedure. To enter a 1-2-3 function in a worksheet, follow this general four-step process:

1. Press @, the character that identifies a function.

2. Type the function name.

3. Type within parentheses any inputs, or arguments, that the function needs.

4. Press ↵Enter.

An example of a function is @AVG. If you type the function **@AVG(1,2,3)** 1-2-3 returns the calculated result 2, the average of the three arguments—the numbers 1, 2, and 3.

Some functions do not require arguments. For example, the mathematical function @PI returns the value of π; and the mathematical function @RAND produces a random decimal number between 0 and 1.

Using Mathematical and Trigonometric Functions

1-2-3's nine mathematical functions and eight trigonometric functions are useful in engineering and scientific applications. These functions are also convenient tools and can be used to perform a variety of standard arithmetic operations, such as rounding values or calculating square roots.

Table 7.1 lists the mathematical and trigonometric functions, their arguments, and the operations they perform. The sections that follow cover the @INT and @ROUND mathematical functions in detail.

Table 7.1
Mathematical and Trigonometric Functions

Function	Description
@ABS(*number* or *cell_reference*)	Computes the absolute value of the argument
@ACOS(*angle*)	Calculates the arccosine, given an angle in radians
@ASIN(*angle*)	Calculates the arcsine, given an angle in radians

continued

Table 7.1 (*continued*)

Function	Description
@ATAN(*angle*)	Calculates the arctangent, given an angle in radians
@ATAN2(*number1, number2*)	Calculates the four-quadrant arctangent
@COS(*angle*)	Calculates the cosine, given an angle in radians
@EXP(*number* or *cell_reference*)	Computes the number *e* raised to the power of the argument
@INT(*number* or *cell_reference*)	Returns the integer portion of a number
@LN(*number* or *cell_reference*)	Calculates the natural logarithm of a number
@LOG(*number* or *cell_reference*)	Calculates the common, or base 10, logarithm of a number
@MOD (*number, divisor*)	Computes the remainder of a division operation
@PI	Returns the value of π
@RAND	Generates a random decimal number between 0 and 1
@ROUND(*number* or *cell_reference, precision*)	Rounds a number to a specified precision
@SIN(*angle*)	Calculates the sine, given an angle in radians
@SQRT(*number* or *cell_reference*)	Computes the positive square root of a number
@TAN(*angle*)	Calculates the tangent, given an angle in radians

7

Computing Integers with @INT

The @INT function converts a decimal number into an integer, or whole number. @INT creates an integer by truncating, or removing, the decimal portion of a number (without rounding). @INT uses the following syntax:

@INT(*number* or *cell_reference*)

@INT has one argument, which can be either a numeric value or a cell reference to a numeric value. The result of applying @INT to the values 3.1, 4.5, and 5.9 yields integer values of 3, 4, and 5, respectively.

@INT is useful for computations in which the decimal portion of a number is irrelevant or insignificant. Suppose, for example, that you have $1,000 to invest in XYZ company and that shares of XYZ sell for $17 each. You divide 1,000 by 17 to compute the total number of shares that you can buy. Because you cannot buy a fractional share, you can use @INT to truncate the decimal portion.

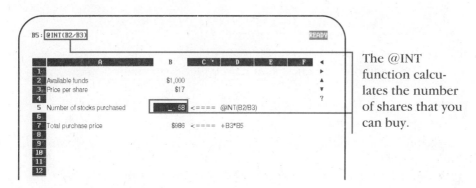

The @INT function calculates the number of shares that you can buy.

Rounding Numbers with @ROUND

The @ROUND function rounds values to the precision you specify. The function uses two arguments: the value you want to round and the precision you want to use in the rounding. @ROUND uses the following syntax:

@ROUND(*number* or *cell_reference,precision*)

The first argument can be a numeric value or a cell reference to a numeric value. The *precision* argument determines the number of decimal places and can be an integer between –15 and +15. You use positive precision values to specify positions to the right of the decimal place. Negative values specify positions to the left of the decimal place. A precision value of 0 rounds decimal values to the nearest integer.

241

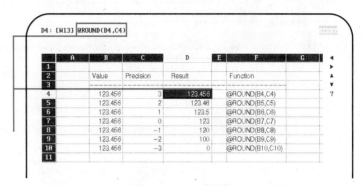

The @ROUND function rounds values to a specified precision.

Note: The @ROUND function and the /**R**ange **F**ormat command perform differently. /**R**ange **F**ormat alters only how 1-2-3 displays the cell's contents; @ROUND actually changes the contents of a cell.

7 Using Date and Time Functions

The 11 date and time functions enable you to convert dates, such as November 26, 1991, and times, such as 6:00 p.m., to serial numbers. You can then use the serial numbers to perform date and time arithmetic. These functions are valuable tools when dates and times affect calculations and logic in your worksheets.

1-2-3's internal calendar begins with the serial number 1, which represents January 1, 1900. The calendar ends with 73050, which represents December 31, 2099. 1-2-3 represents a single day with an increment of 1; therefore, 1-2-3 represents January 2, 1900, as 2. To display that serial number as a text date, format the cell with the /**R**ange **F**ormat **D**ate command.

Table 7.2 summarizes the date and time functions available. The sections that follow review examples of the @DATE, @DATEVALUE, and @NOW functions.

Table 7.2
Date and Time Functions

Function	Description
@DATE(*year,month,day*)	Calculates the serial number of the specified date
@DATEVALUE(*date_string*)	Converts a date expressed as a string into a serial number

242

Function	Description
@DAY(*date_number*)	Extracts the day number from a serial number
@HOUR(*time_number*)	Extracts the hour number from a serial number
@MINUTE(*time_number*)	Extracts the minute number from a serial number
@MONTH(*date_number*)	Extracts the month number from a serial number
@NOW	Calculates the serial date and time from the current system date and time
@SECOND(*time_number*)	Extracts the seconds from a serial number
@TIME(*hour,minutes,seconds*)	Calculates the serial number of the specified time
@TIMEVALUE(*time_string*)	Converts a time expressed as a string into a serial number
@YEAR(*date_number*)	Extracts the year number from a serial number

7

Converting Date Values to Serial Numbers with @DATE

To use dates in arithmetic operations, first convert the dates to serial numbers. You can then use those serial numbers in arithmetic operations and sorting. The most frequently used date function is @DATE, which converts any date into a serial number. You use the resulting number in calculations or display it as a date in 1-2-3. @DATE uses the following syntax:

@DATE(*year,month,day*)

You use numbers to identify a year, month, and day. For example, you enter the date November 26, 1991, into the @DATE function as @DATE(91,11,26). The serial number that results is 33568.

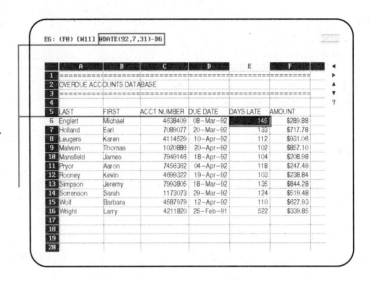

The @DATE function calculates the number of days a bill is overdue as of July 31, 1992.

Note: The numbers you enter to represent the year, month, and day must create a valid date. If the date is not valid, 1-2-3 returns ERR. For example, 1-2-3 allows you to specify February 29 only during leap years. You never can specify February 30.

Converting Date Strings to Serial Numbers with @DATEVALUE

@DATEVALUE computes the serial number for a date text string typed into a referenced cell. The text string must use one of the date formats recognized by 1-2-3. @DATEVALUE requires the following syntax:

@DATEVALUE(*date_string*)

If 1-2-3 cannot recognize the format used for the argument, the function results in ERR. After you enter the function, use the /Range Format Date command to display the serial date number as a text date.

7

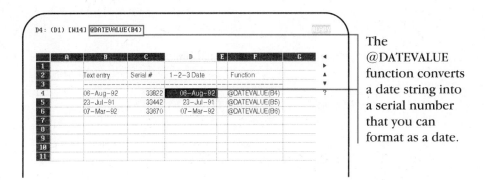

The @DATEVALUE function converts a date string into a serial number that you can format as a date.

Finding the Current Date and Time with @NOW

The @NOW function displays as a serial number both the current system date and the current system time. The numbers to the left of the decimal point specify the date. The numbers to the right of the decimal point define the time. This function, which requires no arguments, provides a convenient tool for adding dates to worksheets and reports.

After you enter the @NOW function, use the /**R**ange **F**ormat **D**ate command to display the serial date number as a text date or time.

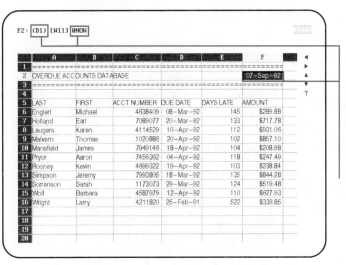

The @NOW function, formatted as a date, inserts the current date in a worksheet.

7

Using Financial Functions

The 11 financial functions enable you to perform a variety of business-related calculations. These calculations include discounting cash flows, computing loan amortization, calculating depreciation, and analyzing the return on investments. This set of functions helps you perform investment analysis and accounting, or budgeting for depreciable assets.

Table 7.3 summarizes the financial functions available in 1-2-3. The sections that follow describe the @PMT, @PV, and @FV functions in greater detail.

Table 7.3
Financial Functions

Function	Description
@CTERM(*interest, future_value, present_value*)	Calculates the number of periods required for a present value amount to grow to a future value amount given a periodic interest rate
@DDB(*cost,salvage, life,period*)	Calculates depreciation using the double-declining balance method
@FV(*payments, interest,term*)	Calculates the future value of a series of equal payments compounded at the periodic interest rate
@IRR(*estimate,range*)	Calculates the internal rate of return on an investment
@NPV(*interest,range*)	Calculates the present value of a series of future cash flows at equal intervals when payments are discounted by the periodic interest rate
@PMT(*principal, interest,term*)	Calculates the loan payment amount
@PV(*payments, interest,term*)	Calculates the present value of a series of future cash flows of equal payments discounted by the periodic interest rate
@RATE(*future_value, present_value,term*)	Calculates the periodic rate required to increase the present value amount to the future value amount in a specified length of time

7

Function	Description
@SLN(*cost,salvage,life*)	Calculates straight-line depreciation for one period
@SYD(*cost,salvage, life, period*)	Calculates sum-of-the-years' digits depreciation for a specified period
@TERM(*payments, interest, future_value*)	Calculates the number of payment periods necessary to accumulate the future value when payments compound at the periodic interest rate

Calculating Loan Payment Amounts with @PMT

You use the @PMT function to calculate the periodic payments necessary to pay the principal on a loan with a given interest rate and time period. Therefore, to use @PMT, you need to know the total loan amount (principal), periodic interest rate, and term, as shown in the following syntax:

   @PMT(*principal,interest,term*)

Express the interest rate and the term in the same units of time. For example, if you make monthly payments, you should use the annual interest rate divided by 12. The term should be the number of months you will be making payments. @PMT operates on the assumption that payments are made at the end of each period.

To calculate the monthly car payment on a $10,000 car loan, you can use the @PMT function. The loan is repaid over 48 months, and the interest rate is 10.5%.

7

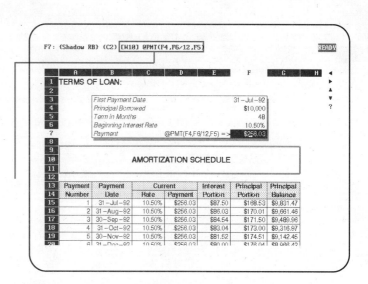

The @PMT function calculates loan payments.

---

7 Calculating Present and Future Values with @PV and @FV

@PV calculates the present value of a series of future cash flows of equal payments discounted by the periodic interest rate. Express the interest rate and the term in the same units of time. The @PV function uses the following syntax:

   @PV(*payments,interest,term*)

@PV can determine whether to receive contest winnings immediately in one lump sum or as a specified amount annually, for example.

The @FV function calculates the amount a current amount will grow to, based on a specified interest rate and the number of years. Again, express the interest rate and the term in the same units of time. @FV uses the following syntax:

   @FV(*payments,interest,term*)

You can use @FV to calculate the future value of a savings account that makes equal automatic deposits on a monthly basis. Simply specify the amount of deduction per month (payments), the monthly interest rate, and the specified number of months (term).

Using Statistical Functions

A set of seven statistical functions enables you to perform all the standard statistical calculations on data in your worksheet or in a 1-2-3 database. You can find minimum and maximum values, calculate averages, and compute the standard deviation and variance.

The attribute of all statistical functions is a list that can be value(s), cell reference(s), range(s), and formula(s). If the list contains more than one item, separate the items with commas, as in the following example:

    @SUM(B5..B20,B30..B40,B55,10%*B80,1000)

Table 7.4 lists the functions, their arguments, and the statistical operations they perform. The sections that follow cover the @AVG, @COUNT, @MAX, and @MIN statistical functions. (The functions section of Chapter 3 illustrates the @SUM function, the most commonly used 1-2-3 function.)

Table 7.4
Statistical Functions

Function	Description
@AVG(*list*)	Calculates the arithmetic mean (average) of a list of values
@COUNT(*list*)	Counts the number of cells that contain entries
@MAX(*list*)	Returns the maximum value in a list of values
@MIN(*list*)	Returns the minimum value in a list of values
@STD(*list*)	Calculates the population standard deviation of a list of values
@SUM(*list*)	Sums a list of values
@VAR(*list*)	Calculates the population variance of a list of values

Note: The statistical functions perform differently when you specify cells as ranges instead of individually. When you specify a range of cells, 1-2-3 ignores empty cells within the specified range. When you specify cells individually, however, 1-2-3 takes empty cells into consideration for the particular functions mentioned. Also, when you specify cells, keep in mind that 1-2-3 treats cells containing labels as zeros. This is the case when the cell is part of a range or when you specify the cell individually. For this reason, do not erase cells by pressing the space bar.

Computing the Arithmetic Mean with @AVG

To calculate the average of a set of values, add all the values and then divide
the sum by the number of values. Essentially, the @AVG function produces
the same result as if you divided @SUM(*list*) by @COUNT(*list*). The @AVG
function is a helpful tool for calculating the commonly used arithmetic mean,
or average. Use the following syntax for this function:

> @AVG(*list*)

The *list* argument can contain any combination of values, cell addresses,
single and multiple ranges, and range names.

The @AVG function can calculate the mean price-per-share of an imaginary
company. The function's argument includes the list of stock prices. 1-2-3
ignores any empty cells in the list when calculating the average.

The @AVG
function calcu-
lates the average
price-per-share of
stock.

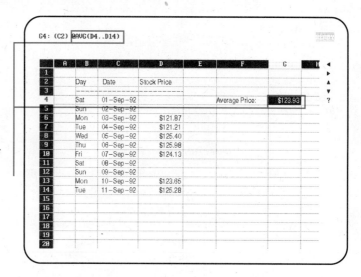

Counting Cell Entries with @COUNT

The @COUNT function totals the number of cells that contain entries of any
kind, including labels, label-prefix characters, and the values ERR and NA. Use
the following syntax for @COUNT:

> @COUNT(*list*)

The *list* argument can contain any combination of values, cell addresses, single and multiple ranges, and range names. For example, you can use @COUNT to show the number of share prices included in the @AVG calculation of the prior example.

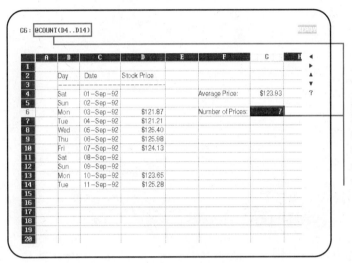

The @COUNT function calculates the number of prices per share used in the average calculation.

Note: Be sure to include only ranges as the argument in the @COUNT function. If you specify an individual cell, 1-2-3 counts that cell as if it has an entry, even if the cell is empty.

Finding Maximum and Minimum Values with @MAX and @MIN

The @MAX function finds the largest value included in the *list* argument. The @MIN function finds the smallest value included in the *list* argument. These functions use the following syntax:

> @MAX(*list*)

> @MIN(*list*)

The @MAX and @MIN functions can help you find the highest and the lowest prices in the stock prices example. Although the example shows only seven values, the true power of these functions is clear when your list consists of several hundred items.

251

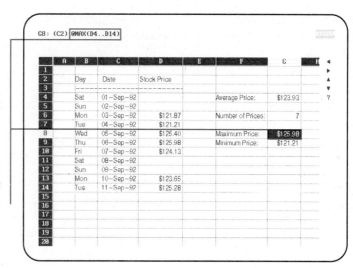

The highlighted @MAX function shows the highest price-per-share. The @MIN function in cell G9 shows the lowest stock price in the list.

7 Using Database Functions

1-2-3's seven database functions are similar to the statistical functions, but they require different arguments to work with database ranges. Like other functions, the database functions perform—in one simple statement—calculations that otherwise require several statements. This efficiency and ease of application make these functions excellent tools for manipulating 1-2-3 databases. Table 7.5 describes the database functions.

The general syntax of each of these functions is as follows:

@DSUM(*input_range,offset,criteria_range*)

The input range and criteria range are the same as those used by the /Data Query command. The input range specifies the database or the part of a database to be searched, and the criteria range specifies which records are to be selected. The offset indicates which field to select from the database records; the offset value must be either zero or a positive integer. A value of zero indicates the first column in the database, a one indicates the second column, and so on.

Table 7.5
Database Functions

Function	Description
@DAVG	Calculates the arithmetic mean (average) of items in a list
@DCOUNT	Counts the number of entries in a list
@DMAX	Returns the maximum value among items in a list
@DMIN	Returns the minimum value among items in a list
@DSTD	Calculates the standard deviation of items in a list
@DSUM	Sums the values of items in a list
@DVAR	Computes the variance of items in a list

Suppose that you want to compute database statistics of the average interest rates offered by money market funds for a given week. 1-2-3's database functions enable you to find the count, sum, average, variance, standard deviation, maximum, and minimum rates of return.

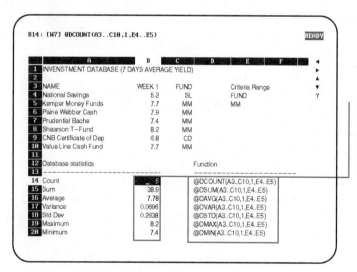

Examples of database functions used here with an investment database.

As displayed in the control panel, the input range is A3..C10, the offset of 1 indicates column B, and the criteria range is E4..E5. In the lower part of the example, the database functions are in column B (shown in text format in column D).

Using Logical Functions

Each of 1-2-3's nine logical functions enables you to test whether a condition is true or false. Many of these functions operate in a similar manner—by returning a 1 if the test is true or a 0 if the test is false. These logical tests are important for creating decision-making functions; the results of these functions depend on conditions elsewhere in the worksheet.

Table 7.6 summarizes the logical functions that 1-2-3 provides. The text that follows describes the @IF, @TRUE, and @FALSE logical functions in more detail.

Table 7.6
Logical Functions

Function	*Description*
@FALSE	Returns the logical value 0, for false
@IF(*condition,true,false*)	Tests a condition and returns one result if the condition is true and another result if the condition is false
@ISAAF(*name*)	Tests for a defined add-in program
@ISAPP(*name*)	Tests for an attached add-in program
@ISERR(*cell_reference*)	Tests whether the argument results in ERR
@ISNA(*cell_reference*)	Tests whether the argument results in NA
@ISNUMBER(*cell_reference*)	Tests whether the argument is a number
@ISSTRING(*cell_reference*)	Tests whether the argument is a string
@TRUE	Returns the logical value 1, for true

Creating Conditional Tests with @IF

The @IF function represents a powerful tool—one you can use both to manipulate text within your worksheets and to affect calculations. For example, you can use an @IF statement to test the following condition:

Is the inventory on hand below 1,000 units? You can return one value or label if the answer to the question is true, or another value or label if the answer is false. The @IF function uses the following syntax:

@IF(*condition,true,false*)

The @IF function can use six operators when testing conditions. The following list shows the operators and their corresponding descriptions.

Operator	Description
>	Greater than
<	Less than
=	Equal to
>=	Greater than or equal to
<=	Less than or equal to
<>	Not equal to

In addition, you can perform more complex conditional tests. Adding logical operators enables you to test multiple conditions in one @IF function. These operators and their descriptions are the following.

Operator	Description
#AND#	Tests two conditions, both of which must be true in order for the entire test to be true
#NOT#	Tests that a condition is not true
#OR#	Tests two conditions; if either condition is true, the entire test condition is true

The @IF function can check whether a specified cell's content is between 4 and 10, whether a cell contains a specified text string, and whether a 1-2-3 date falls before or after the current date. The results of these tests depend on whether the condition evaluates as true or false.

7

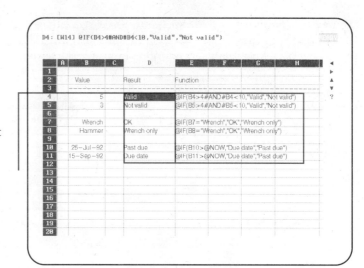

D4: [W14] @IF(B4>4#AND#B4<10,"Valid","Not valid")

Examples of the @IF function test for specified values or labels.

Checking for Errors with @TRUE and @FALSE

You use the @TRUE and @FALSE functions to check for errors. Neither function requires arguments, but each is useful for providing documentation for formulas and advanced macro commands. The @TRUE function always returns the value 1—the logical value for true. The @FALSE function always returns the value 0—the logical value for false. A common use for these functions is in combination with functions requiring a logical value, such as the following @IF formula:

@IF(B4>4#AND#B4<10,@TRUE,@FALSE)

This formula, similar to the formulas used in the previous example, returns the value of 1 (true) if cell B4 contains a value between 4 and 10; otherwise, returns a 0 (false).

Using String Functions

Another set of 1-2-3 functions includes the 19 string functions that manipulate text. You can use string functions to repeat text characters, convert letters in a string to uppercase or lowercase, change strings into numbers, and change numbers into strings. String functions also are important when you prepare 1-2-3 data for use in other programs, such as word processing programs.

Included with the string functions are a few special functions for working with the Lotus International Character Set (LICS). The complete set of LICS characters, listed in the 1-2-3 documentation, includes everything from the copyright sign (©) to the lowercase *e* with the grave accent (è).

Table 7.7 summarizes the string functions available in 1-2-3. The sections that follow discuss the @LOWER, @UPPER, @PROPER, and @REPEAT string functions in more detail.

Table 7.7
String Functions

Function	Description
@CHAR(*number*)	Converts a code number into the corresponding LICS character
@CLEAN(*string*)	Removes nonprintable characters from the specified string
@CODE(*string*)	Returns the LICS code that corresponds to the first character of the specified string
@EXACT(*string1,string2*)	Returns 1 (true) if arguments are exact matches; otherwise, returns 0 (false)
@FIND(*search_string, string,start_number*)	Locates the start position of one string within another string
@LEFT(*string,number*)	Returns the specified number of characters from the left side of a string
@LENGTH(*string*)	Returns the number of characters in the string
@LOWER(*string*)	Converts all characters in the string to lowercase
@MID(*string,start_ number,number*)	Returns a specified number of characters from the middle of another string, beginning at the specified starting position
@N(*range*)	Returns as a value the contents of the cell in the upper left corner of a range

continued

7

257

Table 7.7 (*continued*)

Function	Description
@PROPER(*string*)	Converts the first character in each word of the string to uppercase, and the remaining characters in each word to lowercase
@REPEAT(*string,number*)	Duplicates the string the specified number of times in a cell
@REPLACE(*original_string, start_number,number, new_string*)	Replaces a number of characters in the original string with new string characters, starting at the character identified by the start position
@RIGHT(*string,number*)	Returns the specified number of characters from the right side of the string
@S(*range*)	Returns as a label the contents of the cell in the upper left corner of a range
@STRING(*number, decimal_places*)	Converts a value to a string with the specified number of decimal places
@TRIM(*string*)	Removes blank spaces from the string
@UPPER(*string*)	Converts all characters in the string to uppercase
@VALUE(*string*)	Converts the string to a value

Strings are labels or portions of labels. Strings used within functions consist of characters enclosed in quotation marks, such as "Total." Some functions produce strings, but other functions produce numeric results. If a function's result is not of the data type you need, use @STRING to convert a numeric value to a string, or @VALUE to convert a string to a numeric value.

Converting the Case of Strings with @LOWER, @UPPER, and @PROPER

1-2-3 offers three different functions for converting the case of a string value. The @LOWER and @UPPER functions convert all characters in the referenced string to lowercase and uppercase, respectively. The @PROPER function

258

converts characters in the string to proper capitalization—with the first letter in uppercase and all remaining letters in lowercase. The general syntax of these functions is as follows:

@LOWER(*string*)

@UPPER(*string*)

@PROPER(*string*)

These three functions work with strings or references to strings. If a cell contains a number or is empty, 1-2-3 returns ERR for these functions.

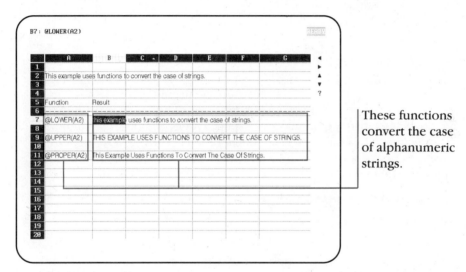

These functions convert the case of alphanumeric strings.

7

The text versions of the formulas appear in column A, and the formulas and their results are in column B.

You can use @LOWER, @UPPER, or @PROPER to modify the contents of a database so that all entries in a field appear with the same capitalization. This technique produces reports with a consistent appearance. To be sure that 1-2-3 sorts data with different capitalizations correctly, create a column using one of these functions that references the data and sort on this new column.

Repeating Strings with @REPEAT

The @REPEAT function repeats a string a specified number of times, much as the backslash (\) repeats strings to fill a single cell. However, @REPEAT has some distinct advantages over the backslash. With @REPEAT, you can repeat the string the precise number of times you want. If the result is wider than the cell width, the result displays in empty adjacent cells to the right. @REPEAT uses the following syntax:

> @REPEAT(*string,number*)

The *number* argument indicates the number of times you want to repeat a string in a cell. For example, if you want to repeat the string -**- four times, you can enter the following function:

> @REPEAT("-**-",4)

The resulting string will appear as: -**--**--**--**-.

Using Special Functions

1-2-3 provides a set of 12 special functions. You use these special tools to perform a variety of tasks. For example, two special functions return up to 10 different characteristics of a cell. Other special functions count the number of rows or columns in a range. Special functions also enable you to trap worksheet errors and use specified keys in the functions' arguments to look up values in tables or lists.

Table 7.8 lists 1-2-3's special functions. The sections that follow discuss the @ERR, @NA, @HLOOKUP, and @VLOOKUP commands.

Table 7.8
Special Functions

Function	Description
@@(*location*)	Returns the contents of the cell referenced in the specified location
@?	Indicates an unknown add-in function referred to in a formula; results when you load the worksheet before the add-in program (1-2-3 shows @? in the control panel and displays NA in the cell) **Note:** You cannot enter @? in a cell.
@CELL(*attribute,range*)	Returns an attribute of the cell in the upper left corner of the range

Function	Description
@CELLPOINTER(*attribute*)	Returns an attribute of the current cell
@CHOOSE(*offset*,*list*)	Locates in a list the entry specified by the offset number
@COLS(*range*)	Counts the number of columns in a range
@ERR	Displays ERR in the cell
@HLOOKUP(*key*,*range*, *row_offset*)	Locates the number in a table and returns a value from that row of the range
@INDEX(*range*,*column_ offset*, *row_offset*)	Returns the contents of a cell specified by the intersection of a row and column within a range
@NA	Displays NA in the cell
@ROWS(*range*)	Counts the number of rows in a range
@VLOOKUP(*key*,*range*, *column_offset*)	Locates the number in a lookup table and returns a value from that column of the range

7

Trapping Errors with @ERR and @NA

When you create 1-2-3 applications, you may want to use @ERR or @NA to distinguish certain cell entries. Formulas that depend on cells with @NA or @ERR will return NA or ERR. Suppose, for example, that you are creating a checkbook-balancing worksheet in which checks with dollar amounts less than or equal to zero are unacceptable. One way to show that these checks are unacceptable is to use @ERR to signal that fact. You can use the following version of the @IF function:

@IF(B9<=0,@ERR,B9)

This statement says, "If the amount in cell B9 is less than or equal to zero, then display ERR in that cell; otherwise, display the amount."

In an inventory database, you can place the @NA function in cells to show uncounted inventory items. You can also use @IF and @NA together, as in the following example:

@IF(C4=0,@NA,C4)

This statement says, "If the value in cell C4 is equal to zero, display NA in that cell; otherwise display the value."

Finding Table Entries with @HLOOKUP and @VLOOKUP

The @HLOOKUP and @VLOOKUP functions retrieve a string or value from a table, based on a specified key used to find the information. The operation and format of the two functions are essentially the same except that @HLOOKUP searches horizontal tables and @VLOOKUP searches vertical tables. These functions use the following syntax:

@HLOOKUP(*key,range,row_offset*)

@VLOOKUP(*key,range,column_offset*)

The *key* argument is the string or value that tells 1-2-3 which column (@HLOOKUP) or row (@VLOOKUP) to search. The key strings or values belong in the first row or column. Numeric keys must be in ascending order for the functions to work properly. The *range* argument is the area that makes up the entire lookup table. The *row_offset* or *column_offset* argument specifies from which row (@HLOOKUP) or column (@VLOOKUP) to retrieve data. The offset argument is always a number, ranging from 0 to the highest number (minus one) of columns or rows in the lookup table.

The @HLOOKUP and @VLOOKUP functions are useful for finding any type of value you would have to look up manually in a table. Examples include tax amounts, shipping zones, and interest charges.

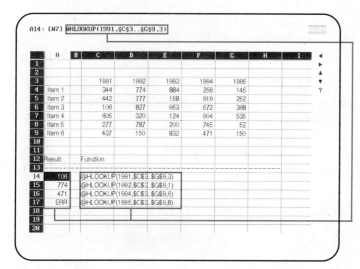

The @HLOOKUP function retrieves values from a table.

7

Summary

This chapter described the functions that 1-2-3 provides to make formula and worksheet construction easier and more error-free. After you become accustomed to using these functions, you can use them regularly in your worksheets. Use the tables of this chapter as a reference for the available functions, their syntax, and the types of arguments they require.

Specifically, you learned the following key information about 1-2-3:

- 1-2-3 includes built-in functions that can be divided into eight different categories. These functions perform a variety of powerful calculations that save the user much time when building worksheets.

- Enter 1-2-3 functions by typing the @ sign, followed by the function name and any required arguments within parentheses. Press Enter to complete the process.

- The mathematical and trigonometric functions perform standard arithmetic operations, such as computing the integer with @INT and rounding numbers with @ROUND.

- The date and time functions convert dates and times to serial numbers that can be used in sorting and arithmetic calculations. Examples include @NOW, @DATE, and @DATEVALUE. You can use @NOW to stamp the date on a worksheet or report.

- The financial functions calculate cash flows, loans, annuities, and asset depreciation. The @PMT function calculates loan payments, while the @PV and @FV functions calculate present and future values, respectively.

- The statistical functions perform standard statistical calculations on lists. For example, @AVG calculates the average of values in a list. @COUNT counts the total number of entries in a list. @MAX and @MIN find the maximum and minimum values in a list.

- The database functions are similar to the statistical functions, but calculate and query databases.

- The logical functions test whether a condition is true or false. The @IF function returns a different value or label depending on the outcome of a specified condition. You can use the @TRUE and @FALSE functions in conditional tests to display a 1 (true) or a 0 (false).

- Use the string functions to manipulate text. For example, the @LOWER, @UPPER, and @PROPER functions convert the case of a specified label. The @REPEAT function repeats a string a specified number of times.

- The special functions perform a variety of worksheet tasks. The @ERR and @NA functions trap errors or distinguish certain cell entries. The @HLOOKUP and @VLOOKUP functions return values from a specified row and column of a table.

In the next chapter, you learn how to print reports created in 1-2-3. This chapter also discusses the various options available for enhancing reports.

7

Printing Reports

8

1-2-3 is a powerful tool for developing information presented in a column-and-row format. You can enter and edit your worksheet and database files on-screen as well as store the input on disk. To make good use of your data, however, you often need it in printed form. Examples include a target production schedule, a summary report to your supervisor, or a detailed reorder list to central stores.

Using 1-2-3's /Print command, you can access different options to meet your printing needs. You can choose to write directly from 1-2-3 to the printer by using the /Print Printer command sequence. Or you can use the alternative /Print File or Encoded *filename* sequence to create a print file on disk. Later, you can produce a printout of the file from within 1-2-3 or from DOS. Alternatively, you can merge the file into a word processing file. You can use /Print Background in conjunction with the BPRINT program to print while you do other work.

You can use the add-in program Wysiwyg to take advantage of presentation-quality printing features not found in the standard 1-2-3 /Print commands. Printing reports with Wysiwyg is the subject of the next chapter.

Printing draft-quality reports

Controlling paper movement

Changing the page layout

Printing a listing of cell contents

Clearing print options

Key Terms in This Chapter

Print defaults	Preset, standard specifications for a 1-2-3 print job.
Encoded file	A file that you print to a disk. An encoded file has all the instructions necessary to output highlighted text and graphs to a specific printer.
Print Settings dialog box	The dialog box that appears on-screen when you select /**Print**. The dialog box shows you the current printer settings and allows you to change them on-screen.
Borders	One or more rows or columns of data or labels that 1-2-3 repeats on a multiple-page report.
Header	Information displayed on one line at the top of a page. A header may include a date and a page number.
Footer	Information displayed on one line at the bottom of a page. A footer may include a date and a page number.

8

Using the Mouse

To use a mouse with 1-2-3 Release 2.3, you need a mouse, mouse software, and a graphics monitor and graphics card that support a mouse. You can use a mouse to select commands and files, specify ranges, move the cell pointer within the worksheet, and make selections in a dialog box. Refer to the following sections of the specified chapters for further information on using the mouse.

- Chapter 2—"Understanding Mouse Terminology"
- Chapter 3—"Mouse Control of the Cell Pointer"
          "Using Dialog Boxes"
          "Using the Mouse To Select Menu Commands"
- Chapter 4—"Using the Mouse To Specify Ranges"

To help you learn the basics of printing, this chapter assumes that

- You have not changed 1-2-3's preset printing defaults.
- You produce reports on 8 1/2-by-11-inch paper.
- You send data to the printer in most cases.
- You want to use basic report-enhancement techniques such as hiding columns and rows, adding headers and footers, and repeating column and row headings.

If you want to change 1-2-3's default settings, consult Que's *Using 1-2-3 for DOS Release 2.3*, Special Edition.

Getting Started from the /Print Menu

Every print command in 1-2-3 starts from the /**P**rint option of the 1-2-3 main menu. After choosing /**P**rint, you must select one of the next options: **P**rinter, **F**ile, **E**ncoded, or **B**ackground.

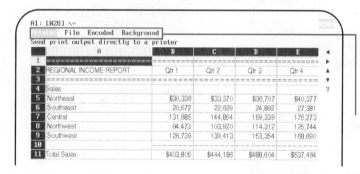

The /**P**rint command options in the control panel.

To send your report directly to the current printer, select **P**rinter.

To create a text file on disk, select **F**ile. A text file can contain data but no graphs or special printer codes. Later, you can print the text file from the operating system prompt.

To create a disk file that includes instructions on printing, choose **E**ncoded. An encoded file can contain data, graphs, and printer codes for 1-2-3 print options, such as fonts, colors, and line spacing. You can print an encoded file from the operating system prompt, but such a file is not suitable for transferring data to another program.

267

To create an encoded file that prints while you continue working in 1-2-3, choose **B**ackground. If you don't choose **B**ackground, you have to wait while 1-2-3 finishes printing before you work on your worksheet. Before you select the **B**ackground option, you must start the program BPRINT. To use BPRINT, follow these steps:

1. Exit 1-2-3 by selecting /**Q**uit.

2. If necessary, change to the directory containing the 1-2-3 program (for example, type **CD \123R23** and press ⏎Enter).

3. At the 1-2-3 directory prompt, type **BPRINT** and press ⏎Enter.

4. Type **123** and press ⏎Enter to return to the 1-2-3 program.

If you choose **F**ile, **En**coded, or **B**ackground from the /**P**rint menu, you must respond to the prompt for a file name. Type a name that contains up to eight characters. You need not add a file extension because 1-2-3 automatically assigns the PRN (print file) or ENC (encoded file) extension. You can specify a different extension if you want.

You use an encoded file for printing at another time or from another computer while preserving all the special print options available in 1-2-3. When you create an encoded file, be sure that the selected printer is the same as the one you eventually use to print the file. An encoded file contains printer codes that control special printer features, such as fonts and line spacing. Because these codes are printer-specific, an encoded file created for one printer may not print correctly on another printer. The printer control codes embedded in the encoded file make sure that the final output looks the same as output printed directly from 1-2-3. To print an encoded file, you use the operating system COPY command with the /B option. Consider the following example:

```
COPY C:\123R23\SALES.ENC/B LPT1:
```

This command prints the file SALES.ENC, located in the directory C:\123R23, on the printer connected to the port LPT1 (usually the default printer port). Other printer ports are LPT2, COM1, and COM2.

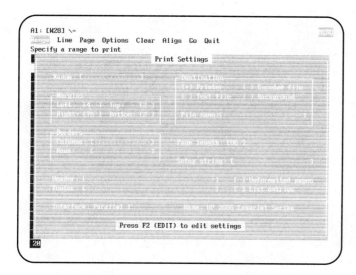

After you select **Printer**, **File**, **Encoded**, or **Background**, the Print Settings dialog box appears.

You can toggle between the Print Settings dialog box and the worksheet by pressing F6.

Table 8.1 outlines the various options on the /**Print Printer** menu. Regardless of which options you select, you must choose **Range** and specify a range to print. Select **Go** and then **Quit** to return to the worksheet. All other selections are optional.

Table 8.1
Selections on the /Print Printer Menu

Selection	Description
Range	Indicates the section of the worksheet to print or save to disk as a print file
Line	Adjusts the paper line-by-line in the printer
Page	Adjusts the paper page-by-page in the printer
Options	Determines settings to enhance the appearance of the printout; you can use this menu item or the Print Settings dialog box

continued

Table 8.1 (*continued*)

Selection	Description
Clear	Erases previous settings
Align	Signals the printer position at the top of the print page
Go	Starts printing to the printer or a disk file
Quit	Exits the menu and returns 1-2-3 to READY mode

Printing Draft-Quality Reports

Printing does not have to be an arduous task. With 1-2-3, you can print quick reports by issuing a few simple commands. In this section, you learn a variety of printing techniques. Specifically, you learn how to print a draft-quality report of one page or less. You also learn to use the Print Settings dialog box and print a multipage report with borders.

Printing a One-Page Report

If you work with default print settings and haven't entered other print settings during the current worksheet session, printing one page or less involves only the following few steps:

1. Specify to print to the printer or a file.
2. Highlight the range to print.
3. Choose the command to begin printing.

Two other steps may be necessary if you or someone else has changed the default settings or entered new print settings. First, you can check the default settings by selecting /Worksheet Global Default Printer. A quick review of this dialog box shows whether the printer and page layout settings are the ones you need. Second, you can clear any settings that another user entered by selecting /Print Printer Clear All. All settings return to the default settings. (A later section of this chapter covers clearing print settings.)

8

If you are certain that all default settings are correct and no other settings have been entered, you can print a draft-quality report of one page or less by completing the following steps:

1. Check to see that your printer is on-line and that you have positioned the paper properly.

2. Select /**P**rint **P**rinter.

3. Select **R**ange to specify a range to print from the worksheet.

4. Indicate what part of the worksheet you want to print by typing cell references or highlighting the area. Then press ↵Enter.

   Note: In addition to the arrow keys, you can use the PgUp, PgDn, and End keys to set ranges when you print. If you want to set a range that includes the entire active area of the worksheet, press Home to move to the top left corner. Then anchor the range (.), and move the cell pointer to the lower right corner of the active area with End Home.

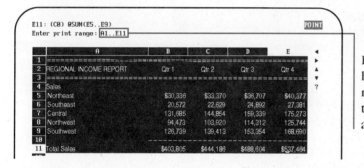

In this example, highlight the range A1..E11 as the range to print, and press ↵Enter.

5. After you highlight the range you want to print, select **A**lign.

   Choosing **A**lign ensures that printing begins at the top of each page. Before printing, always make sure that you have correctly positioned your printer paper.

6. To begin printing, select **G**o.

   The **G**o option sends your worksheet data to the printer.

7. After the printer finishes, select **P**age to advance to the top of the next page or eject the page from a laser printer.

8. Select **Q**uit to return to READY mode.

8

This draft-quality report of less than one page prints with 1-2-3's default settings.

```
=====================================================================
REGIONAL INCOME REPORT          Qtr 1      Qtr 2      Qtr 3      Qtr 4
=========================    ========   ========   ========   ========
Sales
  Northeast                   $30,336    $33,370    $36,707    $40,377
  Southeast                    20,572     22,629     24,892     27,381
  Central                     131,685    144,854    159,339    175,273
  Northwest                    94,473    103,920    114,312    125,744
  Southwest                   126,739    139,413    153,354    168,690
                            ---------  ---------  ---------  ---------
Total Sales                  $403,805   $444,186   $488,604   $537,464
```

8

If you press Enter after selecting the **G**o option, the file prints a second time. If this accidentally occurs, you can stop printing by pressing Ctrl-Break. Even if the area of your worksheet to print is larger than one page, you can use the basic steps for printing one-page reports. However, setting the print range so that a new page begins where you want can be tricky. Therefore, if you want to print a section of a large worksheet, you may need to change the **B**orders option in the Print Settings dialog box or by using /**P**rint **P**rinter **O**ptions **B**orders. The **B**orders option enables you to repeat certain labels on each page.

Print ranges can also be selected from the Print Settings dialog box. However, it requires fewer steps to specify print ranges through the **R**ange option. The next section of this chapter discusses how to use the Print Settings dialog box to specify other print settings quickly and easily.

Using the Print Settings Dialog Box

You can use the Print Settings dialog box to view or change many print options. Specific procedures for changing print options are discussed later in this chapter.

The main parts of the dialog box include option buttons, check boxes, and text boxes.

To use the Print Settings dialog box, follow these steps:

1. Press F2 (Edit) or click the left mouse button.

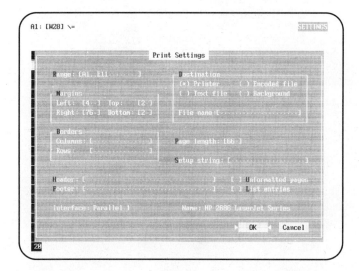

1-2-3 highlights one letter (usually the first letter) of each option. The main **Print** menu disappears when you activate the dialog box.

2. To select an option button or check box, press the highlighted letter of each option until your choice is made.

   Or

   Click the left mouse button on your choice.

   For example, to choose **Text** file as the destination, select **Destination Text** file or click the left mouse button on the **Text** file option button. An asterisk (*) indicates your choice.

   To choose unformatted pages, select **Unformatted** pages or click the left mouse button on the corresponding check box. An x indicates your choice.

   Note: To unmark a check box, select the check box again. The x should disappear.

3. To use a text box, press the highlighted letter of each option until the cursor is in the text box or click the left mouse button on your choice.

4. Type the text in the box and press ↵Enter .

   For example, type **130** as the right margin.

5. Where the text box calls for a range (**R**ange or **B**orders), you can select the range in one of the following ways:

   • Type the cell references for the range in the text box and press ⏎Enter.

   • Or, type the range name in the text box and press ⏎Enter.

   • Or, press F4 to go to POINT mode, highlight the range, and press ⏎Enter.

6. When you finish selecting all options in the Print Settings dialog box, press ⏎Enter or click the left mouse button on OK. The main **Print** menu reappears.

7. To print the selected range, select **A**lign **G**o from the menu.

A completed Print Settings dialog box.

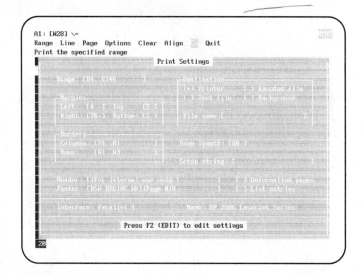

8. Select **P**age to advance (or eject) the paper; then select **Q**uit to return to READY mode.

Printing Two or More Pages with Borders

If you want to print information correctly when splitting data between pages, remember that 1-2-3 treats numeric and text data differently. 1-2-3 prints numbers completely because they span only one cell. However, text—such as long labels that lie across several cells—may split awkwardly from one page to the next.

When printing two or more pages, you can repeat certain columns or rows on each printed page. 1-2-3 defines the repeated columns and rows as *borders*.

To repeat column or row borders on each page when printing, follow these steps:

1. Select /**P**rint **P**rinter.

2. Press F2 or click the left mouse button in the dialog box to edit the settings.

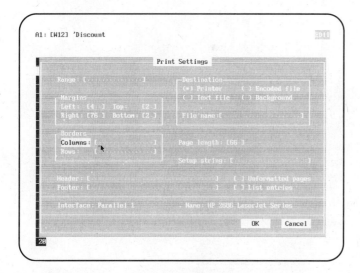

1-2-3 highlights a character from each option on the dialog box.

8

3. Select **B**orders.

   The **B**orders option enables you to select row or column borders to repeat on each page of the printout.

   1-2-3 asks whether you want to locate the labels down one or more columns or across one or more rows.

4. Select either **C**olumns or **R**ows.

   Suppose that you want to print a report on two or more pages and repeat labels displayed in a column. To do this, select **C**olumns. To print a report on two or more pages and repeat labels displayed across a row, select **R**ows.

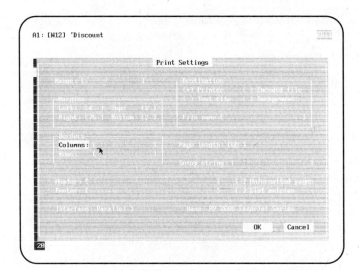

In this example,
select Columns.

5. Show which rows or columns you want printed on each page by
   typing the cell reference or range name of the rows or columns.

   Or

   Press F4 and highlight the rows or columns and press ↵Enter.

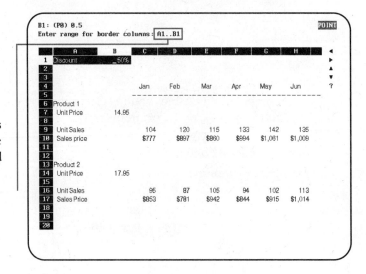

For columns A
and B to appear
as a border, press
F4, highlight the
range A1..B1, and
press ↵Enter.

6. To return to the main Print menu, press ↵Enter.
7. To choose the range to print, select Range.

8. Highlight the desired print range and press ⏎Enter.

   Note: Do not include in your print range the borders you want repeated on each page. 1-2-3 automatically prints the borders on every page of the printout. If you include the borders in the print range, 1-2-3 prints them twice on each page.

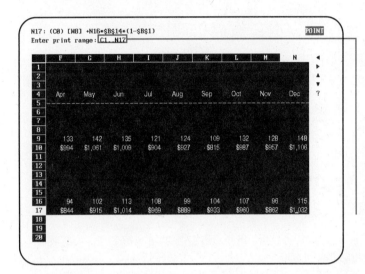

In this example, highlight the range to print as C1..N17 and press ⏎Enter. Note that this range does not include the columns A and B specified as borders.

8

9. Select **Align G**o.

10. After the printer finishes printing, select **P**age to advance to the top of the next page or eject the page from a laser printer.

11. Select **Q**uit.

```
Discount        50%

                 Jan    Feb    Mar    Apr    May    Jun
                ------ ------ ------ ------ ------ ------
Product 1
  Unit Price   14.95

  Unit Sales     104    120    115    133    142    135
  Sales price   $777   $897   $860   $994 $1,061 $1,009

Product 2
  Unit Price   17.95

  Unit Sales      95     87    105     94    102    113
  Sales Price   $853   $781   $942   $844   $915 $1,014
```

This first page of a two-page report has column borders repeated on each page.

```
Discount          50%

                        Jul    Aug    Sep    Oct    Nov    Dec
                      ------ ------ ------ ------ ------- ------
          Product 1
            Unit Price  14.95

            Unit Sales      121    124    109    132    128    148
            Sales price    $904   $927   $815   $987   $957 $1,106

          Product 2
            Unit Price  17.95

            Unit Sales      108     99    104    107     96    115
            Sales Price    $969   $889   $933   $960   $862 $1,032
```

This is the second
page of the report
with borders.

Excluding Segments within a Designated Print Range

Because the /**Print** commands require that you specify a range to print, you
can print only rectangular blocks from the worksheet. You can, however,
suppress the display of cell contents within the range. You can hide entire
rows or columns, or you can remove from view a segment that spans only part
of a row or a column. You can hide a column (or range) of sensitive financial
information. You can also compress the worksheet so that the most important
data fits on a one-page report.

Excluding Columns

As you learned in Chapter 5, you can use /**W**orksheet **C**olumn **H**ide to mark
columns you don't want to appear on-screen. If you include these marked
columns in a print range, they do not appear on the printout.

To print a worksheet range and exclude one or more columns within that
range, follow these steps:

1. Select /**W**orksheet **C**olumn **H**ide.

2. When the prompt Specify column to hide: appears, highlight the
   column or columns you want to hide. Then press   .

278

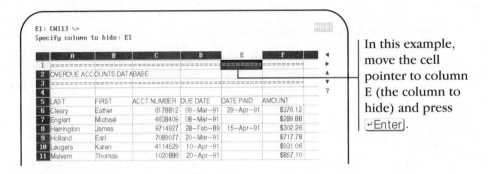

In this example, move the cell pointer to column E (the column to hide) and press ↵Enter.

3. Select /**Print** **P**rinter **R**ange.

4. Type or highlight the range you want to print, and then press ↵Enter.

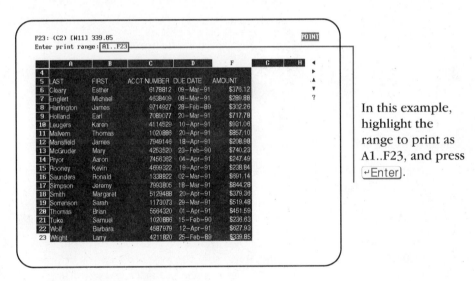

In this example, highlight the range to print as A1..F23, and press ↵Enter.

5. Select **Align G**o **P**age **Q**uit.

Note: To restore hidden columns, select /**W**orksheet **C**olumn **D**isplay. When the hidden columns (marked with an asterisk) reappear on-screen, you can specify which column or columns to display.

279

```
================================================================
OVERDUE ACCOUNTS DATABASE
================================================================

LAST         FIRST      ACCT NUMBER   DUE DATE    AMOUNT
Cleary       Esther          6178812   09-Mar-91   $376.12
Englert      Michael         4638409   08-Mar-91   $289.88
Harrington   James           9714927   28-Feb-89   $302.26
Holland      Earl            7089077   20-Mar-91   $717.78
Leugers      Karen           4114529   10-Apr-91   $931.06
Malvern      Thomas          1020886   20-Apr-91   $857.10
Mansfield    James           7949146   18-Apr-91   $208.98
McGruder     Mary            4253520   23-Feb-90   $740.23
Pryor        Aaron           7456362   04-Apr-91   $247.49
Rooney       Kevin           4699322   19-Apr-91   $238.84
Saunders     Ronald          1338822   02-Mar-91   $691.14
Simpson      Jeremy          7993805   18-Mar-91   $844.28
Smith        Margaret        5129488   20-Apr-91   $379.36
Sorrenson    Sarah           1173073   29-Mar-91   $519.48
Thomas       Brian           5564320   01-Apr-91   $451.59
Tuke         Samuel          1020886   15-Feb-90   $236.63
Wolf         Barbara         4587979   12-Apr-91   $627.93
Wright       Larry           4211820   25-Feb-89   $339.85
```

The printed report excludes the information from the hidden column.

8

Excluding Rows

To prevent specific rows of the worksheet from printing, you must mark these rows with a symbol for nonprinting. You enter the symbol for nonprinting by typing two vertical bars (||) in the first column of the print range in each row you want to exclude.

After you type both vertical bars, only one appears on-screen, and neither vertical bar appears on the printout. If the row you want to exclude contains data in the first column of the print range, you must insert a new column for the vertical bars. Keep in mind that the column with the vertical bars must be the first column of the print range. To avoid alignment problems when inserting this new column, use /Worksheet Column Hide to suppress printing of the column.

To print a worksheet range and suppress one or more rows within that range, follow these steps:

1. Move the cell pointer to the row you want to suppress from the printout—in the first column of the print range.

   Note: If the first cells in the rows marked for omission already contain data, use /Worksheet Insert Column to insert a blank column to the left of the print range.

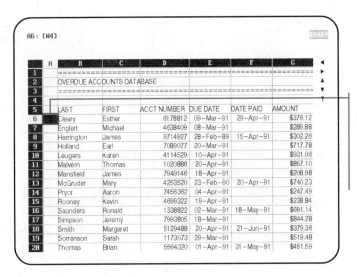

Move the cell pointer to the first cell in row 6, the first row to suppress from the printout.

2. Type || (the symbol for nonprinting), and then press ⏎Enter.

The symbol for nonprinting appears as a single bar in the worksheet.

3. Repeat steps 1 and 2 until you mark all rows to suppress from the printout with two vertical bars.

4. To define the range to print, select **/Print Printer Range**.

5. Type or highlight the range you want to print, and press ⏎Enter. You must include the column with the vertical bars as the first column in the print range.

8

281

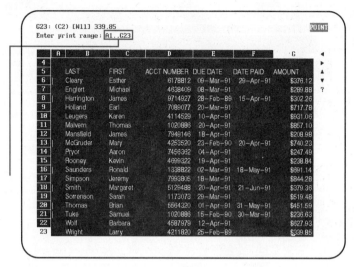

In this example, highlight the range to print as A1..G23 and press ↵Enter.

6. If you insert a new column for the vertical bars, hide the column to avoid alignment problems in your printout. To do this, select **Q**uit from the main **P**rint menu. Then highlight the new column, select **/W**orksheet **C**olumn **H**ide, and press ↵Enter. Then select **/P**rint **P**rinter to access the main **P**rint menu again, and continue with the next step.

Note: You must hide the column with the vertical bars before printing to avoid alignment problems. The marked rows are suppressed although the symbols for nonprinting are not visible on-screen.

7. Select **A**lign **G**o **P**age **Q**uit.

Rows marked with two vertical bars in the first column of the print range do not appear in the printed output.

```
================================================================
OVERDUE ACCOUNTS DATABASE
================================================================

LAST       FIRST     ACCT NUMBER  DUE DATE    DATE PAID   AMOUNT
Englert    Michael      4638409   08-Mar-91               $289.88
Holland    Earl         7089077   20-Mar-91               $717.78
Leugers    Karen        4114529   10-Apr-91               $931.06
Malvern    Thomas       1020886   20-Apr-91               $857.10
Mansfield  James        7949146   18-Apr-91               $208.98
Pryor      Aaron        7456362   04-Apr-91               $247.49
Rooney     Kevin        4699322   19-Apr-91               $238.84
Simpson    Jeremy       7993805   18-Mar-91               $844.28
Sorrenson  Sarah        1173073   29-Mar-91               $519.48
Wolf       Barbara      4587979   12-Apr-91               $627.93
Wright     Larry        4211820   25-Feb-89               $339.85
```

To restore the worksheet after you finish printing, remove the vertical bars from the marked rows. If you inserted a column for the vertical bars, display the column again, if necessary, with /Worksheet Column Display. Then delete the column with /Worksheet Column Delete.

Excluding Ranges

If you want to hide an area that partially spans one or more rows and columns, follow these steps:

1. Select /**R**ange **F**ormat **H**idden.

2. Specify the range you want to hide by highlighting the range and pressing ⏎Enter).

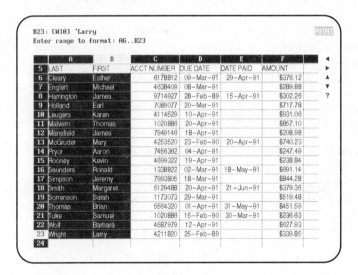

In this example, highlight the range to hide as A6..B23 and press ⏎Enter).

3. To choose the range to print, select /**P**rint **P**rinter **R**ange.

4. Type or highlight the range you want to print and press ⏎Enter). Be sure to include the hidden range within the range to print.

5. Select **A**lign **G**o **P**age **Q**uit.

```
=================================================================
OVERDUE ACCOUNTS DATABASE
=================================================================

LAST        FIRST      ACCT NUMBER  DUE DATE   DATE PAID   AMOUNT
                       6178812      09-Mar-91  29-Apr-91   $376.12
                       4638409      08-Mar-91              $289.88
                       9714927      28-Feb-89  15-Apr-91   $302.26
                       7089077      20-Mar-91              $717.78
                       4114529      10-Apr-91              $931.06
                       1020886      20-Apr-91              $857.10
                       7949146      18-Apr-91              $208.98
                       4253520      23-Feb-90  20-Apr-91   $740.23
                       7456362      04-Apr-91              $247.49
                       4699322      19-Apr-91              $238.84
                       1338822      02-Mar-91  18-May-91   $691.14
                       7993805      18-Mar-91              $844.28
                       5129488      20-Apr-91  21-Jun-91   $379.36
                       1173073      29-Mar-91              $519.48
                       5564320      01-Apr-91  31-May-91   $451.59
                       1020886      15-Feb-90  30-Mar-91   $236.63
                       4587979      12-Apr-91              $627.93
                       4211820      25-Feb-89              $339.85
```

1-2-3 suppresses the range hidden with /**R**ange **F**ormat **H**idden from the printout.

8

After you finish printing, restore the hidden range to the global format with the /**R**ange **F**ormat **R**eset command.

If you find yourself repeating print operations (hiding the same columns, setting and resetting ranges), you can save time and minimize frustration with print macros. Chapter 14 explains the basics about macros. For more detailed information, see Que's *Using 1-2-3 for DOS Release 2.3*, Special Edition.

Controlling Paper Movement

If you print a report shorter than full-page length, the printer does not automatically advance to the top of the next page. Instead, the next print operation begins where the preceding operation ended. Similarly, if you print a report with more than one page, 1-2-3 inserts page breaks in the document between pages. But the paper does not advance to the top of the next page after 1-2-3 has printed the last page. You can, however, control movement of the paper in your printer from within 1-2-3. You can specify the "top" of a page in any paper position, advance the paper by line or by page, and precisely insert page breaks.

Using the Line, Page, and Align Options

If you are using continuous-feed paper, position the paper so that the print head is at the top of the page. Then turn on the printer. If your printer is already on, turn it off and then on again. Do not advance the paper manually once the printer is on. 1-2-3 coordinates a line counter with the current page-length setting. Because 1-2-3 does not count any lines you advance manually, page breaks could crop up in strange places.

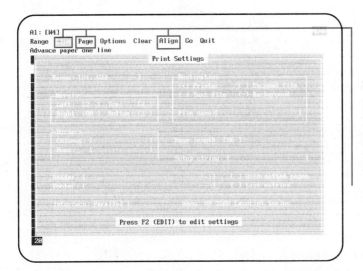

You control the movement of the paper in your printer with the Line, **Page**, and Align options.

8

The Line option of the main **Print** menu advances the paper one line at a time. The **Page** option advances paper one complete page a time. You use the **Align** option to set the beginning of a page.

To advance paper one line at a time, issue the **/Print Printer Line** command. This command sequence causes the printer to skip a line; you can use this command to separate several small printed ranges that fit on one page. To advance paper one line at a time, follow these steps:

1. Select **/Print Printer**.

2. Select Line for each line you want to advance.

If you want to advance to a new page after printing less than a full page, select **/Print Printer Page**. Whenever you issue this command, the printer skips to a new page. (Note that the following section shows how you can embed in the print range a page-break symbol that instructs 1-2-3 to advance automatically.)

Use /**P**rint **P**rinter **A**lign to align the paper perforation with the print head and to set (or reset) correct page breaks.

Whenever you begin a print job at the top of a page, always select **Align** before printing. To align the printer and set the beginning of a page, select /**P**rint **P**rinter **A**lign.

Setting Page Breaks within the Worksheet

As discussed in Chapter 5, insert page breaks in the worksheet with the /**W**orksheet **P**age command. Execute this command with the cell pointer at the first column of the range to print. The cell pointer should also be in the row that should begin the new page. The command automatically inserts a new blank row containing a page-break symbol (|::) in the cell at the cell pointer.

An alternative to using /**W**orksheet **P**age is to add page breaks to your document manually. To do this, insert a blank row into your worksheet where you want a page break. Then type a page-break symbol (|::) in a blank cell in the first column of the print range in that row. The contents of cells in any row marked by the page-break symbol do not print.

When you print the range containing the page-break symbol, 1-2-3 automatically advances the paper at that point. 1-2-3 then begins to print the data after the page-break symbol on a new page.

Note: Be careful when entering page breaks into the worksheet, either manually or with the /**W**orksheet **P**age command. You can accidentally delete the wrong row after you finish printing. Avoid accidents by typing the page-break symbol in the first column in the print range of a blank row. Check to be sure that the row is blank by using the End key and the arrow keys to scan across the row. Alternately, add a new row with /**W**orksheet **I**nsert **R**ow.

Adding Headers and Footers

If you prepare a report for distribution, you can add some simple enhancements. This section discusses how to add headers and footers to your reports. The following section covers changing the page layout.

1-2-3 reserves three lines in a document for a header and an additional three lines for a footer. If specified, headers and footers appear at the top and bottom of each page of your printout. You can keep the six lines reserved for these options (regardless of whether you use them). Or you can drop all six lines by selecting the /**Print Printer Options Other** Unformatted command, or modifying the Print Settings dialog box (illustrated later in this chapter).

The **H**eader and **F**ooter options are in the Print Settings dialog box. The header or footer can be up to 240 characters of text within one line of your printed output. You can also position the header and footer at the left, right, or center of the page. However, the size of both the paper and the printed characters limits the size of the header and footer lines. For example, when printing on 8 1/2-by-11-inch paper with 1/2-inch margins and 10-characters-per-inch type, you can print only 75 characters in the header and footer.

1-2-3 prints the header text on the first line after any blank top margin lines. 1-2-3 follows the header by two blank header lines for spacing. 1-2-3 prints the footer text line above any blank bottom margin lines and below two blank footer lines (for spacing).

You can manually enter all features of the text. However, 1-2-3 provides special characters for controlling page numbers, the current date, and the positioning of text within a header or footer. The following list shows the characters that you use to place page numbers and dates in headers, and to set the alignment of the header.

Character	Function
#	Automatically prints consecutive page numbers, starting with 1
@	Automatically prints the current date
|	Automatically separates text (absence of a | symbol left-justifies all text); the first | symbol centers the text that follows and the second | symbol right-justifies remaining text
\	When followed by a cell address or range name, left-aligns and fills the header or footer with the contents of the indicated cell

To add a header or footer, follow these steps:

1. Select /**Print Printer**.
2. Press [F2] or click the left mouse button in the dialog box to edit the settings.
3. Select **R**ange; type or highlight the desired print range and press [⏎Enter]. **Note:** To *highlight* the range, you must first press [F4] to clear the dialog box. For example, press [F4], highlight the range A1..E11, and press [⏎Enter].

287

4. Select **Header** or **Footer** in the dialog box. For example, select **Header** to add a header to the report.

5. In the text box, type the header text and codes for date and page number, and press ⏎Enter. For example, type @ | **NATIONAL MICRO** | # and press ⏎Enter.

@ | NATIONAL MICRO |

@ tells 1-2-3 to include the date in your header (or footer). Make sure that you set your computer to the correct date.

| tells 1-2-3 how to align the different items in the header (or footer) line.

tells 1-2-3 to print a page number.

6. To return to the main **Print** menu, press ⏎Enter again or click the left mouse button on OK.

7. Select **Align G**o **Page Q**uit.

8

The header appears at the top of the printed report.

```
13-Mar-92                    NATIONAL MICRO                              1

=========================================================================
REGIONAL INCOME REPORT        Qtr 1      Qtr 2      Qtr 3      Qtr 4
=========================================================================
Sales
  Northeast                 $30,336    $33,370    $36,707    $40,377
  Southeast                  20,572     22,629     24,892     27,381
  Central                   131,685    144,854    159,339    175,273
  Northwest                  94,473    103,920    114,312    125,744
  Southwest                 126,739    139,413    153,354    168,690
                           --------   --------   --------   --------
Total Sales                $403,805   $444,186   $488,604   $537,464
```

288

To add the same header by using the menu alone, select /**P**rint **P**rinter **O**ptions **H**eader, type the text, and press Enter. Return to the **P**rint menu by selecting **Q**uit, and then select **A**lign **G**o **P**age **Q**uit.

1-2-3, to a limited extent, can insert the contents of a cell into a header or footer. When the prompt to enter a header or footer appears, use the backslash character (\) followed by a cell address or existing range name. Your printed output contains that cell's contents in the header or footer. You cannot, however, use this capability effectively when you want to segment a header or footer into left, center, and right portions. Note the effect of using an address in the following header lines. Each entry would be typed in the Header text box.

Entry	*Result*
\A1	Prints the contents of cell A1 left-justified
|\A1	Prints the string \A1 (not the contents of cell A1) centered within the header
@|\A1	Prints the date left-justified and the string \A1 (not the contents of cell A1) centered
\A3..A6	Prints the contents of cell A3 only, not the range A3..A6
\SALES	Prints the contents of the range named SALES, if it exists; otherwise, prints nothing in the header

Whenever the print range exceeds one single page, 1-2-3 repeats the header on each succeeding page, and the page number increases by one. If you have used the special page-number character (#) and want to print your report a second time before you leave the main **P**rint menu, reset the page counter and set the top of the form by selecting **A**lign before you choose **G**o.

If the centered or right-justified text in your header or footer doesn't print, look at the right-margin setting (discussed in the next section). Make sure that the right margin is appropriate for the current type size and paper width. To change the header, repeat the sequence to establish the text, pressing Esc to remove the existing header from the control panel or dialog box. (You can delete a header or footer without removing other specified options.)

To print a footer on the last page of a report (or on a single-page report), you must use the **P**age command. If you select the **Q**uit command from the main **P**rint menu without issuing the **P**age command, this final footer does not print. You can, however, reissue the /**P**rint **P**rinter command and select **P**age. In this case, the footer prints.

8

289

Changing the Page Layout

Before you change the page layout defaults, be aware of the current settings.
1-2-3 initially assumes 8 1/2-by-11-inch paper, a printer output of 6 lines per
inch, and the default page length of 66 lines. 1-2-3 reserves 2 lines at the top
and bottom of each page for the top and bottom margins. Also, 1-2-3 automatically reserves 3 lines at the top and 3 lines at the bottom for headers and
footers. The header or footer takes 1 line, and 2 lines are for spacing before or
after the main text. Therefore, on a default page length of 66 lines, only 56
lines are available for other text.

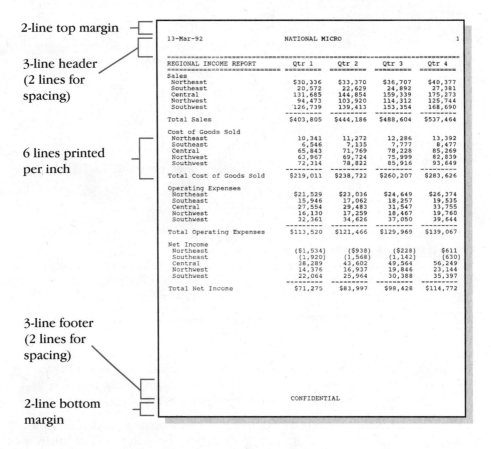

2-line top margin

3-line header
(2 lines for
spacing)

6 lines printed
per inch

3-line footer
(2 lines for
spacing)

2-line bottom
margin

13-Mar-92	NATIONAL MICRO			1
REGIONAL INCOME REPORT	Qtr 1	Qtr 2	Qtr 3	Qtr 4
Sales				
Northeast	$30,336	$33,370	$36,707	$40,377
Southeast	20,572	22,629	24,892	27,381
Central	131,685	144,854	159,339	175,273
Northwest	94,473	103,920	114,312	125,744
Southwest	126,739	139,413	153,354	168,690
Total Sales	$403,805	$444,186	$488,604	$537,464
Cost of Goods Sold				
Northeast	10,341	11,272	12,286	13,392
Southeast	6,546	7,135	7,777	8,477
Central	65,843	71,769	78,228	85,269
Northwest	63,967	69,724	75,999	82,839
Southwest	72,314	78,822	85,916	93,649
Total Cost of Goods Sold	$219,011	$238,722	$260,207	$283,626
Operating Expenses				
Northeast	$21,529	$23,036	$24,649	$26,374
Southeast	15,946	17,062	18,257	19,535
Central	27,554	29,483	31,547	33,755
Northwest	16,130	17,259	18,467	19,760
Southwest	32,361	34,626	37,050	39,644
Total Operating Expenses	$113,520	$121,466	$129,969	$139,067
Net Income				
Northeast	($1,534)	($938)	($228)	$611
Southeast	(1,920)	(1,568)	(1,142)	(630)
Central	38,289	43,602	49,564	56,249
Northwest	14,376	16,937	19,846	23,144
Southwest	22,064	25,964	30,388	35,397
Total Net Income	$71,275	$83,997	$98,428	$114,772

CONFIDENTIAL

If you want to check the default settings for margins and page length, select
/Worksheet Global Default Printer.

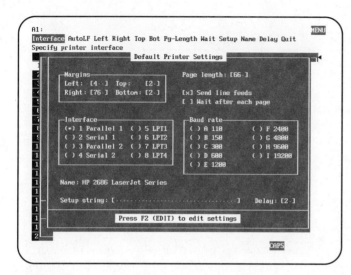

The Default
Printer Settings
dialog box
appears on-
screen, showing
the current
margins and page
length.

To change the page layout of the current worksheet, follow these steps:

1. Select /**Print Printer**.

2. Press F2 or click the left mouse button in the dialog box to edit the
    settings.

3. Select **Margins** in the Print Settings dialog box.

    The **Margins** option allows you to change the size of the margins in the
    printed report.

4. Select **Left**, **Right**, **Top**, or **Bottom**.

5. Type a value in the text box and press ↵Enter.

Be sure that you set left and right margins consistent with the width of your
paper and the printer's pitch (characters per inch). The right margin must be
greater than the left margin. And make sure that settings for the top and
bottom margins are consistent with the paper's length and the established
number of lines per inch. 1-2-3 shows the options in table 8.2 when you
change margin settings.

8

Table 8.2
Selections for Changing Margin Settings

Selection	Setting Range	Minimum Option
Left	0..240	0
Right	0..240	240
Top	0..32	0
Bottom	0..32	0

Note: In addition to the options in the dialog box, the /**Print Printer Options Margins None** command sets all options to the minimum amount.

To maximize the output on every printed page of a large worksheet, you can select Unformatted pages in the Print Settings dialog box. This option ignores margins, headers, and footers. This chapter later covers this command in the section "Preparing Output for Other Programs." You can also use setup strings that condense print and increase the number of lines per inch.

Printing a Listing of Cell Contents

You can spend hours developing and debugging a model worksheet and additional time entering and verifying data. You should safeguard your work by making backup copies of your important files on disk. You can also print a listing of the cell contents of important worksheets. Be aware, however, that this print job can eat up lots of time (and paper) if you have a large worksheet.

You can produce printed documentation of cell contents by selecting the List entries option in the Print Settings dialog box. Choosing List entries produces a list with one cell per line showing the Wysiwyg format, cell format, the width of the cell (if different from the default), the cell-protection status, and the contents of cells (including any formulas) in the print range. With List not checked, the data prints as it is on-screen.

To print a cell-by-cell listing of the contents of a particular range, follow these steps:

1. Select /**Print Printer**.

2. Press F2 or click the left mouse button in the dialog box to edit the settings.

3. Select the **List** entries option in the Print Settings dialog box. An x in the check box indicates that your output will show cell contents, one line at a time. An empty check box indicates that the range will print as it appears on-screen.

   In this example, select **List** entries.

4. Select **R**ange, type or highlight the range of cells you want printed, and then press ⏎Enter.

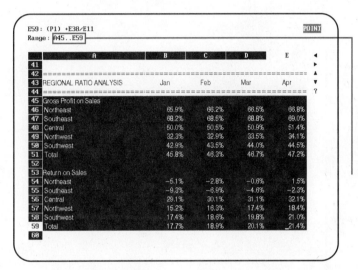

In this example, highlight the range A45..E59 as the range to print and press ⏎Enter.

5. Return to the main **P**rint menu by pressing ⏎Enter or clicking on OK.

6. Select **Align G**o **P**age **Q**uit.

1-2-3 lists each entry in the resulting printout in the following format.

Each entry begins with the location of the cell.

The entry ends with the actual contents of the cell, in this case a formula.

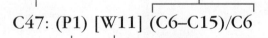

C47: (P1) [W11] (C6–C15)/C6

If the format of the cell is different from the default global format, 1-2-3 prints within parentheses a notation for the cell's format. For example, (P1) indicates that the cell was formatted (with a /**R**ange **F**ormat command) as **P**ercent with **1** decimal place.

If the column width of the cell is different from the default global column width, 1-2-3 indicates within square brackets the column width. For example, [W11] indicates that the column is set specifically to be 11 characters wide.

8

293

1-2-3 prints the contents of each cell, moving horizontally across each row of the print range.

```
A45: [W28] 'Gross Profit on Sales
A46: [W28] ' Northeast
B46: (P1) (B5-B14)/B5
C46: (P1) [W11] (C5-C14)/C5
D46: (P1) [W11] (D5-D14)/D5
E46: (P1) (E5-E14)/E5
A47: [W28] ' Southeast
B47: (P1) (B6-B15)/B6
C47: (P1) [W11] (C6-C15)/C6
D47: (P1) [W11] (D6-D15)/D6
E47: (P1) (E6-E15)/E6
A48: [W28] ' Central
B48: (P1) (B7-B16)/B7
C48: (P1) [W11] (C7-C16)/C7
D48: (P1) [W11] (D7-D16)/D7
E48: (P1) (E7-E16)/E7
A49: [W28] ' Northwest
B49: (P1) (B8-B17)/B8
C49: (P1) [W11] (C8-C17)/C8
D49: (P1) [W11] (D8-D17)/D8
E49: (P1) (E8-E17)/E8
A50: [W28] ' Southwest
B50: (P1) (B9-B18)/B9
C50: (P1) [W11] (C9-C18)/C9
D50: (P1) [W11] (D9-D18)/D9
E50: (P1) (E9-E18)/E9
A51: [W28] ' Total
B51: (P1) (B11-B20)/B11
C51: (P1) [W11] (C11-C20)/C11
D51: (P1) [W11] (D11-D20)/D11
E51: (P1) (E11-E20)/E11
A53: [W28] 'Return on Sales
A54: [W28] ' Northeast
B54: (P1) +B32/B5
C54: (P1) [W11] +C32/C5
D54: (P1) [W11] +D32/D5
E54: (P1) +E32/E5
A55: [W28] ' Southeast
B55: (P1) +B33/B6
C55: (P1) [W11] +C33/C6
D55: (P1) [W11] +D33/D6
E55: (P1) +E33/E6
A56: [W28] ' Central
B56: (P1) +B34/B7
C56: (P1) [W11] +C34/C7
D56: (P1) [W11] +D34/D7
E56: (P1) +E34/E7
A57: [W28] ' Northwest
B57: (P1) +B35/B8
C57: (P1) [W11] +C35/C8
D57: (P1) [W11] +D35/D8
E57: (P1) +E35/E8
A58: [W28] ' Southwest
B58: (P1) +B36/B9
C58: (P1) [W11] +C36/C9
D58: (P1) [W11] +D36/D9
```

If you unprotected the cell with the /**R**ange **U**nprot command, an uppercase U appears following the cell format. Cells that you protected with /**R**ange **P**rot do not have the U or any other character present in this location.

Clearing the Print Options

When you select **P**rint options, 1-2-3 automatically saves the settings you specify with the worksheet when you select /**F**ile **S**ave. Saving the settings with the worksheet for a future print job is a good practice, rather than clearing them after each printing. You can then quickly make minor changes to the existing settings.

At times, however, you would benefit by clearing all or some of the print settings. You can do this with the /**P**rint **P**rinter **C**lear command. For example, you may want to print a report in the same worksheet from which you printed earlier, but specify a different print range. You can use /**P**rint **P**rinter **C**lear **R**ange to eliminate only the range setting. All other print settings remain intact. The /**P**rint **P**rinter **C**lear **A**ll command can prove to be helpful when a report isn't printing properly.

To clear some or all print settings, follow these steps:

1. Select /**P**rint **P**rinter **C**lear.

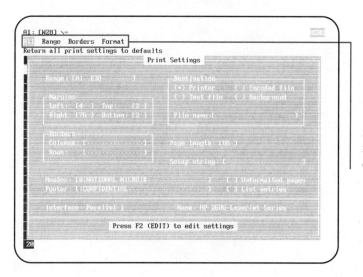

1-2-3 displays the menu selections for clearing print options.

2. Choose the desired option by selecting **A**ll, **R**ange, **B**orders, or **F**ormat. Table 8.3 describes each selection.

Table 8.3
Selections on the /Print Printer Clear Menu

Selection	Description
All	Clears every print option, including the print range.
Range	Removes only the previous print-range specification.
Borders	Cancels only columns and rows specified as borders.
Format	Returns **M**argins, **P**g-Length, and **S**etup string settings to the default settings displayed in the /**W**orksheet **G**lobal **D**efault **P**rinter screen.

Preparing Output for Other Programs

Many word processing and other software packages import ASCII text files. You can successfully export 1-2-3 files to other programs if you select several options in the Print Settings dialog box that eliminate unwanted print options. The primary option you use during this procedure is Unformatted pages. This section shows you how to use this command to create a PRN file that you can later import to another program.

To prepare output for other programs, follow these steps:

1. Select /**P**rint **F**ile to print to a disk rather than to a printer.
2. Specify a file name with up to eight characters to direct output to a PRN file rather than to a printer. Then press ⏎Enter.

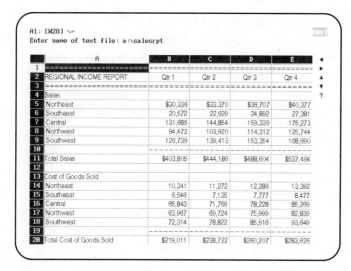

```
A1: [W28] \=
Enter name of text file: a:\salesrpt                          EDIT
```

	A	B	C	D	E
1	==================	====	=========	========	=======
2	REGIONAL INCOME REPORT	Qtr 1	Qtr 2	Qtr 3	Qtr 4
3	==================	====	=========	========	=======
4	Sales				
5	Northeast	$30,336	$33,370	$36,707	$40,377
6	Southeast	20,572	22,629	24,892	27,381
7	Central	131,685	144,854	159,339	175,273
8	Northwest	94,473	103,920	114,312	125,744
9	Southwest	126,739	139,413	153,354	168,690
10					
11	Total Sales	$403,805	$444,186	$488,604	$537,464
12					
13	Cost of Goods Sold				
14	Northeast	10,341	11,272	12,286	13,392
15	Southeast	6,546	7,135	7,777	8,477
16	Central	65,843	71,769	78,228	85,269
17	Northwest	63,967	69,724	75,999	82,839
18	Southwest	72,314	78,822	85,916	93,649
19					
20	Total Cost of Goods Sold	$219,011	$238,722	$260,207	$283,626

In this example, type **a:\salesrpt** and press ⏎Enter to direct the output to a PRN file named SALESRPT on drive A.

3. Press F2 or click the left mouse button in the dialog box to edit the settings.

4. Select **R**ange, specify the range you want to send to the PRN file, and press ⏎Enter.

   In this example, select **R**ange and press F4 to clear the dialog box. Then highlight the range A1..E11 and press ⏎Enter.

5. Select the Unformatted pages option.

   The **U**nformatted pages option removes all headers, footers, and page breaks from a print operation.

6. Return to the main **P**rint menu by pressing ⏎Enter or clicking on OK.

7. To create the PRN file on disk, select **G**o.

   Note: The **A**lign and **P**age commands are not necessary when you create a PRN file. You do not use printer paper for this command.

8. To return to READY mode, select **Q**uit.

9. Follow the instructions in your word processing or other software package to import the specially prepared 1-2-3 disk files.

8

Summary

This chapter showed you how to print reports by selecting the /Print command from 1-2-3's main menu. You can use the /Print **P**rinter command to print a report to a printer, or the /Print **F**ile *filename* or /Print **E**ncoded command to create a PRN or encoded file on disk that you or someone else can print later. Additionally, you can return to the worksheet while you print by using /Print **B**ackground.

You learned how to print a document of one page or less. You learned how to add borders to a multipage report and to hide worksheet segments within the print range. You also learned how to control paper movement with the **L**ine, **P**age, and **A**lign options. Additionally, you learned how to create page breaks within a worksheet.

The chapter showed ways to enhance printouts. You can add headers and footers that can include the date and a page number. You can also change the layout of a page by adjusting the margins and the page length.

Specifically, you learned the following key information about 1-2-3:

■ The /Print **P**rinter command allows you to print reports on a printer. The /Print **F**ile *filename* command allows you to "print" a range to a file that you can import to other software packages.

■ The /Print **E**ncoded command allows you to print a range to a file as well. However, the commands to control the printer are also in the file. You can later print this file from your operating system, and it will contain all your printing enhancements.

■ The /Print **B**ackground command allows you to do other work in 1-2-3 while printing your encoded worksheet. Before you select **B**ackground, you must first start the program BPRINT.

■ The Print Settings dialog box allows you to see and change your current print options on one screen. You can use the keyboard or mouse to select options.

■ The **B**orders option in the Print Settings dialog box enables you to print specified rows or columns on each page of a printed report.

■ When you are printing reports, you can hide specific rows, columns, or ranges. Hide columns by selecting /**W**orksheet **C**olumn **H**ide after you specify a print range. Hide rows by entering the symbol for nonprinting—two vertical bars (||)—in the first cell of the row. Hide ranges with the command /**R**ange **F**ormat **H**idden.

8

298

■ The /Print Printer Line command advances the paper one line in the printer. The /Print Printer Page command advances the paper to the top of the next page.

■ The /Print Printer Align command makes sure that printing begins at the top of all succeeding pages after the first. Before printing, always make sure that you have correctly positioned your printer paper.

■ If you want to add a header or footer, use the Header or Footer text box in the Print Settings dialog box. To add a page number, include a # in the header or footer. To add today's date, include @.

■ The Margins text box allows you to change the left, right, top, or bottom margin for your printout.

■ The List entries check box allows you to print a cell-by-cell listing of a specified range. The listing includes the Wysiwyg format, cell's location, format, width, protection status, and contents (including formulas). Unmarking the List entries check box tells 1-2-3 to print the cell contents as they appear on-screen.

■ The Unformatted pages check box allows extra lines to print on the page by dropping margins and page breaks from the printout.

■ The /Print Printer Clear command clears some or all of a worksheet's print settings. /Print Printer Clear Range clears only the specified print range. /Print Printer Clear All clears all settings, including the print range, borders, margins, and other settings.

8

The next chapter shows you how to use the Wysiwyg add-in program to enhance the appearance of your printed output. You learn how to incorporate different sizes and styles of typefaces, shading, outlining, grids, and much more.

Printing with Wysiwyg

9

Using Wysiwyg and 1-2-3 together

Selecting fonts

Using shading and lines

Sizing images

Formatting characters

Managing formats

How you present yourself and your work determines your ability to convince other people. To be successful, people keep fit, smile, and dress for success.

1-2-3 now offers an option to "dress up" your work. Lotus calls this option Wysiwyg, an acronym for "what-you-see-is-what-you-get." This add-in offers a spreadsheet publishing choice to users of 1-2-3 Release 2.3. In this environment, the screen reflects fancy formatting (for example, lines, shading, and fonts). Also, the worksheet prints exactly as it appears on-screen.

Wysiwyg enables you to produce printed 1-2-3 reports that incorporate a variety of type fonts, lines, shadings, and other formatting features, such as boldface, italics, underlining, and color. You also can change the appearance of text and graphics on the monitor for easier viewing and editing. Through menu choices, you can also quickly change between portrait and landscape modes for certain printers; add worksheet column and row indicators to your printout; add a grid; and compress a range so that it will automatically fit on one page.

In addition to enhanced text formatting, Wysiwyg enables you to embed 1-2-3 graphs in your printouts and use a graphics editor to embellish your graphs. Chapter 12 covers the graphing aspects of Wysiwyg.

Key Terms in This Chapter

Typeface   The design of a character set, such as Swiss or Dutch.

Font   A character set displaying a particular size and style of typeface, such as 12-point Swiss.

Point size   The size of a particular font. One point is equal to 1/72 of an inch; therefore, 12-point Swiss is about 1/6 of an inch high.

Soft fonts   Soft fonts are provided with Wysiwyg. These include various sizes and styles of Swiss, Dutch, Courier, and a symbol font set.

Wysiwyg   "What-you-see-is-what-you-get." This spreadsheet publishing add-in allows you to see on-screen graphical changes (fonts, outlining, bold) as you make them on the worksheet.

Using the Mouse

9

To use a mouse with 1-2-3 Release 2.3, you need a mouse, mouse software, and a graphics monitor and graphics card that support a mouse. You can use a mouse to select commands and files, specify ranges, move the cell pointer within the worksheet, and make selections in a dialog box. Refer to the following sections of the specified chapters for further information on using the mouse.

- Chapter 2—"Understanding Mouse Terminology"
- Chapter 3—"Mouse Control of the Cell Pointer"
            "Using Dialog Boxes"
            "Using the Mouse To Select Menu Commands"
- Chapter 4—"Using the Mouse To Specify Ranges"

Comparing Reports Printed with 1-2-3 and Wysiwyg

If you compare a worksheet printed with 1-2-3's /Print commands and one printed with Wysiwyg's :Print commands, you see a dramatic difference.

```
TERMS OF LOAN:

        First Payment Date           31-Jul-92
        Principal Borrowed           $10,000
        Term in Months               48
        Beginning Interest Rate      10.50%
        Payment                      $256.03

AMORTIZATION SCHEDULE


Payment   Payment    Current              Interest Principal Principal
Number    Date       Rate      Payment    Portion  Portion   Balance
      1   31-Jul-92  10.50%   $256.03     $87.50   $168.53   $9,831.47
      2   31-Aug-92  10.50%   $256.03     $86.03   $170.01   $9,661.46
      3   30-Sep-92  10.50%   $256.03     $84.54   $171.50   $9,489.96
      4   31-Oct-92  10.50%   $256.03     $83.04   $173.00   $9,316.97
      5   30-Nov-92  10.50%   $256.03     $81.52   $174.51   $9,142.45
      6   31-Dec-92  10.50%   $256.03     $80.00   $176.04   $8,966.42
      7   31-Jan-93  10.50%   $256.03     $78.46   $177.58   $8,788.84
      8   03-Mar-93  10.50%   $256.03     $76.90   $179.13   $8,609.71
      9   03-Apr-93  10.50%   $256.03     $75.33   $180.70   $8,429.01
     10   04-May-93  10.50%   $256.03     $73.75   $182.28   $8,246.73
     11   04-Jun-93  10.50%   $256.03     $72.16   $183.87   $8,062.85
     12   05-Jul-93  10.50%   $256.03     $70.55   $185.48   $7,877.37
     13   05-Aug-93  10.50%   $256.03     $68.93   $187.11   $7,690.26
     14   05-Sep-93  10.50%   $256.03     $67.29   $188.74   $7,501.52
     15   06-Oct-93  10.50%   $256.03     $65.64   $190.40   $7,311.12
     16   06-Nov-93  10.50%   $256.03     $63.97   $192.06   $7,119.06
     17   07-Dec-93  10.50%   $256.03     $62.29   $193.74   $6,925.32
     18   07-Jan-94  10.50%   $256.03     $60.60   $195.44   $6,729.88
     19   07-Feb-94  10.50%   $256.03     $58.89   $197.15   $6,532.74
     20   10-Mar-94  10.50%   $256.03     $57.16   $198.87   $6,333.86
     21   10-Apr-94  10.50%   $256.03     $55.42   $200.61   $6,133.25
```

1-2-3's /Print commands created this report.

9

Wysiwyg's **:Print** commands created this report.

TERMS OF LOAN:

First Payment Date	31 – Jul – 92
Principal Borrowed	$10,000
Term in Months	48
Beginning Interest Rate	10.50%
Payment	$256.03

AMORTIZATION SCHEDULE

Payment Number	Payment Date	Current Rate	Current Payment	Interest Portion	Principal Portion	Principal Balance
1	31 – Jul – 92	10.50%	$256.03	$87.50	$168.53	$9,831.47
2	31 – Aug – 92	10.50%	$256.03	$86.03	$170.01	$9,661.46
3	30 – Sep – 92	10.50%	$256.03	$84.54	$171.50	$9,489.96
4	31 – Oct – 92	10.50%	$256.03	$83.04	$173.00	$9,316.97
5	30 – Nov – 92	10.50%	$256.03	$81.52	$174.51	$9,142.45
6	31 – Dec – 92	10.50%	$256.03	$80.00	$176.04	$8,966.42
7	31 – Jan – 93	10.50%	$256.03	$78.46	$177.58	$8,788.84
8	03 – Mar – 93	10.50%	$256.03	$76.90	$179.13	$8,609.71
9	03 – Apr – 93	10.50%	$256.03	$75.33	$180.70	$8,429.01
10	04 – May – 93	10.50%	$256.03	$73.75	$182.28	$8,246.73
11	04 – Jun – 93	10.50%	$256.03	$72.16	$183.87	$8,062.85
12	05 – Jul – 93	10.50%	$256.03	$70.55	$185.48	$7,877.37
13	05 – Aug – 93	10.50%	$256.03	$68.93	$187.11	$7,690.26
14	05 – Sep – 93	10.50%	$256.03	$67.29	$188.74	$7,501.52
15	06 – Oct – 93	10.50%	$256.03	$65.64	$190.40	$7,311.12
16	06 – Nov – 93	10.50%	$256.03	$63.97	$192.06	$7,119.06
17	07 – Dec – 93	10.50%	$256.03	$62.29	$193.74	$6,925.32
18	07 – Jan – 94	10.50%	$256.03	$60.60	$195.44	$6,729.88
19	07 – Feb – 94	10.50%	$256.03	$58.89	$197.15	$6,532.74
20	10 – Mar – 94	10.50%	$256.03	$57.16	$198.87	$6,333.86
21	10 – Apr – 94	10.50%	$256.03	$55.42	$200.61	$6,133.25

9

Understanding How 1-2-3 and Wysiwyg Work Together

1-2-3 Release 2.3 integrates closely with Wysiwyg—much better than Allways integrates with Release 2.2. You do not need to switch between the graphical and the standard interface because there is now only one interface: the graphical. When you start Wysiwyg, the screen looks similar to the following figures. You can now move the cell pointer, make cell entries, bring up the menu with the slash key, and do many more things that are discussed later.

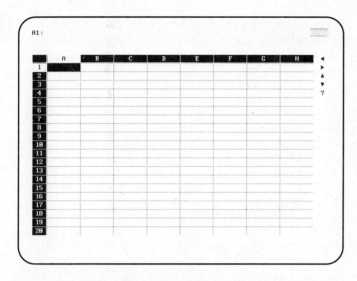

The worksheet screen is displayed here with Wysiwyg loaded.

In Wysiwyg, you have two menus available to you. As always, the slash key displays the standard 1-2-3 menu. The MENU mode indicator appears and, for color monitors, the default highlighted menu choice is blue. To display the Wysiwyg menu, press the colon (:).The WYSIWYG mode indicator appears and, for color monitors, the highlighted menu choice is magenta. Use Esc to back out of any displayed menu.

9

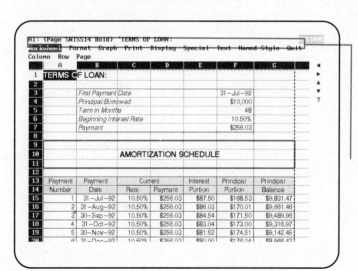

The Wysiwyg menu is displayed here.

Another way to display the menus is with the mouse. A menu automatically appears when you place the mouse pointer in the control panel. The menu that displays depends on which menu you used last; to switch to the other menu, press the right mouse button. The right mouse button switches you back and forth between the two menus.

Wysiwyg menus work the same way as 1-2-3 menus: select a command by typing the first letter, clicking on the command with the left mouse button, or highlighting the command and pressing Enter. Wysiwyg options are explained throughout this chapter.

Saving Your Wysiwyg Formatting

Wysiwyg stores the enhanced formatting information in its own file, separate from the worksheet file. The Wysiwyg file has the same first name as your 1-2-3 file, but with an FMT extension. For example, if you save a worksheet file called BUDGET.WK1 with Wysiwyg attached, Wysiwyg saves an associated BUDGET.FMT file. This file contains all the formatting enhancements selected with Wysiwyg.

Wysiwyg saves enhanced formatting only when you use the 1-2-3 /**F**ile **S**ave command to save the current 1-2-3 worksheet. If you choose Alt-F10 (or /**A**dd-In) **D**etach, you erase Wysiwyg from memory and therefore can no longer save enhanced formatting. If you detach Wysiwyg before you save the worksheet, the program does not update your FMT file and you may lose much of your special formatting. To review the procedures for starting Wysiwyg automatically or manually, see Chapter 2.

Do not modify the structure of a Wysiwyg-formatted worksheet without attaching Wysiwyg. If you delete, insert, or move anything, the formatting will not match the same cells the next time you attach Wysiwyg.

Learning To Format with Wysiwyg

The heart of Wysiwyg's power is its capability to add professional formatting touches. The 1-2-3 formats—numeric display and label alignment—carry through automatically to Wysiwyg. Wysiwyg's formats determine the printed typeface, character size, boldface, and other stylistic features, such as lines and shading.

Wysiwyg's additional formats provide many ways to enhance the appearance of printed text. To assign a Wysiwyg format to a cell or range, use the Wysiwyg **:F**ormat command. To determine the format of a cell, move the cell pointer to the cell. The format displays at the top of the screen, next to the current cell address. If you use Wysiwyg in graphics mode (the default), you actually see the formatting on the screen.

Selecting from a Variety of Fonts

One of the highlights of Wysiwyg is its capability to use different fonts. A *font* consists of a typeface (for example, Times Roman) and a point size. A *point* is a unit of measurement used in publishing, equal to 1/72 of an inch. The larger the point size, the larger the type. Your choice of fonts depends on your printer; Wysiwyg can use any font your printer can print.

Wysiwyg comes with four soft fonts: Swiss, Dutch, Courier, and XSymbol. A *soft font* is a file on disk that specifies to a printer how to make a font. Your program sends soft fonts to the printer's memory before it prints the document, so that the printer can use the information to print the document. If you have a dot-matrix printer, Wysiwyg uses its graphics mode to produce these fonts. If you have a laser printer, Wysiwyg downloads these four fonts automatically to your printer when you use them. Your printer, however, may not have enough memory for many different fonts or larger point sizes.

If your printer provides additional fonts, these fonts also are available to Wysiwyg. The HP LaserJet comes with two built-in fonts (Courier and Line Printer), and you can purchase dozens of cartridges to access additional fonts.

Each worksheet can use up to eight different fonts. Wysiwyg stores these eight fonts in a *font set*. The default fonts are Swiss, Dutch, and XSymbol. If you want to change the sizes of these fonts or change to Courier, you can replace any of the default fonts.

With Wysiwyg, you can format each cell or range of cells with a different font, and you can use up to eight fonts for a single worksheet. By default, however, Wysiwyg assigns all cells to font 1.

9

Examples of Wysiwyg's default fonts are shown here.

FONT	WYSIWYG DEFAULT FONT SET
1	Bitstream Swiss 12 Point
2	Bitstream Swiss 14 Point
3	Bitstream Swiss 24 Point
4	Bitstream Dutch 6 point
5	Bitstream Dutch 8 point
6	Bitstream Dutch 10 point
7	Bitstream Dutch 12 point
8	➡ ➤ ➢ ➣ ➡ ➡ ▸ ➡ ⇨ ⇦ ⇨ ⇨ ⇨ ⇨ ⇨ ⤵ ⤴ ↖ ↗ ↙ ↘ ↖

Changing the Font for a Range of the Worksheet

You assign a font to a cell or range with the Wysiwyg **:**Format **F**ont command. To perform this procedure, follow these steps:

1. Select **:**Format.

The Wysiwyg Format menu is displayed.

```
A1: (SWISS14 Bold) 'TERMS OF LOAN:
Font  Bold  Italics  Underline  Color  Lines  Shade  Reset  Quit
1 2  3 4  5 6  7 8  Replace  Default  Library
     A         B            C        D        E        F         G        H
 1  TERMS OF LOAN:
 2
 3           First Payment Date                       31-Jul-92
 4           Principal Borrowed                       $10,000
 5           Term in Months                                48
 6           Beginning Interest Rate                   10.50%
 7           Payment                                  $256.03
 8
 9
10                     AMORTIZATION SCHEDULE
11
12
13  Payment  Payment       Current         Interest  Principal  Principal
14  Number   Date      Rate    Payment      Portion   Portion    Balance
15      1    31-Jul-92  10.50%  $256.03      $87.50    $168.53   $9,831.47
16      2    31-Aug-92  10.50%  $256.03      $86.03    $170.01   $9,661.46
17      3    30-Sep-92  10.50%  $256.03      $84.54    $171.50   $9,489.96
18      4    31-Oct-92  10.50%  $256.03      $83.04    $173.00   $9,316.97
19      5    30-Nov-92  10.50%  $256.03      $81.52    $174.51   $9,142.45
20      6    31-Dec-92  10.50%  $256.03      $90.00    $176.04   $8,966.42
```

2. Select **F**ont.

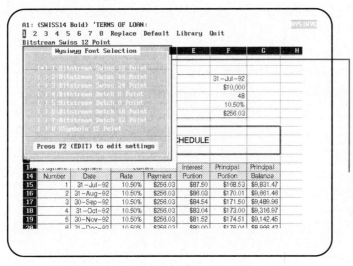

The **Font** menu lists the eight default fonts by typeface and point size.

3. Type the number of the font desired or use the dialog box to choose the desired font.

4. Indicate the range where you want the font by highlighting the range (as you would in 1-2-3); then press ↵Enter.

If necessary, Wysiwyg adjusts the height of the row to conform to the tallest point size present.

9

Choosing Alternative Fonts for the Entire Worksheet

If you want to replace all occurrences of one font with another, regardless of where they occur in the worksheet, use the command sequence **:Format Font Replace**. This command lists the fonts from which you can choose.

To change one font used throughout the worksheet to a different one, follow these steps:

1. Select **:Format Font Replace.**
2. Type the number of the font to change and press ⏎Enter
3. Select the new typeface from the following menu:
   Swiss Dutch Courier XSymbol Other
4. Type the new point size and press ⏎Enter.
5. Select **Quit** twice to return to READY mode.

Two factors determine the available typeface and point sizes. First, typeface and point size depend on which fonts you generated when you installed 1-2-3. Second, they depend on which fonts your printer supports (including soft fonts and cartridges). If you select a font that your printer cannot use, Wysiwyg substitutes a similar typeface.

This range of fonts includes point sizes from 3 to 72, font cartridges, and downloadable fonts.

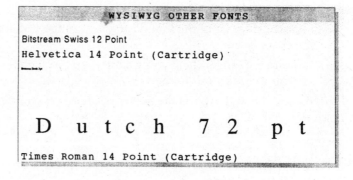

The XSymbol font contains *dingbats*, special characters such as arrows and circled numbers. For example, if you enter a lowercase *a* in a cell and format it to XSymbol font, the screen displays a right arrow.

XSymbol Font Characters					
@CHAR Code	Alphanumeric Typeface	Xsymbol Typeface	@CHAR Code	Alphanumeric Typeface	Xsymbol Typeface
33	!	❡	80	P	❼
34	"	❢	81	Q	❽
35	#	❣	82	R	❾
36	$	❤	83	S	❿
37	%	❥	84	T	➔
38	&	❦	85	U	→
39	'	❧	86	V	↔
40	(	♣	87	W	↕
41	)	♦	88	X	➘
42	*	♥	89	Y	➙
43	+	♠	90	Z	➚
44	,	①	91	[	➛
45	–	②	92	\	➜
46	.	③	93	]	➝
47	/	④	94	^	➞
48	0	⑤	95	_	➟
49	1	⑥	96	`	➠
50	2	⑦	97	a	➡
51	3	⑧	98	b	➢
52	4	⑨	99	c	➣
53	5	⑩	100	d	➤
54	6	❶	101	e	➥
55	7	❷	102	f	➦
56	8	❸	103	g	➧
57	9	❹	104	h	➨
58	:	❺	105	i	➩
59	;	❻	106	j	➪
60	<	❼	107	k	➫
61	=	❽	108	l	➬
62	>	❾	109	m	➭
63	?	❿	110	n	➮
64	@	①	111	o	➯
65	A	②	112	p	
66	B	③	113	q	➱
67	C	④	114	r	➲
68	D	⑤	115	s	➳
69	E	⑥	116	t	➴
70	F	⑦	117	u	➵
71	G	⑧	118	v	➶
72	H	⑨	119	w	➷
73	I	⑩	120	x	➸
74	J	❶	121	y	➹
75	K	❷	122	z	➺
76	L	❸	123	{	➻
77	M	❹	124	|	➼
78	N	❺	125	}	➽
79	O	❻	126	~	➾

Letters and numbers, as well as characters (dingbats) formatted with the XSymbol font are shown here.

9

All cells automatically display font 1. Thus, when you replace font 1 with a different font, all cells not assigned to other font numbers change to the new font.

After experimenting with Wysiwyg, you may decide that a particular group of fonts is the one you normally want to use. Wysiwyg lets you store font selections in a file so that you can access those fonts later.

To store a set of fonts in a file, follow these steps:

1. Select **:Format Font Library Save**.
2. Type the name of the file and press ⏎Enter. Wysiwyg saves your file with an AFS extension.

To recall these groups of fonts, use the **:Format Font Library Retrieve** command.

If you find that you frequently retrieve the same font library, make it the default font set. To do this, retrieve the font library you want as the default and select **:Format Font Default Update**.

Using Shading

The **:Format Shade** command enables you to highlight important areas on the printed worksheet. The net income row and heading in the following figure stand out because of the background shading.

Headings and important values are emphasized with light and dark shades.

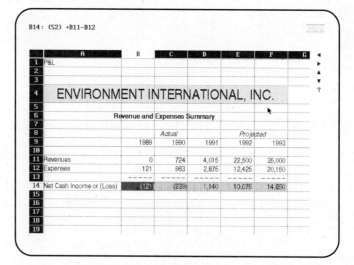

312

Using Light and Dark Shading

If you use light or dark shading on cells with data, the contents will remain visible through the shading. To shade a range with light or dark shading, use the **:Format Shade Light** or **:Format Shade Dark** command.

To highlight or accent portions of a worksheet with light or dark shading, follow these steps:

1. Select **:Format Shade**.

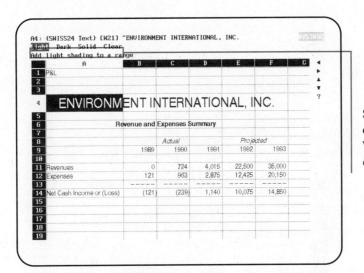

Shading options offered in Wysiwyg are displayed.

2. If you want light shading, select **Light**. If you want dark shading, select **Dark**.

3. Highlight the range you want to shade and press ⏎Enter.

9

In this example,
highlight the
range A4..F4 and
press ⏎Enter).

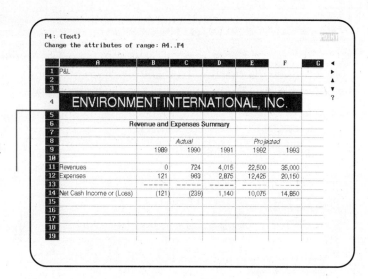

9

The shading
appears
on-screen.

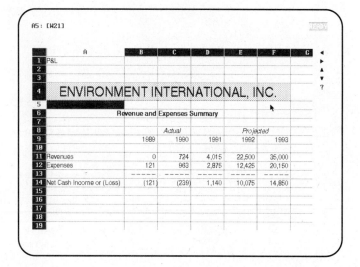

Using Solid Shading

Use the Solid shade only on blank cells to create solid lines. You cannot see
the cell contents if you assign Solid to cells containing data. When you want to
create a thick, dark line, select **:Format Shade Solid**. Then use **:Worksheet
Row Set-Height** to shrink the height of the row to the desired line thickness.

314

To add solid shading, follow these steps:

1. Select **:Format Shade Solid**.

2. Highlight the range you want to shade and press ⏎Enter.

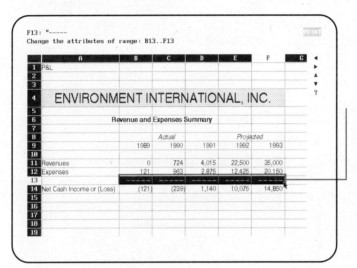

In this example, highlight the range B13..F13 and press ⏎Enter.

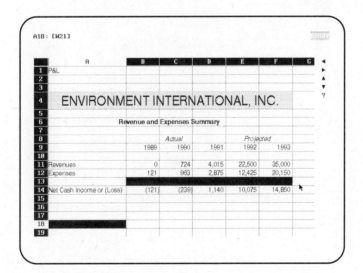

The result of solid shading is shown on-screen.

9

To change the height of the row where solid shading occurs, follow these steps:

1. Select **:Worksheet Row Set-Height**.

2. At the prompt `Select the rows to set height to:` highlight one cell from each row to change height.

3. At the prompt `Enter new row height in points (1..255):` use ↑ to shorten the height of the row and see this change displayed on-screen.

4. Press ↵Enter to accept the height.

In this example, press ↑ until the control panel displays 2; then press ↵Enter.

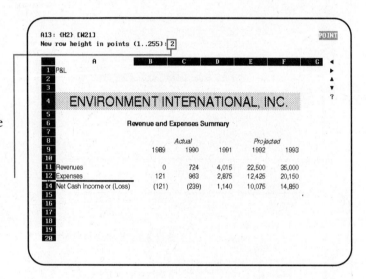

9

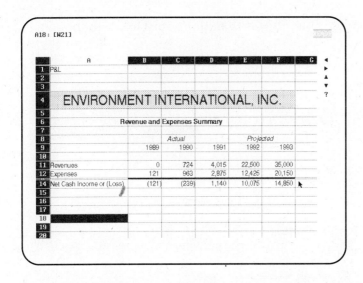

The row height in this example is 2 points (the default is 14).

To change the height of a row using a mouse, follow these steps:

1. Move the tip of the mouse arrow to the line below the row indicator in the worksheet frame.

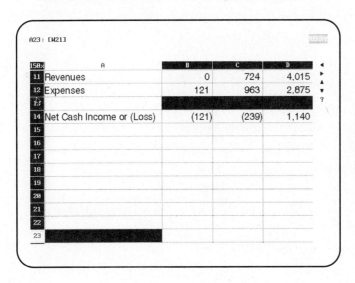

In this zoomed example, point to the line between rows 12 and 13.

9

317

2. Click the left mouse button and drag the horizontal line up or down.

Move the mouse pointer up to decrease the row height in this zoomed display.

```
A23: [W21]                                              READY
┌─────────────────────────────────────────────────────────────┐
│150%          A              B        C        D        ◄
│ 11 Revenues                 0       724      4,015     ►  ▲
│ 12 Expenses               121       963      2,875     ▼
│ 13                                                     ?
│ 14 Net Cash Income or (Loss)   (121)   (239)   1,140
│ 15
│ 16
```

3. Release the left mouse button.

The changed row height is shown with a zoomed display.

```
A14: [W21] 'Net Cash Income or (Loss)                   READY
┌─────────────────────────────────────────────────────────────┐
│150%          A            · B ·       C        D        ◄
│ 11 Revenues                 0       724      4,015     ►  ▲
│ 12 Expenses               121       963      2,875     ▼
│ 13                                                     ?
│ 14 Net Cash Income or (Loss) ↖ (121)   (239)   1,140
│ 15
│ 16
│ 17
```

Removing Existing Shading

You remove existing shading by using the command **:Format Shade Clear** and indicating the desired range.

To remove existing shading, follow these steps:

1. Select **:Format Shade Clear**.
2. Highlight the range from which you want to remove shading and press ⏎Enter).

318

Using Underlining and Boldface

You can use Wysiwyg to add underlining and boldface to cell entries. The
:Format **U**nderline and **:F**ormat **B**old commands, discussed in the sections
that follow, are useful for emphasizing important areas of the worksheet and
increasing the visual impact of printed reports.

Using Underlining

Three styles of underlining are available in Wysiwyg: single, double, and wide.
Wysiwyg's underlining capability is superior to the limited underlining available in 1-2-3, which merely repeats the minus sign or equal sign in a separate
cell. Wysiwyg gives you the kind of solid underlining you can create on paper
with a pencil and ruler. Underlining will display in the control panel—{U1},
for example—but not in the cell if there is no data in that cell.

To underline a range, follow these steps:

1. Select **:F**ormat **U**nderline.

2. Select **S**ingle, **D**ouble, or **W**ide.

3. Highlight or type the range(s) to underline and press ⏎Enter.

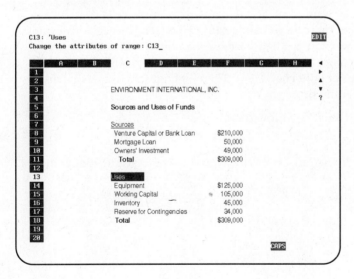

In this example,
type **C7, C13,
F11, F18** and
press ⏎Enter.
As you type each
comma, Wysiwyg
underlines the
cell and allows
you to indicate
another cell or
range.

The result
of single
underlining is
shown on-screen.

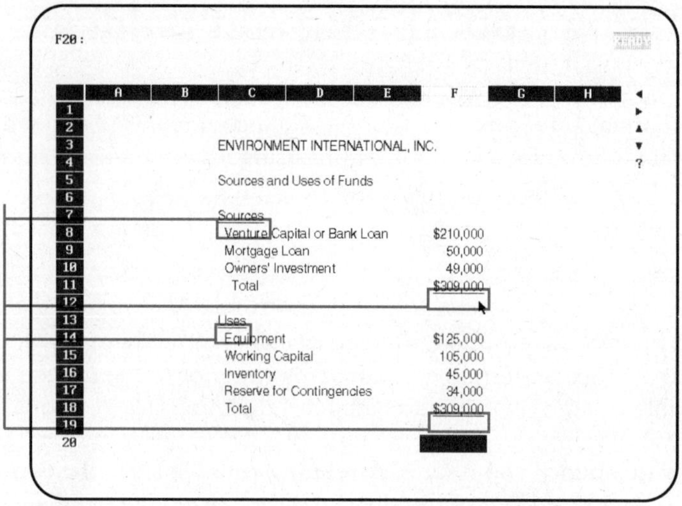

To remove existing underlining, use the command **:Format Underline Clear**.

Using Boldface

For emphasis, you may want to make the contents of some cells darker than other cells. With Wysiwyg, you can choose any cell or range of cells you want to appear darker. When you use light or dark shading in cells with data, you can see the contents more clearly if the characters are bold. Use the **:Format Bold** command to select bold characters. Then highlight the range of cells to appear in bold type at the prompt.

To create boldface characters, follow these steps:

1. Select **:Format Bold Set**.
2. Highlight or type the range(s) where you want boldface to appear and press ⏎Enter.

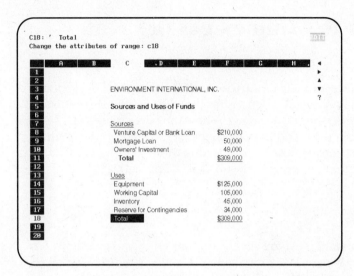

In this example, select cell C5, type a comma, select C11, type a comma, select C18, and press

↵Enter.

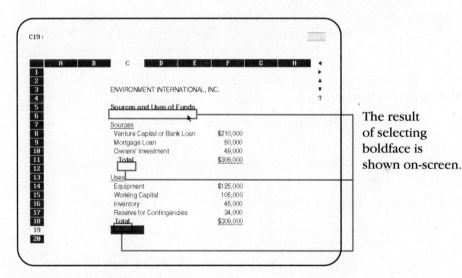

The result of selecting boldface is shown on-screen.

To remove existing boldface, use the command **:Format Bold Clear** and specify the range for which you want to remove boldface.

Using Lines To Outline Cells or Create Grid Lines

With Wysiwyg, you have a variety of ways to use lines to enclose or separate parts of the worksheet. Access the options for outlining particular cells with the **:Format Lines** command. If you want to show the boundaries of all cells in the worksheet, you can print grid lines by choosing the Grid option on the Wysiwyg Print Settings dialog box (or by selecting **:Print Settings Grid**). If you want grid lines displayed on-screen, select **:Display Options Grid Yes**.

Outlining Cells

When you select **:Format Lines**, you see the options **Outline, Left, Right, Top, Bottom, All, Double, Wide, Clear,** and **Shadow.** Usually, you surround all cells in a given range by selecting All or draw lines around the perimeter of a range by choosing Outline. To create a three-dimensional appearance, choose Shadow. If you want to put a single cell in a box, you can use either **:Format Lines Outline** or **:Format Lines All**. A shaded range will be more clearly defined if you surround it by using **:Format Lines Outline**. Remove existing lines with **:Format Lines Clear**. The control panel prompts you for the kinds of lines you want cleared.

To draw lines on all sides of the cells in a range, follow these steps:

1. Select **:Format Lines All**.
2. Highlight the range of cells where you want to show lines around each cell, and then press ⏎Enter.

To draw lines on the perimeter (outline) of the cells in a range, follow these steps:

1. Select **:Format Lines Outline**.
2. Highlight the range of cells to outline, and then press ⏎Enter.

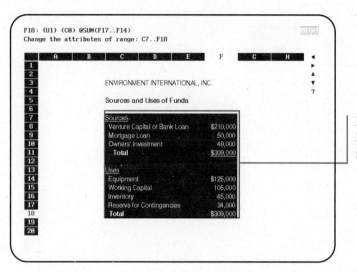

In this example, highlight the range C7..F18.

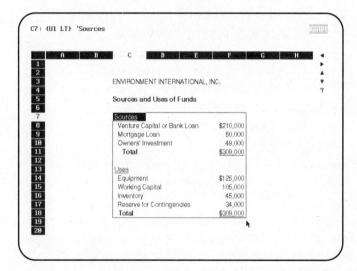

The information is outlined in a block.

9

To draw a shadow around a range and create a three-dimensional appearance, follow these steps:

1. Select **:Format Lines Shadow Set**.

2. Highlight the range of cells to shadow, and then press ⏎Enter.

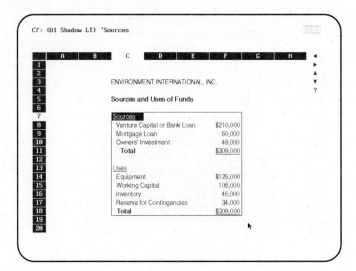

The result of
selecting Shadow
appears
on-screen.

To clear the shadow, use the **:Format Lines Shadow Clear** command and
specify the range from which you want to remove the shadow.

Creating Grid Lines

You can surround every cell in the worksheet with lines if you select **:Format
Lines All** and highlight all cells. Although this process displays cell boundaries
clearly, the result can appear cluttered.

You can display grid lines on-screen by using the **:Display Options Grid Yes**
command. This command, however, will not print the grid lines.

To print cell boundaries without letting the lines dominate the text, select
:Print and then select the **Grid** check box in the Wysiwyg Print Settings dialog
box or select **:Print Settings Grid**. This command draws lightly-dotted lines for
all column and row separations. You cannot use grid lines for a selected range
of cells; the **Grid** option affects the entire worksheet.

To create grid lines throughout the worksheet, follow these steps:

1. Select **:Print**. The Wysiwyg Print Settings dialog box appears.
2. Select **Settings Grid**; or access the dialog box by pressing (F2), and
   then select **Settings Grid**.

324

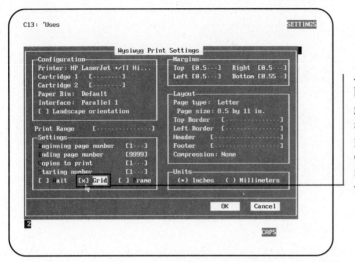

An x in the check box indicates that grid lines will appear in your printed report; an empty box indicates otherwise.

Grid lines surround all cells in the worksheet, including labels that cross cell boundaries and graphs added to the worksheet.

Changing the Size of the Image On-Screen

By shrinking the display of your worksheet on-screen, you get a larger view of your worksheet and can see more cells. By magnifying the display, you can see the image more clearly. This is helpful if you have eye problems or if you are showing your display to a group of people. Using the :Display Zoom command, you can shrink the image on-screen so that characters are as small as 25 percent of their usual size, or you can magnify images so that characters expand up to 400 percent of normal size. The :Display Zoom command has no effect on printed output.

To change the size of the image on-screen, follow these steps:

1. Select :Display Zoom.

2. Select the size you want from among the following options:

   Tiny Small Normal Large Huge Manual

   If you select the Manual option, type a number from 25 to 400 (1/4 normal size up to 4 times normal size).

3. Select Quit to return to a modified screen size.

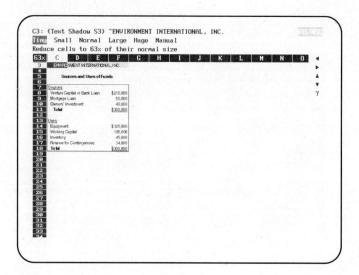

The **T**iny option displays the image on-screen at 63% of normal size.

9

The **H**uge option displays the image on-screen at 150% of normal size.

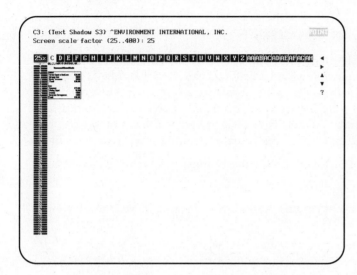

The Manual option lets you choose the size of the on-screen image from 25%…

…to 400% of normal size.

327

Formatting Sequences

The options on the **:Format** menu enable you to format cells and ranges. To format individual characters within a cell, you can use *formatting sequences*. Using these sequences, you can bold or italicize a single word in a cell, for example. Formatting sequences are codes you enter as you are entering or editing text in the control panel. The codes appear in the control panel, but Wysiwyg replaces the codes with the actual formatting when you press Enter.

To format a word within a cell, follow these steps:

1. Press F2 to change to EDIT mode.

2. Press Ctrl A (for attribute). A solid triangle appears within the control panel.

3. Type the one- or two-character code for the attribute. Table 9.1 lists these codes. Be sure to type the correct upper- or lowercase characters.

4. To end the formatting sequence, press Ctrl N at the end of the word. An upside-down solid triangle appears within the control panel.

Table 9.1
Character Codes for Attributes

Code	Description	Code	Description
b	Bold	5c	Cyan
i	Italic	6c	Yellow
u	Superscript	7c	Magenta
d	Subscript	8c	Reverse colors
o	Outline	1F	Font 1
f	Flashing	2F	Font 2
x	Flip x-axis	3F	Font 3
y	Flip y-axis	4F	Font 4
1c	Default color	5F	Font 5
2c	Red	6F	Font 6
3c	Green	7F	Font 7
4c	Dark blue	8F	Font 8

9

Code	Description	Code	Description
1_	Single underline	4_	Box around characters
2_	Double underline	5_	Strike-through characters
3_	Wide underline		

To specify multiple attributes, press Ctrl-A and the first attribute code, followed by Ctrl-A and the second code. For example, to bold and italicize a word, press Ctrl-A and type **b**, and then press Ctrl-A and type **i**. If you just want to cancel one of the attributes, press Ctrl-E followed by the attribute code you want to end (for example, **i** for italic). To end all formatting sequences, press Ctrl-N.

Managing Your Formats

Because formatting is the heart of Wysiwyg, the program offers several commands for dealing with the formats assigned to your cells. You can copy and move formats—not the cell contents, but the formats associated with the cell. You can assign a name to the set of formatting instructions in a cell, and then apply this format to any range. You can save *all* the formats associated with the file and then apply this format to another file.

Copying Formats

If you want to format one cell or range with the same highlighting features as another formatted cell or range, you can use the **:S**pecial Copy command to copy the formatting instructions. For example, if you have formatted a range as 14-point Swiss, in boldface with shading and an outline, you can save a lot of time by copying the format to another range rather than using four separate **:F**ormat commands. The command copies formats only, not cell contents. 1-2-3's /Copy command copies cell contents *and* formats (with Wysiwyg attached). **:S**pecial Copy copies the following formats: font, boldface, italics, underline, shade, color, and lines.

9

329

To copy a format from one range to another range of cells, follow these steps:

1. Select **:S**pecial **C**opy.
2. Highlight the range of cells you want to copy *from* and press ⏎Enter.
3. Highlight the range of cells you want to copy *to* and press ⏎Enter.

Using Named-Styles

Another way to apply a format from one cell to another is by creating and using named-styles. You should create named-styles for the formats you use frequently. Suppose, for example, that your worksheet contains 10 subheadings and you want them to be in 14-point Swiss bold with a heavy shade. To ease formatting and ensure consistency, you can name this particular formatting style HEAD and then apply this style to all headings.

Another advantage to using named-styles is that you can make format changes rapidly. If you decide that you want your headings to have a light shade instead of a heavy one, you need to change the format of only one cell.

To define a style, format a cell with the desired attributes and then follow these steps:

1. Select **:N**amed-Style **D**efine.
2. Choose any number from 1 to 8.

Type **1** to choose the first style to define.

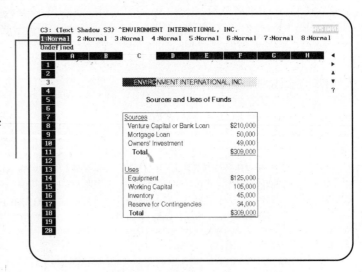

3. Highlight the cell you want as the defined style, and then press
   ⏎Enter.

4. Press ◂Backspace to remove the existing style name (if any).

5. Type the name of the style and press ⏎Enter.

6. Type a description for the style and press ⏎Enter.

   The description appears on the third line of the display panel when
   you select the named-style.

To apply a format style to a cell or range, follow these steps:

1. Select :**N**amed-Style.

2. Choose the style you want from the resulting menu.

3. Highlight the range of cells to receive the style, and then press ⏎Enter.

Typing Long Text in Wysiwyg

Many people use 1-2-3 to type short letters and memos. Traditionally, typing
and editing in a spreadsheet was much more cumbersome than typing in a
word processor—until Wysiwyg came along. You can now type directly into
the worksheet, and Wysiwyg automatically word-wraps when you get to the
end of the line. You can position the cursor on any character in the text range,
and edit the characters—insert, delete, overtype, or format them.

In addition to typing letters and memos, you can use :**T**ext **E**dit to type a
paragraph or two of descriptive information about the purpose of a
worksheet.

Typing or Correcting Text

You can use the :**T**ext **E**dit command to modify existing worksheet labels or to
type new text. When you select :**T**ext **E**dit, the control panel prompts you for a
text range. Be sure to include the complete width and length of the range you
want to edit. If you want to insert text, you need to include blank rows or
columns in your text range. Otherwise, you see the error message `Text input
range full`. If this happens, press Esc to return to READY mode. Then
redefine your text range.

9

331

To define a range to accept text, follow these steps:

1. Select :Text Edit.

2. Highlight the range of cells to receive text, and then press ⏎Enter.

In this example, highlight the range H4..J19 and press ⏎Enter.

```
J19:                                                              EDIT
Select text range: H4..J19

          C      D        E        F        G      H      I      J      ◄
     3   ENVIRONMENT INTERNATIONAL, INC.                                ►
     4                                                                  ▲
     5         Sources and Uses of Funds                                ▼
     6                                                                  ?
     7   Sources
     8   Venture Capital or Bank Loan    $210,000
     9   Mortgage Loan                     50,000
    10   Owners' Investment                49,000
    11      Total                        $309,000
    12
    13   Uses
    14   Equipment                      $125,000
    15   Working Capital                 105,000
    16   Inventory                        45,000
    17   Reserve for Contingencies        34,000
    18      Total                       $309,000
    19
    20
    21
    22
```

9

Several important changes occur when you are in the text editor. First, the cell pointer disappears and becomes a small vertical-line cursor. The arrow keys move the cursor within the defined text range. Second, the mode indicator displays TEXT. Third, once you start typing or moving the cursor, the control panel displays the following information: the cell with the current line of text, the cursor's row and column number position, and the line's alignment (left-aligned, centered, and so forth). The row number corresponds to the row in the defined text range, not the actual worksheet row. For example, if row 4 of the worksheet is the first row in the current text range, the row number is 1. The column number refers to the number of characters from the beginning of the line.

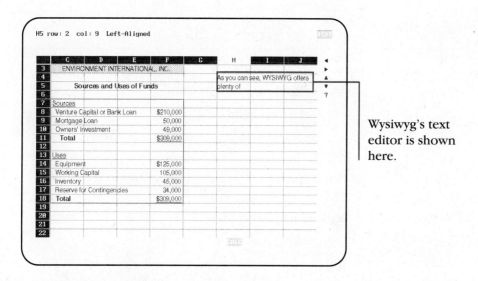

H5 row: 2 col: 9 Left-Aligned

	C	D	E	F	G	H	I	J
3	ENVIRONMENT INTERNATIONAL, INC.							
4						As you can see, WYSIWYG offers		
5	Sources and Uses of Funds					plenty of		
6								
7	Sources							
8	Venture Capital or Bank Loan			$210,000				
9	Mortgage Loan			50,000				
10	Owners' Investment			49,000				
11	Total			$309,000				
12								
13	Uses							
14	Equipment			$125,000				
15	Working Capital			105,000				
16	Inventory			45,000				
17	Reserve for Contingencies			34,000				
18	Total			$309,000				
19								
20								
21								
22								

Wysiwyg's text editor is shown here.

As you type new text, the words automatically wrap to the next line. When you want to start a new paragraph, you have three choices, depending on how you want the text to look:

- Press ⏎Enter twice, leaving a blank line between paragraphs.
- Press ⏎Enter once, and press the space bar one or more times at the beginning of the paragraph.
- Press Ctrl⏎Enter to insert a paragraph symbol.

Table 9.2 lists the cursor movement and editing keys you can use in **:Text Edit**. Many of these keys are similar to the ones you use in 1-2-3's EDIT mode.

9

Table 9.2
:Text Edit Cursor Movements and Editing Keys

Key	Description
Ctrl ←	Beginning of the previous word
Ctrl →	End of the next word
PgDn	Next screen or end of text range if it all fits on one screen
PgUp	Previous screen or beginning of text range if it all fits on one screen
Home	Beginning of line
Home Home	Beginning of paragraph
End	End of line
End End	End of paragraph
←Backspace	Deletes character to the left of the cursor
Del	Deletes character to the right of the cursor
Ins	Toggles between insert mode (the default) and overtype mode (OVR status indicator appears)
←Enter	Begins a new line
Ctrl ←Enter	Begins a new paragraph
F3	Displays a format menu
Esc	Returns to READY mode

When you finish typing and editing the text, press Esc to exit the text editor. In READY mode, you can see that Wysiwyg entered each line of text into cells in the first column of the text range.

Formatting Characters

Earlier in this chapter, you learned how to use formatting sequences to assign attributes to individual characters in a cell. (Press Ctrl-A and a code, and then

9

334

press Ctrl-N to end the attribute.) The text editor offers an easier way to format characters—with the F3 key. You don't need to remember codes because pressing F3 displays a menu.

To add formatting attributes with :Text Edit, follow these steps:

1. Select :Text Edit.

2. Highlight the range of cells to modify, and then press ⏎Enter. Be sure to include the entire width of the long labels, not just the column you type them into.

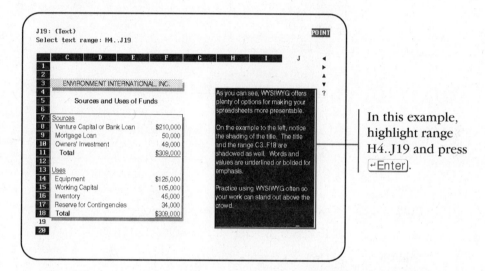

In this example, highlight range H4..J19 and press ⏎Enter.

3. Place the cursor to the left of the first character you want to format.

   In this example, move the cursor to *your* in the third paragraph.

4. Press F3.

9

The font at-
tributes menu
appears in the
control panel.

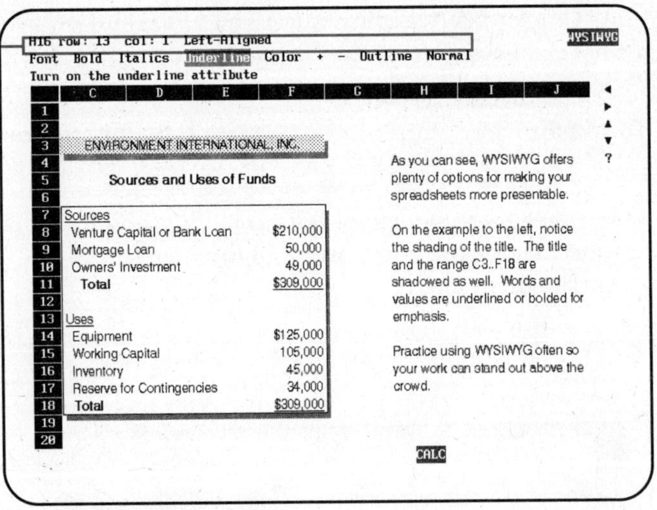

5. Choose the desired attribute from the resulting menu:

Selection	Description
Font	Changes the font
Bold	Boldfaces the text
Italics	Italicizes the text
Underline	Draws a single underline under the text
Color	Chooses a color for the text
+	Superscripts the text
–	Subscripts the text
Outline	Traces the outside of each letter in the line
Normal	Removes any formatting

Choose **Underline** for this example.

9

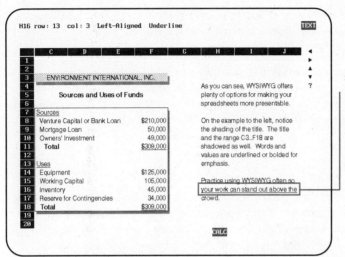

The attribute affects the data right of the cursor to the end of the line.

6. To indicate where you want the attribute to stop, place the cursor to the right of the last character and press F3. In this example, place the cursor to the right of the word your.

7. Press N for **Normal** to remove the highlighting from the rest of the line.

9

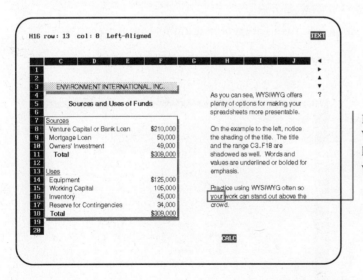

In this example, Wysiwyg underlines only the word your.

337

Because some of the attributes change the size of characters, paragraphs may no longer be neatly aligned after you format. When this happens, use the **:Text Reformat** command to adjust the paragraphs.

Wysiwyg does not limit character formatting to existing text; you can also apply attributes as you type new text in **:Text Edit** mode. Just press F3 and select the format before you begin typing. When you want to discontinue the attribute, press F3 and choose **Normal**.

Aligning Labels

Wysiwyg's **:Text Align** command is an elaborate version of 1-2-3's **/Range Label [Left, Right, Center]** command. 1-2-3's command aligns a label within the current column width. If the label exceeds the column width, 1-2-3 aligns it on the left. Wysiwyg's command aligns a label within a specified range—you can center a label across a range of cells to center it over the worksheet.

To align a range of text, follow these steps:

1. Select **:Text Align**.
2. Choose **Left**, **Right**, **Center**, or **Even**.

   Left is the default alignment. Even stretches the text between the left and right edge of the specified range. Wysiwyg inserts spaces between words to create smooth margins.
3. Highlight the range of cells to align text, and then press ⏎Enter.

In this example, the range C3..F5 is highlighted.

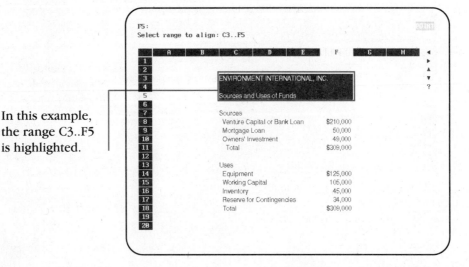

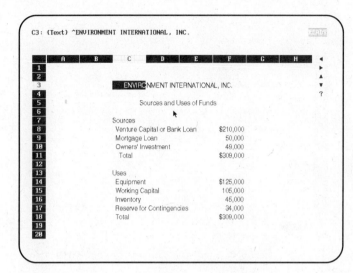

The result of
centering the text
in a range is
shown here.

Wysiwyg uses the following symbols to identify each type of alignment:

'   Left

"   Right

^   Center

| Even

These symbols match the label alignment symbols inserted with the /Range
Label command. The symbols have different functions, however, when the cell
is formatted as text in Wysiwyg because you can affect a range, not just a single
cell. You can insert these symbols manually in 1-2-3's EDIT mode, as long as
the cell has the {Text} attribute.

When you are editing in Wysiwyg's text editor, the control panel displays the
symbol for alignment of the current line (left-aligned, centered, and so on).

Reformatting Paragraphs

One of the advantages to using the text editor is that you can easily correct
typing mistakes, reword a passage, or insert additional text. Once you start
editing and formatting, however, your paragraphs no longer align. For instance, some lines may be too short.

9

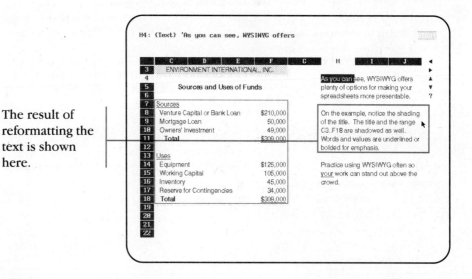

C21:   READY

	C	D	E	F	G	H	I	J	◄
3	ENVIRONMENT INTERNATIONAL, INC.
4
5	Sources and Uses of Funds
6
7	Sources
8	Venture Capital or Bank Loan	$210,000
9	Mortgage Loan	50,000
10	Owners' Investment	49,000
11	Total	$309,000
12
13	Uses
14	Equipment	$125,000
15	Working Capital	105,000
16	Inventory	45,000
17	Reserve for Contingencies	34,000
18	Total	$309,000

As you can see, WYSIWYG offers plenty of options for making your spreadsheets more presentable.

On the example, notice the shading of the title. The title and the range C3..F18 are shadowed as well. Words and values are underlined or bolded for emphasis.

Practice using WYSIWYG often so your work can stand out above the crowd.

Text in this example requires reformatting to correct alignment.

To reformat a paragraph, follow these steps:

1. If necessary, return to READY mode by pressing Esc.
2. Select :Text Reformat.
3. Wysiwyg automatically highlights the range you last indicated in the :Text Edit command. If this range is acceptable, press ↵Enter.
4. To indicate a different range, press Esc or ←Backspace; then highlight the new range and press ↵Enter.

H4: {Text} 'As you can see, WYSIWYG offers   READY

The result of reformatting the text is shown here.

340

Another reason to use the **:Text Reformat** command is to align the text into more columns. Suppose, for example, that the range currently spans four columns and you want to extend it to six. To make longer lines of text, include these extra columns in your reformat range.

Completing the Printing Process

After you finish formatting a report with Wysiwyg, you can easily print it with the **:Print Go** command. Before you print, you must specify a print range with the **:Print Range** command; then select **Go** from the Wysiwyg **:Print** menu to begin printing. If you choose to print your report at a later time, you can instead select **:Print File**, which creates an encoded file on disk with the ENC extension. Print the file using the DOS COPY command (for example, **COPY REVENUE/B LPT1**). You can also print to the background—allowing you to work in 1-2-3 while Wysiwyg prints the worksheet. Select **:Print Background** to print to the background.

To print a report created with Wysiwyg, follow these steps:

1. Select **:Print Range**.
2. Select **Set** and highlight the range you want to print (if necessary, select **Clear** to clear the current print range); or press F2 to activate the Wysiwyg Print Settings dialog box, select **Range**, and specify the print range.
3. Press Enter (twice if you used the dialog box).
4. Select **Go** to begin printing.

   If you select **:Print Range Set** and specify a print range, Wysiwyg displays the print range boundaries and page breaks as dashed lines on-screen.

Preview Printing to the Screen

The **:Print Preview** command gives you an idea of what your worksheet looks like before you print it on paper. This option displays your print range, one page at a time. Press any key to display subsequent pages and to return to the **:Print** menu.

To preview your document, follow these steps:

1. Select the print range and layout settings you want.
2. Select **:Print Preview**.

9

3. If multiple pages exist, press any key to view the next page(s) until you are returned to the **:P**rint menu.

Forcing a Print Range to One Page

The **:P**rint **L**ayout **C**ompression **A**utomatic command offers an ideal way to fit a large worksheet onto one page. Rather than guess at the font size needed to print a report on a single page, you can use this option. Wysiwyg will then determine how much it needs to reduce the font size.

To compress the print range to fit on one page, follow these steps:

1. Select **:P**rint.
2. On the Wysiwyg Print Settings dialog box, select **L**ayout **C**ompression.
3. From the pop-up dialog screen that appears, select Automatic to fit the range on one page.

The Wysiwyg Print Settings dialog box is shown here with Automatic print compression selected.

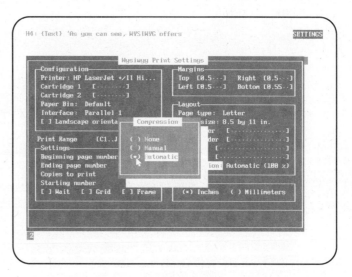

You can use additional Wysiwyg **:P**rint **L**ayout options to choose the paper size, change margins, add headers and footers, and add borders to the printout.

The Wysiwyg **:P**rint **C**onfig options enable you to change the current printer and interface. Depending on your selected printer, other **C**onfig options may be available. These options enable you to select the orientation (**P**ortrait or **L**andscape) of your printout, the font cartridges you use, and the paper-feed option.

Use the **:Print Settings** options to select which pages of a multipage report to print, the page number of the first page, the number of copies to print, whether to print the worksheet grid and frame, and whether to pause the printer for a paper change before printing pages.

Summary

In this chapter you learned how to use Wysiwyg to enhance your 1-2-3 worksheets when you print them. You can add boldface, italics, shading, underlining, grids, outlines, word-wrapped text, and symbols to your printed reports. These enhancements, which appear on-screen while you are formatting the worksheet, let you visualize how the report will appear when printed. Also, you can use different type sizes and styles to emphasize and enhance the text in your report.

Specifically, you learned the following key information about 1-2-3:

- To attach Wysiwyg, press Alt-F10 (or select /Add-In), select **Attach**, and choose WYSIWYG.ADN. To display the separate Wysiwyg menu, press **:**.

- The **:Format Font** command enables you to change the font for a specified range in the worksheet. If you want to use a different font throughout the entire worksheet, you can do so with the **:Format Font Replace** command.

- The **:Format Lines** command draws lines around the perimeter of a range, as well as lines in the left, right, top, or bottom of a range. An additional option enables you to create a drop shadow for a range, producing a three-dimensional effect.

- You can set grid lines to print or display on your screen. To print grid lines, select **:Print** and choose the **Grid** option on the Wysiwyg Print Settings dialog box. To display grid lines on-screen only, choose the **:Display Options Grid** command.

- The **:Display Zoom** command can shrink or magnify images on the screen so that characters appear much smaller or larger than normal size. This command does not affect the printed output.

- The **:Special Copy** command enables you to copy formatting from one cell to another cell or range of cells. Alternatively, you can use the **:Format Font Library** command to save or retrieve formatting.

9

343

■ The **:Text Edit** command enables you to type words on your worksheet using word-wrap and gives you the ability to enhance individual words of a cell. Once in **:Text Edit** mode, you can press F3 to format text.

■ The **:Text Align** command can align text in a cell or range of cells. **:Text Reformat** is used to reformat a range of labels into paragraph form.

■ The **:Print Range** command enables you to select the Wysiwyg print range. The **G**o option on the Wysiwyg **:P**rint menu prints the specified range to the printer. The **P**review option enables you to see an on-screen preview of the document before it prints.

■ The **:Print Layout Compression A**utomatic command automatically compresses a large worksheet range to print on a single page.

The next chapter describes how to manage files. You learn about protecting files with passwords, working with partial files, and importing files from other programs.

9

Managing Files

10

In Chapter 3, you learned some of the basic file management tasks. You learned to name, save, and retrieve files. This chapter covers some of the other valuable procedures for managing files. For example, you learn how to protect files with passwords so that unauthorized users cannot access the files. Only those who know the current password can change or delete it.

This chapter also covers how to save and retrieve parts of files. You learn how to extract a section of data from one worksheet to a separate worksheet. Additionally, you learn how to combine parts of several files into one master file. This capability is useful for consolidating data from similar worksheets. Individual cells can contain formulas that reference information in another worksheet on disk. 1-2-3 automatically updates these linked cells when you retrieve a file containing the links.

You also learn how to list and preview different types of files on-screen. You can change the default drive and directory (either permanently or temporarily for the current 1-2-3 session). You can delete worksheets and other 1-2-3 files. Finally, you learn how to import files from outside programs into 1-2-3 using 1-2-3's Translate utility.

Protecting files with passwords

Saving and retrieving partial files

Linking files

Listing files

Using the Viewer add-in

Specifying a drive and directory

Deleting files

Importing files

Key Terms in This Chapter

Password	A string of up to 15 characters used to limit access to worksheet files.
File linking	A 1-2-3 feature that enables you to use formulas in the current worksheet to refer to values in other worksheets.
ASCII file	A text (or print) file, created in another program, that 1-2-3 can import into a worksheet with the /File Import command.
Template	An empty master file with labels and formulas but no data. Use a template to create new worksheets or combine data from multiple files.
File reservation	The capacity for one user at a time to save changes to a file in a multiuser network.
Read-only	A file that can be viewed only; changes to the original file cannot be saved.

Using the Mouse

10

To use a mouse with 1-2-3 Release 2.3, you need a mouse, mouse software, and a graphics monitor and graphics card that support a mouse. You can use a mouse to select commands and files, specify ranges, move the cell pointer within the worksheet, and make selections in a dialog box. Refer to the following sections of the specified chapters for further information on using the mouse.

- Chapter 2—"Understanding Mouse Terminology"
- Chapter 3—"Mouse Control of the Cell Pointer"
    "Using Dialog Boxes"
    "Using the Mouse To Select Menu Commands"
- Chapter 4—"Using the Mouse To Specify Ranges"

Protecting Files with Passwords

You can protect your files by using 1-2-3's password-protection system. By specifying passwords when you save files, you can prevent access to the protected files by unauthorized users. The only persons who can retrieve the protected files are those who know the passwords. This feature is particularly useful for confidential information such as sales and payroll data.

Creating a Password

You can create a password with the /File Save command. To assign a password to a worksheet, follow these steps when saving a file:

1. Select /File Save.

2. When the prompt Enter name of file to save: appears, type the file name, leave a space, press P, and press Enter.

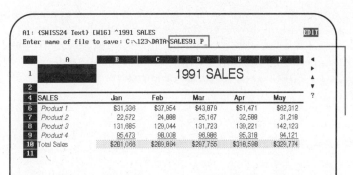

In this example, SALES91 receives a password.

10

3. When the prompt Enter password: appears, type your password and press Enter.

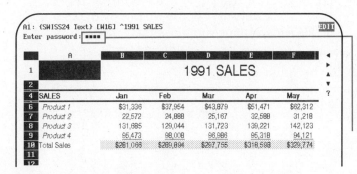

The password never appears on-screen. As you type, graphic blocks are used to hide characters.

347

4. When the prompt `Verify password:` appears, type the password once more and press ⏎Enter.

The passwords must match exactly (including case) or you must start the procedure again.

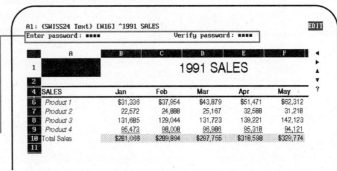

At this point, 1-2-3 saves the file with the new password. Only those who know the password can now retrieve the file.

You can enter any character in a 1-2-3 password, which can contain as many as 15 characters. You must be careful, however, because 1-2-3 accepts only the password you first entered. Uppercase or lowercase letters must be exactly the same. For example, if you entered **pdfund** as your password, 1-2-3 will not retrieve the file if you type **PDFUND** or **PDfund**. Be sure to remember your password or write it down.

10

Retrieving a Password-Protected File

To open a protected file, use the /**File Retrieve** command and type the password. To retrieve a file protected with a password, follow these steps:

1. Select /**File Retrieve**.

2. If you have made changes to the current worksheet and have not used /**File Save**, 1-2-3 informs you that changes have not been saved. Choose **Yes** to retrieve the file anyway. Choose **No** to stop the command; then save the file and continue with this procedure.

3. Select the file to retrieve by highlighting or typing the file name, and then press ⏎Enter.

4. When the prompt `Enter password:` appears, type your password exactly as you created it; then press ⏎Enter.

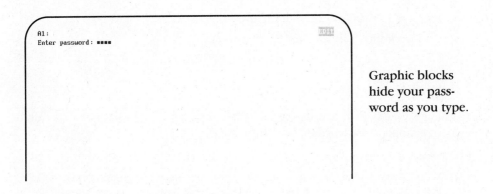

Graphic blocks hide your password as you type.

If you enter the password correctly, the worksheet appears. If you enter the wrong password, however, the words Incorrect password appear in a pop-up screen, and the mode indicator flashes ERROR. Press Esc or Enter to return to a blank worksheet.

Deleting a Password

You can delete a password by first retrieving the file with the password you want to delete. Then, when you are ready to save the file, select the /File Save command and erase the [PASSWORD PROTECTED] message.

To delete password protection from a file you have just retrieved, follow these steps:

1. Select /File Save.

10

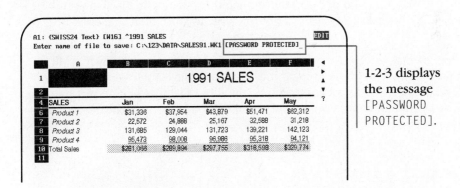

1-2-3 displays the message [PASSWORD PROTECTED].

2. When the prompt Enter name of file to save: appears, erase [PASSWORD PROTECTED] by pressing ◆Backspace or Esc.

3. Press ⏎Enter to save the file without the password.

4. Choose **R**eplace to update the file on disk.

Changing a Password

To change a password, first delete the existing password and then enter a new one. To change a password, follow these steps:

1. Select /**F**ile **S**ave.

2. When the prompt Enter name of file to save: appears, erase [PASSWORD PROTECTED] by pressing ⬅Backspace or Esc.

3. Leave a space after the file name, press P, and press ⏎Enter.

4. When the prompt Enter password: appears, type the password and press ⏎Enter.

5. At the prompt Verify password: type the password once more and press ⏎Enter.

6. Choose **R**eplace to update the file on disk. 1-2-3 saves the file with the new password.

Saving and Retrieving Partial Files

Sometimes you may want to store only part of a worksheet (a range of cells, for instance) in a separate file on disk. For example, you may need to extract payments from an expense report or revenues from an income statement. You can use /**F**ile **X**tract to perform these operations. Extracting is also useful for breaking up worksheet files that are too large to store on a single disk.

Conversely, you may have several worksheets with similar information. Suppose that you own a store in which each department is its own profit center. At the end of the month, you want to retrieve a partial file from each department's worksheet and combine the files to get the overall picture of the store's profit and loss. You can use the /**F**ile **C**ombine command to perform this operation.

Extracting Data

With the /**F**ile **X**tract command, you can save formulas or the current values of formulas in a range in a worksheet. Both options (**F**ormulas and **V**alues)

10

create a separate worksheet file that you can reload in 1-2-3 with the /File Retrieve command.

The /File Xtract command requires that you specify the portion of the worksheet you want to save. The range can be as small as a cell or as large as the entire worksheet.

To copy a part of your worksheet to a separate file, follow these steps:

1. Select /File Xtract.

2. To extract data and preserve any formulas in the extract range, select Formulas; or to extract data and convert formulas to values, select Values.

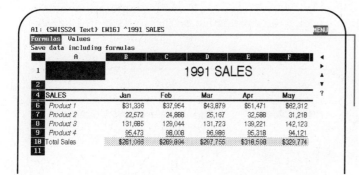

For this example, select Formulas.

3. When the prompt `Enter name of file to extract to:` appears, type a name for the file to hold the extracted data and press ↵Enter.

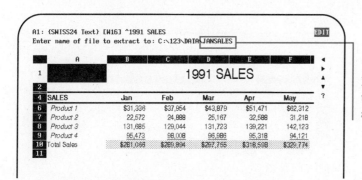

In this example, type JANSALES and press ↵Enter.

4. When the prompt `Enter extract range:` appears, highlight the range you want to extract and press ↵Enter.

10

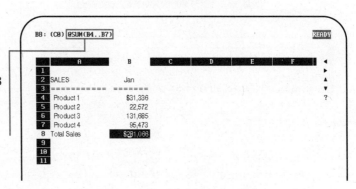

In this example,
highlight the
range A3..B10 and
press ⏎Enter.

5. If the extracted file already exists, choose **R**eplace to update the file on
disk or **B**ackup to back up the existing file on disk and save the current
file.

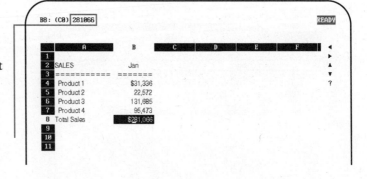

1-2-3 retains the
formula in cell B8
(displayed in the
control panel) in
the new file.

In this example,
select /**File X**tract
Values. 1-2-3
converts the
formula in B8 to
a value.

10

If you save only the current values with /File **X**tract Values, remember that the resulting worksheet file will contain numbers but no formulas. The /File **X**tract Formulas command preserves any formulas that are in the extract range.

When you select the /File **X**tract Values command, you can lock the current values in a worksheet. Think of this process as taking a snapshot of the current worksheet. You can then reload the new, values-only file into the worksheet and quickly perform operations that do not require formulas (such as printing and graphing). Before using /File **X**tract Values, however, be sure to press Calc (F9) if the CALC indicator appears at the bottom of the screen, to be sure that 1-2-3 will extract the correct formula values.

Combining Files

Another task you may need to perform is to copy ranges of cells from other worksheets and place them in strategic spots in your current worksheet. For example, if you work in a large firm, you may want to combine quarterly sales information by region into one consolidated worksheet.

A simple technique for this kind of consolidation is to start with a copy of an empty master file, or template. A template can contain exactly the same labels as the combined worksheets, but the area containing the specific data values is blank. When you start with a blank template, you can copy the first quarterly sales worksheet to the template, leaving the original worksheet untouched. Copying a range of cells also can be helpful when you want to combine divisional data in a single consolidated worksheet.

The command used to combine data from different files is /File **C**ombine. The **C**opy option of this command copies the worksheet or range on top of the current worksheet. The **A**dd option adds the values from the combined worksheet or range to the values in the current worksheet. The **S**ubtract option decreases the values in the current worksheet by the values in the combined worksheet or range.

To combine data from different files, follow these steps:

1. Retrieve the blank template file into which you want to combine files with /File **R**etrieve.

10

353

In this example, because the range B4..E8 is blank, all the formulas in row 10 evaluate to zero.

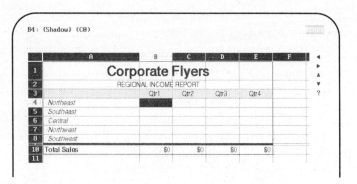

2. Position the cell pointer on the first cell of the range to receive the combined data.

3. Select /**F**ile **C**ombine.

4. Select **C**opy to copy a worksheet or range from another file to the existing worksheet or select **A**dd to add the incoming values in a worksheet or range to the values in the existing worksheet or range. To decrease the existing values in a worksheet or range by the values in an incoming worksheet or range, select **S**ubtract.

In this example, select **C**opy.

5. If you want to copy an entire incoming file, choose **E**ntire-File. To copy a specific range from an incoming file, choose **N**amed/Specified-Range.

10

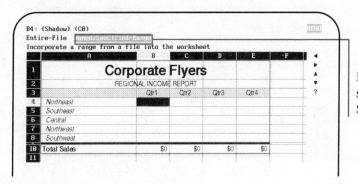

In this example, select **Named/ Specified-Range.**

6. Type the range name or location of the incoming range and press ⏎Enter. (If you select the **Entire-File** option, 1-2-3 does not prompt you to enter a range.)

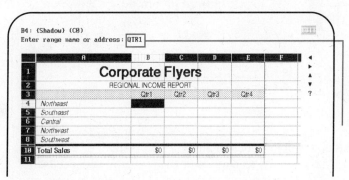

In this example, type the range name **QTR1** and press ⏎Enter.

7. When the prompt `Enter name of file to combine:` appears, indicate the name of the file containing the data and press ⏎Enter.

10

The first quarter data is now in the range B4..B8. 1-2-3 automatically updates the formula in cell B10.

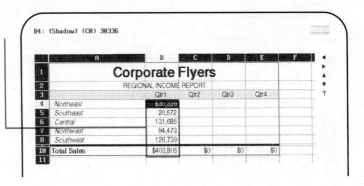

After you combine data for all quarters, the template is filled. The formulas in row 10 display values.

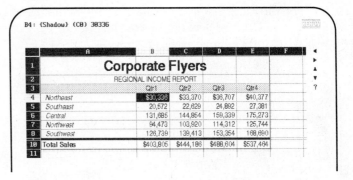

The **C**opy option of /**F**ile **C**ombine pulls in an entire worksheet or named range and causes the new contents to write over the corresponding cells in the current worksheet. The **C**opy command does not affect cells in the current worksheet that correspond to blank cells in the target file. (Note the important distinction between blank cells and cells containing a space in the target file or range.)

10

356

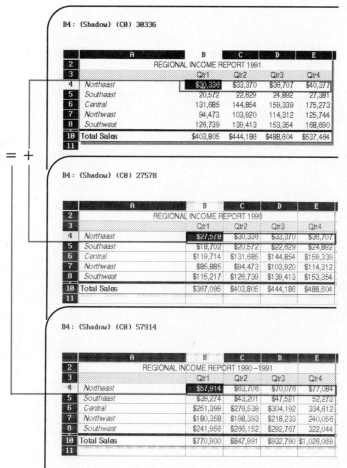

B4: {Shadow} (C0) 30336

	A	B	C	D	E
2		REGIONAL INCOME REPORT 1991			
3		Qtr1	Qtr2	Qtr3	Qtr4
4	Northeast	$30,336	$33,370	$36,707	$40,377
5	Southeast	20,572	22,629	24,892	27,381
6	Central	131,685	144,854	159,339	175,273
7	Northwest	94,473	103,920	114,312	125,744
8	Southwest	126,739	139,413	153,354	168,690
10	Total Sales	$403,805	$444,186	$488,604	$537,464
11					

= +

B4: {Shadow} (C0) 27578

	A	B	C	D	E
2		REGIONAL INCOME REPORT 1990			
3		Qtr1	Qtr2	Qtr3	Qtr4
4	Northeast	$27,578	$30,336	$33,370	$36,707
5	Southeast	$18,702	$20,572	$22,629	$24,892
6	Central	$119,714	$131,685	$144,854	$159,339
7	Northwest	$85,885	$94,473	$103,920	$114,312
8	Southwest	$115,217	$126,739	$139,413	$153,354
10	Total Sales	$367,095	$403,805	$444,186	$488,604
11					

B4: {Shadow} (C0) 57914

	A	B	C	D	E
2		REGIONAL INCOME REPORT 1990–1991			
3		Qtr1	Qtr2	Qtr3	Qtr4
4	Northeast	$57,914	$63,706	$70,076	$77,084
5	Southeast	$39,274	$43,201	$47,521	52,273
6	Central	$251,399	$276,539	$304,192	334,612
7	Northwest	$180,358	$198,393	$218,233	240,056
8	Southwest	$241,956	$266,152	$292,767	322,044
10	Total Sales	$770,900	$847,991	$932,790	$1,026,069
11					

In this example, the Add option is selected. The values in the center worksheet (the worksheet to be combined) are added to the values in the corresponding cells of the top worksheet (the current worksheet) to create a worksheet of combined values.

10

Add pulls in the values from another worksheet or range and adds these values to the corresponding cells in the current worksheet. The Add command affects only blank worksheet cells or cells containing numeric values. In the current worksheet, cells that contain formulas or labels do not change.

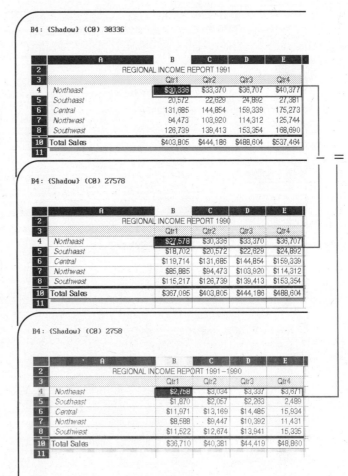

In this example, select the Subtract option. 1-2-3 subtracts the values in the center worksheet from the values in the corresponding cells in the top worksheet to create a worksheet of combined values.

Subtract pulls in an entire worksheet or a named range and subtracts the values from the corresponding cells in the current worksheet. When an existing cell is blank, 1-2-3 subtracts the incoming value. Like Add, Subtract affects only blank cells or cells that contain numeric values. In the current worksheet, cells containing formulas or labels do not change.

Linking Cells between Files

1-2-3 enables you to use formulas to link a range in one worksheet to a cell in another. The cell that receives the information is the *target cell*. The range that sends the information is the *source range*. You can save linked cells with

/**F**ile **S**ave. 1-2-3 automatically updates the linked formulas when you retrieve the file. (Cell linking is unavailable with versions before 1-2-3 Release 2.2.) With the Viewer add-in (Release 2.3 only) you can quickly point to the cell you want to link.

Use /**F**ile **C**ombine when you want to copy information from file to file. The cell linkage feature is automatic and requires no active use of commands.

Establishing a Link

1-2-3 performs links within the target cell, using a special kind of formula. To begin the formula, type a plus sign (**+**) followed by two less-than symbols (**<<**). Next enter the name of the source file (including the directory name if the file is not in the current directory). Then type two greater-than symbols (**>>**). Finally, type the address or range name of the source cell.

Another way to link files is with the Viewer add-in of Release 2.3. You can move to source cells in other files as you type a formula. If the files with the source cells have long path names, using Viewer is easier than typing file names.

The entry +<<MIAMI>>B17 in cell B8 of a worksheet is an example of a file-linking formula. The formula means that B8 is to contain the data found in cell B17 of the file MIAMI.WK1 in the current directory. When this cell entry is complete, data copying occurs at once. For the link to become permanent and automatic (occurring with every /**F**ile **R**etrieve), use /**F**ile **S**ave.

10

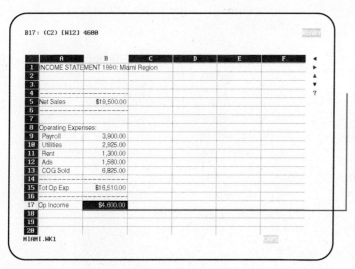

The income statement worksheet for the Miami region contains a source cell: B17.

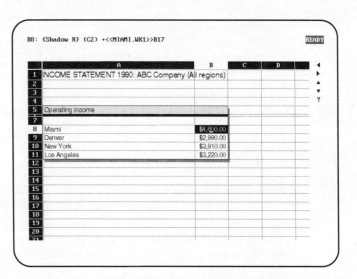

The target file is the income statement worksheet for all regions. This file uses existing information from the Miami file (as well as the files for Denver, New York, and Los Angeles).

Cell B8 links to cell B17 of the file named MIAMI.WK1. The remaining data cells in the target file also link to their respective worksheets. Whenever you retrieve the target file, 1-2-3 automatically updates cells B8 through B11 with information from the source files.

When you alter a source cell, 1-2-3 does not immediately copy its contents to the linked target cell or cells. In fact, a source cell may go through many changes and you can save the file many times, yet the target cell might not reflect any of these interim values. 1-2-3 only updates the contents of the target file when you retrieve the file containing the target cell or when you issue the /**F**ile **A**dmin Link-Refresh command.

Using the Viewer Add-In To Link Files

If you don't remember what cell you want to link to in another file, finding the cell can be time consuming. You need to save and exit your current file, retrieve the file to be linked, locate the cell reference, and retrieve the target file. 1-2-3 Release 2.3 provides the Viewer add-in to solve this problem.

To attach the Viewer add-in, follow these steps:

1. Press Alt F10 (or select /**A**dd-in). **Note:** You may need to change directories if Viewer is located in a different directory.

2. Select **A**ttach.

3. Type or highlight **VIEWER.ADN** and press Enter.

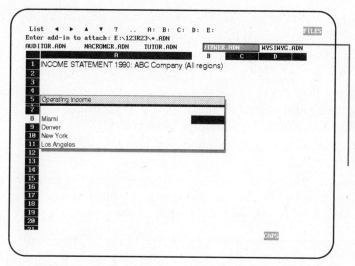

In this example, highlight VIEWER.ADN and press ⏎Enter.

4. Choose a function key to assign to the Viewer add-in.

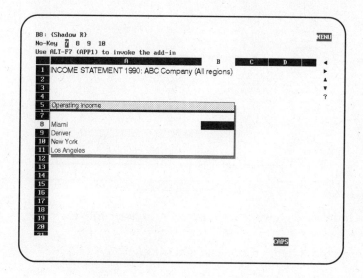

In this example, select **7** to assign Viewer to the Alt-F7 key.

5. Select **Quit** to return to READY mode.

To link to a file on disk, follow these steps:

1. Move the cell pointer to the cell in the current worksheet where you want to link to another file.

361

2. Invoke the Viewer add-in by pressing the Alt-function key combination you assigned to Viewer.

   In this example, press Alt F7.

3. Select **Link**.

4. A list of worksheet files and/or directories appears on the left side of the screen. To change the drive and directory, use an arrow key to move the highest to a parent directory or a subdirectory.

   The Viewer screen displays directories between less-than (<) and greater-than (>) symbols.

5. When you reach the desired directory and drive, use ↑ and ↓ to find the file you want to link. As you move the pointer, a picture of the highlighted worksheet appears on the right side of the screen.

The list of files appears on the left of the screen; a view of each highlighted file appears on the right side of the screen.

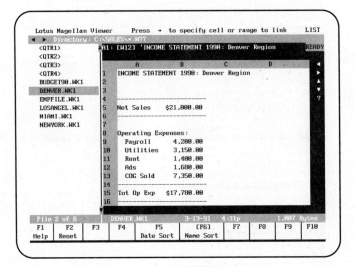

6. When you reach the desired worksheet, press → to move into the worksheet file.

7. Move to the desired cell in the worksheet and press ↵Enter.

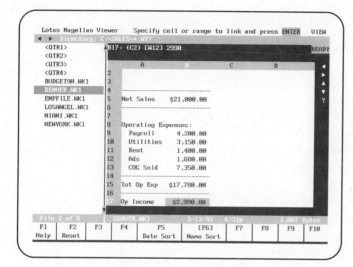

In this example, move the pointer to cell B17 in DENVER.WK1 and press ⏎Enter.

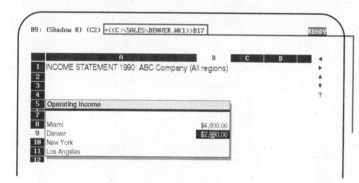

1-2-3 links cell B17 from DENVER.WK1 to the current worksheet.

Listing Linked Files

The command /File List Linked provides a list of all files linked to the current worksheet. The /File List Linked command does not give you the addresses of either the target cells or source cells.

To list the files linked to the current worksheet, select /File List Linked. The resulting screen lists all other files that have links to the current file.

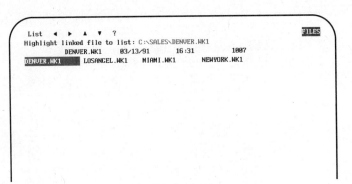

In this example, four files are linked to the current file.

Refreshing Links

If you use 1-2-3 in a network or multiuser environment, someone else may alter files that contain source cells for the worksheet you are using. In this case, you may want periodic updating of your target cells. Use the /File Admin Link-Refresh command to update all target cells in the current worksheet to reflect the contents of source cells.

To update or "refresh" the cells linked to the current worksheet, select /File Admin Link-Refresh.

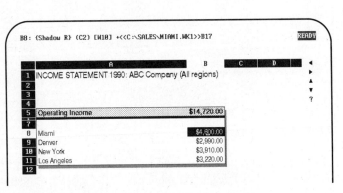

Use the Link-Refresh option to update the values of cells linked to other worksheets.

Listing Different Types of Files

1-2-3 can list all the names of a certain type of file in the current drive and directory with the /File List command. When you list files, you can specify worksheet, print, or graph files; any type of files; or linked files.

To display a list of files in the current drive and directory, follow these steps:

1. Select /File List.

2. Select the type of file you want to list: **Worksheet**, **Print**, **Graph**, **Other**, or **Linked**. After you choose an option, 1-2-3 displays the list of files.

To list only worksheet files (files with a WK? extension), choose **Worksheet**. To list only print files (files with a PRN extension), choose **Print**. Select **Graph** to list only graph files (files with a PIC extension). Choose **Other** to list all types of files (files with any extension). To list only files linked to the current worksheet, choose **Linked**.

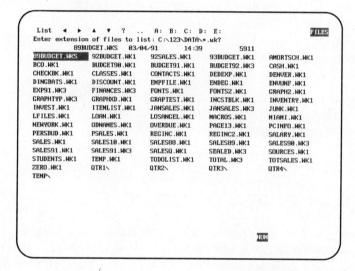

In this example, 1-2-3 displays all WK? files in the current directory after you select **Worksheet**.

Using Viewer To List and Retrieve Files

You can also use the Viewer add-in of Release 2.3 to list and retrieve files. This is especially helpful if you don't remember the name of a file. After you attach Viewer with the Alt F10 (or /Add-in) **Attach** command, follow these steps to list or retrieve a file:

1. Invoke the Viewer add-in by pressing the Alt-function key you assigned to Viewer.

   In this example, press Alt F7.

2. Select **Retrieve** if you want to retrieve a file or **Browse** if you only want to look at the files.

3. If you select **Retrieve** and have made changes to your file since your last save, 1-2-3 warns you that you have not saved your worksheet. Select **No** to start over to allow you to save your file or **Yes** to go ahead and retrieve a file anyway.

4. A list of files appears on the left side of the screen. To change the drive and directory, use the arrow keys to move to a parent directory or a subdirectory.

5. When you reach the desired directory and drive, use ⬆ and ⬇ to look at each file. As you move the pointer, Viewer shows a picture of the worksheet on the right side of the screen.

   The list of files appears on the left of the screen; a view of each high-lighted file appears on the right side of the screen.

6. If you are retrieving a file, press ⏎Enter when the desired file name is highlighted. Pressing ⏎Enter while browsing returns you to READY mode in the current worksheet.

Note: When you use **Retrieve**, Viewer shows only worksheet files. When you use **Browse**, Viewer shows all files. You can also see the contents of text files. Other files such as word processing or database files may show odd characters as well as text.

Specifying a Drive and Directory

Use the /**Worksheet Global Default Directory** or the /**File Directory** commands to change the drive and directory. After installing 1-2-3, the default directory is the one containing the 1-2-3 program files. /**Worksheet Global Default Directory** can change the default drive and directory to one that contains your data files. /**File Directory**, on the other hand, changes the drive and directory temporarily—for only the current worksheet session.

To change the default directory, follow these steps:

1. Select /**Worksheet Global Default**. The Default Settings dialog box shows the current default directory.

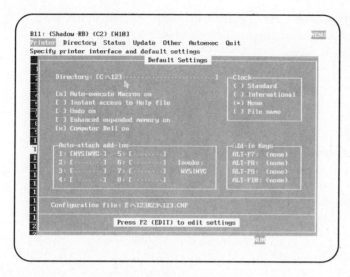

In this example,
C:\123 is the
default directory.

2. Select **Directory** on the dialog box. Use ◆Backspace to clear the current default directory.

3. Type the new default directory name and press ↵Enter. Remember to precede the directory name with the drive letter, a colon (:), and a backslash (\).

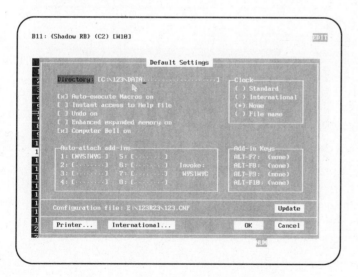

In this example,
press Esc, type
C:\123\DATA and
press ↵Enter.

4. Select Update. This command updates a program file that allows 1-2-3 to use the new default directory in future sessions.

5. Select **Quit** to return to READY mode.

To specify a directory with the menu commands, select /**Worksheet Global Default Directory** and press Enter. Then type the directory and select **Update** and **Quit**.

With a hard disk, you can use the default directory setting to your advantage. As in the preceding example, you can set the default directory to C:\123\DATA. When you want to retrieve a file, 1-2-3 displays all the subdirectories and files within the C:\123\DATA directory. After you choose the proper directory, 1-2-3 again displays the subdirectories and files stored in that directory so that you can make a choice. Setting the default directory this way saves time if you use worksheets in different subdirectories.

If you are working with files in a different directory than the one you normally use, you can change the directory temporarily with the /**File Directory** command. This command overrides the default directory for the current session only.

To change the current directory temporarily, follow these steps:

1. Select /**File Directory**. The control panel shows the current directory.

In this example, C:\SALES is the current directory.

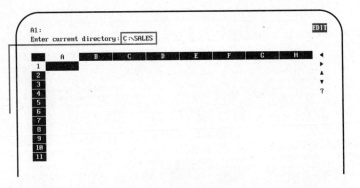

2. Type the new directory name and press ↵Enter (the current directory name automatically clears when you start typing). Remember to precede the directory name with the drive letter, colon, and backslash.

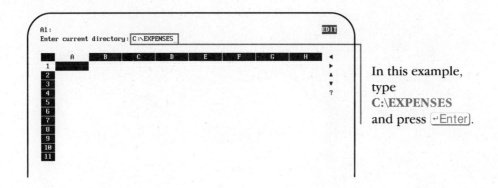

```
A1:                                                    EDIT
Enter current directory: C:\EXPENSES
```

In this example,
type
C:\EXPENSES
and press ↵Enter.

1-2-3 changes the directory for the current session only. The next time you access 1-2-3, the default directory again becomes the current directory.

Deleting Files

When you save files to a floppy disk, you sometimes find that the disk is full. To alert you, 1-2-3 displays the message `Disk full` in a pop-up screen, and the mode indicator flashes ERROR. To save the current file, you must either swap disks or delete one or more of the files occupying space on the disk.

You have two ways to delete stored files in 1-2-3. You can use the /File **Erase** command within 1-2-3. Or, you can access DOS with the /**System** command and erase the file with the DOS ERASE or DEL (DELETE) command.

To delete a file from within 1-2-3, follow these steps:

1. Select /**File Erase**.
2. Select the type of file you want to erase: **Worksheet**, **Print**, **Graph**, or **Other**. To erase a worksheet file (a file with a WK1 or WKS extension), choose **Worksheet**. To erase a print file (a file with a PRN extension), choose **Print**. To erase a graph file (a file with a PIC extension), choose **Graph**. To erase any type of file, choose **Other**.

10

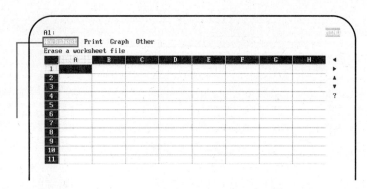

In this example, choose **W**orksheet.

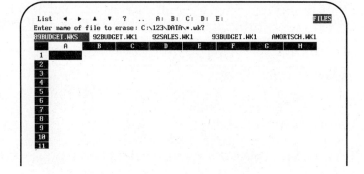

Depending on your selection, 1-2-3 displays files with the appropriate extension(s).

3. Press ⌐F3⌐ (Name) to display a full-screen listing of files in the current directory.

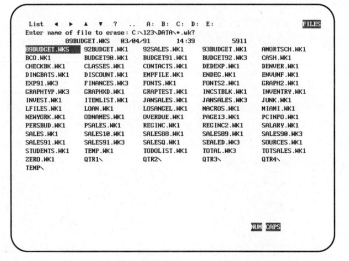

In this example, a full-screen listing shows all worksheet files.

10

4. Highlight the file you want to erase, or type its name; then press
   ⏎Enter.

5. When the **No/Yes** menu appears, select **Yes** to complete the erase
   operation, or select **No** to cancel the command without erasing.

You can use the wild-card characters described in Chapter 3 to display all the
files of a certain type that you want to delete. These characters are the same
familiar wild-card characters used for DOS and other commands throughout
1-2-3. The following list shows some examples of using wild-card characters:

* Matches the remaining characters of a file name. For example, C*
  matches CHICAGO, CASHFLOW, and CENTERS.

? Matches all characters in a single position in a file name. For
  example, SALES8? matches SALES88 and SALES89, but not SALES90
  or SALES.

Be careful when you use the /**File Erase** command. After you delete a file, you
cannot recover it with 1-2-3. Always double check before you delete a file.

Importing Files into 1-2-3

A powerful 1-2-3 feature is its capacity to transfer data between 1-2-3 and
other programs. To perform a transfer, use the /**File Import** command and
select Unformatted pages on the dialog box after you choose /**Print File**. (See
Chapter 8 for a discussion of the Unformatted print option.) Additionally, you
can use the Translate utility.

Importing ASCII Text Files

Use the /**File Import** command to copy standard ASCII files to specific loca-
tions in the current worksheet. For example, PRN (print) files are standard
ASCII text files created to print after the current 1-2-3 session. Other standard
ASCII files include those produced by various word processing, BASIC, and
database programs. These programs, like 1-2-3, can produce and retrieve
ASCII files.

To import an ASCII text file to 1-2-3, follow these steps:

1. Select /**File Import**.

2. Select **Text** or **Numbers**.

10

Use the **Text** option for importing an ASCII file created by your word processing software. Use the **Numbers** option when you import delimited files—ASCII files that contain separator characters to distinguish items of data.

If you select **Text**, 1-2-3 displays all PRN files in the current directory.

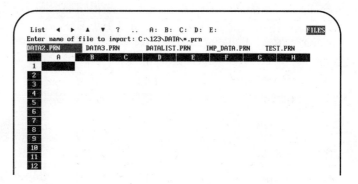

3. To display files in a different drive or directory, or with a different extension, type the appropriate drive, directory, and extension.

4. Use wild-card characters (* or ?) and extensions as needed; then press ⏎Enter to display the desired files.

5. Highlight the name of the text file you want to import; then press ⏎Enter. For example, highlight the file name IMP_DATA.PRN, and press ⏎Enter.

10

1-2-3 imports the ASCII text file.

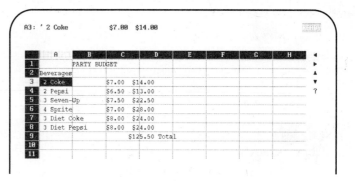

If you select /**File Import Numbers**, 1-2-3 places numbers and delimited text—separated by commas, colons, semicolons, or spaces—into separate columns. If you import a file with the **Numbers** option, 1-2-3 imports only those column headings that are surrounded by quotation marks.

If you have Wysiwyg loaded, imported text files may appear out of alignment. To make sure that text characters line up, change to a nonproportional font such as Courier with the **:Format Font** command.

Importing Files from Other Programs

Use the Translate utility to import files into 1-2-3 from other programs such as dBASE II, dBASE III, Multiplan (SYLK), and VisiCalc. Also use Translate to export 1-2-3 files to dBASE II, dBASE III, DIF and other file formats. (Many presentation-graphics packages use DIF files.)

The Translate utility provides good communication with dBASE, including dBASE IV (which the menu does not list but which you can access by selecting dBASE III). The Translate utility also provides translation capabilities among all Lotus products, allowing free interchange of worksheets between Symphony and earlier releases of 1-2-3.

To use the Translate utility, follow these steps:

1. Select **Translate** from the Lotus 1-2-3 Access menu.

2. Select the format (program) from which you want to translate by highlighting your selection and pressing ⏎Enter .

3. Select the format (program) to which you want to translate by highlighting your selection and pressing ⏎Enter .

4. Based on your choice of format, a list of files appears. (As a format choice, for example, you can choose *.WK1 for a 1-2-3 file or *.DBF for a dBASE file.)

5. Select the file name you want to translate by highlighting the file name and pressing ⏎Enter , or press Esc to edit the subdirectory or file name.

10

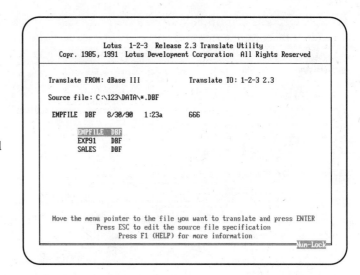

In this example, highlight EMPFILE.DBF and press ⏎Enter .

6. Type the name of the new file and press ⏎Enter , or just press ⏎Enter to accept the default file name shown.

10

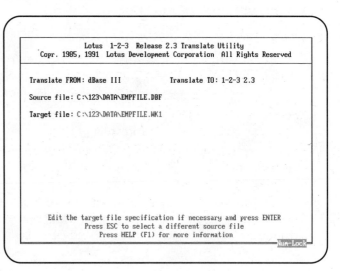

In this example, press ⏎Enter to accept EMPFILE.WK1 as the translated file name.

7. At the resulting menu, select **Yes** to proceed with the translation.

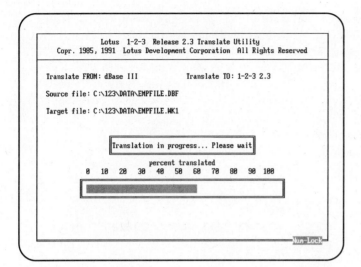

As you begin the translation process, an indicator appears on-screen, informing you that the translation is in progress.

8. When the translation is complete, press Esc twice to reach a menu giving you the option to leave the Translate utility. To exit, select **Yes**.

Writing a List of Files into the Worksheet

1-2-3 uses the /**F**ile **A**dmin **T**able command to create a table of information about files on disk or files linked to the current file. This table appears in a specified range in the worksheet.

The **T**able command lists varied information about the files, depending on the type of file you select. Make certain that the specified location in the worksheet is blank. 1-2-3 writes over the existing data to create the table. The following breakdown shows the information you can find:

*   When you select the **W**orksheet, **P**rint, **G**raph, or **O**ther option, 1-2-3 lists basic information about each file. You see listed the name and extension of each file, the last date and time each file was saved, and its disk size in bytes.

*   **L**inked displays basic file information along with the path and the file name of each linked file.

To write a table of information in the worksheet, follow these steps:

1. Select /**F**ile **A**dmin **T**able.

10

375

2. Select the type of file you want to list: Worksheet, **P**rint, **G**raph, **O**ther, or **L**inked. To list only worksheet files (files with a WK1 or WKS extension), choose **W**orksheet. To list only print files (files with a PRN extension), choose **P**rint. To list only graph files (files with a PIC extension), choose **G**raph. To list all types of files (files with any extension), choose **O**ther. To list only files linked to the current worksheet, choose **L**inked.

3. Type the drive and directory and press ⏎Enter, or simply press ⏎Enter to accept the current drive and directory.

In this example,
to list the default
directory, press
⏎Enter.

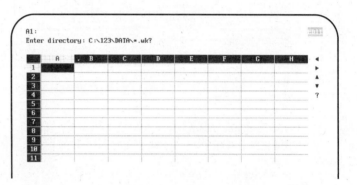

4. At the `Enter range for table:` prompt, type or highlight the address of the top left corner of the range where the directory will appear and press ⏎Enter. 1-2-3 displays the list of files.

10

This screen is the
result of the /**F**ile
Admin **T**able
Worksheet
command.

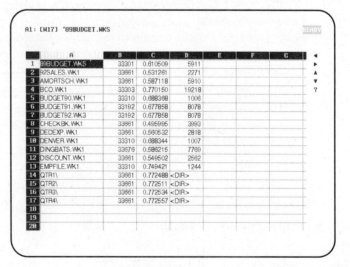

For the information to be clear, you may need to increase the width of columns with the /**W**orksheet **C**olumn **S**et-Width command. You should also format the second column with /**R**ange **F**ormat **D**ate and the third column with /**R**ange **F**ormat **D**ate **T**ime.

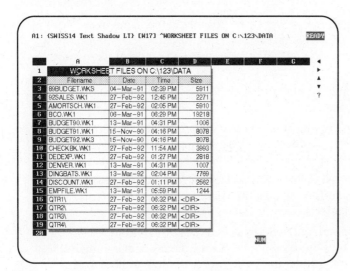

A1: {SWISS14 Text Shadow LT} [W17] ^WORKSHEET FILES ON C:\123\DATA   READY

	A	B	C	D
1	WORKSHEET FILES ON C:\123\DATA			
2	Filename	Date	Time	Size
3	89BUDGET.WKS	04–Mar–91	02:39 PM	5911
4	92SALES.WK1	27–Feb–92	12:45 PM	2271
5	AMORTSCH.WK1	27–Feb–92	02:05 PM	5910
6	BCO.WK1	06–Mar–91	06:29 PM	19218
7	BUDGET90.WK1	13–Mar–91	04:31 PM	1006
8	BUDGET91.WK1	15–Nov–90	04:16 PM	8078
9	BUDGET92.WK3	15–Nov–90	04:16 PM	8078
10	CHECKBK.WK1	27–Feb–92	11:54 AM	3993
11	DEDEXP.WK1	27–Feb–92	01:27 PM	2818
12	DENVER.WK1	13–Mar–91	04:31 PM	1007
13	DINGBATS.WK1	13–Mar–92	02:04 PM	7769
14	DISCOUNT.WK1	27–Feb–92	01:11 PM	2562
15	EMPFILE.WK1	13–Mar–91	05:59 PM	1244
16	QTR1\	27–Feb–92	06:32 PM	<DIR>
17	QTR2\	27–Feb–92	06:32 PM	<DIR>
18	QTR3\	27–Feb–92	06:32 PM	<DIR>
19	QTR4\	27–Feb–92	06:32 PM	<DIR>
20				

NUM

This example shows the result of the /**F**ile **A**dmin **T**able **W**orksheet command after formatting.

Summary

Knowing how to manage files is essential for the efficient use of 1-2-3. Aside from the basic tasks of naming, saving, and retrieving files you learned in Chapter 3, you need to perform other file management tasks. This chapter showed you how to protect files with passwords. You also learned how to save partial files when you want to extract or combine portions of a worksheet. You learned how you can list and delete files with ease if you know how to specify drives, subdirectories, and file names accurately. You even learned how you can import files from other software programs.

Specifically, you learned the following key information about 1-2-3:

- You can add passwords to your files with the /**F**ile **S**ave command so that only those who know the exact password can retrieve your file.

- The /**F**ile **X**tract command enables you to save part of the worksheet file. You can save either the formulas existing in a range of cells or the current values of the formulas in the range.

10

■ The /File **Combine** command enables you to combine data from different files. You can copy the source worksheet or range on top of the current worksheet. You can also add or subtract values from the combined worksheet or range with the values in the current worksheet.

■ You link cells in different files by enclosing the file name in two less-than and greater-than signs, such as +<<MIAMI>>B5. Alternatively, you can use the Viewer add-in in Release 2.3 to quickly link to another file.

■ The /File **List Linked** command provides a listing of all files linked to the current worksheet.

■ The /File **Admin Link-Refresh** command updates all target cells in the current worksheet to reflect the current contents of the source cells. This command is particularly helpful for users on a network.

■ You can use the /**Worksheet Global Default Directory** and the /**File Directory** commands to change the current drive and directory. The latter command affects only the current session of 1-2-3.

■ The /File **Erase** command deletes stored files from within 1-2-3. You can also delete files by accessing DOS with the /**System** command. Then you erase the files at the DOS level with the ERASE or DEL command.

■ The /File **Import** command allows the transfer of data between 1-2-3 and other programs. Use this command to copy standard ASCII files to specific locations in the current worksheet.

■ Use the Translate utility, available from the Lotus 1-2-3 Access menu, for converting other programs to 1-2-3's format.

■ The /File **Admin Table** command enables you to write a list of file information in your worksheet.

The next chapter shows you how to create graphs within 1-2-3. You learn about the graph creation process and how to select graph types and data ranges. Also included are steps to enhance the appearance of a graph and to save a graph to disk for later printing.

10

Creating and Printing Graphs

11

Even if 1-2-3 provided only spreadsheet capabilities, the program would be extremely powerful. More information can be quickly assembled and tabulated electronically than can possibly be developed manually. But despite the importance of keeping detailed worksheets that show real or projected data, that information can be worthless if you can't readily understand it.

To help decision-makers who are pressed for time or unable to draw conclusions from countless rows of numeric data, and who may benefit from seeing key figures displayed graphically, 1-2-3 offers graphics capabilities. The program has seven types of basic business graphs as well as options for enhancing the graphs' appearance. You can quickly design and alter graphs as worksheet data changes. This capability means that graphs may be changed almost as fast as 1-2-3 recalculates the data.

Key Terms in This Chapter

Graph type   The manner in which data is represented graphically.

X-axis   The horizontal bottom edge of a graph.

Y-axis   The vertical left edge of a graph.

Origin   The intersection of the x- and y-axes.

Legend   The description of the shading, color, or symbols assigned to data ranges in line or bar graphs. The legend appears across the bottom of the graph.

Tick marks   The small marks on the axes of a graph, which indicate the increments between the minimum and maximum graph values.

Indicator   An automatic label that 1-2-3 provides on the y-axis showing the scaling factor of the data. For example, (Thousands) or (Millions).

Zero line   The line that extends through zero on the y-axis or the x-axis. Negative values are below or to the left of the zero line. Positive values are above or to the right of the zero line. You choose whether or not to display the zero lines.

Frame   A set of four lines creating a box that surrounds the graph. You can remove any or all of the lines.

Data labels   Text or values that you can add to data points on the graph.

11

You create graphs with 1-2-3's /Graph commands. Although the program has a number of options, you need to specify only a graph type and a single data range to create a basic graph. After providing the required information, you select the View option from the /Graph menu. This command plots the graph to the screen, temporarily replacing the worksheet until you press a key.

You can perform true graphics "what if" analyses with 1-2-3. In fact, you can use the Graph (F10) key to replot a graph after making changes in the worksheet, without having to redefine the graph with the /Graph commands. This replotting immediately shows the effects of changes on the current graph.

In this chapter, you learn to create a basic graph, to create seven types of graphs from the data in your worksheet, and to enhance your graphs. You also learn to name and save your graphs in a worksheet file that you can retrieve and modify at any time. The last part of the chapter shows you how to print graphs with the PrintGraph program provided with Releases 2.01, 2.2, and 2.3.

Graphing commands are also available in Wysiwyg in Release 2.3. However, the options on the :Graph menu are primarily for further enhancing the graphs you create from 1-2-3's /Graph menu. Wysiwyg contains a built-in graphics editor that you can use to annotate your graphs. With Wysiwyg, you can also insert a graph in any worksheet range; draw arrows, lines, circles, and other shapes; and print graphs and worksheet data on the same page. Chapter 12 covers how to use the Wysiwyg :Graph commands to enhance your 1-2-3 graphs.

Using the Mouse

To use a mouse with 1-2-3 Release 2.3, you need a mouse, mouse software, and a graphics monitor and graphics card that support a mouse. You can use a mouse to select commands and files, specify ranges, move the cell pointer within the worksheet, or make selections in a dialog box. Refer to the following sections of the specified chapters for further information on using the mouse.

- Chapter 2—"Understanding Mouse Terminology"
- Chapter 3—"Mouse Control of the Cell Pointer"
    "Using Dialog Boxes"
    "Using the Mouse To Select Menu Commands"
- Chapter 4—"Using the Mouse To Specify Ranges"

An Overview of Creating a Graph

Before creating your first graph, you must determine whether your hardware supports viewing and printing graphs, whether your 1-2-3 software is correctly installed for graphics, and whether the worksheet on-screen contains data you want to graph. And you should understand which type of graph is best suited for presenting specific numeric data in picture form.

11

You can use 1-2-3's graphics feature to create and view a graph, store its specifications for later use, and print the graph. Creating and storing a graph requires only that you have the 1-2-3 software installed on your equipment, that you correctly select options from the /Graph menu, and that you save these options with the associated worksheet file.

Hardware Requirements

To view a graph on-screen, you need a graphics monitor or a monitor with a graphics-display adapter. Without this monitor, you can construct and save a 1-2-3 graph, but you must print the graph to view it. To print a graph, you need a graphics printer supported by 1-2-3.

The Graph Creation Process

To create a 1-2-3 graph, begin by selecting the /Graph command while the worksheet containing the data you want to graph is displayed.

Selecting /Graph produces a menu and the Graph Settings dialog box.

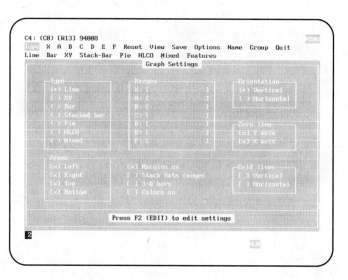

11

Each option on the /Graph menu is described in table 11.1. Options common to the Graph Settings dialog box are also described there. Later in the chapter, table 11.4 describes more options in the dialog box.

Table 11.1
Selections on the /Graph Menu

Selection	Description
Type	Provides options for creating seven types of graphs: line, bar, XY, stacked bar, pie, HLCO, or mixed; you can use the dialog box or the menu to choose this option
X	Specifies the range to be used as x-axis labels or values, or labels of pie slices; you can use the dialog box or the menu to choose this option
A through F	Specifies the ranges containing the numeric data to graph; you can use the dialog box or the menu to choose these options
Reset	Clears the current graph settings
View	Displays a full-screen view of the current graph
Save	Saves a graph in the file format needed for using the graph with other programs
Options	Provides choices for labeling, enhancing, or customizing a graph; you can use the menu or dialog box to choose graph options
Name	Lets you assign a name to one or more graphs and store the graph settings so that you can redisplay the graph(s) whenever you retrieve the worksheet file
Group	Lets you define a range of contiguous cells to be the X and A through F ranges
Quit	Quits the /Graph menu and returns the worksheet to READY mode

You use some of these commands every time you create a graph. Other commands or options are used less frequently; you use these commands when you need to enhance or customize your graph. If you do not need to enhance or customize the graph, creating a graph that displays nothing more than data points is easy. Only the following four steps are required to produce a simple graph:

1. Select the type of graph (if different from the default type, which is line) by selecting the appropriate type in the Graph Settings dialog box or from the /Graph Type menu.

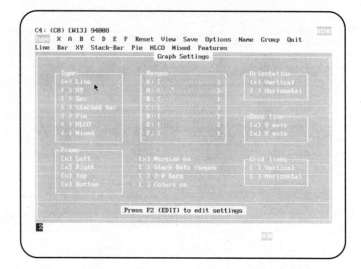

For this example, accept the default of **Line**.

2. Indicate the data ranges from your worksheet that you want to graph by selecting one or more of the **A–F** options from the Graph Settings dialog box or the /Graph menu.

To graph the quarterly sales for Product 1, select **A**. Then highlight the range C4..F4 and press ⏎Enter.

	A	B	C	D	E	F
2	SALES		Qtr 1	Qtr 2	Qtr 3	Qtr 4
4	Product 1		$94,008	$113,862	$131,637	$154,413
5	Product 2		67,716	74,664	75,501	97,764
6	Product 3		395,055	387,132	395,169	417,663
7	Product 4		286,419	294,024	290,958	285,954
9	Total Sales		$843,198	$869,682	$893,265	$955,794

F4: (C0) [W13] 154413
Enter first data range: C4..F4

3. Use the **X** range in the Graph Settings dialog box or the /Graph **X** command to indicate the data range for labeling the tick marks along the x-axis in a line, bar, stacked-bar, mixed, or HLCO graph; for labeling each part of a pie graph; and for plotting the independent variable in an XY graph.

11

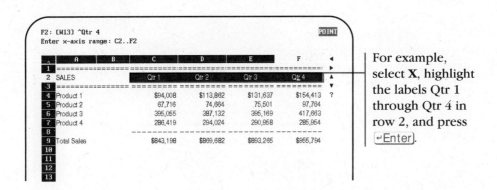

For example, select **X**, highlight the labels Qtr 1 through Qtr 4 in row 2, and press ↵Enter.

You can combine steps 2 and 3 into a one-step operation if all ranges (X, A–E) are adjacent. Use the /Graph Group command to set all contiguous data ranges at once. This option is described later in the chapter.

4. Display the graph on the screen by selecting the View command from the /Graph menu or by pressing F10 (Graph). Press any key to return to the graph settings dialog box.

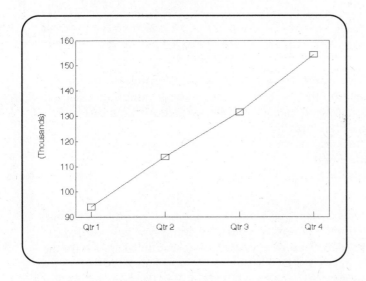

The resulting line graph is the default graph type.

After you have created a basic graph using the preceding four steps, you can choose from among numerous options to change the graph type and add titles, labels, grid lines, and legends. The following graph, for example, has been enhanced in a number of ways.

11

Because 1-2-3 sets a scale based on minimum and maximum values, the program automatically displays a numeric indicator, such as (Thousands), along the y-axis.

1-2-3 automatically provides tick marks.

The y-axis measures the amount along the vertical axis.

1-2-3 automatically scales the adjacent numbers on the y-axis, based on the minimum and maximum values of the graphed data.

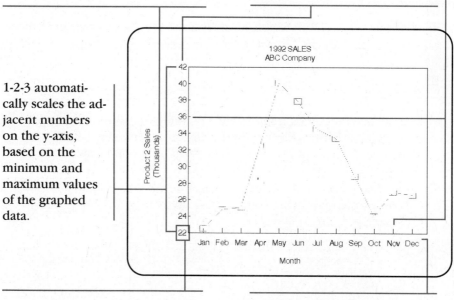

The origin of the x- and y-axes. Notice that if the origin on the graph is not zero, the upward trend will seem larger than it really is. Use an origin of zero to provide a more accurate picture of the trend.

The x-axis represents the time period of the amount measured along the horizontal axis.

You learn more about the many ways you can enhance a graph later in this chapter. Specifically, you learn how to select the graph type you need and how to indicate which data from your worksheet you want to appear on the graph.

11

Using the Graph Settings Dialog Box

In addition to the /Graph menu, the Graph Settings dialog box appears when you choose /Graph. You can use this dialog box to change graph options. Later in this chapter, procedures for changing specific graph options are discussed.

The three main ways to change an option on the dialog box involve option buttons, check boxes, and text boxes.

To use the dialog box, follow these steps:

1. After selecting /Graph, press F2 (Edit) or click the left mouse button in the dialog box.

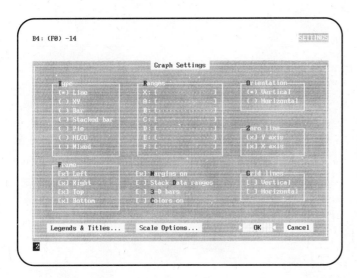

1-2-3 highlights a character from each option (usually the first letter). Also, the /Graph menu disappears when you activate the dialog box.

2. To select an option button or check box, press the highlighted letter of each option; or click the left mouse button on your choice.

11

For example, to choose a bar graph, select **Type Bar** or click the mouse button on the **B**ar option button. An asterisk indicates your choice.

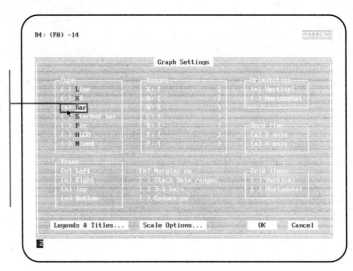

To make the bars appear three-dimensional, select **3-D bars** or click the left mouse button on the check box. An x indicates your choice.

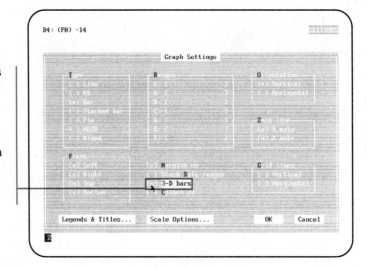

11

Note: To unmark a check box, select the check box again.

3. To use a text box, press the highlighted letter of each option until the pointer is in the text box or click the left mouse button on your choice.

4. Type the text in the box and press ↵Enter.

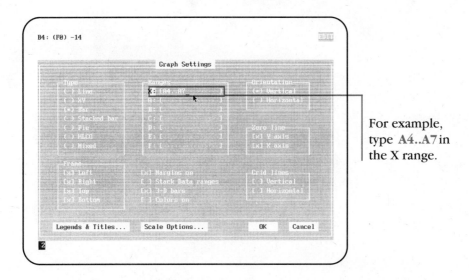

For example, type **A4..A7** in the X range.

When the text box requires a range (**R**anges), you also can select the range in one of the following ways:

Type the cell references of the range (or a range name) in the text box and press ⏎Enter.

Or

Press F4 to go to POINT mode, highlight the range, and press ⏎Enter.

5. To change other options, select **L**egends & Titles or **S**cale Options. Select the desired options and choose OK to return to the Graph Settings dialog box.

6. When you finish selecting all options on the Graph Settings dialog box, select OK. The /**G**raph menu reappears in the control panel.

7. Continue by choosing options from the /**G**raph menu, such as **V**iew, **S**ave, **N**ame, or **Q**uit.

11

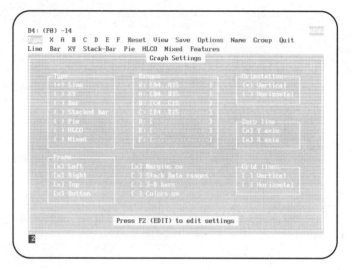

A completed
Graph Settings
dialog box is
shown here.

Selecting a Graph Type

1-2-3's graphic capabilities increase the program's power by giving you a way
to represent your data visually. Do you want to see whether there is a trend in
the latest sales increase of a particular product? A 1-2-3 graph can show you
the answer quickly, when deciphering that type of information from columns
of numbers would be difficult. 1-2-3 offers seven basic graph types: line, bar,
XY, stacked bar, pie, HLCO (high-low-close-open), and mixed. Selecting one
of the seven available graph types is easy.

11

When you select
/Graph, 1-2-3
displays the
Graph Settings
dialog box.
Choose the type
from the options
in the upper left
corner.

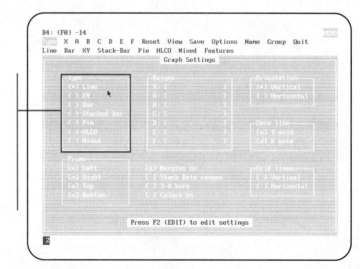

A line graph is best used for showing numeric data across time.

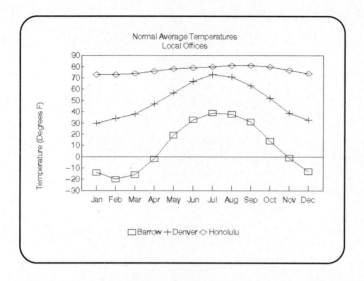

For example, you can show temperature at different stations with a line graph.

An XY graph compares one numeric data series to another across time, to determine whether one set of values (the dependent variable) depends on the other (the independent variable).

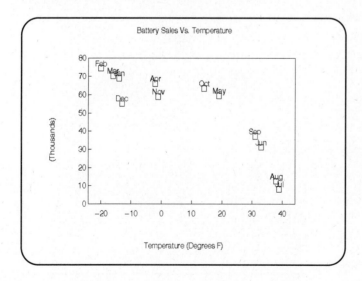

Use an XY graph, for example, to plot total sales and temperature to assess whether sales data appears to depend on temperature.

11

A bar graph shows the trend of numeric data across time.

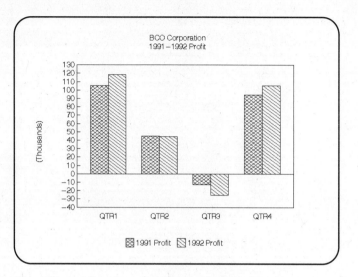

For example, you can track the progress of company profits with a bar graph.

A stacked-bar graph shows two or more data series that total 100 percent of a specific numeric category. (Do not use this type of graph if your data contains negative numbers.)

Use a stacked-bar graph, for example, to graph data series for three company divisions (displayed one above the other) to depict the proportion each represents of total revenue for each quarter. This graph also shows the 3-D option.

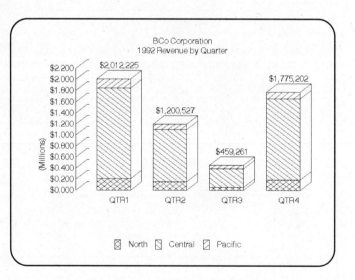

11

A pie graph is used to graph only one data series in which the components total 100 percent of a specific numeric category. (Do not use this type of graph if your data contains negative numbers.)

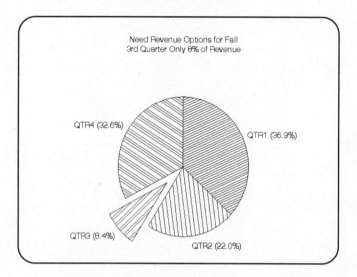

Use a pie graph, for example, to graph the percentage of total sales by quarter.

An HLCO (high-low-close-open) graph can be used to graph stock trends—showing changes in the high, low, closing, and opening prices over time. HLCO graphs can be used for tracking other data trends as well, such as sales information. In HLCO graphs, the top of the line represents the high value, and the bottom represents the low value. The left tick mark represents the opening values, while the right tick mark represents the closing values.

11

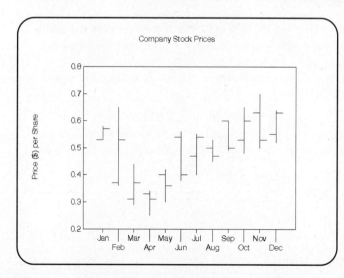

Use an HLCO graph, for example, to show the high, low, closing, and opening prices of a particular stock.

A mixed graph combines a bar graph and a line graph to display two types of data.

Use the bars of a mixed graph, for example, to show profits by division. Use a line to show the total company profit.

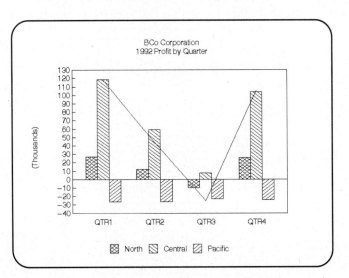

To understand which type will best display specific numeric data, you must know something about plotting points on a graph. All graphs (except pie graphs) have two axes: the x-axis (the horizontal bottom edge) and the y-axis (the vertical left edge). 1-2-3 automatically provides tick marks for the axes. The program also scales the adjacent numbers on the y-axis, based on the minimum and maximum figures included in the plotted data range(s).

Every point plotted on a graph has a unique location (x,y): x represents the time period or the amount measured along the horizontal axis; y measures the corresponding amount along the vertical axis. The intersection of the x-axis and the y-axis is called the *origin*. To avoid the misinterpretation of graph results and to make graphs easier to compare, use a zero origin in your graphs. Later in this chapter, you learn how to manually change the upper or lower limits of the scale initially set by 1-2-3.

Of the seven 1-2-3 graph types, all but the pie graph display both x- and y-axes. Line, bar, stacked-bar, HLCO, and mixed graphs display values (centered on the tick marks) along the y-axis only. The XY graph displays values on both axes.

11

Specifying Data Ranges

Because more than one type of graph can accomplish the desired presentation, you need to consider what data ranges you want to graph and the relationships among data you want to show. To create a graph, you must specify the range(s) of cells from the current worksheet to be used as data series.

To enter a data series from the Graph Settings dialog box, choose from the options **X**, **A**, **B**, **C**, **D**, **E**, or **F**.

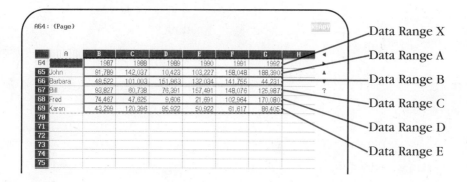

You have the option of defining each data range on the worksheet separately or defining all the data Ranges you want to plot at one time. To define one data range at a time, you fill in the Ranges section of the dialog box. If all the ranges you want to plot are contiguous (next to each other without any intervening rows or columns), select **G**roup from the /**G**raph menu to define all the ranges at once.

Defining One Data Range at a Time

If the ranges you want to plot are located in various parts of the worksheet—that is, the ranges are not all contiguous—you must define one range at a time. You can do so by choosing from among the options **X** and **A–F**.

To specify the data ranges containing x-axis and y-axis data, follow these steps:

1. Select /**G**raph.

2. Choose from the following selections the ranges for x- or y-axis data or labels:

11

Graph Type

Range	Line, Bar Stacked-Bar	XY	Pie	HLCO	Mixed
X	X-axis labels	Independent variable (x-axis)	Slice labels	X-axis labels	X-axis labels
A	1st data range	Dependent variable (y-axis)	Slice values	High	1st bar
B	2nd data range		Shading, color, and explosion	Low	2nd bar
C	3rd data range			Close	3rd bar
D	4th data range			Open	1st line
E	5th data range				2nd line
F	6th data range				3rd line

3. When you select one of the **X** or **A–F** text boxes, 1-2-3 allows you to type in the ranges. If you want to point to the range, press F4 while the cursor is in the text box, highlight the data range, and press ↵Enter.

In this example, highlight the **A** range B65..G65 and press ↵Enter.

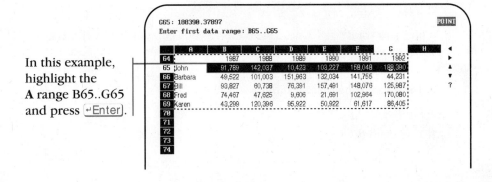

11

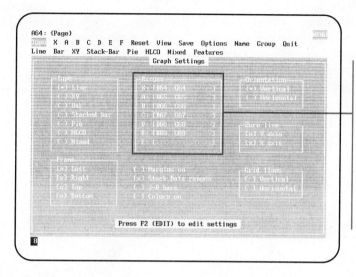

This example shows a completed Ranges section of the Graph Settings dialog box with the **X** range and five data series (**A–E**). You can enter as many as six data series.

4. After you finish choosing graph options, select OK. The /Graph menu reappears.

5. To view the graph, select **View**.

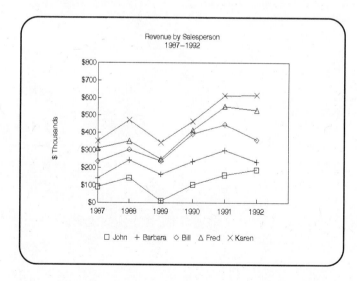

The completed graph shows five lines.

11

You can specify the ranges in any order; the range selected will always correspond with the letter assigned in the selection process. Use the **X** option to plot the time or amount measured along the x-axis. The data points in each data series are marked by a unique symbol.

397

These six symbols, which correspond to specific data ranges from A through F, are displayed in table 11.2. You can choose whether or not to display these symbols by selecting the Legends and Titles command button and choosing Format. This option is covered later in the chapter. Shading within bar, stacked-bar, pie, and mixed graphs is also covered in the following pages.

Table 11.2
Data Range Symbols for Line Graphs

Data Range	Line Graph Symbol
A	□
B	+
C	◇
D	△
E	✕
F	▽

With bar, stacked-bar, or mixed graphs, you can also enter as many as six data series in the Graph Settings dialog box.

In a bar graph, multiple data ranges appear in the graph from left to right in order of data ranges A through F.

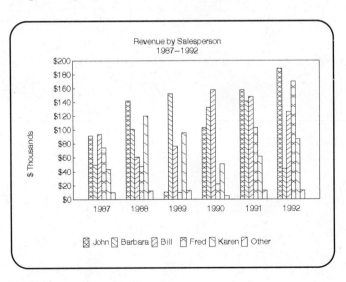

398

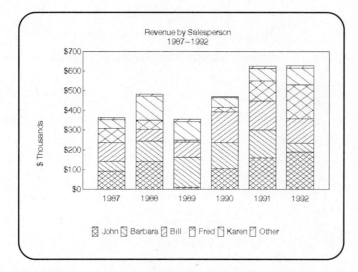

In a stacked-bar graph, multiple data ranges appear on the graph from bottom to top in order of data ranges A through F.

In bar, stacked-bar, and mixed graphs, the **X** option lets you indicate the time or amount measured along the x-axis. Every data series displayed in monochrome (one color) has unique shading. Data series displayed in color are assigned up to six different colors. Refer to table 11.3 for assignments of the patterns and colors used in bar, stacked-bar, and mixed graphs. Note that the colors listed in the table are those displayed on a VGA monitor (other monitors may display different results).

Table 11.3
Data Range Patterns and Colors for Bar Graphs

Data Range	*Bar Graph Pattern*	*Wysiwyg Bar Graph Color*
A		Blue
B		Green
C		Light Blue
D		Red
E		Magenta
F		Yellow

11

With XY graphs, to enter the data series being plotted as the independent variable, select **X** in the Graph Settings dialog box and specify the range.

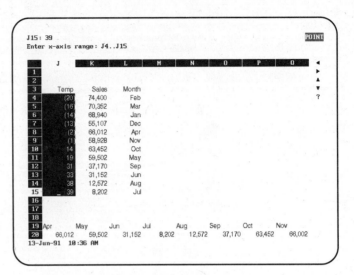

Plot at least one dependent variable (you would usually select **A**). The unique symbols that mark the data points depend on which data series (**A–F**) is selected.

With pie graphs, choose **X** to identify each piece of the pie. Then enter only one data series by selecting **A** from the Graph Settings dialog box. Other than the **X** and **A** options, the only other option in the **X** and **A–F** selections you need for creating a pie graph is **B**. By selecting **B**, you can shade and "explode" pieces of the pie.

To shade pieces of the pie graph, select a range of cells containing values between 1 and 8—corresponding to data range **A** of the graph.

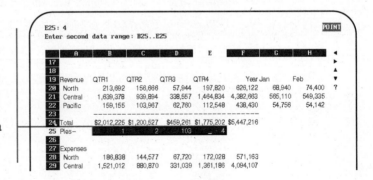

To explode a piece of the pie, add 100 to this number. Select **B** from the menu and highlight the range of numbers.

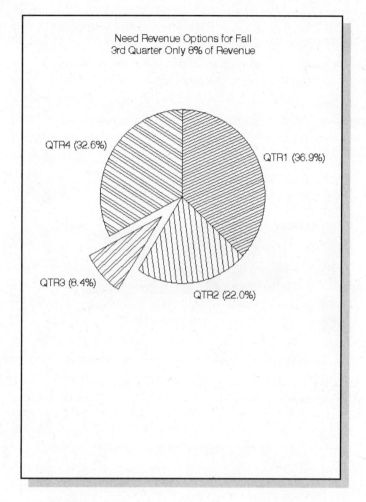

Need Revenue Options for Fall
3rd Quarter Only 8% of Revenue

QTR4 (32.6%)

QTR1 (36.9%)

QTR3 (8.4%)

QTR2 (22.0%)

The printed pie graph shows some of the different types of shading and one exploded slice.

11

Defining All Data Ranges at Once

If the **X** and the **A–F** ranges are in one contiguous range, you can use the **Group** command on the **/Graph** menu to define all the ranges at once. The command **/Graph Group** gives you a quick way to define the **X** and **A–F** ranges without having to specify them individually. For this option to work properly, the cells for the **X** range must be immediately to the left of or immediately above the **A** range. The cells for ranges **B** through **F**, if present, are adjacent to the **A** range. Once you have defined the location of the range, the command prompts you for a "columnwise" or "rowwise" orientation.

To select all the data ranges for a graph, **X** and **A–F**, when data is in adjacent rows and columns are in consecutive order, follow these steps:

1. Select /**G**raph and choose a graph type from the seven selections in the dialog box. Select OK to redisplay the /**G**raph menu.

2. Select **G**roup.

3. Specify the range that contains **X** and one or more **A** through **F** data ranges, and then press ⏎Enter. The rows or columns must be adjacent and in the order X, A, B, C, and so on.

For this example, specify the group range as B64..G70 and press ⏎Enter.

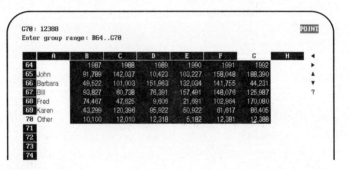

4. Select **C**olumnwise if the data ranges are in columns, or select **R**owwise if the data ranges are in rows.

5. Select **V**iew.

This graph shows the result of selecting **R**owwise orientation with the /**G**raph **G**roup command.

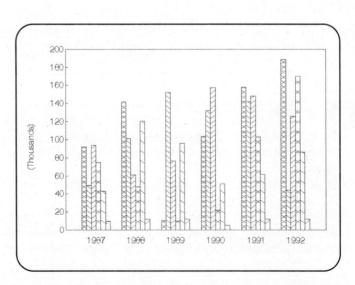

Enhancing the Appearance of a Graph

After you have created a basic graph using the simple four-step procedure described earlier in this chapter, you can improve the appearance of your graph and produce final-quality output suitable for business presentations. By selecting choices from the Graph Settings dialog box or from the /Graph Options menu, you can enhance a graph by adding descriptive labels and numbers, and by changing the default graph display items.

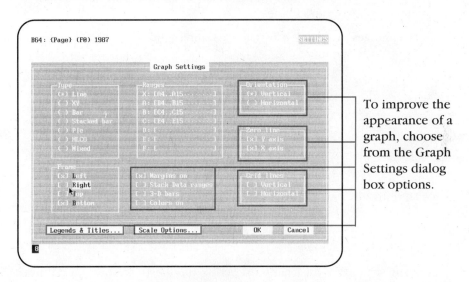

To improve the appearance of a graph, choose from the Graph Settings dialog box options.

Table 11.4 describes Graph Settings dialog box options that allow you to enhance the graph.

Table 11.4
Selections in the Graph Settings Dialog Box

Selection	Description
Frame	Check boxes that let you define a border line around all, part, or none of the graph
Orientation	Option buttons that give you the choice of producing the graph vertically or horizontally
Zero line	A check box that allows you to add or remove the origin or zero line from the x- or y-axis

continued

11

403

Table 11.4 (*continued*)

Selection	Description
Grid lines	A check box that produces spaced vertical or horizontal lines in the graph to orient bars or lines
Margins on	A check box that leaves space between the y-axis and the first and last data points; if this check box is empty, the first and last data points plot against the graph frame
Stack Data ranges	A check box that stacks lines and bars on top of each other
3-D bars	A check box that allows you to produce three-dimensional bars
Colors on	A check box that causes a graph to display and print in color, if the proper equipment is available
Legends & Titles	A command button that generates a pop-up dialog box allowing you to specify additional options
Scale Options	A command button that generates a pop-up dialog box which lets you control the division and format of values along the x-axis or y-axis

The following sections of this chapter describe and illustrate how you can use additional options from the Graph Settings dialog box to create presentation-quality graphs.

As you add enhancements to your graphs, check the results frequently. Press Graph (F10) to check the most recent version of the graph. Press any key to exit the graph display.

Setting the Graph Frame

Normally, you would want the entire graph frame to appear around your graph. However, you may want to vary individual graphs in a presentation. To add or remove lines in the graph frame, follow these steps:

1. Select /Graph.
2. Press F2 (Edit) or click the left mouse button somewhere in the dialog box to display the options in the Graph Settings dialog box.

404

3. Select **Frame** and then select **Left**, **Right**, **Top**, or **Bottom**. An x indicates that the line will be present; an empty check box indicates the line will be absent.

4. To view the graph with a modified graph frame displayed, press F10.

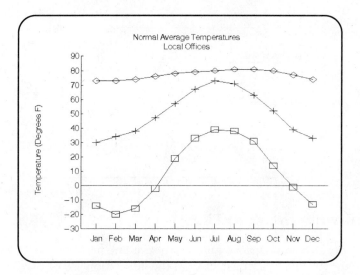

This example shows the effect of removing the top and right lines of the graph frame.

Changing the Orientation

Another way to vary your graphs is through the Orientation option of the Graph Settings dialog box. Graphs normally display with the y-axis vertical and the x-axis horizontal. To reverse this option, select the Horizontal option button in the Graph Settings dialog box.

11

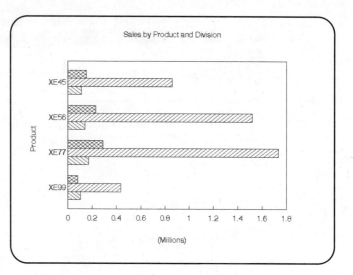

The bars in this graph show a **Horizontal** orientation.

Adding or Removing the Zero Line

For graphs that have positive and negative values, the zero line may be helpful. In other graphs, the zero line may distract from the illustration. To display or remove the zero line running through the 0 on the y-axis or x-axis, follow these steps:

1. Select /**Graph**.

2. Press F2 (Edit) or click the left mouse button somewhere in the dialog box to display the options in the Graph Settings dialog box.

3. Select **Zero line** and then select **Y**-axis or **X**-axis. An x indicates that the line will be present; an empty check box indicates the line will be absent.

4. To view the graph with modified zero lines, press F10.

11

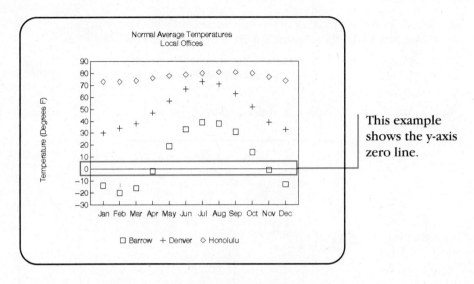

This example shows the y-axis zero line.

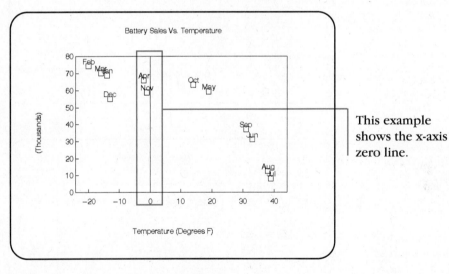

This example shows the x-axis zero line.

11

Setting a Background Grid

Ordinarily, you use the default background (clear—without a grid) for your graphs. Sometimes you may want to impose a grid on a graph so that the data-point amounts are easier to read. To add a grid to your graph, follow these steps:

1. Select /**Graph**.

407

2. Press [F2] (Edit) or click the left mouse button somewhere in the dialog box to display the options in the Graph Settings dialog box.

3. Select **Grid** lines and then select **Vertical** or **Horizontal**. An x indicates that lines will be present; an empty check box indicates the lines will be absent.

4. To view the graph with grid lines displayed, press [F10].

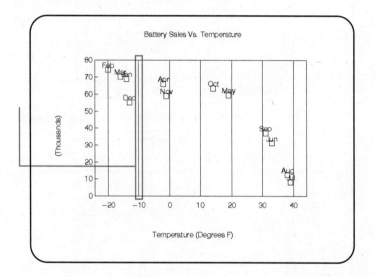

This example shows the result of using vertical grid lines.

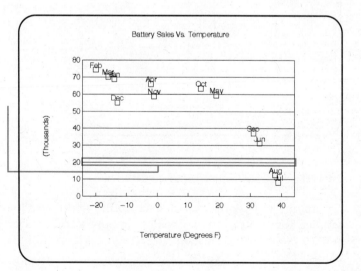

This example shows the result of using horizontal grid lines.

Adding or Removing Graph Margins

Graph margins, or *gutters*, are spaces between the graph frame and the first
and last data points. You can turn the margins on or off. To do so, select the
Margins check box in the Graph Settings dialog box.

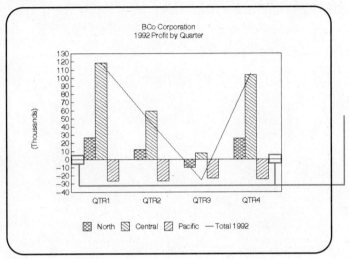

This graph shows
the graph margins.

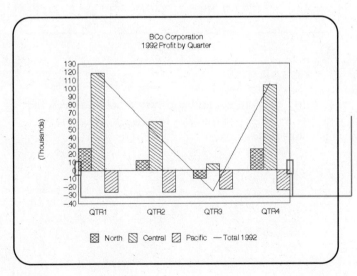

This graph shows
the graph margins
removed.

11

Stacking Data Ranges

Although there is a stacked bar graph type, you may want to stack lines on your graph. When you stack data values, the graph adds the first value to the second. The graph adds the third set of data points to the first two, and so on. The resulting graph shows the total value of all data points as the top line or bar. To stack data points, select the Stack **D**ata ranges check box in the Graph Settings dialog box.

This line graph sums revenue by salesperson. The top line is the total of all sales-people.

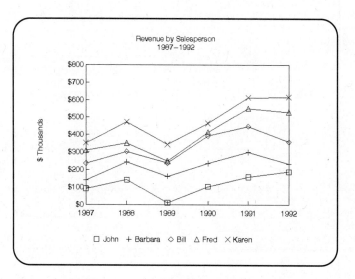

Creating a 3-D Bar Graph

Three dimensional bar graphs can highlight and add variety to your presentations. In Release 2.3, you can create 3-D bar graphs by selecting the **3-D bars** check box in the Graph Settings dialog box.

11

410

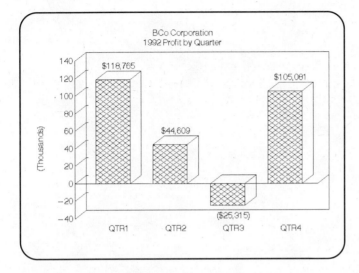

This example shows the 3-D bar effect.

Displaying a Graph in Color

If you have a monitor or output device that displays color, you can turn color on by selecting the **Colors on** check box in the Graph Settings dialog box. To display the graph in monochrome (black and white), unmark the **Colors** check box.

Using the Legends and Titles Dialog Box

In most cases, a graph without explanations is incomplete. To add text and symbols to various parts of the graph, you use the **Legends & Titles** command button to pull up another dialog box.

To access the Graph Legends & Titles dialog box, follow these steps:

1. Select /**Graph**.
2. Press F2 (Edit) or click the left mouse button somewhere in the dialog box to display the options in the Graph Settings dialog box.
3. Select the **Legends & Titles** command button.

11

411

The Graph
Legends & Titles
dialog box is
shown here.

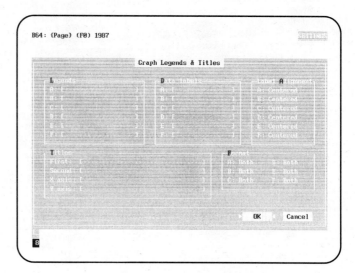

Table 11.5 describes each item in the Graph Legends & Titles dialog box.
Explanations of some of these items follow. For more information, refer to
your Lotus documentation.

Table 11.5

Selections on the Graph Legends & Titles Dialog Box

Selection	Description
Legends	Adds descriptions below the x-axis that link symbols, shadings, or colors to specific y-axis data ranges
Titles	Includes graph titles and axis titles
Data labels	Adds labels that identify different data points within the graph
Label Alignment	Determines the position of data labels relative to data points or bars
Format	Adds the lines and/or symbols that connect or represent data points

You can enter one or two centered titles at the top of the graph, a title below
the x-axis, and a title to the left of the y-axis.

11

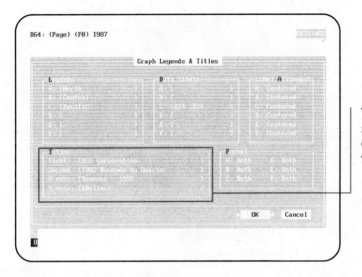

Titles are desig-
nated in the
Graph Legends &
Titles dialog box.

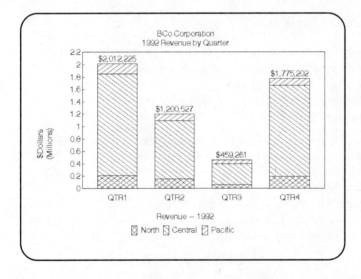

The titles, leg-
ends, and data
labels that can
be added are
displayed in the
designated
locations.

11

You can enter titles by typing a new description, by specifying a range name,
or by referencing the cell location of a label or a number already in the
worksheet.

To add titles to a graph (after you have chosen the graph type and entered
data ranges), complete the following steps:

1. In the Titles area of the Graph Legends & Titles dialog box, choose
   from the following selections:

413

Selection	Description
First	Displays a title on the top line of a graph
Second	Displays a title on the second line of a graph
X-Axis	Displays a title below the x-axis
Y-Axis	Displays a title to the left of the y-axis

Note: The **X-Axis** and **Y-Axis** titles do not apply when you construct a pie graph.

2. To enter a title, type the text and press ⏎Enter or type a \ (backslash) followed by the cell reference or range name containing the title.

3. Repeat steps 1 and 2 for each title desired.

4. To view the graph with the titles displayed, press F10.

Using the Legend Option

Whenever a graph contains more than one set of data, you need to be able to distinguish between those sets. If you are using a color monitor and select Color from the Graph Settings dialog box, 1-2-3 differentiates data series with color. If the Color option is not selected, the data series in line and XY graphs are marked with special symbols.

If you intend to print the graph on a black-and-white printer, even if you have a color monitor, choose **B&W** from the /Graph Options menu or leave the Color option unmarked in the dialog box before saving the graph. A graph saved under the Color option will print all ranges on a black-and-white printer as solid blocks of black. You might choose a data series (**A**, **B**, **C**, **D**, **E**, or **F**) because you want certain symbols, shadings, or colors, or to avoid using certain combinations of symbols or shadings.

To provide explanatory text for data that is represented by symbols or shadings, use the **Legends** option to display legends below the x-axis. To add a legend to your graph, follow these steps:

1. In the Graph Legends & Titles dialog box, select **Legends**, and then select **A**, **B**, **C**, **D**, **E**, or **F**.

2. To enter a legend, type the text and press ⏎Enter; or type a \ (backslash) followed by the cell reference or range name containing the legend.

11

3. Repeat steps 1 and 2 for each legend desired.

4. To view the graph with the legends displayed, press [F10].

You can select Options **Legend R**ange from the **/G**raph menu to select the legends in one step if the text to appear in the legends is in adjacent cells in the worksheet. To select all legends in one step:

1. Select **/G**raph **O**ptions **L**egend **R**ange.

2. Type or highlight the range, and then press [↵Enter].

If you want to edit a legend, change the legend in the Graph Legends & Titles dialog box.

Specifying Connecting Lines or Symbols

The **F**ormat option of the Graph Legends & Titles dialog box is used to display connecting lines and/or symbols on line, XY, HLCO, and mixed graphs.

To add connecting lines and/or symbols, follow these steps:

1. In the Graph Legends & Titles dialog box, select **F**ormat and then select **A**, **B**, **C**, **D**, **E**, or **F**. The Graph Range Formats pop-up screen appears.

2. Select from the following options on the resulting menu:

   Lines **S**ymbols **B**oth **N**either **A**rea

3. To view the graph with the format displayed, press [F10].

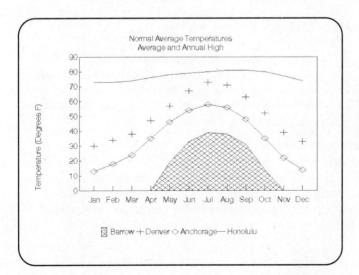

This example shows the result of using different options with four ranges.

11

415

To restore the default format setting for the sample line graph, select **B**oth for each data point in the **F**ormat area of the Graph Legends & Titles dialog box.

Changing Axis Scale Settings

You can use the **S**cale Options command button in the Graph Settings dialog box to alter three distinct default settings associated with the values displayed along a graph's x- and y-axes. These settings let you change the upper and lower limits of the y-axis scale, change the format of y-axis values, and suppress the x- and y-axis scale indicator(s). In addition, you can use this option to change the number of labels displayed along the x-axis.

To display the Graph Scale Settings dialog box, follow these steps:

1. Select /**G**raph.
2. Press F2 (Edit) or click the left mouse button somewhere in the dialog box to display the options in the Graph Settings dialog box.
3. Select the **S**cale Options command button.
4. Make the necessary adjustments to the Graph Scale Settings dialog box.
5. To view the graph with axis scale changes made, press F10.

For more information on changing the axis scale settings, refer to your Lotus documentation or to Que's *Using 1-2-3 for DOS Release 2.3*, Special Edition.

Saving Graphs on Disk

11

To create a disk file of a graph to be used with other programs, use the /**G**raph **S**ave command. This command creates a file with the extension PIC. To save the graph specifications along with the underlying worksheet, first use the /**G**raph **N**ame **C**reate command to name the graph, and then save the worksheet to retain the graph settings by using /**F**ile **S**ave.

Suppose that you have constructed a graph that you want to store for subsequent printing or importing through another program, such as a word processing program. After you verify that the graph type chosen is appropriate for your presentation needs, that the graph data ranges have been specified accurately, and that all desired enhancements have been added, use /**G**raph **S**ave to create a PIC file on disk.

To save a graph as a PIC file so that it can be used with other programs, follow these steps:

1. Select /**G**raph **S**ave.

    1-2-3 prompts you for a file name and displays (across the top of the screen) a list of the PIC files in the current directory.

2. Type a new file name (as many as eight characters long), or use → or ← to highlight a name already listed; then press ↵Enter .

    Note: You can press F3 to display a full-screen listing of existing graph names.

3. If you chose an existing name from the list, select **R**eplace to overwrite the old file, or select **C**ancel to avoid overwriting the old file. 1-2-3 automatically adds the PIC extension to the file name for you.

After you have saved the graph settings for printing, you can follow instructions provided with the other program for using the 1-2-3 graph with that program.

Saving Graph Settings

If you want to view on-screen a graph that you created in an earlier graphing session, you must have given the graph a name when you originally constructed the graph. You also must have saved the worksheet, unless the same worksheet is still active. To name a graph, you issue the /**G**raph **N**ame **C**reate command. Use the /**G**raph **N**ame options to save the graph along with the underlying worksheet or to retrieve or delete a named graph you have saved.

Only one graph at a time can be the current graph. If you want to save a graph that you have just completed (for subsequent recall to the screen) as well as build a new graph, you must first issue the /**G**raph **N**ame **C**reate command. The only way to store a graph for later screen display is to issue this command, which instructs 1-2-3 to remember the specifications used to define the current graph. If you do not name a graph and subsequently either reset the graph or change the specifications, you cannot restore the original graph without having to rebuild it.

To use the graph name settings, follow these steps:

1. Select /**G**raph **N**ame.

2. Select from the following options the graph naming activity you want to perform:

11

417

Selection	Description
Use	Displays a graph whose settings have already been saved with /**Graph Name Create**; this option allows you to recall any named graph from within the active worksheet
Create	Creates a name for the currently defined graph so that you can later access and modify the graph
Delete	Erases an individual graph name and the settings associated with that graph
Reset	Erases all graph names
Table	Produces a listing directly in the worksheet of all graph names, their types (pie, bar, and so on), and titles (the top line of the graph); use caution to avoid writing over existing data

3. If you selected **Create** in step 2, type a new name (up to 15 characters in length), and then press ⏎Enter. If you selected **Use** or **Delete**, use →⏎ or ←⏎ to highlight in the list the name of the graph you want (press F3 to view a full-screen list of names); then press ⏎Enter. If you selected **Table**, highlight the desired location of the graph name table and press ⏎Enter.

Note: If you want graph names to be stored with their worksheet, remember to save the worksheet file by using /**File Save** after creating the names.

11 Printing Graphs

The first part of this chapter showed you how to create 1-2-3 graphs that are displayed on-screen. The remainder of this chapter shows you how to create printed copies that can be distributed to colleagues, used in business presentations, or filed for future reference. You will learn how to modify the quality, size, and orientation of printed graphs.

Another way to print graphs is through the Release 2.3 Wysiwyg **:Graph Add** and **:Print** commands. These commands allow you to print graphs along with your worksheet data. Chapter 12 includes information on this process.

Accessing and Exiting PrintGraph

Once you create a graph within 1-2-3, you need to access the PrintGraph program to print the graph. This is accomplished directly from DOS or through the Lotus 1-2-3 Access menu. The following sections cover the different ways to access and exit the PrintGraph program.

Accessing the PrintGraph Program

As you learned earlier in this chapter, to print a graph within the PrintGraph program, you must first save the graph in 1-2-3 with /**G**raph **S**ave. So that you can later modify graphs that you create, you must also issue the /**G**raph **N**ame **C**reate command and save the worksheet with /**F**ile **S**ave before you exit 1-2-3.

To access PrintGraph directly from DOS, type **pgraph** at the DOS prompt and press Enter. The PrintGraph program must be in the current directory. If you use a printer driver other than the default 1-2-3 driver, you must type the name of that driver set (**pgraph hp**, for example) to reach the PrintGraph main menu. However, you are more likely to use PrintGraph immediately after you have created a graph.

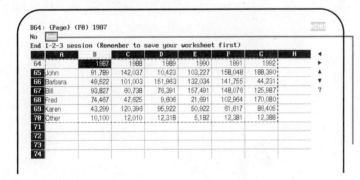

If you originally accessed 1-2-3 by typing **lotus**, select /**Q**uit and then **Yes** to return to the Lotus 1-2-3 Access menu.

11

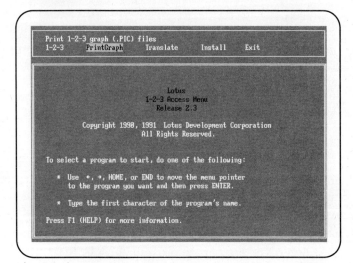

From the Lotus
1-2-3 Access
menu, select
PrintGraph.

When the open-
ing screen of the
PrintGraph
program is
displayed, you
can choose the
options you want
to set and print
your graph.

11

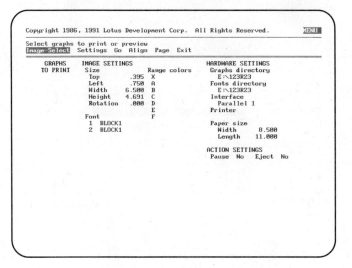

420

Exiting the PrintGraph Program

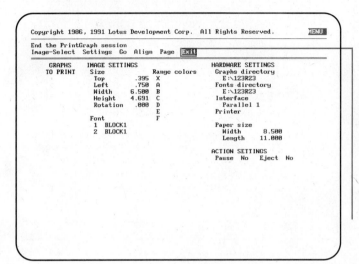

```
Copyright 1986, 1991 Lotus Development Corp.  All Rights Reserved.      MENU

End the PrintGraph session
Image-Select  Settings  Go  Align  Page  Exit

     GRAPHS    IMAGE SETTINGS                    HARDWARE SETTINGS
    TO PRINT   Size             Range colors      Graphs directory
               Top     .395     X                   E:\123R23
               Left    .750     A                 Fonts directory
               Width  6.500     B                   E:\123R23
               Height 4.691     C                 Interface
               Rotation .000    D                   Parallel 1
                                E                 Printer
               Font             F
               1  BLOCK1                          Paper size
               2  BLOCK1                            Width     8.500
                                                    Length   11.000

                                                 ACTION SETTINGS
                                                 Pause  No  Eject  No
```

To leave the PrintGraph program, select **Exit** from the PrintGraph main menu. Then select **Yes** to verify that you want to end your PrintGraph session.

The next screen to appear depends on the method you used to access PrintGraph. If you entered PrintGraph by typing **pgraph** from the DOS prompt, the DOS prompt is restored. If you entered PrintGraph from the Lotus 1-2-3 Access menu, the Access menu reappears. Select **Exit** from the Access menu to restore the DOS prompt.

If you want to enter 1-2-3 after you have exited PrintGraph and restored the DOS prompt, type **123** or **lotus** and press Enter. If you typed **lotus**, select **1-2-3** from the Access menu.

Understanding the PrintGraph Menu

Like 1-2-3, the PrintGraph program is menu-driven. The menu screens not only provide instructions for printing graph (PIC) files, but also information about current print conditions.

11

The first three
text lines, which
display a copy-
right message and
two levels of
current menu
options, always
remain on-screen.
In the settings
sheet area, below
the double line,
selections are
continually
updated.

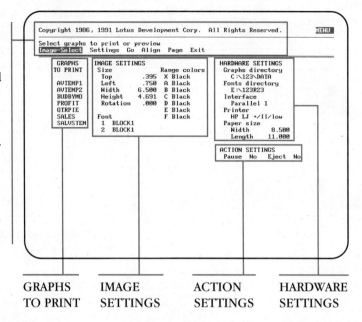

```
Copyright 1986, 1991 Lotus Development Corp.  All Rights Reserved.        MENU
Select graphs to print or preview
Image-Select  Settings  Go  Align  Page  Exit
  GRAPHS     IMAGE SETTINGS                HARDWARE SETTINGS
  TO PRINT   Size           Range colors     Graphs directory
             Top       .395  X Black            C:\123\DATA
  AVTEMP1    Left      .750  A Black         Fonts directory
  AVTEMP2    Width    6.500  B Black            E:\123R23
  BUDBYMO    Height   4.691  C Black         Interface
  PROFIT     Rotation  .000  D Black            Parallel 1
  QTRPIE                     E Black         Printer
  SALES      Font            F Black            HP LJ +/II/low
  SALVSTEM   1  BLOCK1                       Paper size
             2  BLOCK1                          Width      8.500
                                               Length    11.000

                                            ACTION SETTINGS
                                            Pause  No   Eject  No
```

| GRAPHS | IMAGE | ACTION | HARDWARE |
| TO PRINT | SETTINGS | SETTINGS | SETTINGS |

Before you begin printing a graph, make sure that you check the settings
sheet. The settings displayed in the settings sheet are organized into four
areas that are related to either the **Image-Select** or **Settings** options of the
PrintGraph menu.

A list of graphs selected for printing appears under GRAPHS TO PRINT on the
left side of the settings sheet. To make changes in the other three settings
sheet areas, you first select **Settings** from the PrintGraph main menu. When
you select **Settings**, a menu of options appears (see table 11.6).

11

Table 11.6
Selections on the PrintGraph Settings Menu

Selection	Description
Image	Changes the size, font, and color of the graph; the updated revisions are displayed in the IMAGE SETTINGS area of the settings sheet
Hardware	Alters the paper size, printer, or disk-drive specifications displayed in the HARDWARE SETTINGS area
Action	Moves to a new page and pauses while you change specifications for the next graph

Selection	Description
Save	Allows you to save the current settings in a configuration file, to be used when starting PrintGraph
Reset	Restores the settings to those saved in the configuration file
Quit	Returns you to the PrintGraph main menu

Printing a Basic Graph

Printing a graph can be simple if you accept PrintGraph's default print settings. If you have specified the correct hardware configuration, you can produce a half-size, block-style typeface, black-and-white graph on 8 1/2-by-11-inch continuous-feed paper simply by marking a graph for printing and then printing it.

Suppose, for example, that you want to print a bar graph with the file name AVTEMP1.PIC. Before you begin the printing procedure, make sure that the current printer and interface specifications accurately reflect your hardware, that you're using continuous-feed paper, and that the printer is on-line and the print head is positioned at the page's top. (The sections that follow explain the graph printing process in detail.) Then use the following steps to print the graph with the default settings.

To print a graph using PrintGraph's default settings, follow these steps:

1. Access PrintGraph using one of the methods described earlier.

2. From the PrintGraph main menu, select **I**mage-Select.

3. Move the pointer to the name of the graph(s) you want to print and press the space bar. A # appears next to the selected graph.

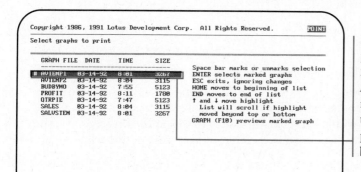

For example, to print the graph file named AVTEMP1.PIC, move the pointer to AVTEMP1 and press the space bar.

423

4. Press ⏎Enter to select the graph and return to the PrintGraph menu.

5. Select **Align** to let PrintGraph know that the paper is correctly aligned at the top of the page.

6. Select **G**o to print the graph.

The printed graph is centered upright (zero degrees rotation) on the paper and fills the top half of an 8 1/2-by-11-inch page. The titles are printed in the default BLOCK1 font.

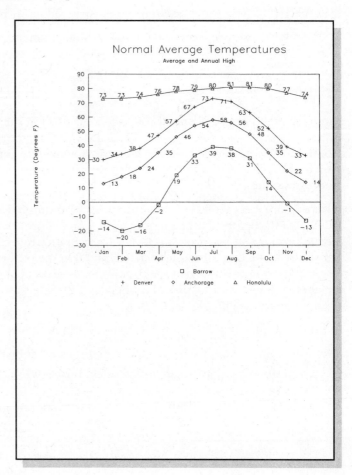

Note: A printed graph looks different from its on-screen display. The two titles at the top of the graph in the on-screen version appear to be the same size, but the first title automatically appears larger in a printed graph. Another variation can occur within the y-axis—the tick marks in the on-screen version are occasionally scaled in increments different from that of the printed graph.

A third potential difference between an on-screen display and the printed graph is in the legends. In versions of 1-2-3 prior to Release 2.2, legends may spread out so that the first and last items in the legends are not printed. You can solve the problem by reducing the amount of text in each legend.

If you want to enhance this default graph, you can do so by using any or all of PrintGraph's many special features. These special capabilities (which are not available in the main 1-2-3 program) include the enlargement, reduction, and rotation of graph printouts and the use of different colors and fonts. These enhancement options are described in the sections that follow.

Changing the Appearance of the Printed Graph

You can enhance a basic graph you have created with PrintGraph's default settings in a number of ways. You can change the appearance of the printed graph by adjusting its size and orientation, by selecting different fonts, and by choosing alternate colors. When you select **Settings Image** from the PrintGraph menu, 1-2-3 provides the options **Size**, **Font**, and **Range-Colors** (as well as **Quit**). Use these options, respectively, to change the size of a graph, to specify one or two print typefaces on a single graph, and to select colors for the different data ranges. The settings for these options are displayed in the middle of the PrintGraph settings sheet under IMAGE SETTINGS. Refer to your Lotus documentation for more information on these options.

Setting Up Your Hardware for Printing

There is more to printing than just inserting a sheet of paper in a printer and pressing a key. Although the printing process is governed to some extent by your hardware and software, most of the initial decisions are up to you. You need to make decisions about the disk drives containing the print files, the printer type and name, and the size of the paper. The hardware settings are displayed in the settings sheet's far right column.

11

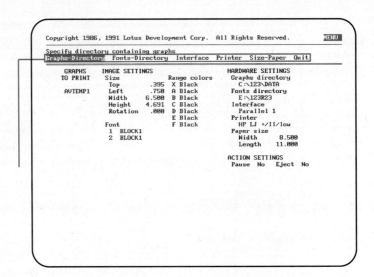

Copyright 1986, 1991 Lotus Development Corp. All Rights Reserved.   MENU

Specify directory containing graphs
Graphs-Directory Fonts-Directory Interface Printer Size-Paper Quit

```
   GRAPHS    IMAGE SETTINGS                      HARDWARE SETTINGS
  TO PRINT   Size             Range colors        Graphs directory
              Top       .395  X Black              C:\123\DATA
  AVTEMP1     Left      .750  A Black             Fonts directory
              Width    6.500  B Black              E:\123R23
              Height   4.691  C Black             Interface
              Rotation  .000  D Black              Parallel 1
                             E Black             Printer
             Font                  F Black         HP LJ +/II/low
              1  BLOCK1                           Paper size
              2  BLOCK1                            Width     8.500
                                                   Length   11.000

                                                 ACTION SETTINGS
                                                   Pause  No   Eject  No
```

When you select
Settings Hard-
ware, this menu
appears.

The **G**raphs-Directory and **F**onts-Directory options pertain to disk-drive
specifications; **I**nterface and **P**rinter determine the current printer name and
type; and **S**ize-Paper permits you to specify the paper width and length in
inches.

Controlling Printing Actions

In addition to specifying hardware settings, you can control printing actions
by indicating certain settings before you start the printing process. In particular, you can make the printer pause between graphs, and you can decide
whether you want the paper ejected after each graph. These ACTION
SETTINGS are displayed in the far right column of the settings sheet. Refer to
your Lotus documentation for more information.

Completing the Print Cycle

After you create a graph and specify which options you want to use when
printing, you can save the PrintGraph settings (if you want to use them again
later), preview the graph on-screen (optional), and print the graph.

11

426

Saving PrintGraph Settings

After you establish the current **I**mage, **H**ardware, and **A**ction settings, you can select **S**ettings **S**ave if you want to use these settings in a later PrintGraph session. The current options are then written to a file named PGRAPH.CNF, which is read whenever PrintGraph is loaded.

To save the current PrintGraph settings for use in a later session, follow these steps:

1. From the PrintGraph main menu, select **S**ettings **S**ave.

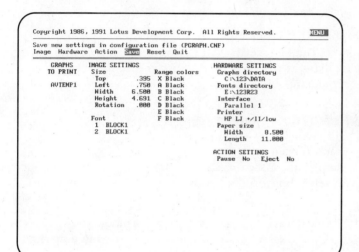

The current settings are stored in a file named PGRAPH.CNF, and are used whenever PrintGraph is loaded (until you modify and save the settings again).

2. Select **Q**uit to return to the PrintGraph main menu.

Select **S**ettings **R**eset to restore all **I**mage, **H**ardware, and **A**ction settings to PrintGraph's default settings or to the options most recently saved. Note, however, that graphs selected to print with the **I**mage-**S**elect command are not reset when you issue **S**ettings **R**eset.

Previewing a Graph

Before printing a graph, you may want to first view the graph on-screen—especially when you cannot remember the name of the specific graph you want to print. Instead of returning to 1-2-3, you can view the graph from within PrintGraph just before printing.

11

427

To preview a graph from within PrintGraph, follow these steps:

1. From the PrintGraph main menu, select **Image-Select**. A list of all PIC files in the current **Graphs-Directory** appears on-screen.

2. Highlight the name of the graph you want to view and press F10 (Graph).

   To verify that the graph shown is the one you want to print, you can use the F10 (Graph) key to preview every graph listed.

3. Press any key to remove the graph from the screen.

4. Repeat steps 2 and 3 to view additional graphs on-screen. Then press Esc to return to the PrintGraph main menu.

When previewing graphs within PrintGraph, the size, font, and rotation options are not displayed. But the preview does give a good idea of what the printed graph will look like—in some instances, a better idea than you can get with the /Graph View command within 1-2-3.

Selecting and Printing Graphs

Selecting graphs you want to print from the list of PIC files is easy. To mark the files for printing, simply follow the directions that appear on the right side of the screen when you select **Image-Select** from the PrintGraph main menu.

Use the direction keys to position the highlight bar on the graph you want to select. Then press the space bar to mark the file with a # symbol. The space bar acts as a toggle key; use the same action to remove any unwanted marks. If necessary, continue to mark additional graphs. After you press Enter to accept the currently marked graphs for printing, the updated settings sheet is displayed again, listing all selected graph names under GRAPHS TO PRINT.

The PrintGraph main menu's **Align** option sets the program's built-in top-of-page marker. Regularly selecting **Align** before selecting **Go** is a good practice. The **Page** option advances the paper one page at a time. At the end of a printing session, this useful option advances continuous-feed paper to help you remove the printed output.

To print a graph, select **Go** from the PrintGraph main menu. After you select **Go**, you will see in the screen's menu area messages indicating that picture and font files are loading. Then 1-2-3 will print the graphs. If you want to interrupt the process of printing a graph or series of graphs, press Ctrl-Break. Then press Esc to access the PrintGraph menu options.

11

Summary

This chapter has shown you how to create and print graphs. You learned the basic steps for creating a graph and how to select any one of 1-2-3's seven types of graphs: line, XY, bar, stacked-bar, pie, HLCO, and mixed. You learned, too, how to improve the appearance of graphs.

So that you could use graphs with another program and PrintGraph, the chapter showed you how to create a PIC file on disk. You learned how to use the PrintGraph program to print graphs created within 1-2-3. You learned how to access and exit PrintGraph, and also how to print a basic graph in six simple steps. Then you learned how to enhance the appearance of a printed graph. You were also shown how to set up your hardware to allow printing of graphs. Finally, you learned how to save your PrintGraph settings, preview a graph before printing, and actually begin the printing process.

Specifically, you learned the following key information about 1-2-3:

- The 1-2-3 /Graph menu allows you to create graphs associated with data in the 1-2-3 worksheet and brings up the Graph Settings dialog box.

- The Type option of the Graph Settings dialog box enables you to select from seven different types of graphs. Which graph type is most appropriate depends on your data and your graphing needs.

- You can choose the data ranges to be displayed in a graph with the Ranges X and A–F options of the Graph Settings dialog box. The /Graph Group command allows you to select all data ranges at once, as long as they form a contiguous block of cells in the worksheet.

- The Graph Settings dialog box also allows you to select from many different options that can be used to enhance the appearance of your graph. You can use this dialog box to add or remove parts of the graph frame, change the orientation of the graph, add or delete the zero and grid lines, stack data ranges, create 3-D bar graphs, turn margins (gutters) on or off, and turn colors on or off.

- The Legends & Titles command button in the Graph Settings dialog box brings up another dialog box, which allows you to enter titles, legends, and data labels for your graph. You can also align data labels and change the format of line graphs.

- The Scale Options command button in the Graph Settings dialog box brings up another dialog box, which allows you to change the scale of the axes.

11

■ The /Graph Save command saves the graph as a PIC file on disk. This file can then be used with other programs, such as word processing programs.

■ The /Graph Name command enables you to use existing graph specifications, create a new graph name, delete a graph name, reset all graph names, and display a table of graph names in the worksheet.

■ To modify a graph in a later session of 1-2-3, you must use the /Graph Name Create command and then save the file with /File Save. Otherwise, your graph specifications will be lost, even if a PIC file has been created with /Graph Save.

■ The PrintGraph program allows you to print graphs saved with /Graph Save.

■ You can access the PrintGraph program in two ways: by typing **pgraph** directly from DOS, or by selecting **P**rintGraph from the Lotus 1-2-3 Access menu.

■ To leave the PrintGraph program, select **E**xit from the PrintGraph main menu. If you entered 1-2-3 from the Access menu, you return to that screen. Otherwise, you return to the DOS prompt.

■ The PrintGraph screen consists of three text lines at the top of the screen: a copyright message and two levels of current menu options. The lower area of the screen, which contains the settings sheet, displays the results of option selections. This settings sheet is composed of four areas: GRAPHS TO PRINT, IMAGE SETTINGS, HARDWARE SETTINGS, and ACTION SETTINGS.

■ The Image-Select option of the PrintGraph main menu allows you to select which graphs from the current directory are to be printed. You also use this option to preview a graph on-screen before it is printed.

■ The Settings **I**mage command is used to change the size and orientation (rotation) of the printed graph. This command is also used to select different fonts and colors to be displayed in a graph.

■ The Settings **H**ardware command allows you to change the directories where PrintGraph looks to find your graph files and the font program files. You also use this command to select or change the printer or plotter used to print the graphs, and change the paper size from the default of 8 1/2 inches by 11 inches.

■ The Settings **S**ave command is used to save any **I**mage, **H**ardware, or **A**ction settings you change so that you can use these settings in other PrintGraph sessions. **Settings R**eset returns the PrintGraph settings to the default, or to the settings most recently saved.

11

■ The **A**lign and **G**o options on the PrintGraph main menu allow you to tell PrintGraph that the paper is properly aligned in the printer, and to begin printing, respectively. The **P**age option on the main menu is used to advance the paper in the printer to the top of the next page before or after printing.

The next chapter shows you how to use Wysiwyg to print and modify graphs.

11

Enhancing and Printing Graphs in Wysiwyg

12

In the last chapter you learned how to create and print graphs with 1-2-3's /Graph and /Print commands. As you see in this chapter, Wysiwyg offers its own set of graphing commands. However, the Wysiwyg :Graph commands are not for creating graphs—they are primarily for embellishing graphs you create in 1-2-3 and other graphics programs. (You can even create your own drawings.) A graphics editor lets you add geometric shapes, rotate and flip objects, and perform other advanced operations.

Adding a graph

Replacing a graph

Repositioning a graph

Using the graphics editor

Key Terms in This Chapter

Graphic	A current graph, named graph, PIC file, Metafile, or blank placeholder you add to your worksheet with **:Graph Add**.
Graphics editing window	A screen that appears when you select **:Graph Edit**, enabling you to add and change objects on your graphic.
Selection indicators	Small boxes that appear on the edges of an object selected for editing.
Selected objects	Objects that you can change together.
Bounding box	A rectangle shown on-screen in graphics editor mode that outlines an object you move or change.

Using the Mouse

To use a mouse with 1-2-3 Release 2.3, you need a mouse, mouse software, and a graphics monitor and graphics card that support a mouse. You can use a mouse to select commands and files, specify ranges, move the cell pointer within the worksheet, and make selections in a dialog box. Refer to the following sections of the specified chapters for further information on using the mouse.

- Chapter 2—"Understanding Mouse Terminology"
- Chapter 3—"Mouse Control of the Cell Pointer"
  "Using Dialog Boxes"
  "Using the Mouse To Select Menu Commands"
- Chapter 4—"Using the Mouse To Specify Ranges"

12

Adding a Graph

Before you can include a 1-2-3 graph in a Wysiwyg-formatted report, you must add the graph to the worksheet with the :Graph Add command. With this command, you define the worksheet range where you want the graph to appear—and you actually see the graph in the worksheet.

To add a graph into the worksheet, follow these steps:

1. Select :Graph Add.

2. Select one of the following options:

   Select **Current** to insert the current 1-2-3 graph (the same graph that appears when you press F10).

   Select **Named** to insert a 1-2-3 graph that you named with the /Graph Name Create command.

   Select **PIC** to insert a 1-2-3 graph created with the /Graph Save command. The file has the extension PIC.

   Select **Metafile** to insert a Metafile graphic. 1-2-3 Release 3 or an external graphics package created this file, and it has the extension CGM.

   Select **Blank** to insert an empty placeholder. Use this option if you have not yet created the graph, but want to reserve space for it. You also can use it to create your own graphic drawing.

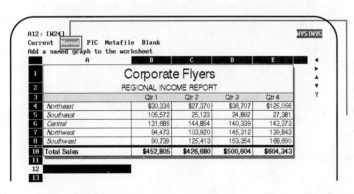

In this example, choose **Named**.

12

Choose the **Current** option only if the worksheet contains a single graph. If the worksheet has multiple graphs, 1-2-3 replaces the graph with the new current graph every time you use the command /Graph Name Use. When the worksheet contains more than one graph, you can save time by naming the graph before adding it.

3. If you chose **Named**, **PIC**, or **Metafile**, Wysiwyg prompts you for the name of the graph. Type the name or highlight one of the graphs listed; then press ↵Enter.

In this example, choose the named graph REG INCOME by highlighting the name and pressing ↵Enter.

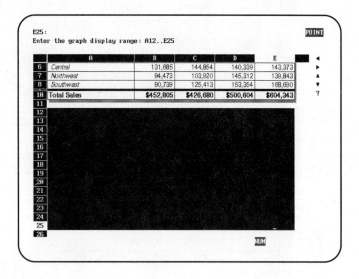

4. When the prompt appears, indicate the range to accept the graph.

In this example, press ⌐.⌐ (period) to anchor the range at A12. Move the cell pointer to E25 and then press ↵Enter.

5. To exit the Wysiwyg menu, select **Quit**.

12

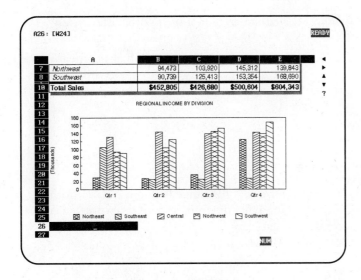

The graph appears in the worksheet.

Before you add a graph to the middle of a worksheet report, insert blank rows or columns where you want the graph to appear. Otherwise the graph overlays worksheet data. The graph range should include only blank cells; be sure that you insert enough rows and columns to make the graph the size you want.

Replacing a Graph

If you add the wrong graph or create a different graph you want to insert in that same-sized range, you can replace the existing graph with another. You do not need to remove one graph before adding another in the same location.

To replace a graph, follow these steps:

1. Select **:Graph Settings Graph**.

2. Indicate the graph you want to replace by moving the cell pointer to one cell in the graph range and pressing ⏎Enter. If your cell pointer is not near the graph, press F3 (Name) and select the graph name from a list.

3. Select the type of graphic (**Current**, **Named**, **P**IC, **Metafile**, or **B**lank).

4. If you chose **Named**, **P**IC, or **Metafile**, Wysiwyg prompts you for the name of the graph.

12

5. Type the name or move the cursor to one of the graphs listed; then press ⏎Enter.

Any enhancements (such as annotations) to the initial graph also appear in the new graph. If you don't want these enhancements in the new graph, use **:G**raph **R**emove to delete the initial graph. Insert the new graph with **:G**raph **A**dd.

Repositioning a Graph

After adding a graph, you may realize that the range isn't appropriate for your graph, or you may want it positioned in a different area of the worksheet. The **:G**raph menu offers several commands for changing your graph's position. You can move, resize, or remove the graph.

If your worksheet is large or has many graphs, you can use the **:G**raph **G**oto command to move to a graph before editing it. To go to a graph on your worksheet, follow these steps:

1. Select **:G**raph **G**oto.
2. Move the cursor to select the graph name from the list. Press F3 (Name) to see a full-screen list.
3. Press ⏎Enter.

Moving a Graph

To move a graph from one worksheet location to another, use the **:G**raph **M**ove command. This command retains the graph's original size and shape (number of rows and columns). The only change is the graph's position in the worksheet.

To move a graph in the worksheet, follow these steps:

1. Select **:G**raph **M**ove.
2. Indicate the graph by moving the cell pointer to one cell in the graph range and pressing ⏎Enter. If your cell pointer is not near the graph, press F3 (Name), select the graph name from a list, and then press ⏎Enter.
3. Type the name or move the cell pointer to the upper left corner of the target range and press ⏎Enter. (You needn't highlight the entire range.)

12

Resizing a Graph

After you add a graph, you may realize that the range you specified is either too large or too small for your graph. The **:Graph Settings R**ange command lets you resize an existing graph.

To change the size of a graph, follow these steps:

1. Select **:Graph Settings R**ange.
2. Indicate the graph you want to resize. Move the cell pointer to one cell in the graph range and press ⏎Enter, or press F3 and select the graph name from a list. 1-2-3 highlights the current graph range.
3. Type the new range, or move the cell pointer to highlight a larger or smaller area. If you want to specify a new range to be different from the existing one, press Esc or ◆Backspace. Then move the cursor and specify the new range.
4. Press ⏎Enter after you have set the new range.

Removing a Graph

To erase a graph from the worksheet report, follow these steps:

1. Select **:G**raph **R**emove.
2. Indicate the graph you want to remove. Move the cell pointer to one cell in the graph range or press F3 and select the graph name from the list.

Using the Graphics Editor

Included in Wysiwyg is a graphics editor that enables you to add and manipulate graphic objects. Using this graphics editor, you can add text, arrows, boxes, and other geometric shapes. After adding these objects, you can modify, rearrange, duplicate, and transform them.

To place a graph in the graphics editing window, follow these steps:

1. Select **:G**raph **E**dit.
2. Indicate the graph you want to change. Move the cell pointer to one cell in the graph range and press ⏎Enter, or press F3 and select the graph name from the list.

12

To use a mouse to place the graph in the graphics editing window, follow these steps:

1. Select **:Graph Edit**.
2. Place the mouse pointer on the graphic, and then double-click the left mouse button.

The graph is displayed in the graphics editing window.

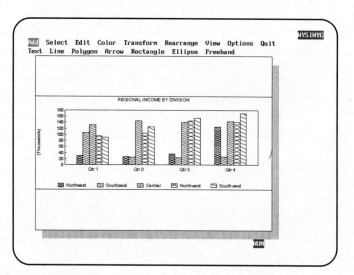

When you are in the graphics editing window, you are almost in a different world. You see only your graphic—not your worksheet. This lets you concentrate on your task at hand: enhancing your graphic. Furthermore, the editing menu permanently remains at the top of the screen; the Esc key or right mouse button does not clear the menu. The only way to exit from the graphics editor is to choose the **Q**uit menu option or press Ctrl-Break.

Note: The Undo command does not work on options in the **:Graph Edit** menu.

Adding Objects

Wysiwyg lets you add the following types of objects to your graphic: text, lines, polygons, arrows, rectangles, and ellipses. You can also draw freehand. These objects help you add text to explain your graphs. For example, you can add a brief explanation of why a data point is unusually high or low.

440

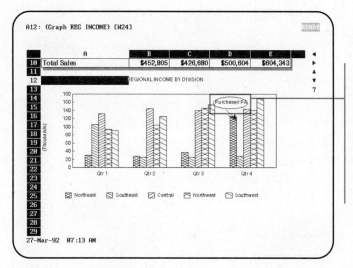

This graph, annotated with the graphics editor, shows how text, an arrow, and an ellipse point out a value on the graph.

Adding Text

You do not type the text directly on the graph. Instead, you add the text in two steps. First, type the text at the Text: prompt at the top of the screen. Second, position the complete phrase where you like. The text phrase can be up to 240 characters long.

To add text to your graph, follow these steps:

1. From the :**Graph Edit** menu, select **Add**.
2. Select **Text**.

441

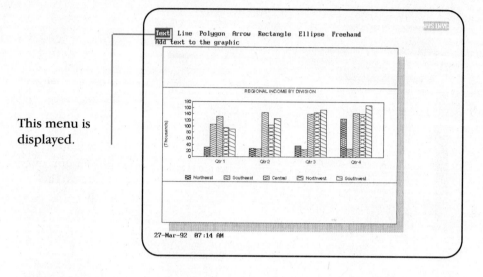

This menu is
displayed.

3. Type the text you want. To insert the contents of a cell, press $\boxed{\setminus}$ followed by the cell's coordinates or range name.

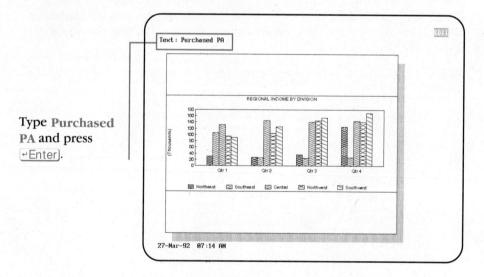

Type **Purchased**
PA and press
$\boxed{\text{↵Enter}}$.

4. Position the pointer where you want the text to go. Either move the pointer with the arrow keys and press $\boxed{\text{↵Enter}}$, or move the pointer with the mouse and click the left mouse button.

Note: The arrow keys move in such small increments that you will probably prefer to use the mouse if you have one.

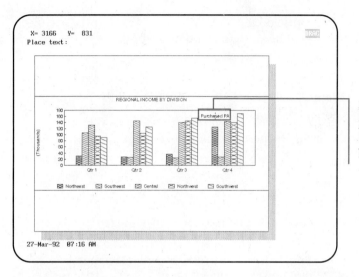

For this example, place Purchased PA above the first bar in quarter 4.

Small, filled-in squares, called *selection indicators*, surround the text. These boxes mean that you selected the object and can perform another operation on it (such as move it, change its font, and so forth). To change the font, use the **Edit Font** command. To change the content of the text, use the **Edit Text** command.

The text you add can include formatting sequences (for example, bold, italic, outline, or fonts). See the section "Formatting Sequences" in Chapter 9 for further information.

Adding Lines and Arrows

The process of drawing lines and drawing arrows is the same. The only difference is the arrow's arrowhead at the second point of the line.

To draw a line or arrow using the keyboard, follow these steps:

1. From the **:G**raph Edit menu, select **Add**.
2. Select **L**ine or **A**rrow.

443

3. When the screen prompts you to `Move to the first point:` use the arrow keys to move the pointer to one end of the line.

4. Press the space bar to anchor this point.

5. When the screen prompts you to `Stretch to the next point:` use the arrow keys to move the pointer to the other end of the line.

6. Press `⏎Enter` to complete the line.

To draw a line or arrow using the mouse, follow these steps:

1. From the **:Graph Edit** menu, select **Add**.

2. Select **Line** or **Arrow**.

   For this example, select **Arrow**.

3. Move the mouse pointer to the first point and click the left mouse button.

4. At the `Stretch to the next point:` prompt, move the mouse pointer to the next point and click the left mouse button twice to complete the line.

The arrow shows on-screen and the selection indicator appears in the center of the line, in zoomed mode.

If you are adding an arrow, the arrowhead points from the end of the line (the second point you indicated). To switch the direction of the arrow, use the **Edit Arrowheads** option. To change the line width, use the **Edit Width** option.

You can connect several lines by pressing the space bar or clicking the left mouse button for each line ending. When you finish drawing lines, click the left mouse button twice or press Enter.

When drawing horizontal, vertical, or diagonal lines, you notice that drawing straight lines is difficult; the lines look somewhat jagged. To prevent this jagged look, press and hold down the Shift key before you anchor the last point. The line segment automatically snaps to 45-degree angles, allowing you to draw perfectly straight lines.

Adding Polygons

A polygon is a multisided object. The object can have as many connecting lines as you want. With Wysiwyg commands, you can connect automatically the last line drawn to the first line. The steps for creating a polygon are similar to creating lines and arrows.

To create a polygon, follow these steps:

1. From the :Graph Edit menu, select Add.

2. Select Polygon.

3. When the screen prompts you to Move to the first point: use the mouse or arrow keys to move the pointer to one end of the line.

4. Press the left mouse button or space bar to anchor this point.

5. When the screen prompts you to Stretch to the next point: use the mouse or arrow keys to move the pointer to the opposite end of the first line.

6. Press the left mouse button or space bar to anchor this point.

7. Repeat steps 5 and 6 for each point of the polygon.

8. Click the left mouse button twice or press ⏎Enter to complete the polygon.

12

Adding Rectangles and Ellipses

Use the **R**ectangle and **E**llipse options on the **:Graph Edit Add** menu to enclose text and other objects in your graphic.

This graph is annotated with text, a rectangle, and an ellipse.

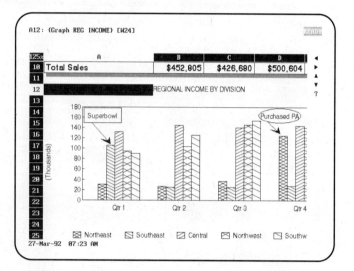

To draw rectangles and ellipses with the keyboard, follow these steps:

1. From the **:Graph Edit** menu, select **A**dd.
2. Select **R**ectangle or **E**llipse.
3. Place the pointer on the upper left corner of the area where you want to place the object.
4. Press the space bar to anchor the corner.
5. Use the arrow keys to stretch the box to its desired size. (A box appears regardless of whether you are drawing a rectangle or ellipse. This is the *bounding box*.)
6. Press ⏎Enter.

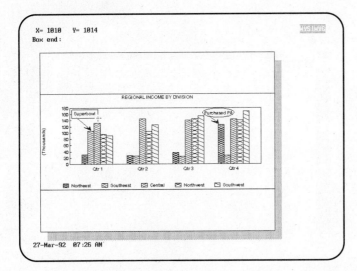

Whether you are creating a rectangle or an ellipse, a rectangle (the bounding box) appears until you release the mouse button.

To draw rectangles and ellipses with a mouse, follow these steps:

1. From the **:Graph Edit** menu, select **Add**.
2. Select **Rectangle** or **Ellipse**.
3. Click and hold the left mouse button in the upper left corner of the object.
4. Drag the mouse to create the desired size.
5. Release the button. Wysiwyg draws the shape you chose.

The middle of each side of the rectangle or ellipse has selection indicators. To change the type of line (solid, dashed, or dotted) used in the rectangle or ellipse, select Edit Line-Style from the **:Graph Edit** menu.

To create a circle when you choose **Ellipse**, or a square when you choose **Rectangle**, hold the Shift key before you set the object size. The object may not appear perfectly circular or square on-screen, but will print accurately.

Adding Objects Freehand

When you use the Freehand option on the **:Graph Edit Add** menu, it is like drawing with a pencil on the screen. Unless you have artistic ability, freehand drawing resembles freehand scribbling; therefore, you may want to leave this option to the professionals.

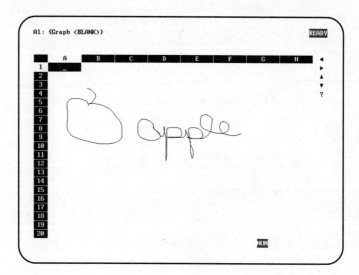

This is an example of freehand drawing (scribbling).

You must have a mouse to draw freehand. To draw freehand, follow these steps:

1. From the **:Graph Edit** menu, select **Add**.
2. Select **Freehand**.
3. Place the pointer where you want to begin drawing.
4. Click and hold the left mouse button, and move the mouse to draw.
5. Release the mouse button when you finish drawing a segment of the graphic.

Each segment of the freehand drawing displays a selection indicator. To change the type of line (solid, dashed, or dotted), select **Edit Line-Style** from the **:Graph Edit** menu.

Selecting Objects

There is much you can do to your objects after you add them to your graphic. For example, you can change the line-style and font. You can also move, delete, or copy the objects. No matter what you want to change, you must first select the object. If you just added the object, Wysiwyg selects it automatically. Selection indicators, small filled-in boxes, show that you selected the object(s).

Normally, you select the object before issuing a command. If you issue a command without selecting an object, Wysiwyg prompts you to point to what you want.

Selecting Objects with the Mouse

To select one object with the mouse, follow these steps:

1. With the main **:Graph Edit** menu displayed, move the mouse pointer to the object.
2. Click the left mouse button.

Check the selection indicators to make sure that they are around the object you want to change. If two objects are close together, you may need to click several times. Wysiwyg selects the correct object.

Sometimes you want to select more than one object. For example, you may want to change the font of all the text you have added.

To select multiple objects with the mouse, follow these steps:

1. With the main **:Graph Edit** menu displayed, move the mouse pointer to the first object.
2. Hold down the ⟨⇧Shift⟩ key as you click the left mouse button on each object. If you accidentally select the wrong object, keep the ⟨⇧Shift⟩ key down and click on the object again.

Selecting Objects with the Keyboard

To select one object with the keyboard, follow these steps:

1. From the **:Graph Edit** menu, choose **Select One**.
2. When Wysiwyg prompts you to `Point to desired object:` use the arrow keys to move the pointer to the object and press ⟨⏎Enter⟩. The selection indicators appear around the object.

Another way to select an object is with the **:Graph Edit Select Cycle** command. Use this option to select one or multiple objects.

To select multiple objects with the keyboard, follow these steps:

1. From the **:Graph Edit** menu, choose **Select Cycle**.
2. To select an object, press an arrow key. The object displays small boxes similar to selection indicators.
3. To select or deselect the object, press the space bar.
4. Repeat steps 2 and 3 until you have selected all the objects you want; then press ⟨⏎Enter⟩.

12

Mouse users may want to use the Cycle option if they are having trouble selecting an object that is close to another object. You may not be able to identify an object with a click of the mouse. The Cycle option enables you to select or skip every object in the graphic.

The Select menu offers several other ways to select objects. All selects all the objects you have added except the graphic itself. None deselects everything— the objects and your graphic. Graph selects only your underlying graphic. More/Less lets you select an additional object or deselect one of the currently selected objects. If you point to an unselected object, Wysiwyg selects it. If you already selected the object, Wysiwyg removes the selection.

Editing Text in the Graph

The Edit Text option on the :Graph Edit menu lets you edit text that you added with the Add Text command. You cannot edit text (for example, titles and legends) that was part of the worksheet graph, PIC, or Metafile graphic you inserted. You can select text before or during the editing process. If you select text before editing, skip step 2 in the following procedure.

To begin editing text on the graph, follow these steps:

1. From the :Graph Edit menu, select Edit Text.

2. If you have not preselected text, Wysiwyg displays the prompt `Select text to edit:`. Move to the text to edit and press `⏎Enter`. A copy of the text appears at the top of the screen.

3. To correct or insert text on the graph, choose one or more of the following options:

   Move the cursor and type text to insert text.

   Press `Ins` to type over text.

   Press `Del` to delete the character at the cursor.

   Press `←Backspace` to delete the character before the cursor.

   Press `End` to move to the end of the line.

   Press `Home` to move to the beginning of the line.

4. When you finish editing the graph, press `⏎Enter`. The correct text appears on-screen.

12

Adding Patterns and Colors

The **Color** option on the **:Graph Edit** menu enables you to assign colors or patterns to the following areas of your graphic:

Selection	Description
Lines	Lines, arrows, and object outlines
Inside	The space inside the rectangle, ellipse, or polygon
Text	Text added with **Add Text** (not legends or titles you entered with /Graph commands)
Map	Changes the default colors (up to 8) available for the graphic
Background	The area behind the graphic

To change the color of lines or text, follow these steps:

1. From the **:Graph Edit** menu, select **Color**.

2. Select **Lines** or **Text**.

3. Choose from a menu of the following colors:

   Black White Red Green Dark-Blue Cyan Yellow Magenta Hidden

4. If you have not preselected lines or text, Wysiwyg displays the prompt `Select objects to color:`. Move to the line or text to appear in color and press ⏎Enter.

To change the color or pattern inside objects, follow these steps:

1. From the **:Graph Edit** menu, select **Color**.

2. Select **Inside**.

   A color palette appears on your color monitor.

12

451

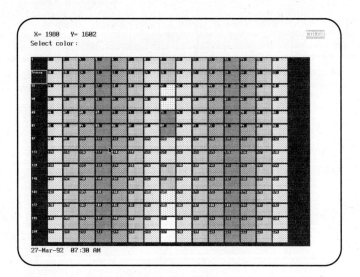

If you have a
monochrome
monitor, the
palette displays
patterns.

3. Type the number, or click on the desired color/pattern.

4. If you have not preselected lines or text, Wysiwyg displays the prompt
   `Select objects to color:`. Move to the object where you want the
   change and press `⏎Enter`.

To change the background color, follow these steps:

1. From the **:Graph E**dit menu, select **C**olor.

2. Select **B**ackground.

   A color palette appears on your screen. Monochrome monitors display
   a palette of different patterns.

3. Type the number and press `⏎Enter`, or click on the color/pattern you
   want.

Changing Colors of Graph Elements

To change the colors or patterns of any elements in your 1-2-3 graph, you can
use color mapping.

The **C**olor **M**ap option of the **:Graph E**dit menu allows you to change the fill
colors and patterns of the underlying graphic. For example, suppose that you
don't like a bar's green shading. You can use color mapping to adjust this
shade or to use a different pattern. You cannot use this option to change the
color of the lines or text.

You can change up to eight different colors. The **Map** menu shows the choices with the numbers 1 through 8. How do you know which color in your graph corresponds to which number on the menu? Unfortunately, trial and error is the answer. Wysiwyg does not tell you which color goes with which menu choice until after you choose the number. For example, if you want to change a green bar, you have to try 1 through 8 until you see green on the color map.

To change a graph color or pattern, follow these steps:

1. From the **:G**raph **E**dit menu, select **Color Map.**

2. Select a number from 1 to 8. A color palette appears on your color monitor. Monochrome monitors display a palette of different patterns. The palette shows the current color/pattern with a box.

3. Type the number and press ⏎Enter or click on the desired color/ pattern. If you change your mind, press Esc and try another number.

If you have a color monitor and a black-and-white printer, you may want to view the graph in black and white before you print. This allows you to see the contrast when the colors translate into gray shades. Use the **:D**isplay **M**ode **B&W** command to change to a black-and-white display.

Rearranging Objects

The **Rearrange** option on the **:G**raph **E**dit menu lets you delete, copy, and move objects you added to your graphic with **:G**raph **E**dit **A**dd. Before you choose one of the **Rearrange** options, select the object(s) you want to re-arrange. See "Selecting Objects" earlier in this chapter for details on preselecting objects with the mouse or the **S**elect menu.

Deleting and Restoring Objects

The **Rearrange Delete** option on the **:G**raph **E**dit menu removes the selected object(s) from the graphic. Be careful; Wysiwyg does not ask you to confirm your intention to delete. However, you can retrieve the last deleted object or group of objects with the **Rearrange Restore** command.

To delete selected objects, follow these steps:

1. Select objects using one of the procedures in the "Select Objects" section of this chapter.

2. From the **:G**raph **E**dit menu, select **Rearrange Delete.**

12

As an alternative to using the **Rearrange Delete** command, you can simply select the object and press Del.

To restore the objects you deleted (last deletion only), select **Rearrange Restore** from the **:G**raph **E**dit menu. Suppose, for example, that you select three objects and then choose **Rearrange Delete**. Wysiwyg deletes all three objects. If you choose **Rearrange Restore**, Wysiwyg retrieves all three objects into their original locations. However, if you select and delete a line, and then select and delete a rectangle, you cannot restore the deleted line.

You can also press the Ins key on the numeric keypad to restore the most recently deleted object(s). Do not select any objects when you press Ins, or Wysiwyg will copy the selected object.

Moving Objects

To reposition an object with the keyboard, follow these steps:

1. From the **:G**raph **E**dit menu, select **Rearrange Move**.

Move is an option on the **Rearrange** menu.

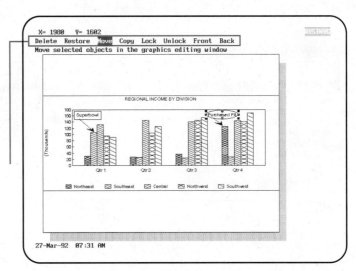

2. If you haven't already done so, Wysiwyg asks you to select the objects to move. Use the arrow keys to move the pointer to the object and press ⏎Enter.

3. After you make your selection, a copy of your object appears inside a dotted rectangle (the bounding box). A hand also appears inside the bounding box, indicating that you are moving the object.

4. Use the arrow keys to move the bounding box to the target location; then press ⏎Enter.

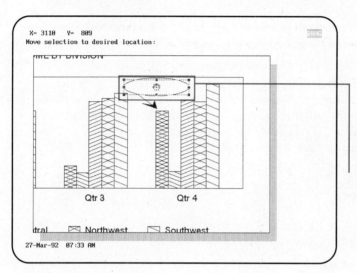

An object is being moved with the bounding box and hand.

To move an object using a mouse, follow these steps:

1. If necessary, click the left mouse button to select the object to be moved.

2. Click and hold the left mouse button on the object.

3. While holding down the left mouse button, drag the object to the desired location and release the mouse button.

Copying Objects

After you create an object, you may want to copy it to another location on your worksheet. Using the **Rearrange Copy** option of the **:Graph Edit** menu ensures that two or more objects have the exact same size, color, line-styles, and rotation options. For example, if you create a shaded rectangle with wide lines, the copy of the rectangle is also shaded and has wide lines.

To copy an object, follow these steps:

1. From the **:Graph Edit** menu, select **Rearrange**.

12

455

2. Select **C**opy.

   If you preselected an object before you chose the **R**earrange **C**opy command, Wysiwyg places a duplicate slightly to the right of and below the original object. If you did not select an object before you chose the **C**opy command, Wysiwyg prompts you to select the objects to copy.

Note that the **C**opy command does not prompt you for a target location. You must use the **R**earrange **M**ove command to put the object into place. Thus, copying is a two-step process.

Rather than using the **R**earrange **C**opy command, you can simply select the object and press the Ins key. Like the **C**opy command, Ins places the duplicated object next to the original. You have to use the **M**ove command to put the object into position. If you don't have an object selected when you press Ins, Wysiwyg restores the last deleted object.

Sizing an Object

You can change the size (height and width) of any added objects except text. To change the text size, specify a different font with the **E**dit **F**ont command.

To change the size of an object, follow these steps:

1. From the **:G**raph **E**dit menu, select **T**ransform **S**ize.

   Wysiwyg surrounds the selected object with a bounding box. Wysiwyg anchors the upper left corner of the box, and the pointer is in the lower right corner.

2. Change the size of the object by pressing the arrow keys until the bounding box is the desired size.

3. When the desired size is reached, press ↵Enter.

12

Rotating an Object

The **T**ransform menu offers two ways to rotate an object. The **Q**uarter-Turn option rotates the selected object(s) in 90-degree increments. Wysiwyg makes the turns in a counterclockwise direction.

If you need to rotate an object in increments other than 90 degrees, use the **T**ransform **R**otate option. You can rotate the selected object(s) to any angle.

To rotate selected objects by any amount, follow these steps:

1. From the **:Graph Edit** menu, select **T**ransform **R**otate.

    An axis extends from the center of the object to outside the bounding box. Think of this axis as a handle that pulls the object in the direction you press the arrow keys.

2. Use ⎡↑⎤ and ⎡←⎤ to rotate the object.

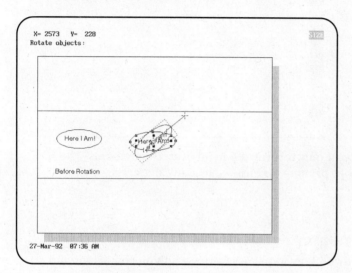

As you rotate, the original object remains intact, and a copy of the object rotates.

3. Press ⎡↵Enter⎤ to finish the rotation. Wysiwyg replaces the original with the rotated copy.

12

457

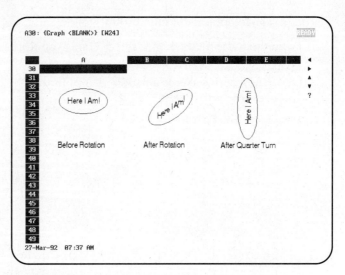

This example shows a figure and text rotated with the Transform **R**otate and Transform **Q**uarter-Turn options.

Some printers can print only text rotated in 90-degree increments. The HP LaserJet and PostScript printers can print text at any angle.

Summary

This chapter showed you how to use Wysiwyg's graphing commands and options. At the simplest level, you can insert a graph to include it with a Wysiwyg-formatted report. You can then take the 1-2-3 graph and add comments to point out key data values. At another level, you can use the graphics editor to create your own graphic drawings with text and geometric objects.

Specifically, you learned the following key information about 1-2-3:

- To add a graph to a worksheet range, use **:G**raph **A**dd.
- To replace a graph on the worksheet with a different graph, use **:G**raph **S**ettings **G**raph.
- The **:G**raph **M**ove command allows you to move a graph to a different position in the worksheet.
- To change the size of a graph in a worksheet, use **:G**raph **S**ettings **R**ange.
- To delete a graph from a worksheet range, use **:G**raph **R**emove.
- The graphics editor enables you to add and modify objects on a graph. These objects include text, lines, arrows, rectangles, and ellipses.

12

458

- To reach the graphics editor window, select **:Graph Edit**. The graph will appear on the screen with a new menu. To return to the worksheet, select **Quit**.

- Add objects to a graph with the **:Graph Edit Add** command. Then choose **Text, Line, Polygon, Arrow, Rectangle, Ellipse,** or **Freehand**.

- To select objects using the mouse in the **:Graph Edit** window, click the left mouse button on the object. To select multiple objects, hold down the Shift key as you select.

- To select objects using the keyboard in the **:Graph Edit** window, choose **Select**. The **One** option allows you to select one item. The **Cycle** option allows you to select multiple items.

- When you want to edit text you have added to the graph, choose the **:Graph Edit Edit Text** command.

- The **:Graph Edit Color** command allows you to change colors of text and objects you added to the graph, the graph background, and the original parts of a graph.

- The **Rearrange Delete** option on the **:Graph Edit** menu allows you to delete selected objects. The **Rearrange Restore** option enables you to restore the objects if necessary.

- To move an object in a graph, choose **:Graph Edit Rearrange Move**.

- To copy an object in the graph, choose **:Graph Edit Rearrange Copy**.

- The **:Graph Edit Transform** command enables you to **Size** or **Rotate** an object.

The next chapter shows you how to use the database features of 1-2-3. You will learn terms associated with a database as well as commands allowing you to sort, find, and extract information from your worksheet database.

12

Managing Data

13

In addition to the electronic spreadsheet and business graphics, 1-2-3 provides a third element: data management. 1-2-3's database feature is fast, easy to access, and relatively simple to use.

You can easily access the 1-2-3 database because Lotus has made the entire database visible from the worksheet. You can view the contents of the whole database by using worksheet windows and direction keys to scroll through the database.

The relative ease of use is a result of integrating data management with the program's spreadsheet and graphics functions. The procedures for adding, changing, and deleting items in a database are the same as those for manipulating cells within a worksheet. Creating graphs from ranges in a database is as easy as creating them in a worksheet.

Planning and building a database

Modifying a database

Sorting database records

Searching for and listing particular records

Key Terms in This Chapter

Database	A collection of data organized so that you can list, sort, or search its contents.
Field	One information item, such as an address or a name.
Field name	The label in the first row of a database that identifies the contents of the field or column.
Record	A collection of associated fields. In 1-2-3, a record is a row of cells within a database.
Key field	A column (or field) that determines the sorting order for rows in a database.
Input range	The range of the database on which 1-2-3 performs database operations.
Output range	The range to which 1-2-3 copies data when extracted from the database.
Criteria range	The range of the database in which you enter range search criteria.

Using the Mouse

To use a mouse with 1-2-3 Release 2.3, you need a mouse, mouse software, and a graphics monitor and graphics card that support a mouse. You can use a mouse to select commands and files, specify ranges, move the cell pointer within the worksheet, or make selections in a dialog box. Refer to the following sections of the specified chapters for further information on using the mouse.

- Chapter 2—"Understanding Mouse Terminology"
- Chapter 3—"Mouse Control of the Cell Pointer"
    "Using Dialog Boxes"
    "Using the Mouse To Select Menu Commands"
- Chapter 4—"Using the Mouse To Specify Ranges"

13

What Is a Database?

A database is a collection of data organized so that you can list, sort, or search its contents. The list of data may contain any kind of information, from addresses to tax-deductible payments. A Rolodex is one form of a database. Other examples of databases include address books and a file cabinet of employee records.

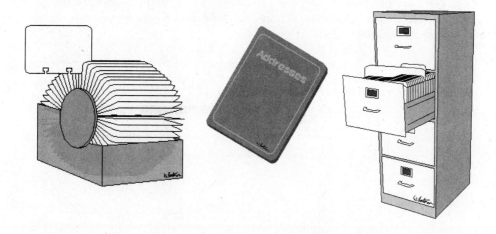

In 1-2-3, the word *database* means a range of cells that spans at least one column and more than one row. This definition, however, does not distinguish between a database and any other range of cells in a worksheet. Because a database is actually a list, its manner of organization distinguishes it from an ordinary range. As a list must be organized to be useful, you have to arrange a database so that the information is easy to access.

The smallest unit in a database is a field, or single data item. For example, if you were to develop an information database of customer accounts that are overdue, you might include the following fields of information:

Customer Last Name	Area Code
Customer First Name	Telephone Number
Street Address	Account Number
City	Payment Due Date
State	Date Paid
ZIP Code	Amount Due

13

A database record is a collection of associated fields. For example, the accumulation of all data about one customer forms one record. In 1-2-3, a record is a row of cells within a database, and a field is one type of information, such as City.

You must set up a database so that you can access the information it contains. Retrieval of information usually involves relying on key fields. A database key field is any field (or column) on which you base a list, sort, or search operation. For example, you can use the ZIP code as a key field to sort the data in the overdue accounts database. Then you could assign contact representatives to specific geographic areas.

A database key field

A database record

A database field

A database input range

Capabilities of the 1-2-3 Database

Building a database in 1-2-3 is no different from building any other worksheet. After you build the database, you can perform a variety of functions with it. You can accomplish some of the tasks in a 1-2-3 database with standard 1-2-3 commands. For example, you can add records and fields using simple worksheet commands such as /Worksheet Insert. Editing data in the database is the same as editing worksheet cells. Highlight the cell, press Edit (F2), and correct it.

You can also sort data. You sort with just a primary key, or both a primary and secondary key, in ascending or descending order. In addition, you can perform various mathematical analyses on a field of data over a specified range of records. For example, you can count the number of items in a database that match a set of criteria. You can compute a mean, variance, or standard deviation. You can also find the maximum or minimum value in the range. The capacity to perform statistical analysis on a database is an advanced feature of database management systems on any microcomputer.

Other database operations specifically require database commands, such as /Data Query Find and /Data Query Unique. Data commands can help you search the database and remove duplications.

You have several options for defining selection criteria with 1-2-3. The criteria range can contain up to 32 cells across the worksheet, with each cell containing criteria. You can use numbers, text, and complex formulas as criteria.

1-2-3 also has a special set of statistical functions that operate only on information stored in the database. Like the /Data Query commands, the statistical functions use criteria to determine on which records they operate. The database functions include @DCOUNT, @DSUM, @DAVG, @DVAR, @DSTD, @DMAX, and @DMIN.

Understanding the /Data Menu

You use the /Data menu for many of 1-2-3's data management tasks. All other options from the 1-2-3 main menu work as well on databases as they do on worksheets. When you select /Data from the 1-2-3 main menu, the control panel displays the following options:

Fill Table Sort Query Distribution Matrix Regression Parse

Table 13.1 describes each of these options.

Table 13.1
Selections on the /Data Menu

Selection	Description
Fill	Fills a specified range with values; you can choose the increment by which 1-2-3 increases or decreases successive numbers
Table	Substitutes different values for a variable used in a formula; often used for "what if" analyses
Sort	Organizes the database in ascending or descending order based on one or two specified key fields

continued

13

Table 13.1 (*continued*)

Selection	Description
Query	Offers different options for performing search operations and manipulating the found data items
Distribution	Finds how often specific data occurs in a database
Matrix	Lets you solve systems of simultaneous linear equations and manipulate the resulting solutions
Regression	Performs multiple regression analysis on X and Y values
Parse	Separates long labels resulting from /File **Import** into discrete text and numeric cell entries

In the /Data menu, the **Sort** and **Query** (search) options are true data management operations. **Sort** allows you to specify the order in which you want the records of the database organized. For example, you can sort by number, by name, or by date. With **Query**, you can perform many search operations, allowing you to display a specific record quickly without having to scan a multitude of records.

Using the /Data Dialog Boxes

When you select /Data **Sort**, /Data **Query**, /Data **Regression**, or /Data **Parse**, a dialog box appears. These dialog boxes allow you to view and change your current settings for these commands.

To use a dialog box, follow these steps:

1. Select /Data **Sort**, /Data **Query**, /Data **Regression**, or /Data **Parse**.

2. Press F2 (Edit) or click the left mouse button somewhere in the dialog box to activate the dialog box.

   1-2-3 highlights one character of each option (usually the first letter). The menu also disappears when you activate the dialog box.

3. To select an option, press the highlighted letter, or click the left mouse button on your choice.

4. When the text box requires a range (/Data **Sort** Data-Range or /Data **Query** Input-range, for instance), you can select the range in one of the following ways:

- Type the cell references for the range (or the range name) in the text box and press ⏎Enter.
- Press F4 to go to POINT mode, highlight the range, and press ⏎Enter.

5. When you finish selecting all options in the dialog box, press ⏎Enter or click the left mouse button on OK. The menu reappears in the control panel.

Planning and Building a Database

Before you begin to create a database in 1-2-3, you should determine the categories (fields) of information you want to include. You can determine these fields by planning what kind of output you expect to produce from your data. Next, decide which area of the worksheet to use. Then create a database by specifying field names across a row. Finally, enter data in cells beneath these names, as you would for any other 1-2-3 application. Entering database contents is simple. The most critical step in creating a database is choosing your fields accurately.

Determining Required Output

1-2-3's data-retrieval techniques rely on finding data by field names. Before you begin typing the kinds of data items you think you may need, write down the output you expect from the database. You also need to consider any source documents already in use that can provide input to the file.

Before you set up the items in your database, be sure to consider how you might look for data in each field. For example, consider how you will look for a particular information item. Will you search by date? By last name? Knowing beforehand how you will use your database will save time that you would lose if you have to redesign the database.

After you decide on the fields, select the appropriate column width (which you can later modify) and determine whether you will enter the data as a number, label, or date.

13

467

Overdue Accounts Database		
Item	Column Width	Type of Entry
1. Customer Last Name	15	Label
2. Customer First Name	10	Label
3. Street Address	25	Label
4. City	15	Label
5. State	7	Label
6. ZIP Code	6	Label
7. Area Code	6	Number
8. Telephone Number	11	Label
9. Account Number	10	Number
10. Payment Due Date	11	Date
11. Date Paid	11	Date
12. Amount Due	12	Number

Here are some tips for planning various types of fields (columns) in your database:

- For ease in sorting, put last and first names in separate columns. Optionally, put both names in the same cell and separate the last and first names with a comma.

- Some ZIP codes begin with zero, which would not appear in the cell if you entered it as a value. Enter ZIP codes as labels by preceding them with a label prefix.

- Set up an area code field that is separate from the telephone number field. This helps if you want to search, sort, or extract records by area code.

- Enter a telephone number as a label. This number must be a label because of the hyphen between the first three and last four digits of a telephone number. A hyphen signifies subtraction in a number entered as a value.

13

Be sure to plan your database carefully before you type field names, set column widths and range formats, and enter data. Although you can make changes after you set up your database, planning helps to reduce the time required for making those changes.

Positioning the Database

You can create a database as a new database file or as part of an existing worksheet. If you decide to build a database as part of an existing worksheet, choose an area where inserting or deleting lines won't affect the worksheet or another database.

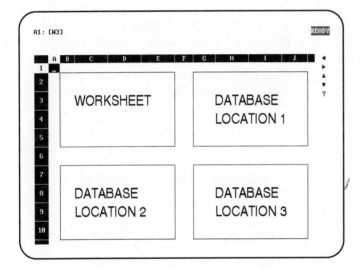

If you place a database to the right of or directly below a worksheet, inserting and deleting rows may affect the worksheet.

An ideal location for a database is in an area where inserting and deleting rows and columns won't affect other applications above, below, to the right of, or to the left of the database.

Entering Data

After you plan your database and decide which area of the worksheet to use, you can start entering data. Build a database by specifying field names as labels across a row. Make sure that each field name is unique and in a separate column.

13

You can use one or more rows for field names, but 1-2-3 processes only the bottom row. Therefore, each field name in the bottom row must be unique. After you enter the field names, enter data in cells as you would for any other 1-2-3 application. Change the column width to fit the information you enter by using the /Worksheet Column Set-Width command.

To build a 1-2-3 database, follow these steps:

1. Choose an area for your database.

   For your first database, you should start with a blank worksheet. If you would rather use an existing worksheet, select an area that is out of the way of the data you have entered.

2. Enter the field names across a single row.

   The field names must be labels, even if they are numeric labels. Although you can use more than one row for the field names, 1-2-3 processes only the values that appear in the bottom row. For example, picture field name DATE DUE in a column with DATE in row 5 and DUE in row 6. 1-2-3 references only DUE as a key field in sort or query operations. Remember that all field names should be unique. Any repetition of names can generate unpredictable results.

This screen shows all field names in the overdue accounts database, displayed with two windows.

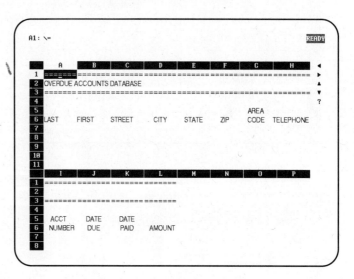

3. Set the column widths and cell display formats.

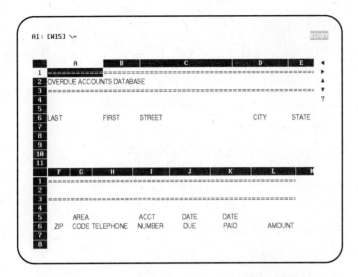

Use /**W**orksheet Column Set-Width to control the width of columns. Use /**R**ange Format to control the way 1-2-3 displays the data.

Note that whenever a right-justified column of numeric data is next to a left-justified column of label information, the data looks crowded. You can insert a blank column and adjust the column width of the blank column to change the spacing between fields.

4. Add records to the database.

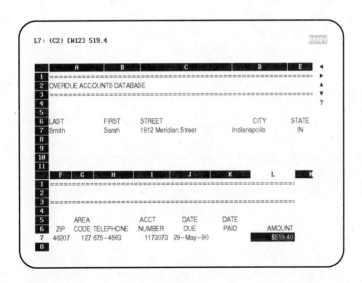

To enter the first record, move the cell pointer to the row directly below the field-names row. Then enter the data across the row in each column (field).

13

Note: There can be no blank rows between the field names and the first row of the database.

Modifying a Database

After you collect the data and decide which field names and types, column widths, and formats to use, creating a database is easy. Thanks to 1-2-3, maintaining the accuracy of the database contents is also simple. Table 13.2 summarizes the commands you use to change a database.

Table 13.2
Commands for Modifying a Database

Action	Command
Add a record	/Worksheet Insert Row
Add a field	/Worksheet Insert Column
Delete a record	/Worksheet Delete Row
Delete a field	/Worksheet Delete Column
Edit a field	Edit (F2)

The process of changing fields in a database is the same as that for altering the contents of cells in any other application. You change the cell contents either by retyping the cell entry or by using the Edit (F2) key and editing the entry.

Other 1-2-3 commands, such as those for copying, moving, and formatting cells, are the same for both database and other worksheet applications. For more information about these commands, see Chapters 4 through 6.

Inserting and Deleting Records

To add and delete records in a database, use the 1-2-3 commands for inserting and deleting rows. Because records correspond to rows, you begin inserting one or more records with the /Worksheet Insert Row command. You then fill in the various fields in each row with the appropriate data. To delete one or more records (rows), you use the /Worksheet Delete Row command.

To insert one or more records (rows) in the database, follow these steps:

1. Select /Worksheet Insert Row.
2. When the prompt Enter row insert range: appears, highlight (or type the cell address of) the location where you want the row (record) inserted.

13

3. Press ⏎Enter .

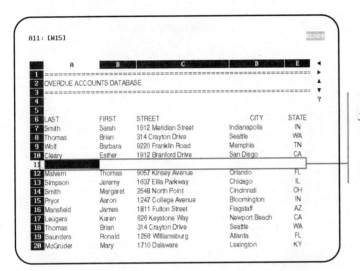

When you press ⏎Enter , a blank row appears, ready for you to enter a new record.

To delete one or more records (rows) from the database, follow these steps:

1. Select /**W**orksheet **D**elete **R**ow.

2. When the prompt Enter range of rows to delete: appears, highlight (or type the cell address of) the rows (records) you want to delete.

3. Press ⏎Enter .

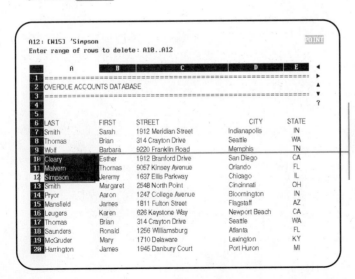

In this example, to delete rows 10 through 12, highlight the rows and press ⏎Enter .

13

473

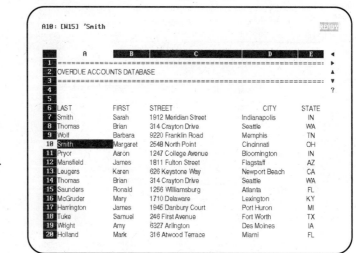

When you press
⏎Enter , 1-2-3
deletes the
records in the
highlighted rows.

You cannot verify the range before you issue the /Worksheet Delete **Row** command. Therefore, be extremely careful when you specify the records to delete. If you want to remove inactive records only, first consider using the /**Data Query Extract** command. Described in a later section, this command lets you store the inactive records in a separate location in the worksheet before you permanently delete the records.

Inserting and Deleting Fields

To add and delete fields in a database, use the 1-2-3 commands for inserting and deleting columns. To add one or more fields, use the /Worksheet **Insert Column** command. To delete one or more fields, use the /Worksheet **Delete Column** command.

To insert one or more new fields (columns) into the database, follow these steps:

1. Select /Worksheet **Insert Column**.

2. When the prompt `Enter column insert range:` appears, highlight (or type the cell address of) the location where you want the column (field) to be inserted; then press ⏎Enter .

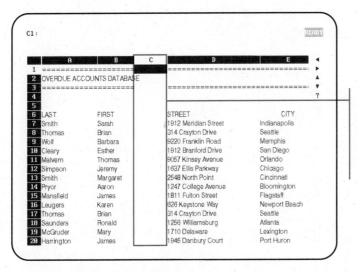

When you press ⏎Enter, a blank column appears. The column is ready for you to enter new data.

Because maintaining data takes up valuable memory, you can remove seldom-used data fields from the database.

To delete one or more fields (columns) from the database, follow these steps:

1. Select /Worksheet **Delete Column**.

2. When the prompt Enter range of columns to delete: appears, highlight the columns (fields) you want to delete; then press ⏎Enter.

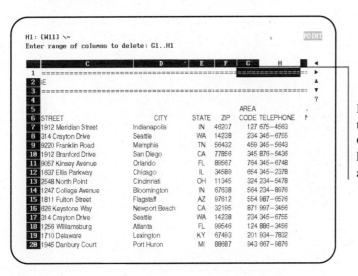

In this example, to delete columns G and H, highlight the columns and press ⏎Enter.

13

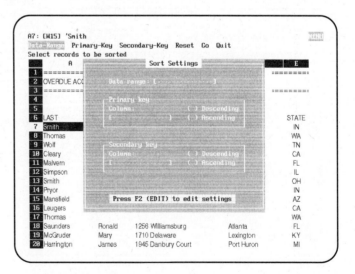

1-2-3 deletes the fields in the highlighted range.

Sorting Database Records

Storing data in a database would be meaningless if you were unable to alphabetize the data or sort it numerically. Sorting is an important function of any database. 1-2-3's data management capability lets you change the order of records by sorting them according to the contents of the fields. To sort data, you use the options available when you select /Data Sort.

The /Data Sort menu and the Sort Settings dialog box are shown here.

13

476

Table 13.3 describes each of these options.

Table 13.3
Selections on the /Data Sort Menu and Sort Settings Dialog Box

Selection	Description
Data-Range	Allows you to specify the range on which the sort operation occurs
Primary-Key	Lets you specify the first item to organize the sort
Secondary-Key	Lets you specify the second item to organize the sort
Reset	Resets the sort options
Go	Starts the search
Quit	Exits the /Data Sort menu

Before you issue a /Data Sort command, save the database to disk. That way, if the sort does not produce the results you expected, you can restore the file to its original order by retrieving it.

To sort a database, follow these steps:

1. Select /Data Sort.

2. Select **Data-Range** from the menu or dialog box and define the range you want to sort.

   This range must be long enough to include all the sorted records and wide enough to include all the fields in each record.

   Note: Do not include the field-names row. (If you are unfamiliar with how to define ranges or how to name them, see Chapter 4.)

   The data range does not have to include all rows in the database. However, it must include all fields (columns) to maintain the proper contents of each record. If some of the database records already have the organization you want, or if you don't want to sort all records, you can sort a portion.

3. Specify the key field(s) for the sort from the menu or dialog box. Then specify ascending or descending order for each key field.

   Key fields are the columns to which you attach the highest precedence when 1-2-3 sorts the database. The column (or field) with the highest

13

477

precedence is the **P**rimary-Key. The field with the next highest precedence is the **S**econdary-Key. You must always set a **P**rimary-Key.
Setting the **S**econdary-Key is optional.

4. Select **G**o to perform the sort.

The One-Key Sort

One of the simplest examples of a database sorted according to a primary key
is the white pages of the telephone book. All the records in the white pages
are in ascending alphabetical order using the last name as the primary key.

Suppose, for example, that you want to reorder records alphabetically on the
LAST name field. To perform a one-key sort operation, follow these steps:

1. Select **/D**ata **S**ort.

2. Select **D**ata-Range from the menu or **D**ata range from the dialog box.

3. Type or highlight the cell address, or enter the range name for the
   range you want to sort. Then press ⏎Enter.

In this example,
highlight the
range for the
entire database,
A7..L24 (exclud-
ing the field
names in row 6)
and press ⏎Enter.

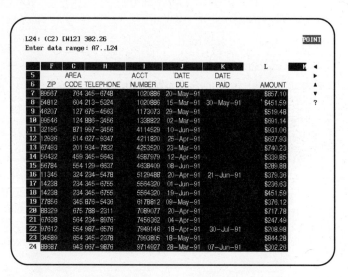

4. From the Sort menu or Sort Settings dialog box, select **P**rimary-Key.

5. Type or point to any cell in the column containing the primary-key
   field on which you want to sort; then press ⏎Enter.

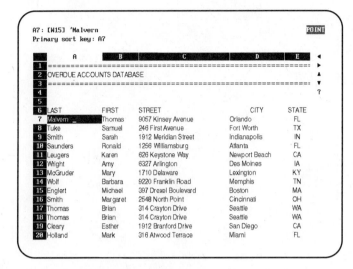

In this example, to sort the database by the LAST (last name) field, highlight any cell in column A. Then press ⏎Enter .

6. Select **A**scending or **D**escending.

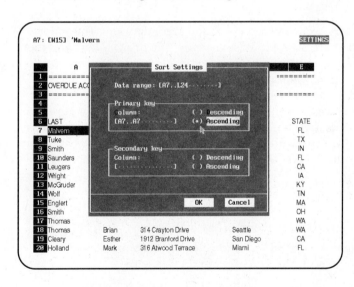

In this example, select **A**scending in the dialog box to sort the database so that 1-2-3 alphabetizes the last names from A to Z.

7. If you are using the dialog box, click the left mouse button on OK or press ⏎Enter to return to the **S**ort menu.

8. Select **G**o to have 1-2-3 sort the database.

13

479

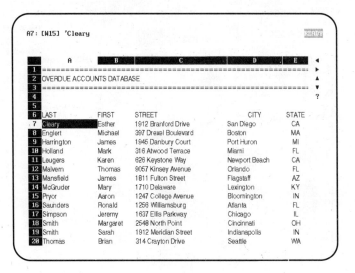

The database displays the result of the one-key sort on the LAST field.

The Two-Key Sort

A two-key database sort uses both a primary and secondary key. The yellow pages sort records first according to business type (the primary key) and then by business name (the secondary key). Another example of a two-key sort (first by one key and then by another key within the first sort order) is an address database. First the address database sorts by state and then by city within state. Suppose, for example, that you want to perform a two-key sort on an overdue accounts database. First, you want to sort records according to due date. Then, when more than one record has the same due date, you want to sort further according to account number.

To perform a two-key sort operation, follow these steps:

1. Select /Data Sort.
2. Select **Data-Range** from the menu or the dialog box.
3. Type or highlight the cell address, or enter the range name for the range you want to sort; then press ⏎Enter .

   For this example, choose the range A7..L24 and press ⏎Enter .
4. From the **S**ort menu or Sort Settings dialog box, select **P**rimary-Key.
5. Type or point to any cell in the column containing the primary-key field on which you want to sort. Then press ⏎Enter .

13

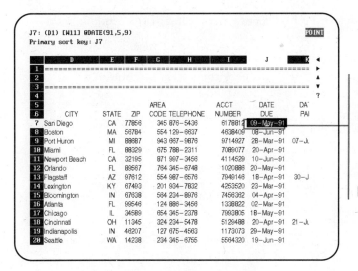

In this example, to first sort the database by the DATE DUE column, highlight any cell in column J and press ↵Enter .

6. Select **A**scending or **D**escending.

   For this example, select **A**scending and press ↵Enter to sort the database so that 1-2-3 arranges the due dates from earliest to most recent.

7. Select **S**econdary-Key from the **S**ort menu or Sort Settings dialog box to have the data sorted a second time within the primary sort order.

8. Type or highlight any cell in the column containing the secondary-key field on which you want to sort. Then press ↵Enter .

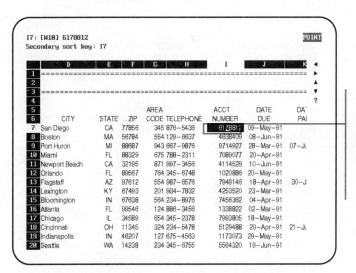

To sort according to ACCT NUMBER after sorting by DATE DUE, highlight any cell in column I and press ↵Enter .

13

9. Indicate the sort order by selecting **A**scending or **D**escending; then press ⏎Enter.

   For this example, select **A**scending.

10. If you are using the dialog box, click the left mouse button on OK or press ⏎Enter to return to the **S**ort menu.

The completed Sort Settings dialog box is shown here.

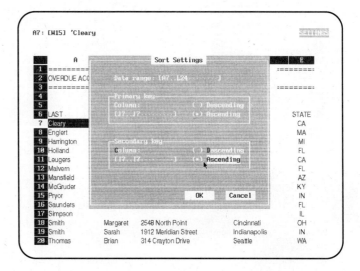

11. Select **G**o to have 1-2-3 sort the database.

The database displays the result of the two-key sort on the DATE DUE and ACCT NUMBER fields. 1-2-3 sorts accounts that are due on the same day according to their account numbers.

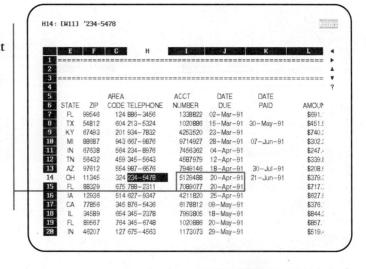

13

482

Tips for Sorting Database Records

Here are a few tips to help you sort database records more successfully.

Tip 1: Don't include blank rows in your data range before you sort the database.

If you accidentally include one or more blank rows in your data range, the blank rows appear at the top of your data range. Therefore, remember to include only rows with data when specifying the data range. However, if your data range includes blank rows, you can delete all the blank rows at one time after you sort the database.

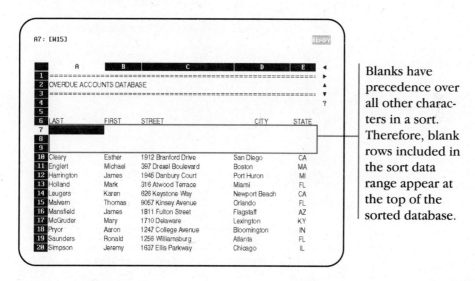

Blanks have precedence over all other characters in a sort. Therefore, blank rows included in the sort data range appear at the top of the sorted database.

Tip 2: Use the /Worksheet Insert Column and /Data Fill commands to create a "counter" field. With this field you can easily re-sort the database to its original order.

After you sort the original contents of the database on any field, you cannot restore the records to their original order. To avoid mistakes and restore the records to the original order, add a counter column to the database before any sort. Include the counter column in the sort range. You can restore the original order by re-sorting on the counter field. The counter field assigns a number to each record so that you can restore the records to their original order.

To create a counter field, follow these steps:

13

483

1. Insert a blank column by selecting /**W**orksheet **I**nsert **C**olumn. You can reduce the column width of this new column with the /**W**orksheet **C**olumn **S**et-Width command.

   In this example, insert a new column at column A.

2. Select /**D**ata **F**ill.

3. Within the blank column, highlight the rows of your database (or the records you want to sort) where you want to enter counter numbers. Then press ↵Enter.

In this example, highlight the range A7..A24 and press ↵Enter.

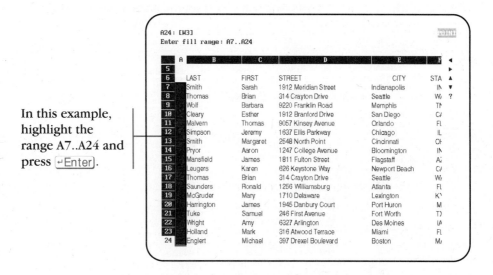

After indicating the /**D**ata **F**ill range, 1-2-3 prompts you for the Start, Step (increment), and Stop numbers.

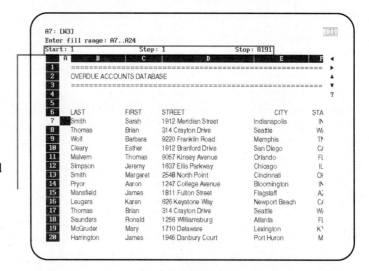

13

4. Press 1 and ↵Enter for the **Start** value, and then press ↵Enter for the default **Step** value of 1. Next, press ↵Enter to accept the default **Stop** value.

Note: Although the default **Stop** value of 8191 is larger than it needs to be, 1-2-3 uses only the numbers necessary to fill the specified range.

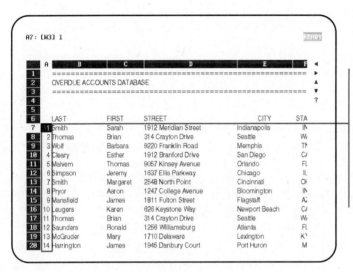

1-2-3 fills the range with consecutive numbers, beginning with 1 and ending with the number of the last highlighted row.

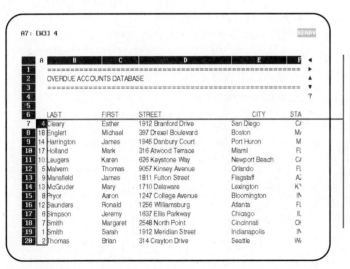

When you sort the database, include the counter column in your data range. To re-sort the database to its original order, use the counter field as your primary-key field.

13

Tip 3: Add new records to the end of the database. Then expand the sort range to include the new records.

You can add a record to an alphabetized name-and-address database without having to insert the record in the correct position manually. Simply add the record to the bottom of the current database, expand the sort data range, and then sort again by last name.

Searching for Records

You have learned how to use the /Data Sort command to reorganize information by sorting records according to key fields. In this section, you learn how to use /Data Query to search for records. You can then edit, extract, or delete those records.

Looking for records that meet one condition is the simplest form of searching a 1-2-3 database. In an inventory database, for example, you can determine when to reorder items. Use a search operation to find any records with an on-hand quantity of fewer than four units. Once you find the information you want, you can extract or copy the found records from the database to another empty section of the worksheet. For example, you can extract all records with a future purchase order date and print the newly extracted area as a record of pending purchases.

With 1-2-3's search operations, you also have the option of looking for only the first occurrence of a specified field value. This allows you to develop a unique list of field entries. For example, you can search and extract a list of the different units of measure. Then you can delete all inventory records for which on-hand quantity equals zero (if you don't want to reorder these items).

Minimum Search Requirements

The /Data Query command lets you search for and extract data that meets specific criteria. After you choose /Data Query, 1-2-3 displays a menu of nine options and a Query Settings dialog box for performing search and extract operations.

13

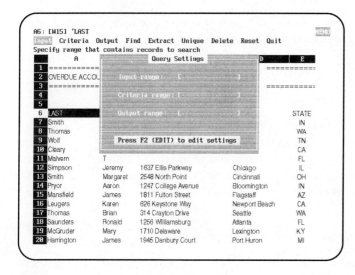

The /**Data Query** menu and the Query Settings dialog box are shown here.

Table 13.4 describes these options.

Table 13.4
Selections on the /Data Query Menu

Selection	Description
Input	Allows you to specify the location of the search area
Criteria	Lets you specify the conditions for searching the database
Output	Allows you to specify the range where you want to locate the records extracted from the database
Find	Finds records based on the specified criteria
Extract	Copies from the database the records matching the specified criteria and places them in the output range
Unique	Eliminates duplicate records in the output range
Delete	Removes from the input range records that match the specified criteria
Reset	Resets the input, criteria, and output ranges
Quit	Returns 1-2-3 to READY mode

13

The first three options specify ranges applicable to the search operation. **Input** and **Criteria** give the locations of the search area and the search conditions. You must specify both in all **Query** operations. You specify the output range with the **Output** option. The output range is necessary when you select a /Data Query command that copies records to an area outside the database. You can enter these ranges through the dialog box or command menu.

The next four options of the /Data Query menu perform a variety of search functions. **Find** moves down through a database and positions the cell pointer on records that match the given criteria. You can enter or change data in the records as you move the cell pointer through them. **Extract** creates copies, in a specified area of the worksheet, of all or some of the fields in certain records that match the given criteria. **Unique** is similar to **Extract**, but ignores duplicates as 1-2-3 copies entries to the output range. **Delete** erases from a database all the records that match the given criteria and closes the remaining gaps.

The last two options of the /Data Query menu are **Reset** and **Quit**. They signal the end of the current search operation. **Reset** removes all previous search-related ranges so that you can specify a different search location, condition, and output range (if applicable). **Quit** restores 1-2-3 to READY mode.

Searching for Specific Records

If you want to search for one or several records that meet certain criteria, you need to make two selections from the /Data Query menu or Query Settings dialog box: **Input** and **Criteria..** Then you select **Find** from the /Data Query menu. Suppose, for example, that you want to search a database containing a list of customers with overdue accounts to find a specific customer. The following sections describe the procedure.

Defining the Input Range

The input range for the /Data Query command is the range of records you want to search. The specified area does not have to include the entire database. Whether you search all or only part of a database, you must include the field-names row in the input range. (In contrast, remember that you do not include the field names in a sort operation.) If field names occupy space on more than one row, specify only the bottom row to start the input range. Do not use a blank row or a dashed line to separate the field names from the database records.

13

488

Select /Data Query Input, and then specify the range by typing or highlighting the range, or by typing an assigned range name. You do not have to specify the range again in later query operations unless the search area changes.

The input range for the database containing a list of overdue accounts includes the entire database and the field names. To define the input range containing the records to search, follow these steps:

1. Select /Data Query.

   The Query Settings dialog box appears.

2. Select Input from the menu or Input range from the dialog box.

3. Specify the range by typing or highlighting the range, or by typing an assigned range name; then press ⏎Enter

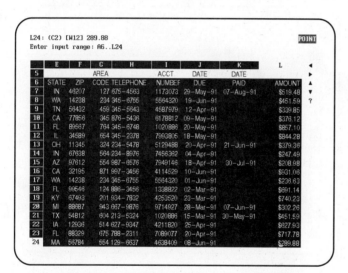

In this example, highlight the range A6..L24 and press ⏎Enter

4. If you are using the dialog box, click the left mouse button on OK or press ⏎Enter to return to the Query menu.

5. To return to READY mode, select Quit.

After you have defined the input range, the next step in a data query operation is to define the criteria range. The next section covers this procedure.

Defining the Criteria Range

To search for data that meets certain conditions, or criteria, you must set up a special range called a criteria range. First find an empty area of the worksheet for your criteria range. Then select /Data Query Criteria.

You can use numbers, labels, or formulas as criteria. A criteria range can be up to 32 columns wide and two or more rows long. The first row must contain the field names of the search criteria, such as STATE. The rows below the unique field names contain the actual criteria, such as OH. The field names of the input range and the criteria range must match exactly.

Suppose that, in an overdue accounts database, you want to identify all records for customers with the last name *Smith*. To define the criteria range containing the search conditions, follow these steps:

1. Begin by locating an area of the worksheet where you can enter the criteria on which you want to search the database. Type the label **CRITERIA RANGE** and press ⏎Enter to mark the area.

In this example, move the cell pointer to cell A27, type **CRITERIA RANGE**, and press ⏎Enter.

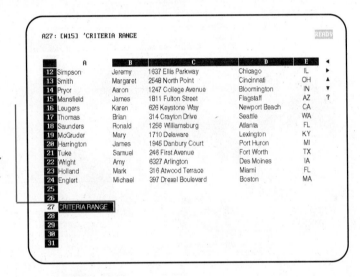

2. Copy the exact field names of your database to the section of the worksheet where you want to locate the criteria range.

   Note: You do not have to include each field name in the criteria range. However, you should copy all field names, because you may choose to enter criteria based on different field names at a later time.

   In this example, copy all field names by issuing the /Copy command and copying the range A6..L6 to cell A28.

3. Type the search criteria just below a field name and press ⏎Enter.

13

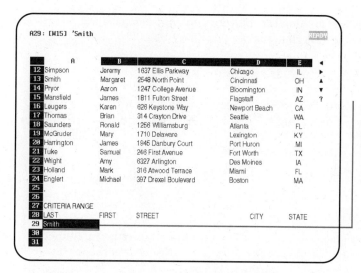

In the cell below the LAST field name, type the last name **Smith** and press ⏎Enter.

4. Select **/Data Query**.

5. Select **Criteria** from the menu or **Criteria range** from the dialog box.

6. Highlight or type the range of cells containing the field names and specific criteria. Then press ⏎Enter.

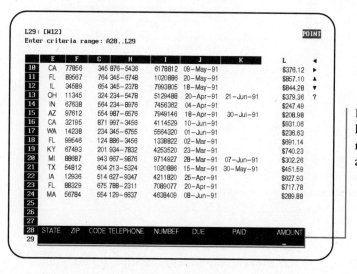

In this example, highlight the range A28..L29 and press ⏎Enter.

7. If you are using the dialog box, click the left mouse button on **OK** or press ⏎Enter to return to the **Query** menu.

8. To return to READY mode, select **Quit**.

13

The next step involves searching for (but not copying) the specified records. The following section covers this step.

Finding Records That Meet the Criteria

After you enter the input and criteria ranges, you have completed the minimum requirements for executing a **F**ind or **D**elete command. Be sure to enter the specific field names above the conditions in the worksheet (in READY mode) before you use /**D**ata **Q**uery **C**riteria.

To search for records that meet the criteria you have specified, follow these steps:

1. Select /**D**ata **Q**uery **F**ind.

   A highlight bar rests on the first record (in the input range) that meets the conditions specified in the criteria range. Notice that the mode indicator changes to FIND during the search.

   If you select /**D**ata **Q**uery **F**ind without the proper input and criteria ranges, 1-2-3 beeps and does nothing.

In this example, the highlight bar rests on the first record that includes `Smith` in the LAST field, in row 7 of the worksheet. The FIND mode indicator appears.

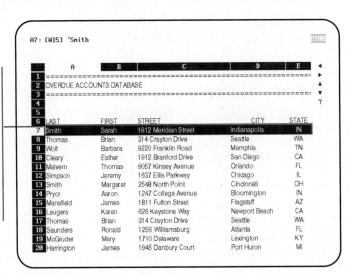

13

2. Press ⬇ to move the highlight bar to the next record that meets the specified criteria. You can continue pressing ⬇ until 1-2-3 highlights the last record that meets the search conditions.

492

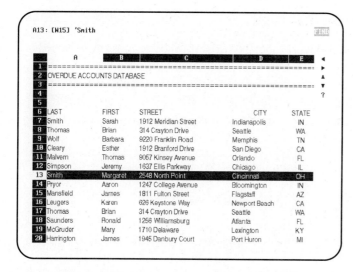

In this example, the highlight bar moves to row 13, the next occurrence of `Smith` in the LAST field of the database.

3. When you want to end the search, press ⏎Enter⏎ or (Esc) to return to the /Data Query menu.

4. To return to READY mode, select **Quit**.

Use the down- and up-arrow keys to position the highlight bar on the next and previous records that meet the search criteria. You can use the Home and End keys to position the highlight bar on the first and last records in the database. This is true even if those records do not fit the search criteria.

In FIND mode, use the right- and left-arrow keys to move the single-character flashing cursor to different fields in the current highlighted record. Then enter new values or use the Edit (F2) key to update the current values in the field.

Listing All Specified Records

The /Data Query Find command has limited use, especially in a large database. The command must scroll through the entire file if you want to view each record that meets the specified criteria. As an alternative to the **Find** command, you can use the **Extract** command. This command copies to a blank area of the worksheet only those records that meet specified conditions. Before you issue the command, you must define the blank area of the worksheet as an output range. You can view a list of all the extracted records or print the range of the newly extracted records. You can even use the /File **Xtract** command to copy only the extracted record range to a new file on disk.

13

Defining the Output Range

Choose a blank area in the worksheet as the output range to receive records copied in an extract operation. In the first row of the output range, type the names of only those fields whose contents you want to extract. You do not have to type these names in the same order as they appear in the database.

The field names in both the criteria and output ranges must match exactly the corresponding field names in the input range. If you enter a database field name incorrectly in the output range, an extract operation based on that field name does not work. For example, FIRSTNAME does not work instead of FIRST. To avoid mismatch errors, use the /Copy command to copy the database field names to the criteria and output ranges.

You can create an open-ended output range by entering only the field-names row as the range. The output range, in this case, can be any size, according to how many records meet the criteria. Or, you can set the exact size of the extract area so that no data located below the area is accidentally overwritten.

To define the output range where 1-2-3 will copy records meeting the specified criteria, follow these steps:

1. Begin by locating an area of the worksheet where you want to copy the records meeting the criteria. Type the label OUTPUT RANGE and press ⏎Enter to mark the area.

2. Copy the exact field names of your database to the section of the worksheet where you want to locate the output range.

   Note: You do not have to extract entire records or maintain the order of field names in the output range. If you do not need to see information for every field in the output range, copy only the desired field names.

13

494

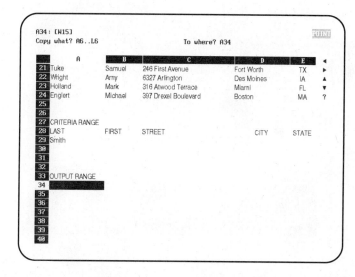

In this example, copy all field names by issuing the /Copy command and copying the range A6..L6 to A34.

3. Select **/Data Query**.

4. Select **Output** from the menu or **Output range** from the dialog box.

5. Type or highlight the range where you want to copy the records and press ↵Enter. You can indicate either an unlimited range or a range limited to a specific block of cells.

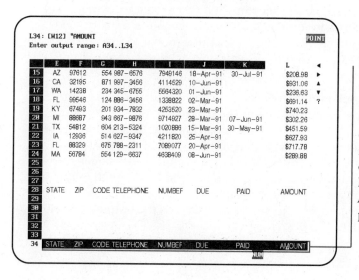

To enter an unlimited output range, highlight only the cells containing field names. In this example, highlight the range A34..L34 and press ↵Enter.

13

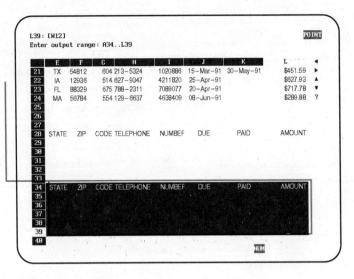

To enter a limited output range, specify additional rows below the field-names row and press ⏎Enter)

6. If you are using the dialog box, click the left mouse button on OK or press ⏎Enter to return to the **Query** menu.

7. To return to READY mode, select **Quit**.

An open-ended output range does not limit the number of incoming records. To create an open-ended range, specify only the row containing the output field names as the output range. Keep in mind that an extract operation first removes all existing data from the output range. If you use only the field-names row, 1-2-3 destroys all data below that row (down to row 8192). Therefore, be sure that you don't have data below the row of field names if you choose an open-ended output range.

To limit the size of the output range, enter the upper left to lower right cell coordinates of the entire output range. The first row in the specified range must contain the field names. The remaining rows must accommodate the maximum number of records you expect to receive from the extract operation. Use this method when you want to keep additional data that is below the extract area. If you do not allow enough room in the fixed-length output area, the extract operation aborts and 1-2-3 displays the message `Too many records for Output range`. Nevertheless, 1-2-3 fills the output area with as many records as will fit.

Executing the Extract Command

Before you can execute the /**Data Query Extract** command, you must type the search conditions in the criteria range of the worksheet. You must also copy the output field names to the output range in the worksheet. Finally, you must specify the input, criteria, and output ranges with the **/Data Query** commands.

To extract (or copy) to the output range records that meet the specified criteria, follow these steps:

1. Select **/Data Query Extract.**

    1-2-3 copies all records that meet the specified criteria in the criteria range to the output area. 1-2-3 keeps the same order as the input range.

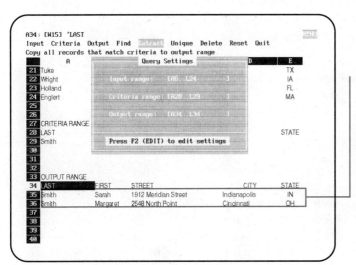

In this example, 1-2-3 copied all records in the LAST field that correspond to the search criteria of Smith to the output range.

2. To return to READY mode, select **Quit.**

To speed the process, you can set up standard input, criteria, and output ranges, and then store the range names for these locations. You can set up a single criteria range that encompasses all the key fields on which you might search. By establishing such a range, you save the time needed to respecify a criteria range for each extract on different field names.

When 1-2-3 is in READY mode, you can press the Query (F7) key to repeat the most recent query operation (**Extract**, in this example). This would eliminate the need to select **/Data Query Extract** again after changing the criteria range. Use the shortcut method only when you do not want to change the locations of the input, criteria, and output ranges.

13

Copying Extracted Records to a New File

If you want to copy extracted records to their own special file, follow these
steps:

1. Select /**File Xtract**.
2. Select either **Formulas** or **Values**, depending on whether the data
    contains formulas you want retained in the new file.
3. Type the name you want to give to the new file and press ⏎Enter.
4. Highlight the range or type the range address of the records you want
    to copy to a new file; then press ⏎Enter.

    For example, highlight the range A34..L36 and press ⏎Enter.

1-2-3 creates a new file containing the data from your extract range. To access
this file, you must issue the /**File Retrieve** command and specify the new file
name.

Creating More Complex Criteria Ranges

In addition to searching for an "exact match" of a specified label within a field
of labels, 1-2-3 permits a wide variety of other types of record searches. For
example, you can search for an exact match in numeric fields. In addition, you
can choose a search criteria that only partially matches the contents of specified fields. You can include formulas in your search criteria. You can also use
multiple criteria that involve searching for specified conditions in more than
one field. Refer to Que's *Using 1-2-3 for DOS Release 2.3*, Special Edition, for
more information on creating more complex criteria ranges.

Performing Other Types of Searches

In addition to **Find** and **Extract**, you can use the **Unique** and **Delete** options of
the /**Data Query** menu to perform searches. By issuing the **Unique** command,
you can produce (in the output range) a copy of only the first occurrence of a
record that meets the specified criteria. The **Delete** command allows you to
update the contents of your 1-2-3 database by deleting all records that meet
the specified criteria. After entering the search conditions, you need to specify
only the input and criteria ranges before you issue the **Delete** command.

13

Searching for Unique Records

Ordinarily, you use the **Unique** command to copy into the output area only a small portion of each record that meets the criteria. For example, if you want a list of states represented in the overdue accounts database, set an output range that includes only the STATE field. To search all records, leave blank the row below the field-names row in the criteria range. Then define the input, criteria, and output ranges and select /**Data Query Unique**. In the following example, the output range includes only the STATE field. The row below the field-names row in the criteria range is blank.

To copy to the output range unique records that meet the criteria you have specified, follow these steps:

1. Select /**Data Query Unique**.

   1-2-3 copies all records that meet the specified criteria in the criteria range to the output area. The order is the same as in the input range.

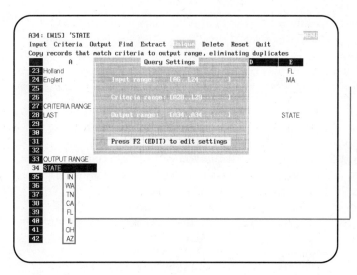

In this example, issuing the Unique command produces a list of the different states represented in the database.

2. To return to READY mode, select **Quit**.

Deleting Specified Records

As discussed earlier, you can use the /**Worksheet Delete Row** command to remove records from a worksheet. An alternative approach is to use the /**Data Query Delete** command to remove from the database unwanted records

499

matching a specified criteria. Before you select **Delete** from the /**D**ata **Q**uery menu, specify the range of records to search (the input range) and the conditions for the deletion (the criteria).

Be extremely careful when you issue the **Delete** command. To give you the opportunity to verify that you indeed want the **Delete** command, 1-2-3 asks you to select **Cancel** or **Delete**. Choose **Cancel** to abort the **Delete** command. Select **Delete** to verify that you want to execute the delete operation.

Although 1-2-3 asks whether you want to delete records, you can't view the records that match the criteria you specified. For this reason, use /**F**ile **S**ave to make a copy of the database. Or you can use the **Extract** command to copy the records you plan to delete and view them. When you are sure that you want to remove the records from the database, proceed with the **Delete** operation.

Summary

Although you can use 1-2-3 for spreadsheet applications, you can also use 1-2-3 for many types of database applications. You create a 1-2-3 database within the worksheet. You also use the same cell pointer and direction keys as you used for other applications. Therefore, you don't have to learn a completely different program when you want to work with a 1-2-3 database.

The /**D**ata command on 1-2-3's main menu leads to commands for performing common database applications. These include sorting data, searching for records that meet specific criteria, and extracting records from the main database. Sorting in 1-2-3 is fast and easy, but you can sort on only up to two fields. When searching for and extracting records, you must create an input range that contains the field names and all records you want to search. You must also create a criteria range to specify the search conditions. When extracting records from a 1-2-3 database, you must also define the output range, where you want to copy the extracted data.

Specifically, you learned the following key information about 1-2-3:

- A *database* consists of records and fields. In 1-2-3, a *record* is a row of cells in the database. A *field* is one type of information within the record, such as a ZIP code.

- 1-2-3's /**D**ata menu contains most of the commands you commonly use to manage and manipulate databases. However, you can also use worksheet options from the 1-2-3 main menu to manage databases.

- Plan a database carefully before you create it. Determine which categories, or fields, of information you want to include. Also decide what type of output you want.

- An ideal location for a database is an area where inserting and deleting rows and columns won't affect other applications above, below, to the right of, or to the left of the database.

- Use /Worksheet Insert Row and /Worksheet Delete Row to add or delete records (rows) in the database. Similarly, use /Worksheet Insert Column and /Worksheet Delete Column to add or delete fields (columns) in the database.

- /Data Sort allows you to change the order of records by sorting them according to the contents of specified key fields. In 1-2-3, you can sort with primary and secondary keys, in ascending or descending order.

- Use the /Data Query command to set up a database, as well as search a database for records matching a specified criteria. Before starting a search, you must first specify an input range and a criteria range with the commands /Data Query Input and /Data Query Criteria, respectively. When using the Extract and Unique options of this command, you must also specify an output range with the /Data Query Output command. Alternatively, you can use the Query Settings dialog box to specify input, criteria, and output ranges.

- The /Data Query Find command positions the cell pointer in records matching a given criteria. You can move the cell pointer to edit cells in a highlighted record.

- The /Data Query Extract command copies records (or specified portions of records) matching a given set of criteria to another area of the worksheet.

- The /Data Query Unique command also copies records to an output range. However, it does not copy duplicate entries based on fields specified in the criteria range.

- The /Data Query Delete command erases from a database the records that match conditions specified in the criteria range. 1-2-3 asks for confirmation before deleting the records.

The next chapter shows you how to create macros. Your ability to create macros allows you to speed up repetitive tasks considerably.

13

Understanding Macros

14

In addition to the capabilities available from the commands in 1-2-3's main menu, another feature makes 1-2-3 the most popular spreadsheet program available today. Macros and the advanced macro commands enable you to automate and customize your applications and thus reduce tasks requiring multiple keystrokes to a two-keystroke operation. Just press two keys and 1-2-3 does the rest, whether you're formatting a range, creating a graph, or printing a worksheet. You also can control and customize worksheet applications by using 1-2-3's advanced macro commands. These 50 built-in commands give you a greater range of control over your 1-2-3 applications.

You can think of simple keystroke macros as the building blocks for advanced macro command programs. When you add advanced macro commands to simple keystroke macros, you can control and automate many of the actions required to build and update 1-2-3 worksheets. At the most sophisticated level, you can use 1-2-3's advanced macro commands as a full-fledged programming language for developing custom applications.

Planning macros

Naming macros

Using the Learn feature

Executing macros

Using automatic macros

Debugging macros

Creating a macro library

Key Terms in This Chapter

Macro	A series of stored keystrokes or commands that 1-2-3 carries out when you press two or more keys.
Program	A list of instructions in a computer programming language, such as 1-2-3's advanced macro commands, which tells the computer what to do.
Advanced macro commands	1-2-3's programming language consisting of more than 50 built-in commands that are not accessible through the 1-2-3 menu system.
Tilde (~)	The symbol used in a macro to signify the Enter keystroke.
Key names	Representations of keyboard keys used in macros. Enclose key names in braces: for example, {EDIT}.
Documented macro or program	A macro or program that contains information explaining each step in the macro or program.
Learn feature	Records keystrokes, enables copying of keystrokes into a worksheet cell as a label, and automatically creates a macro.
Bug	An error in a macro or program.
Debugging	The process of identifying and fixing errors in a macro or program.

In this chapter, you find an introduction to the concept and application of macros. You also will find some simple keystroke macros, which you can retrieve as necessary. For more detailed information on macros and the advanced macro commands, consult Que's *Using 1-2-3 for DOS Release 2.3*, Special Edition, or *1-2-3 Macro Library*, 3rd Edition.

14

What Is a Macro?

A macro, in its most basic form, is a collection of stored keystrokes that you can replay at any time. These keystrokes can be commands or simple text and numeric entries. Macros provide an alternative to typing data and commands from the keyboard. Macros, therefore, can save you time by automating frequently performed tasks.

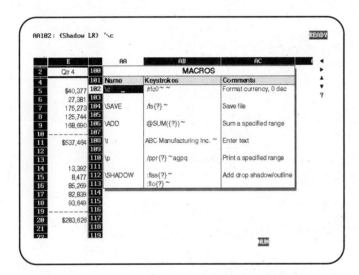

This screen shows six simple keystroke macros in the window on the right. The window on the left displays worksheet data.

A simple macro, for example, can automate the sequence of seven keystrokes which format a cell in Currency format with zero decimal places. You can execute the seven keystrokes in cell AB102 by pressing two keys, Alt and C.

You can name macros in two different ways. One way is to use the backslash key (\) and a single letter. Execute an Alt-*letter* macro by holding down the Alt key and pressing the letter that identifies the macro. This is the only method available for use with versions of 1-2-3 before Release 2.2. In Releases 2.2 and 2.3, you can name macros by using descriptive names of up to 15 characters in length. Access these macros by pressing Run (Alt-F3). When the list of range names appears, highlight the name of the macro you want to use and press Enter.

14

The Elements of Macros

1-2-3 macros follow a specific format, whether they are simple keystroke macros or macros that perform complex tasks. A macro is nothing more than a specially-named text cell. Create all macros by entering into a worksheet cell the keystrokes (or representations of those keystrokes) to store. Suppose that you want to create a simple macro that will format the current cell to appear in Currency format with no decimal places. The macro looks like this:

```
'/rfc0~~
```

The following are the macro elements for the formatting macro, along with descriptions of the actions that result when 1-2-3 executes each element:

Macro Element	Action
'	Tells 1-2-3 that the information which follows is a label.
/	Calls up the 1-2-3 menu.
r	Selects **Range**.
f	Selects **Format**.
c	Selects **Currency**.
0	Tells 1-2-3 to suppress the display of digits to the right of the decimal point.
~~	Functions as two Enter keystrokes. (Each tilde acts as one Enter keystroke.)

You enter this macro into the worksheet in exactly the same way you would any other label. Type a label prefix followed by the characters in the label. The label prefix (displayed only in the control panel) informs 1-2-3 to treat what follows as a label. Every macro that starts with a nontext character (/, \, +, −, or a number) must begin with a label prefix. If you did not use a prefix, 1-2-3 would automatically interpret the next character (/) as a command to execute immediately instead of a label stored in the cell. Any of the three 1-2-3 label prefixes (', ", or ^) works equally well.

The next four characters in the macro represent the command used to create the desired format. After all, /rfc is simply shorthand for **/Range Format Currency**. The 0 (zero) tells 1-2-3 that you want no digits displayed to the right of the decimal point. If you were entering this command from the keyboard, you would type the 0 in response to a prompt.

14

At the end of the macro are two characters called *tildes*. When used in a macro, a tilde (~) represents the Enter key. In this case, the two tildes signal 1-2-3 to press the Enter key twice: to accept the number of decimal places, and to select the current cell as the range to format.

Other elements used in macros include range names and cell addresses. Although you can use these two elements interchangeably, you should use range names instead of cell addresses whenever possible. If you move data included in specified ranges, or insert or delete rows and columns, the range names adjust automatically and the macro continues to refer to the correct cells and ranges. Cell references used in macros do not adjust to any changes made in the worksheet and you must change them manually.

Some macro examples in this chapter include the {?} command. The {?} is actually a type of advanced macro command. Use it to pause the macro so that you can type information, such as a file name, from the keyboard. The macro continues executing when you press the Enter key. For example, a macro that sets column widths can include the {?} command to let you type the new column width when the macro pauses. Then you can press Enter to complete execution of the macro.

Characters in macro commands are not case-sensitive. You can use capitalization wherever you want. For readability, however, this book uses lowercase letters in macros to indicate commands. Range names and key names are in uppercase letters.

Macro Key Names and Special Keys

1-2-3 uses symbols besides the tilde (~) to stand for other keystrokes. You can add to the formatting example key names and special keys that highlight a range as if you were using /**R**ange **F**ormat.

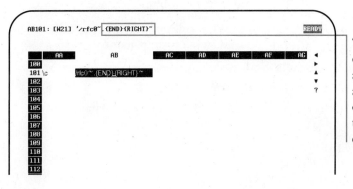

The added part of the macro anchors the range and highlights all occupied cells to the right in the current row.

14

507

This revised macro is similar to the preceding one, except that the
.{END}{RIGHT} portion causes the cell pointer to move. You can use this
version of the macro to format an entire row instead of just one cell.

Once again, notice the apostrophe (') at the beginning of the macro (displayed in the control panel) and the tilde (~) at the end. Notice also the
phrase .{END}{RIGHT} in the macro. The period (.) anchors the cell pointer.
The {END} key name stands for the End key on the keyboard. The {RIGHT}
key name represents the right-arrow key. This phrase has the same effect in
the macro as these three keys would have if you pressed them in sequence
from the keyboard. The cell pointer moves to the next boundary between
blank and occupied cells in the row.

Use representations like these to signify key names and special keys on the
keyboard. In every case, enclose the key name in braces. For example, {UP}
represents the up-arrow key. {ESC} stands for the Esc (Escape) key. {GRAPH}
represents the F10 function key.

Tables 14.1 through 14.4 provide lists of macro key names and special keys
grouped according to their uses. They include function keys, direction keys,
editing keys, and special keys.

Table 14.1
Macro Key Names for Function Keys

Function Key	Key Name	Action
Help (F1)	{HELP}	Accesses 1-2-3's on-line help system
Edit (F2)	{EDIT}	Edits the contents of the current cell
Name (F3)	{NAME}	Displays a list of range names in the current worksheet
Abs (F4)	{ABS}	Converts a relative reference to abso-lute, or an absolute reference to relative
GoTo (F5)	{GOTO}	Jumps the cell pointer to the specified cell address or range name
Window (F6)	{WINDOW}	Moves the cell pointer to the other side of a split screen
Query (F7)	{QUERY}	Repeats the most recent /Data Query operation
Table (F8)	{TABLE}	Repeats the most recent table operation

14

Function Key	Key Name	Action
Calc (F9)	{CALC}	Recalculates the worksheet
Graph (F10)	{GRAPH}	Redraws the current graph on-screen

Table 14.2
Macro Key Names for Direction Keys

Direction Key	Key Name	Action
Up arrow (↑)	{UP} or {U}	Moves the cell pointer up one row
Down arrow (↓)	{DOWN} or {D}	Moves the cell pointer down one row
Left arrow (←)	{LEFT} or {L}	Moves the cell pointer left one column
Right arrow (→)	{RIGHT} or {R}	Moves the cell pointer right one column
Shift-Tab or Ctrl-←	{BIGLEFT}	Moves the cell pointer left one screen
Tab or Ctrl-→	{BIGRIGHT}	Moves the cell pointer right one screen
PgUp or Page Up	{PGUP}	Moves the cell pointer up one screen
PgDn or Page Down	{PGDN}	Moves the cell pointer down one screen
Home	{HOME}	Moves the cell pointer to cell A1; if /Worksheet Titles is on, moves the cell pointer to the top left cell outside the titles area
End	{END}	Used with {UP}, {DOWN}, {LEFT}, or {RIGHT}; the cell pointer moves in the indicated direction to the next boundary between blank cells and cells that hold data Also used with {HOME} to move the cell pointer to the lower right corner of the worksheet

14

Table 14.3
Macro Key Names for Editing Keys

Editing Key	Key Name	Action
Delete (Del)	{DELETE} or {DEL}	Used with {EDIT} to delete a single character from a cell entry
Insert (Ins)	{INSERT} or {INS}	Toggles between insert and overtype modes when you are editing a cell
Esc	{ESCAPE} or {ESC}	Signifies the Esc key
Backspace	{BACKSPACE} or {BS}	Signifies the Backspace key
Ctrl-Break	{BREAK}	Clears the command and returns to READY mode

Table 14.4
Macro Key Names for Special Keys

Special Key	Key Name	Action
/ (menu)	/	Causes the command menu to appear
Enter	~	Signifies the Enter key
~ (Tilde)	{~}	Causes a tilde to appear in the worksheet
{ (Open brace)	{{}	Causes an open brace to appear in the worksheet
} (Close brace)	{}}	Causes a closing brace to appear in the worksheet

Note: A few keys or key combinations do not have a key name to identify them. These include Shift, Caps Lock, Num Lock, Scroll Lock, Print Screen, Compose (Alt-F1), Step (Alt-F2), Run (Alt-F3), and Undo (Alt-F4). You cannot represent any of these keys or key combinations within macros.

14

To specify more than one use of a key name, you can include repetition factors inside the braces. For example, you can use the following statements in macros:

Statement	Action
{PGUP 3}	Press the PgUp key three times
{L 4}	Press the left-arrow key four times
{RIGHT JUMP}	Press the right-arrow key the number of times indicated by the value in the cell named JUMP

Planning Macros

A simple keystroke macro can be thought of as a substitute for keyboard commands. Because of this, the best way to plan a macro is to step through the series of instructions one keystroke at a time. Perform this exercise before you start creating the macro. Take notes about each step as you proceed with the commands on-screen, then translate the keystrokes that you've written into a macro that conforms to the guidelines discussed in this chapter.

Stepping through an operation at the keyboard is an easy way to build simple macros. The more experience you have with 1-2-3 commands, the easier it becomes to "think through" the keystrokes you need to use in a macro.

For more complex macros, the best approach is to break them into smaller macros that execute in a series. Each small macro performs one simple operation, and the series of simple operations together performs the desired application.

This approach starts with the result of an application. What is the application supposed to do or produce? What form must the results take? If you start with the desired results and work backward, you decrease the risk of producing the wrong results with your macro.

Next, consider input. What data do you need? What data is available and in what form? How much work will it take to go from data to results?

Finally, look at the process. How do you analyze available data and, using 1-2-3, produce the desired results? How can you divide calculations into a series of tasks, each of which can have a simple macro?

14

This "divide-and-conquer" method breaks a complex task into smaller and simpler pieces. It is the key to successful development of macros and complex worksheets. Although this method entails some initial work, you will be able to detect and correct errors more easily because you can locate them in a smaller section of the macro.

Positioning Macros in the Worksheet

Usually, you should place macros outside the area occupied by data on your worksheet. This practice helps you avoid accidentally overwriting or erasing part of a macro as you create your model.

Macros should be positioned to the right of and below the main part of the worksheet.

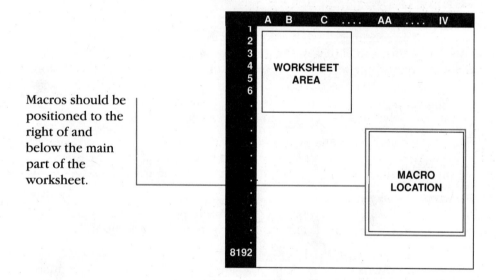

This positioning lessens the chance that you will accidentally include the macro's range in worksheet operations. With this placement, deleting rows or columns in the worksheet area will not affect the cells in the macro location.

1-2-3 has no rule that says you must place your macros in the same place in every worksheet. You may, however, want to make a habit of always placing your macros in a certain column, such as column AA, and well below the usual last row of worksheet data. You will then always know where to look in your applications for the macros if they need to be modified. Also, if your worksheets rarely require more than 26 columns, you don't have to worry about overwriting the macro area with the worksheet data. Such positioning of the macros means that deleting rows or columns from the main part of your worksheet will not affect the cells in the macro location. Finally, column AA is

14

close enough to the home screen that you can easily reach the macro area with the Tab key.

In small worksheets, on the other hand, you may want to put your macros in column I. The macros can be reached from the home screen with a single press of the Tab key when all the columns have a width of nine characters.

You can assign the range name MACROS to the area containing the macros. Using a range name allows you to move to the macro area quickly with the GoTo (F5) key.

Documenting Macros

Professional programmers usually write *documented* programs. This term means that the program contains comments which help to explain each step in the program. In BASIC, these comments are in REM (for REMark) statements. For example, in the following program, the REM statements explain the actions taken by the other statements.

```
10   REM This program adds two numbers
20   REM Enter first number
30   INPUT A
40   REM Enter second number
50   INPUT B
60   REM Add numbers together
70   C=A+B
80   REM Display result
90   Print C
```

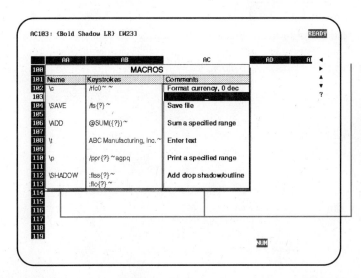

Document your 1-2-3 macros by placing comments in the column to the right of the macro steps. Place the name of the macro to the left of the macro steps.

14

Including comments in your macros will make them far easier to use. Comments are especially useful when you have created complex macros that are important to the worksheet's overall design. Suppose that you have created a complex macro but have not looked at it for a month. Then you decide that you want to change the macro. Without built-in comments, you might have a difficult time remembering what each step of the macro does.

Naming Macros

You must give a macro a name before you can execute it.

Name a macro by using a backslash (\) followed by a single letter (Alt-*letter*). Alternatively, you can name a macro with a backslash and a descriptive name, like a typical range name.

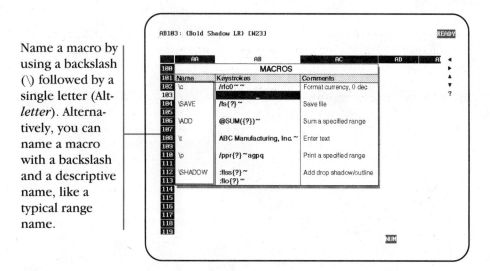

If you choose to use the single-letter naming convention, select a character that in some way helps describe the macro. For example, you could use \c to name a macro that formats a range as currency.

To assign a name to a macro, follow these steps:

1. Select /**R**ange **N**ame **C**reate.
2. Type   and a single letter, and then press Enter; or type a descriptive name of up to 15 characters and press Enter.

   For this example, type \c, and then press Enter.
3. The prompt Enter range: appears. Highlight (or type the cell addresses of) the range where you entered macro commands, and then press Enter.

14

514

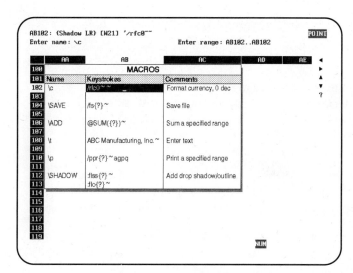

AB102: {Shadow LR} [W21] '/rfc0~~   POINT
Enter name: \c   Enter range: AB102..AB102

	AA	AB	AC	AD	AE
100		MACROS			
101	Name	Keystrokes	Comments		
102	\c	/rfc0~ ~	Format currency, 0 dec		
103					
104	\SAVE	/fs{?}~	Save file		
105					
106	\ADD	@SUM({?})~	Sum a specified range		
107					
108	\t	ABC Manufacturing, Inc.~	Enter text		
109					
110	\p	/ppr{?}~agpq	Print a specified range		
111					
112	\SHADOW	:fss{?}~	Add drop shadow/outline		
113		:flo{?}~			
114					
115					
116					
117					
118					
119					

NUM

In this example, highlight cell AB102 and press ⏎Enter.

This book and the 1-2-3 documentation place the name of the macro in the cell to the immediate left of the macro's first command. If you follow this format, you can use the command /**R**ange **N**ame **L**abels **R**ight to quickly name one or more macros. Specify the range containing the macro names to assign these names to the macros in the adjacent column. This approach works with both descriptive and Alt-*letter* macro names. This command also ensures that you include the name of the macro within the worksheet for easy identification. The /**R**ange **N**ame **L**abels **R**ight command is also useful for naming several macros at once. Otherwise, you would have to name them individually with /**R**ange **N**ame **C**reate.

The advantage of using a single letter for a macro name is that you can activate the macro more quickly from the keyboard. A disadvantage is that a single-letter name doesn't offer as much flexibility in describing what the macro does. Therefore, remembering the name and purpose of a specific macro may be difficult.

To avoid confusing descriptive macro names with other range names, you can also begin descriptive macro names with the backslash (\) character. For example, in this chapter, illustrated macros include one named \SAVE, which you can use to save files. Another macro is \ADD, which uses the @SUM function to add a specified range of values. Yet another descriptive macro, \SHADOW, adds a shadow and outline to a range.

Note: 1-2-3 lets you assign a third type of name to a macro. You can use the name \0 (backslash zero) to create an automatic macro. Automatic macros are discussed later in this chapter.

14

Using the Learn Feature To Record Keystrokes

In Release 2.3, 1-2-3 can keep track of every keystroke and command you issue, and then use this information to build a macro. Instead of creating a macro by typing it manually into worksheet cells, you can use the Learn feature to record all keyboard activity for an indefinite period. The macro is built for you as you step through the procedures you want to include.

To use the Learn feature to record keystrokes, first use the /Worksheet **Learn Range** command to set aside an area in the worksheet where the keystrokes are to be stored. After you designate the range to hold your macro keystrokes, activate recording mode by pressing Learn (Alt-F5). All your commands and keystrokes are stored in the Learn area as you proceed through the operations you want. You can stop recording at any time by pressing Learn (Alt-F5) again. You can resume recording by pressing Learn (Alt-F5) once more.

To record keystrokes for a macro with the Learn feature, follow these steps:

1. Select /Worksheet **Learn Range**.

2. When the prompt `Enter learn range:` appears, highlight a single-column range to hold the keystrokes and press ⏎Enter . Select as many cells as necessary in an area off to the side of your worksheet, and be sure that the area doesn't disturb existing data.

In this example, highlight the range AB101..AB120 and press ⏎Enter . (The macro names can later be added to the appropriate cells in column AA.)

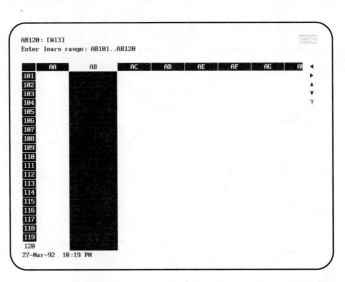

14

3. Move the cell pointer to the worksheet area and press Alt F5 (Learn) to begin recording keystrokes.

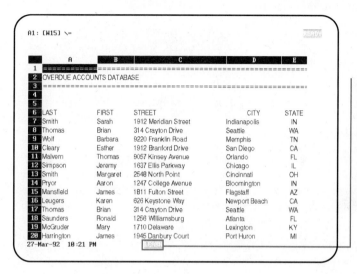

The LEARN indicator, which tells you that your keystrokes are being recorded, appears at the bottom of the screen.

4. Manually type all commands and keystrokes necessary to create your macro.

   For example, you can build a macro that automatically sorts a database. After you record the keystrokes, your database will be sorted, and the Learn range will contain your keystrokes for future use.

5. Press Alt F5 (Learn) to stop recording keystrokes.

To see what you have recorded, move the cell pointer to the Learn range.

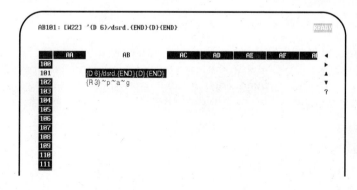

The recorded keystrokes and commands look like a macro you could have typed manually.

14

The column width of the range to which you copy the keystrokes affects the number of keystrokes 1-2-3 copies to each cell. To fit more keystrokes in the macro keystroke column, increase the width of the column.

1-2-3 uses shortcuts when possible. If you press the down-arrow key six times, you might guess that 1-2-3 records the key name {DOWN} six times. Instead, 1-2-3 uses a repetition factor and the most abbreviated form of the key name—in this case, {D 6}.

1-2-3 records the activity of special keys in macro notation. For example, if one of the keys you press while in LEARN mode is the Window (F6) key, the Learn range will contain the macro key name {WINDOW}.

If the size of your Learn range is insufficient to hold the keystrokes being accumulated during LEARN mode, you hear a beep, and the recording activity stops. To continue, simply use the /**W**orksheet **L**earn **R**ange command again to expand the Learn range downward. Press Learn (Alt-F5) when you're ready to continue recording.

When you are satisfied that the recorded activity represents what you want the macro to do, assign a name, such as \SORT, to the first cell of the macro.

Note: When naming macros, you need to name only the *first* cell of the macro, rather than the entire macro range.

At first, you may find using the Learn feature awkward; the Learn range can quickly be filled with irrelevant directional key names and other unwanted commands. If that happens, you can erase the entire contents of the Learn range with the command /**W**orksheet **L**earn **E**rase, and then resume recording with an empty Learn range.

Executing Macros

Alt-*letter* macros named with a backslash and a single letter are the simplest to run. If necessary, move the cell pointer to the appropriate position before you execute the macro. For example, when using a format macro, before running the macro, you must move the cell pointer to the cell you want to format.

To execute an Alt-*letter* macro, follow these steps:

1. Press and hold down the [Alt] key.
2. Press the letter in the macro name.
3. Release both keys.

For example, if you named a macro \a, you invoke it by pressing Alt-A. The \ symbol in the name represents the Alt key. Pressing Alt-A plays back the recorded keystrokes in the macro.

When you identify a macro with a longer descriptive name, it takes only a couple more keystrokes to execute the macro. You must first press Run (Alt-F3) to display a list of range names. Highlight the macro name and then press Enter. The list of names you see when you press Run (Alt-F3) will include range names as well as macro names. To simplify your search for macro names, begin them with a backslash.

To execute a macro with a descriptive name, follow these steps:

1. Press Alt F3 (Run).

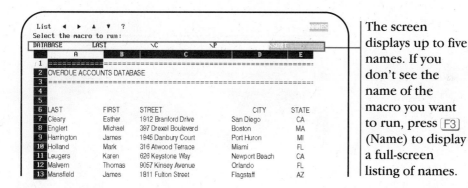

The screen displays up to five names. If you don't see the name of the macro you want to run, press F3 (Name) to display a full-screen listing of names.

2. Highlight the name of the macro you want to execute and press ↵Enter.

As soon as you issue the command to execute a macro, it starts to run. If there are no special instructions (such as a pause) and no bugs are present, the macro continues to run until it finishes. The macro executes each command much faster than if you tried the command manually. You can store many macro keystrokes or commands in a single cell. Some that are especially long, or that include special commands, must be split into two or more cells. When 1-2-3 starts executing a macro, the program begins with the first cell and continues until it executes all the keystrokes stored there. Next, 1-2-3 moves down one cell to continue execution. If the next cell is blank, the program stops. If that cell contains more macro commands, however, 1-2-3 continues reading down the column until it finds the first blank cell.

14

Using an Automatic Macro

1-2-3 allows you to create an automatic macro that will execute automatically when you load the worksheet. You create this macro just like any other. The only difference is its name. The macro that you want to execute automatically must have the name \0 (backslash zero). You can use only one automatic macro in a worksheet.

For example, you can use an automatic macro to position the cell pointer at the upper left corner of a range named DATABASE. The macro can then redefine the range by anchoring the cell pointer and moving it to the right and down to include all contiguous cells. You do not press the Alt key to start the macro in this case. 1-2-3 executes the macro as soon as you retrieve the worksheet.

1-2-3 executes an automatic (\0) macro when you retrieve a file.

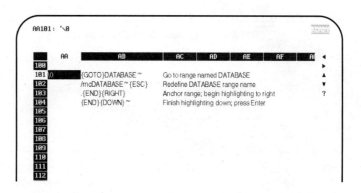

Note that you cannot execute automatic macros with the Alt-0 key combination. If you need to be able to execute the macro from the keyboard, you can use Run (Alt-F3) or you can assign the \0 macro an additional name, such as \a. You then have two identical macros on your system: one that executes automatically, and one that you can execute from the keyboard. This tip is especially useful when testing new automatic macros.

If you do not want to execute an automatic macro when 1-2-3 starts, you can disable this feature. To disable an automatic macro, select /Worksheet Global Default Autoexec No.

14

Debugging and Editing Macros

Almost no program works perfectly the first time. In nearly every case, errors cause programs to malfunction. Programmers call these problems *bugs*. *Debugging* is the process of eliminating bugs.

Like programs written in other programming languages, 1-2-3 macros usually need to be debugged before you can use them. 1-2-3 has a useful feature, STEP mode, that helps make debugging much simpler. When in STEP mode, 1-2-3 executes macros one step at a time. 1-2-3 literally pauses between keystrokes stored in the macro. Using this feature means that you can follow along step-by-step with the macro as it executes.

When you discover an error, you must get out of the macro and return 1-2-3 to READY mode by pressing Esc or Ctrl-Break. Then you can start editing the macro.

Common Errors in Macros

Like all computer programs, macros are literal creatures. They have no capacity to discern an error in the code. For example, you recognize immediately that {GOTI} is a misspelling of {GOTO}. However, a macro cannot make this distinction. The macro tries to interpret the misspelled word and, being unable to, delivers an error message. Here are four reminders to help you avoid some of the most common macro errors:

- Save your worksheet before you execute a macro.
- Verify all syntax and spelling in your macros.
- Include all required tildes (~) to represent Enter keystrokes in macros.
- Use range names in macros whenever possible to avoid problems with incorrect cell references. Cell references in macros are always absolute. They never change when you make modifications in the worksheet.

If a macro is not working correctly, you can use two 1-2-3 features to help you correct worksheet and macro errors. Use the Undo (Alt-F4) feature to "undo" damage to the worksheet created by the faulty execution of a macro. Also, use STEP mode to help pinpoint the location of an error in a macro.

14

521

Undoing Macros

The Undo feature (not available in versions of 1-2-3 before Release 2.2) offers a significant advantage when debugging macros. When a macro doesn't work and appears to have caused major problems within the worksheet, press Undo (Alt-F4). All the steps in the macro will be undone. Remember, the Undo feature restores the worksheet as it was before the last operation. Even though it may contain many steps, 1-2-3 considers a macro as one operation.

If you want to undo a macro, make sure that the Undo feature is active before you actually execute the macro. If necessary, enable Undo with the /Worksheet Global Default Other Undo Enable command. The UNDO indicator should appear at the bottom of the screen. If the macro produces unsatisfactory results, do not perform another operation. Use Undo immediately to reverse the effect of the macro.

Note: There are certain commands that 1-2-3 cannot normally reverse with Undo (Alt-F4). 1-2-3 also cannot reverse these commands within macros. For example, 1-2-3 cannot reverse a macro that includes the /File Save command. Therefore, you should not rely entirely on Undo when you test macros.

Using STEP Mode To Debug Macros

You need to debug most programs before you use them. If you can't locate an error in a macro, enter STEP mode and rerun the macro one step at a time. After each step, the macro pauses and waits for you to type any keystroke before continuing. Although you can use any key, you should use the space bar to step through a macro. As you step through the macro, each command appears in the control panel, and the macro code is displayed at the bottom left of the screen.

To use STEP mode to debug a macro, follow these steps:

1. Press Alt F2 (Step).

14

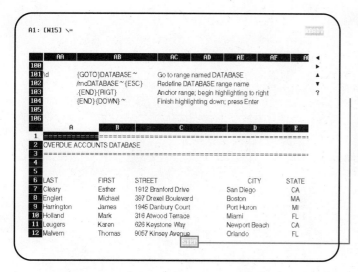

The mode indicator STEP appears at the bottom of the screen.

2. Execute the macro by pressing [Alt] followed by the letter of the macro name. Alternatively, use [Alt] [F3] to select the macro name and press [↵Enter].

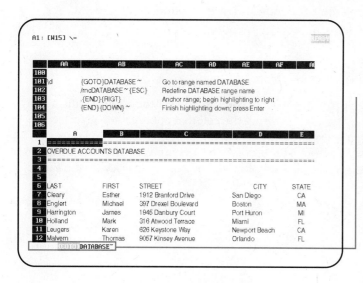

The macro code and its associated address appear at the bottom of the screen as you run the macro in STEP mode.

3. Evaluate each step of the macro, pressing the space bar after you have checked each step.

14

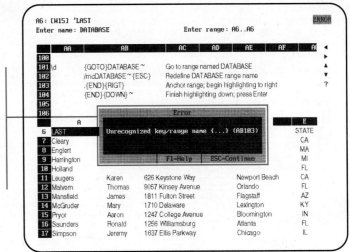

A dialog box displays an error message. In this example, the misspelled key name in cell AB103 caused the error.

4. When you discover an error, press Ctrl Break or Esc to return 1-2-3 to READY mode.

5. When 1-2-3 is in READY mode, edit the macro. You can edit the macro while displaying the STEP indicator at the bottom of the screen.

6. To exit STEP mode, press Alt F2 (Step).

Editing Macros

After you identify an error in a macro, you can correct the error. Fixing an error in a macro is as simple as editing the cell that contains the erroneous code. You don't need to rewrite the entire cell contents. You need only change the element in error. Although editing a complex macro can be much more challenging than editing a simple one, the concept is exactly the same.

14

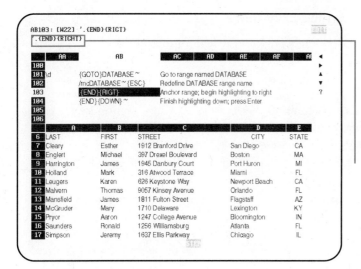

Use the Edit (F2) key to correct the cell that contains the error.

Creating a Macro Library

A macro library is a group of macros that can be used with many different worksheet files. These macros can range from simple keystroke macros to more specialized advanced macro command programs. Macro libraries can save the time necessary to re-create the same macros in different files. After you have created a macro library file, you can copy the macros into the current worksheet.

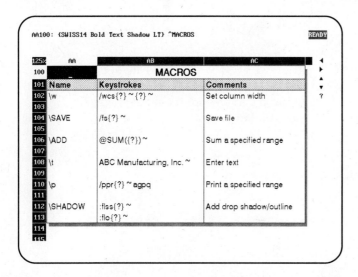

This section introduces six simple keystroke macros that you can create for use in your own macro library.

14

525

To create a macro library file, follow these steps:

1. Start with a blank worksheet, with the cell pointer at the Home position.

2. Begin typing the exact keystrokes displayed in columns AA, AB, and AC. Column AA contains the macro names, column AB contains the actual macros, and column AC contains the documentation for each macro. *Remember to first type a label prefix (such as ') before entering each of the macros in column AB.*

3. Select /**R**ange Name Labels **R**ight to name the macros, specify the range containing all macro names in column AA, and press `←Enter`.

4. Select the /**F**ile **S**ave command to save the macros in a separate file.

When you are ready to copy the macros in the macro library file to your current worksheet, position the cell pointer where you want the macros located (such as column AA), and then issue the /**F**ile Combine Copy **E**ntire-File command. Highlight or type the file name containing the macros, and then press Enter. Rename the macros by using the /**R**ange Name Labels **R**ight command.

Execute one of the Alt-*letter* macros (\w, \t, or \p) by pressing the Alt key followed by the letter key assigned to the macro. Execute one of the macros with a descriptive name (\SAVE or \ADD) by pressing Alt-F3 (Run), selecting the desired macro name, and pressing Enter.

The sections that follow provide a brief explanation of the operation of each macro.

A Macro That Sets Column Widths

Use the \w macro in cell AB102 to change the column width of the current column. Highlight the column whose width you want to change, and then press Alt-W. The macro begins by executing the /**W**orksheet Column Set-Width command. Then, as a result of the {?} command, the macro pauses for input. Enter the desired character width and press Enter. 1-2-3 displays the adjusted column width.

You can modify this macro to change the column width of a range of columns by typing the following in place of the macro in cell AB102:

```
'/wccs{?}~{?}~
```

14

This modified macro executes the command /Worksheet Column Column-Range Set-Width. It then pauses for you to enter the column range and press Enter. The macro pauses again until you type the column width and press Enter. 1-2-3 then displays the range of specified columns with the selected column width.

A Macro That Saves a File

The \SAVE macro in cell AB104 saves the current file in the current directory on disk. To use this macro, press Run (Alt-F3), select \SAVE from the list of macro and range names, and then press Enter. This macro executes the /File Save command and then pauses for you to enter the desired name. After you type the name of the file and press Enter, 1-2-3 begins to save the file. If the file exists, select Replace from the resulting menu to continue saving the file.

A Macro That Sums a Specified Range

The \ADD macro in cell AB106 uses the @SUM function to add values from a specified range. To use this macro, first highlight the cell to contain the result of the formula. Then press Run (Alt-F3), select \ADD from the list of macro and range names, and press Enter. The macro pauses for you to highlight a range of cells that you want to sum. After you select the range and press Enter, the screen displays the formula result.

A Macro That Enters Text

The \t macro in cell AB108 enters a long text label into the current cell. Press Alt-T to execute the macro, and 1-2-3 automatically enters the specified label into the highlighted cell. This macro is straightforward, but very useful for entering any long label that commonly appears throughout the worksheet.

A Macro That Prints a Specified Range

The \p macro in cell AB110 prints a range you specify to the printer and advances the paper to the top of the next page. To run this macro, press Alt-P. The macro executes the /Print Printer Range command. It then pauses for you to specify the desired print range. Highlight the range you want to print and press Enter. Then Align Go Page Quit aligns the paper, prints the range, advances the paper to the top of the page, and returns 1-2-3 to READY mode.

14

If you normally print the same range from a particular worksheet, you can name this print range with /Range Name Create. Then you can use this name in place of {?} in the Alt-P macro. For example, to print a range named PAGE1, use the following macro in place of the macro in cell AB110:

```
'/pprPAGE1~agpq
```

If you use this print macro, remember to redefine the range named PAGE1 whenever you add new data to the print range. If you have multiple named ranges to print, you can copy this cell and change the range references. This macro would print ranges named PAGE1, PAGE2, and PAGE3.

```
'/pprPAGE1~agpq
'/pprPAGE2~agpq
'/pprPAGE3~agpq
```

A Macro That Adds a Drop Shadow

Use the \SHADOW macro in cell AB112 to add a drop shadow and outline around a range you specify. To use this macro, press Run (Alt-F3), select \SHADOW from the list of range names, and press Enter. Then highlight the range for the shadow and select the range for the outline, pressing Enter after each range is selected. Notice that each line of the macro starts with a colon (:). This invokes the Wysiwyg menu and chooses the **Format Lines Shadow Set** and **Format Lines Outline** commands.

Using the Macro Library Manager Add-In

If you would like to save your macros for use with other files, you can use the Macro Library Manager add-in. First, you attach and invoke the Macro Library Manager with the Add-in (Alt-F10) key. After you invoke the Macro Library Manager, choose **Save** to save macros to a macro library. During the current session of 1-2-3, you can invoke a macro in the library with the Alt-*letter* combination or with Alt-F3 and the name of the macro. If you want to use a saved library of macros in another session, load and invoke the macro manager and choose **Load**.

14

528

Summary

This chapter provided the basic information you need to begin creating your own simple keystroke macros. Macros are tools you can use to save time, reduce repetition, and automate your worksheet applications. The chapter identified each of the steps necessary to create macros. It also described ways to document, name, and execute macros. You learned that the Learn feature allows you to create macros by recording keyboard activity. You also learned about automatic (\0) macros, as well as about methods to debug and edit your simple keystroke macros.

Specifically, you learned the following key information about 1-2-3:

■ The elements of macros include actual command keystrokes, key names, range names and cell addresses, and the advanced macro commands.

■ In 1-2-3 macros, tilde (~) represents the Enter key.

■ Enclose macro key names, which represent keyboard keys, within braces, such as {EDIT}. Key names are available for the function keys, direction keys, editing keys, and special keys.

■ You can specify more than one use of a key name by including repetition factors within the braces separated by a space. An example is {DOWN 5} or {D 5}.

■ Take time to plan your macros. Consider the available input and the desired results. Use the keyboard to proceed through your tasks, while jotting down the keystrokes necessary to create simple macros. You can create more complex macros by breaking them into smaller macros consisting of simple operations.

■ Position macros outside of the main area of your worksheet. So that you can quickly find your macros, place them in the same location in each of your worksheets, such as in column AA.

■ Always document your 1-2-3 macros. An easy way to do this is to include comments in the cells to the right of the macro steps. Type the macro name in the cells to the left of macro steps.

■ You can name macros in two different ways. You can use a backslash (\) followed by a single letter or use a backslash and a descriptive name of up to 15 characters. Use the /**R**ange **N**ame **C**reate or /**R**ange **N**ame **L**abels **R**ight command to name your macros.

14

■ The Learn feature of 1-2-3 Release 2.3 lets you create macros automatically by recording your keystrokes and storing them in a specified range. This range must first be defined with the /Worksheet **L**earn **R**ange command. Then use Learn (Alt-F5) to start and stop recording keystrokes.

■ To execute Alt-*letter* macros, press and hold the Alt key while you then press the letter key assigned to the macro. Execute macros with descriptive names by pressing Run (Alt-F3), selecting the macro name, and pressing Enter.

■ Automatic (\0) macros execute automatically when you retrieve a file. You can use only one automatic macro in each worksheet.

■ Access 1-2-3's STEP mode by pressing Step (Alt-F2). Use Step to find macro errors by proceeding through a macro one step at a time. You can sometimes use the Undo feature to reverse the effect of a macro if the macro has caused errors in the worksheet.

■ Edit macros just like any cell entries in the worksheet. Press Edit (F2) and correct each cell containing an error. Rewriting the entire contents of these cells is not necessary.

■ A macro library is a collection of two or more macros saved in a separate file and used with several different files. Use the /**F**ile **C**ombine **C**opy **E**ntire-File command to copy a macro library into the current file.

■ You can use the Macro Library Manager add-in to save the macros in the current worksheet for use with other worksheet files.

14

Installing 1-2-3 Release 2.3

The Install program for installing 1-2-3 Release 2.3 makes installation almost automatic; once you start the program, you follow the on-screen instructions. You must install Release 2.3 on a hard disk; the Install program is designed for this type of installation. You cannot run Release 2.3 from a floppy disk.

The Install program begins by creating several subdirectories on your hard disk. Then the program copies the program files to the new appropriate subdirectory. The program also asks you to select the type of video display you have, as well as the type of printer. Before you install Release 2.3, verify the brand and model of your printer. The program can detect the type of video display you use. Finally, the Install program generates the font files needed to use the Wysiwyg add-in.

Installation takes about 15–20 minutes; you need another 15–20 minutes to generate the basic font set for the Wysiwyg add-in program. When you are ready to begin, turn on your computer and follow the instructions in this appendix.

Checking DOS Configuration

Before you install 1-2-3 Release 2.3 to run under DOS, you must complete a preliminary step: you must make sure that DOS is configured adequately to run 1-2-3.

A

A

To do so, check your CONFIG.SYS file for the FILES statement.
CONFIG.SYS is found on your start-up hard disk in the root directory.
Type **TYPE C:\CONFIG.SYS** and press Enter to see the contents of
CONFIG.SYS (assuming that drive C is your start-up hard disk). The
screen displays something like the following:

```
FILES=25
BUFFERS=20
DEVICE=C:\DOS\ANSI.SYS
```

The FILES statement tells DOS how many files can be open at once. The
minimum number of files you should have is 20 (FILES=20). If you do not
have a FILES statement or if the number of files is less than 20, change the
CONFIG.SYS file. You can edit CONFIG.SYS with any text editor, such as
EDLIN, or with a word processor that can save files as ASCII unformatted text.

Also make sure that your version of DOS is 2.1 or higher and that you have
at least 512K of memory available for 1-2-3 and Wysiwyg (640K is recommended). On the hard disk, you need 7M of available disk space to load 1-2-3
and all of its companion programs (including Wysiwyg). If you do not need to
load all programs, such as the 1-2-3-Go! and Wysiwyg-Go! tutorials, less disk
space is required.

Using the Install Program

After installation is complete, be sure to make backup copies of the original
disks and store the originals in a safe place.

Starting the Install Program

To install 1-2-3 Release 2.3, follow these steps:

1. Place the Install disk in drive A.
2. Type **A:** and press ⏎Enter to switch to drive A.
3. At the DOS A> prompt, type **INSTALL** and press ⏎Enter.
4. Read the information on-screen and press ⏎Enter to continue.

A

Registering Your Original Disks

To make your disks usable for the first time, you must register them by entering and saving your name and company name on the Install disk. When you see the appropriate screen, follow these steps:

1. At the name prompt, type your name and press ⏎Enter.

2. At the company name prompt, type your company name and press ⏎Enter.

3. Choose Yes and press ⏎Enter at the prompt asking whether you want to record this information to disk.

Choosing Files To Install

The next step of the installation procedure asks which auxiliary programs you want to install in addition to 1-2-3. The default is to install all programs except PrintGraph and Translate. If you want to install everything (including PrintGraph and Translate), you must have at least 7M of free disk space.

If you don't have enough memory once you have selected the files to install, **1-2-3 gives you an error message**—not enough space, either end Install and make room on drive, or remove check from any companion program. **Press Enter to continue or Esc to end Install.** (If you press Esc, Install returns you to the A> prompt.)

The list of choices includes the following:

Program	Description
1-2-3	Contains the 1-2-3 program files
Wysiwyg	Adds publishing features to improve the appearance of printouts and graphs
Add-Ins	Adds auditing and file viewing features and a macro library manager to 1-2-3
1-2-3-Go!	Teaches you how to use 1-2-3 with on-screen tutorials
Wysiwyg-Go!	Demonstrates how to use Wysiwyg to create presentation-quality reports and graphs
PrintGraph	Displays and prints graphs created with 1-2-3
Translate	Converts data from other programs to 1-2-3 and vice versa

To mark or unmark any choice, move to the item and press the space bar. This process adds or removes the check mark. When you have selected all items to install, press Enter to continue.

Creating a Directory for the 1-2-3 Files

On the next screen, type the letter of your hard drive and press Enter. Most often, you will install on drive C.

The next screen prompts you for the appropriate directory to contain the 1-2-3 files. Press Enter to accept the default directory of \123R23 or type the new directory and press Enter.

Transferring Files

After you name the drive and directory, the Install program begins transferring files to the hard disk. The program first transfers from disk 1. After transferring the files from that disk, Install prompts you to insert the next disk. Follow the screen prompts to insert the correct disks. **Note:** Because the files on the installation disks are compressed, you cannot directly copy the files from the DOS prompt.

Configuring 1-2-3 for Your Computer

The install program notifies you whether the file transfer was successful. Press Enter to continue. The next screen is the install Main Menu. The first option, Select Your Equipment, is highlighted. Press Enter.

Note: After you install 1-2-3 on your hard disk, you can change the configuration. For example, if you purchase a new printer, you must add the printer to the configuration. In this case, choose Change Selected Equipment from the Main Menu. You may also want to later change or add Wysiwyg fonts. In this case, choose Specify Wysiwyg Options. Refer to your Lotus documentation for more information on each of these procedures.

Install next detects and indicates the type of video display you have. To install your monitor, follow these steps:

1. Record the name displayed and press ⏎Enter to display the Screen Display Selection menu.

2. Your display type should be highlighted. Press ⏎Enter to confirm.

A

3. If your video display offers different modes for displaying information on-screen, Install lists them on the next screen. Highlight the one that best suits your needs and press ⏎Enter.

The next screen asks whether you have a text printer. To install your printer, follow these steps:

1. If you do not have a printer or do not want to install a printer now, select No and press ⏎Enter to continue. Otherwise, press ⏎Enter to select Yes.

2. Highlight the brand of printer you have and press ⏎Enter.

3. Highlight the model of printer you have and press ⏎Enter. If prompted for font cartridges or further choices, move to the choice and press ⏎Enter.

   Install then asks whether you want to install another text printer.

4. If you want to install another text printer, select Yes, press ⏎Enter, and repeat steps 2–4. If you do not want to install another printer at this time, select No and press ⏎Enter.

   Install then asks whether you have a graphics printer.

5. If you have a graphics printer, select Yes, press ⏎Enter, and repeat steps 2–4. If you do not want to install a graphics printer at this time, select No and press ⏎Enter.

Naming Your Driver Set

After you make your display and printer selections, the program prompts you to name your driver set or SET file. The SET file contains all the information from your responses to questions about your display type and printer.

To automatically name your file 123.SET, select No at the prompt and press Enter; or select Yes, name the file something else, and press Enter.

If you name the SET something other than 123.SET, you must supply the SET file's name when you start 1-2-3. For example, if you create a SET file called 60LINE.SET, when you start 1-2-3, type **123 60LINE** and press Enter. If you use the default name of 1-2-3.SET, you don't have to specify the SET name when you start 1-2-3.

Generating Fonts

If you chose to install the Wysiwyg add-in program, you see a screen that tells you the next step is to generate fonts for the Wysiwyg program.

1. Press ⏎Enter to continue.

   Install displays the Generating Fonts menu. From this menu, you choose between a Basic, Medium, or Extended font set. Each successive font set gives you a broader range of fonts and font sizes to choose from when you are in the Wysiwyg add-in, but each font set also takes a longer time to install, and requires more disk space.

2. For now, choose the Basic font set and press ⏎Enter.

   After generating the fonts, Install notifies you whether the font generation was successful.

3. When prompted, press any key to return to the DOS prompt.

Summary of Allways Commands

Allways is an add-in program included with Release 2.2 (Release 2.01 users can buy the program separately). This "spreadsheet publishing" program, which works in conjunction with 1-2-3, enables you to produce professional-looking reports. In addition, Allways enables you to print graphs along with your worksheets—all without leaving 1-2-3.

Note: 1-2-3 Release 2.3 includes the Wysiwyg spreadsheet publishing add-in instead of Allways. Therefore, this Appendix is for 1-2-3 Release 2.2 users (and for 1-2-3 Release 2.01 users who have purchased Allways separately).

Using the Allways Add-In

To use Allways, you must first attach the program, which makes the add-in available for use. Then you must invoke the add-in, which lets you access its commands. An add-in package does not interfere with the operation of 1-2-3; you can switch back and forth between the two without fear of destroying your data. Allways does, however, require a portion of main memory (RAM) for its use. If you are working with an extremely large worksheet, insufficient memory may prevent you from attaching Allways or may limit your freedom to expand the worksheet.

Following are the two ways to attach Allways:

Automatically, by using the command sequence /Worksheet Global Default Other Add-In Set. This sequence of commands ensures that whenever you start using 1-2-3, Allways is automatically attached (available for use). In addition, this command also gives you the option of having Allways automatically invoked (ready for use) when you start 1-2-3. Issue this command once, and use /Worksheet Global Default Update to record the operation on your system.

Each time you want to use the program. If you are concerned about the additional memory Allways requires and don't want to have it attached at all times, use the /Add-In Attach command whenever you need Allways.

Attaching Allways Automatically

To attach Allways using the first method so that the add-in is automatically available every time you use 1-2-3, follow these steps:

1. Select /Worksheet Global Default Other Add-In Set.
2. Select a number for Allways by typing one of the numbers from 1 to 8. (You may attach up to eight add-ins.)
3. Highlight ALLWAYS.ADN from the list of add-ins and press ⏎Enter.
4. Indicate the key to use to invoke Allways. You can select No-Key, 7 (Alt-F7), 8 (Alt-F8), or 9 (Alt-F9).

   Note: Although the 10 option for assigning Alt-F10 to Allways also appears on this menu, it is recommended that you select one of the other four options. This is because the Alt-F10 key combination is sometimes used for other purposes.

5. Select Yes to have Allways automatically invoked whenever you start 1-2-3, or select No if you do *not* want 1-2-3 to automatically invoke when you start 1-2-3.

   Note: Only one add-in program can be automatically invoked when you start 1-2-3.

6. Select Quit to return to the /Worksheet Global Default menu.
7. Select Update to save the default setting in a configuration file.
8. Select Quit to return to READY mode.

Attaching and Invoking Allways Manually

To attach Allways using the second method, which you must repeat *each* time you want to use Allways, follow these steps:

1. Select /**A**dd-In **A**ttach.
2. Highlight ALLWAYS.ADN from the list of add-ins and press (⏎Enter).
3. Indicate the key to use to invoke Allways. You can select **N**o-Key, **7** (Alt-F7), **8** (Alt-F8), or **9** (Alt-F9).

    Note: Although the **10** option for assigning Alt-F10 to Allways also appears on this menu, it is recommended that you select one of the other four options. This is because the Alt-F10 key combination is sometimes used for other purposes.

4. Select **Q**uit to return to READY mode.

To invoke Allways so that you may use it with your current 1-2-3 session, follow these steps:

1. Press the Alt-key combination you selected when attaching Allways; or, if you chose the **N**o-Key option when attaching Allways, follow the remaining steps.
2. Select /**A**dd-In **I**nvoke.
3. Highlight ALLWAYS.ADN from the list of add-ins and press (⏎Enter).

The Allways screen now appears—displaying your worksheet in reverse video with a different typeface than 1-2-3 normally displays. You can return to 1-2-3 at any time by pressing the Esc key.

Allways Command Summary

The remainder of this appendix lists the Allways commands and their actions. For more information on these commands, refer to your Lotus 1-2-3 Release 2.2 documentation. If you are using 1-2-3 Release 2.01, refer to the documentation provided with the Allways program.

You can use certain Alt-key combinations to cycle through some of the format choices in the following list. Using the Alt key is quicker than using the menu commands.

B

B

Action	Commands
Change font for a particular range	/**F**ormat **F**ont, highlight font, **U**se, highlight range, ⏎Enter]; or Alt]1] through Alt]8].
Choose alternative font for entire worksheet	/**F**ormat **F**ont, highlight existing font, **R**eplace; highlight new typeface, ⏎Enter]; highlight point size, ⏎Enter]; **Q**uit.
Shade area of worksheet ·	/**F**ormat **S**hade, **L**ight or **D**ark, highlight range, ⏎Enter]; or Alt]S].
Create a thick line	/**F**ormat **S**hade **S**olid, highlight range, ⏎Enter]; or Alt]S]. Then /**W**orksheet **R**ow **S**et-Height, use ↑] to decrease row height, ⏎Enter].
	Note: Alt-S cycles through all choices; that is, pressing Alt-S once gets **L**ight shading, twice on the same range gets **D**ark, then **S**olid, then **N**one.
Remove existing shading	/**F**ormat **S**hade **C**lear, highlight range, ⏎Enter]; or Alt]S] four times.
Create underline	/**F**ormat **U**nderline, **S**ingle or **D**ouble, highlight range, ⏎Enter]; or Alt]U].
Remove existing underline	/**F**ormat **U**nderline **C**lear, highlight range, ⏎Enter]; or Alt]U].
	Note: Alt-U cycles through the choices **S**ingle, **D**ouble, and **N**one.
Create boldface characters	/**F**ormat **B**old **S**et, highlight range, ⏎Enter]; or Alt]B].
Remove existing boldface	/**F**ormat **B**old **C**lear, highlight range, ⏎Enter]; or Alt]B].
	Note: Alt-B cycles between **S**et and **C**lear.

B

Action	Commands
Outline each cell in range of cells	/**Format Lines All**, highlight range, ⏎Enter; or Alt L.
Outline perimeter of range of cells	/**Format Lines Outline**, highlight range, ⏎Enter; or Alt L.
	Note: Alt-L cycles through **Outline**, **All**, and **None**.
Create grid lines	/**Layout Options Grid Yes**, **Quit**, **Quit**; or Alt G.
	Note: Alt-G toggles between grid and no grid (**On** and **Off**).
Change size of image on-screen	/**Display Zoom**, (**Tiny**, **Small**, **Normal**, **Large**, or **Huge**), **Quit**; or F4 and Alt F4.
	Note: F4 gets smaller; Alt-F4 gets larger.
Combine graph with worksheet	Position cell pointer at location for graph, /**Graph Add**, highlight graph name, ⏎Enter; highlight range for graph, ⏎Enter; **Quit**.
View graph on-screen	/**Display Graphs Yes**; **Quit**.
Remove graph from worksheet	/**Graph Remove**, specify graph name, ⏎Enter; **Quit**.
Print a report with Allways	/**Print Range Set**, highlight range, ⏎Enter, **Go**; **Quit**.

Index

Symbols

Que—The Top Name In Spreadsheet Information!

Find It Fast With Que's Quick References!

Que's Quick References are the compact, easy-to-use guides to essential application information. Written for all users, Quick References include vital command information under easy-to-find alphabetical listings. Quick References are a must for anyone who needs command information fast!

Complete Coverage From A To Z!

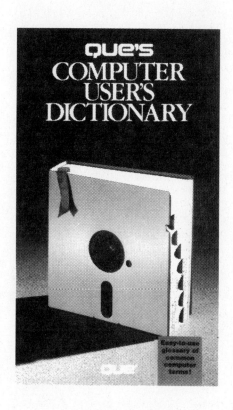

Que's Computer User's Dictionary
Que Development Group

This compact, practical reference contains hundreds of definitions, explanations, examples, and illustrations on topics from programming to desktop publishing. You can master the "language" of computers and learn how to make your personal computers more efficient and more powerful. Filled with tips and cautions, *Que's Computer User's Dictionary* is the perfect resource for anyone who uses a computer.

IBM, Macintosh, Apple, & Programming

Order #1086   **$10.95 USA**

0-88022-540-8, 500 pp., 4 3/4 x 8

**The Ultimate Glossary
Of Computer Terms—
Over 200,000 In Print!**

"Dictionary indeed. This whammer is a mini-encyclopedia...an absolute joy to use...a must for your computer library...."

*Southwest Computer
& Business Equipment Review*

**To Order, Call:
(800) 428-5331 OR (317) 573-2510**

NO POSTAGE
NECESSARY
IF MAILED
IN THE
UNITED STATES

BUSINESS REPLY MAIL
First Class Permit No. 9918   Indianapolis, IN

Postage will be paid by addressee

que.

11711 N. College
Carmel, IN 46032

NO POSTAGE
NECESSARY
IF MAILED
IN THE
UNITED STATES

BUSINESS REPLY MAIL
First Class Permit No. 9918   Indianapolis, IN

Postage will be paid by addressee

que.

11711 N. College
Carmel, IN 46032

Free Catalog!

Mail us this registration form today, and we'll send you a free catalog featuring Que's complete line of best-selling books.

Name of Book _____

Name _____

Title _____

Phone ( ) _____

Company _____

Address _____

City _____

State _____ ZIP _____

Please check the appropriate answers:

1. Where did you buy your Que book?
   - ☐ Bookstore (name: _____)
   - ☐ Computer store (name: _____)
   - ☐ Catalog (name: _____)
   - ☐ Direct from Que
   - ☐ Other: _____

2. How many computer books do you buy a year?
   - ☐ 1 or less
   - ☐ 2-5
   - ☐ 6-10
   - ☐ More than 10

3. How many Que books do you own?
   - ☐ 1
   - ☐ 2-5
   - ☐ 6-10
   - ☐ More than 10

4. How long have you been using this software?
   - ☐ Less than 6 months
   - ☐ 6 months to 1 year
   - ☐ 1-3 years
   - ☐ More than 3 years

5. What influenced your purchase of this Que book?
   - ☐ Personal recommendation
   - ☐ Advertisement
   - ☐ In-store display
   - ☐ Price
   - ☐ Que catalog
   - ☐ Que mailing
   - ☐ Que's reputation
   - ☐ Other: _____

6. How would you rate the overall content of the book?
   - ☐ Very good
   - ☐ Good
   - ☐ Satisfactory
   - ☐ Poor

7. What do you like *best* about this Que book?
   _____
   _____

8. What do you like *least* about this Que book?
   _____
   _____

9. Did you buy this book with your personal funds?
   - ☐ Yes   ☐ No

10. Please feel free to list any other comments you may have about this Que book.
    _____
    _____
    _____

— QUE —

Order Your Que Books Today!

Name _____

Title _____

Company _____

City _____

State _____ ZIP _____

Phone No. ( ) _____

Method of Payment:

Check ☐ (Please enclose in envelope.)

Charge My: VISA ☐   MasterCard ☐

American Express ☐

Charge # _____

Expiration Date _____

Order No.	Title	Qty.	Price	Total

You can **FAX** your order to **1-317-573-2583**. Or call **1-800-428-5331, ext. ORDR** to order direct.
Please add $2.50 per title for shipping and handling.

Subtotal _____

Shipping & Handling _____

Total _____

— QUE —

BUSINESS REPLY MAIL

First Class Permit No. 9918   Indianapolis, IN

Postage will be paid by addressee

11711 N. College
Carmel, IN 46032

BUSINESS REPLY MAIL

First Class Permit No. 9918   Indianapolis, IN

Postage will be paid by addressee

11711 N. College
Carmel, IN 46032